AUGUSTUS VINCENT TACK: *Landscape of the Spirit*

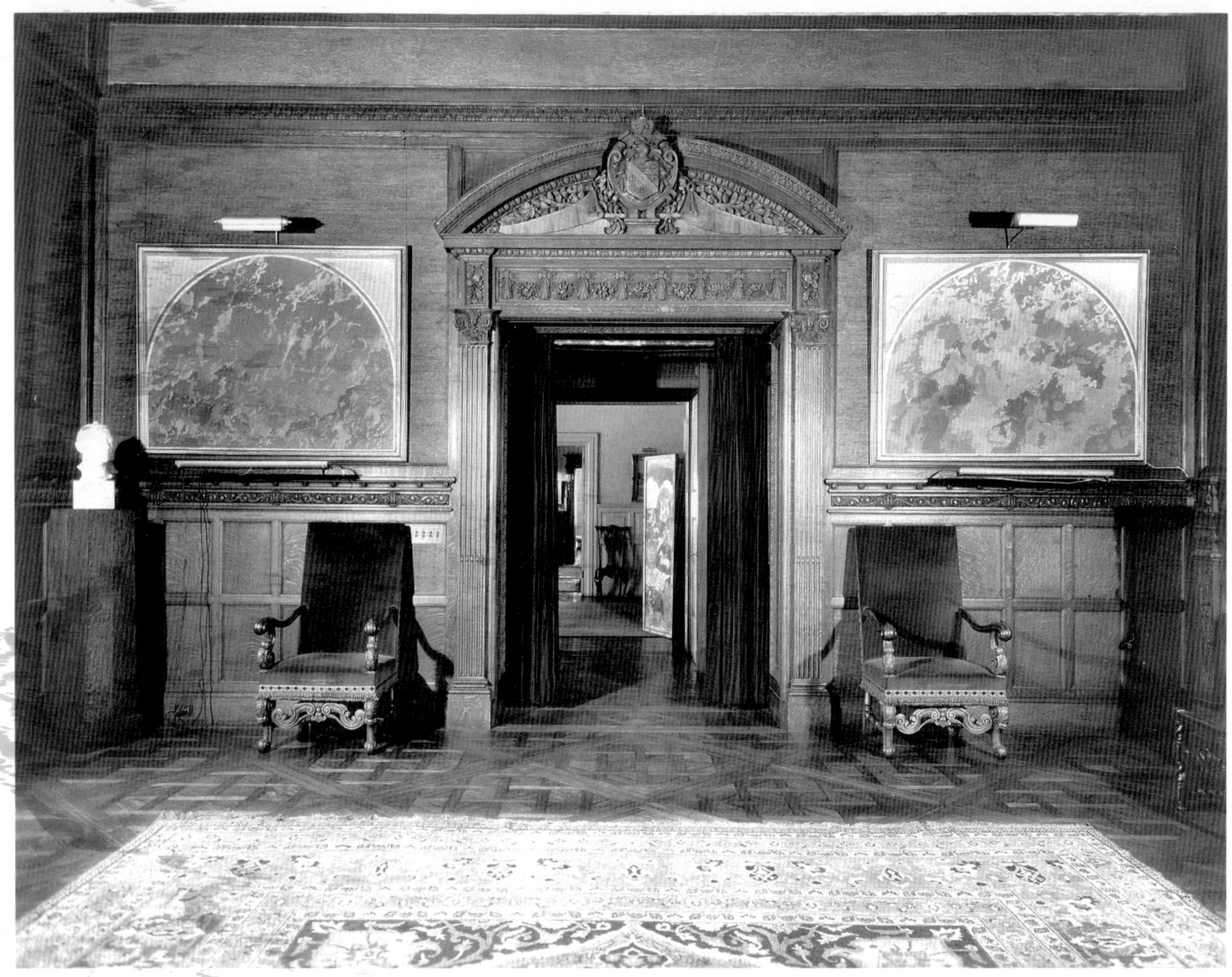

The south wall of the North Library (Music Room), Phillips Memorial Gallery, with Tack's paintings, *Liberation* and *Ecstasy* and screen by Charles Prendergast in dining room beyond, ca. 1930–31. The Phillips Collection Archives.

AUGUSTUS VINCENT TACK

Landscape of the Spirit

Leslie Furth

with essays by Elizabeth V. Chew and David W. Scott

The Phillips Collection, Washington, D.C., 1993

Published by The Phillips Collection,
1600 21st Street, NW, Washington, D.C. 20009

Publication managed by
Stephen Bennett Phillips

Edited by
Ellen Cochran Hirzy and Marcia Schifanelli

Designed by
Susan Lehmann

Design assistant
Mark R. Bacon

Printed by Garamond, Inc.

Cover: Detail, Augustus Vincent Tack, *Outposts of Time I* (cat. 37)

Library of Congress Cataloging-in-Publication Data
Furth, Leslie. 1957-
Augustus Vincent Tack: Landscape of the Spirit/
by Leslie Furth, Elizabeth V. Chew, David Scott.
p. cm.
Exhibition catalog.
Includes bibliographical references.
ISBN 0-943044-19-7: $24.00
1. Tack, Augustus Vincent, 1870–1949--Exhibitions. 2. Painting. Abstract--United States--Exhibitions. 3. Painting--Washington (D.C.) --Exhibitions. 4. Phillips Collection--Exhibitions.
I. Chew, Elizabeth V., 1963- .II. Scott, David, 1916- .
III. Title.
ND237.T32A4 1993
759.13--dc20 93-3596
CIP

Photography of works in The Phillips Collection by Edward Owen, Washington, D.C.

Photograph Credits

fig. 2 Charles J. Miller photographer
fig. 4 The Chicago photographers
fig. 11 Amy Werbel photographer
fig. 12 © 1987, Sotheby's Inc., New York
fig. 13 Peter A. Juley and Son, photographers
fig. 15 Capitol collections, Sidney Spelts Collection
fig. 19 Bryon Harmon Photograph collection
fig. 23 copyright The Frick Collection, New York
fig. 28 Clara E. Sipprell photographer
fig. 32 © 1993, Sotheby's Inc., New York
fig. 33-36 Elizabeth Steele photographer

Contents

Foreword

The work of Augustus Vincent Tack (1870–1949) is well known only to frequent visitors to The Phillips Collection and to a relatively small group of scholars, curators, collectors, and cognoscenti. The reason is that Duncan Phillips bought or commissioned many of Tack's abstract paintings, and later the artist's widow bequeathed more of his work to the museum. As a result, most of Tack's best paintings are virtually impossible to see elsewhere. The Museum of Modern Art, for example, managed to acquire its only painting by the artist in 1979, purchased directly from The Phillips.

Nearly everyone who sees Tack's abstract paintings at The Phillips Collection remembers them. They are much admired and often discussed, but because they are usually seen only in Washington, the artist's importance has been underestimated and understated. Further, little has been published about him, and he fits few of the generally accepted notions about artists who were at the forefront of the modern movement. Fortunately, *Augustus Vincent Tack: Landscape of the Spirit* reveals a wealth of much-needed information about the artist, his development, and his integral contribution to the rise of modern American abstract painting. Moreover, this exhibition is in a long tradition of shows organized by the museum that focus on the work of artists collected by Duncan Phillips and that provide the visual experiences fundamental to our understanding of the art of this century.

Among the many people who made important contributions to the exhibition and the catalogue, I would like to express my deepest gratitude to Laughlin Phillips, chairman of the board and former director; Leslie Furth, principal consultant; Eliza E. Rathbone, chief curator and project director; Elizabeth Chew, assistant curator; and Elizabeth Steele, paintings conservator.

In addition, I would like to extend my sincerest appreciation to the National Endowment for the Arts, which provided a generous grant for conservation of the paintings.

Charles S. Moffett
Director

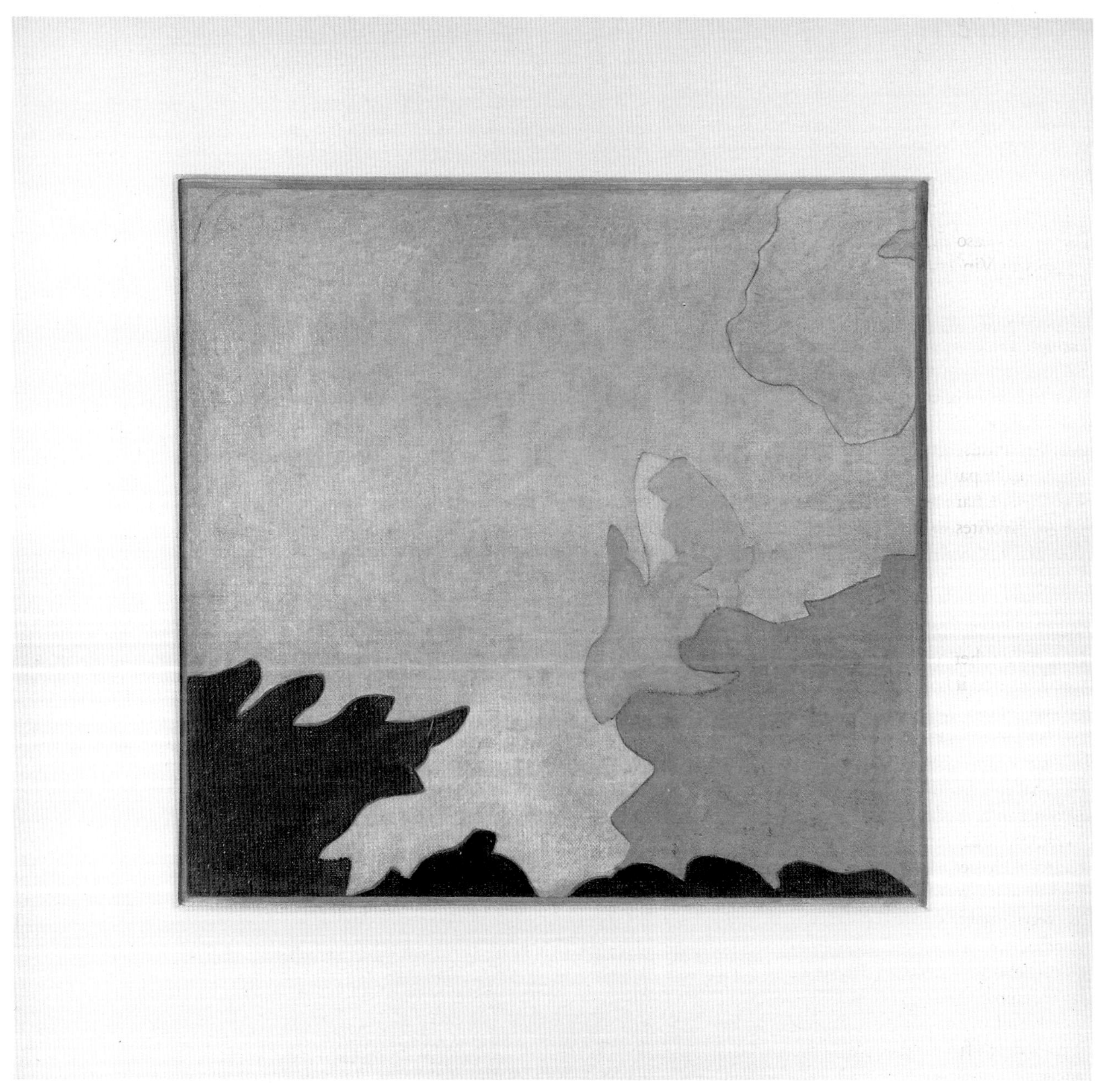

Cat. 48. *Dawn*, between 1934 and 1936, oil on canvas mounted on hardboard, 23 ¾ x 24 ¾ in.

Preface

For many reasons the opening of the exhibition "Augustus Vincent Tack: Landscape of the Spirit" will be greeted not only with excitement but also with considerable curiosity. For though Tack's work has consistently captured the eye and won the admiration of visitors to The Phillips Collection since the 1920s, very few of Tack's mature works belong to other American museum collections. Even at The Phillips, the paintings shown in recent decades have been a handful of Duncan Phillips's particular favorites, which represent the culmination of Tack's achievement in an abstract style. Many visitors are well acquainted with *Storm*, *The Voice of Many Waters*, and *Aspiration*. But where did these unique abstractions come from? No other institution but The Phillips could look to its own storeroom for the answer.

Duncan Phillips and Augustus Vincent Tack saw eye to eye on many accounts. Even before the Phillips Memorial Gallery opened to the public in 1921, Phillips knew and admired Tack. He made him vice-president of the first board of trustees of his fledgling institution, proving his esteem for Tack as advisor as well as creative genius. With characteristic independence, Phillips purchased and commissioned many works by Tack, quickly becoming his foremost patron, with the result that a large number of works came to The Phillips after Tack's death from the estate of the artist's widow.

Seventy-nine works by Tack are included in the permanent collection. Our "embarrassment of riches" has presented us with an equal wealth of challenges. Many works, particularly those predating the 1920s and the emergence of Tack's abstract style, have not been exhibited for more than seventy years. Establishing a chronology for these works alone has been difficult, because Tack signed many of them but dated few. Countless paintings required conservation. Not only does their revived presence lend critical depth to our interpretation of Tack's aesthetic development, but the treatment process brought to light many unique aspects of his technique and materials, described in a special report in this catalogue. The catalogue essays also shed new light on Tack's sources, from the hills around Deerfield, Massachusetts, to the vast panorama of the American West; on his inventive use of photography and his application of mural techniques dating from the Renaissance; and on his fusion of eastern and western traditions.

During the 1970s and 1980s there was a resurgence of interest in Tack's abstract work. In addition to an exhibition of abstractions (drawn exclusively from The Phillips Collection) organized by the University of Texas at Austin in 1972, paintings by Tack began to be included for the first time in major thematic exhibitions, inviting comparison between his abstractions and more recent artistic developments. "Color and Field," organized by the Dayton Art Institute in 1970, was followed in 1976 by "The Natural Paradise: Painting in America 1800–1950" at the Museum of Modern Art, New York. In 1986–87, "The Spiritual in Art," organized by the Los Angeles County Museum of Art, also included work by Tack.

In its emphasis on color and a nonhierarchical allover treatment of the composition, Tack's abstraction may be identified with one salient form of abstract art emerging in the 1960s and 1970s. Cubism never entered into his approach. It is precisely this opposing tradition—stemming from impressionism and the flat patterning of the French symbolists and the Japanese aesthetic—that is fulfilled in Tack and undeniably anticipates more recent color field painting. Yet Tack's inclusion in these survey exhibitions, however appropriate, has been derived from a primarily visual response to his fields of patterned color and from the impact of his work more than its origins. These exhibitions have also necessarily been based on insufficient information. "Augustus Vincent Tack: Landscape of the Spirit" at last positions Tack's work squarely in the context of his own time and experience. In doing so, it reveals how the artist, Janus-faced, reaches as far back as he does forward, becoming one of the most unusual "bridge" figures in the art of this century.

The preparation of this exhibition has been a complex undertaking involving not only extensive research by our principal consultant Leslie Furth, who began her study of Tack's work as a research assistant at The Phillips Collection more than six years ago, but also the guidance of David W. Scott, whose fascination with and understanding of Tack's achievement is long-standing, and the coordination and insight afforded this exhibition and publication by assistant curator Elizabeth Chew. Vivien Greene, Leslie Furth's assistant, also made an invaluable contribution, as did Stephen Phillips, executive assistant to the curatorial department. Few members of the staff of The Phillips Collection have not been involved in this project in some capacity. Most outstanding has been Elizabeth Steele, who devoted many hours to the study and conservation of twenty-six paintings included in the exhibition. Ignacio Moreno has coordinated and overseen all photography by Edward Owen for this publication. Ellen Cochran Hirzy, with the assistance of Marcia Schifanelli, has lent her considerable editing talent to the manuscript, and Susan Lehmann must be thanked for the creativity she has brought to the catalogue design.

An undertaking of this complexity has required the assistance of many individuals outside The Phillips Collection, indeed more than can be thanked here. On behalf of both The Phillips Collection and Leslie Furth, I would like especially to acknowledge the following people: Matthew Armstrong, Cantarel Besson, Father Vincent Butler, Joella de Couessin, Michael Engel, the late John Gernand, Susana Halpine, Dr. George Humphreys, Jeanie James, Katherine Kaplan, Claude Laugier, Dean Lee, Dr. Alain de Leiris, Dr. and Mrs. Arthur S. Localio, Beatrice Orenstein, Veronica Paz, Joël Perocheau, Hugh Phibbs, Paul Racioppi, René de la Rie, Joseph Peter Spang III, the late Justin Singer, James Yarnall, and Mitchell Yokelson. Many institutions have also offered their generous cooperation to this project, including the Archives of American Art, Smithsonian Institution; the Art Students League; the Century Association; Deerfield Academy; the Fogg Art Museum, Harvard University; Historic Deerfield, Inc.; the National Academy of Design; the Nebraska State Capitol; Phillips Academy, Andover; Pocumtuck Valley Memorial Association Library; Tamiment Institute Library, New York University; and the Worcester Art Museum. Finally, we would especially like to acknowledge the descendants of Augustus Vincent Tack and his family who have enriched this project immeasurably: Richard Arms, Mary Ellis Carrere, Theodore Carrere, Margaret Casey, Robert Ellinger, Marion Farley, the late Jean Proctor Tack Kuehn, Mary Marsh, John Moran, Gifford Proctor, Jacques Riboud and family, Mrs. Theodore Robb, Saville Ryan, Richard Harms Tack, and Susan Tillman.

Duncan Phillips recorded in his journal in 1914 his first reaction to Tack's work as "one of those experiences which mark an epoch in one's own mental development." He referred to Tack's landscapes of hills and clouds and observed, "The cloud shadows are flying and we want to fly with them." Already Phillips seemed to touch upon a salient and enduring quality of Tack's work: the invitation to an airborne realm, or the edge of an infinite expanse that lifts us out of ourselves and offers liberation to the spirit.

Eliza E. Rathbone
Chief Curator

Leslie Furth

AUGUSTUS VINCENT TACK

A Mystic's Journey to Abstraction

Art is the evidence of man's yearning to comprehend perfection through his emotions by the complete subjugation of matter to the uses and ends of the spirit.[1]

The seeming contradictions in Augustus Vincent Tack's multifarious oeuvre, which encompassed society portraiture and religious scenes of the most conventional type along with the daringly monumental abstracted landscapes for which he is best known, cast him as one of his era's most enigmatic artists. Isolated eccentric or society bonhomme, Tack remains a shadowy figure whose position and exact contribution to art has been only partially explored and understood. His artistic direction is considered to have paralleled, but remained independent of, the avant-garde, whether through instinct or direct discourse, serendipity or design. On the basis of a shared mystical vision of nature and an abstract approach to landscape, he has been viewed as a bridge between Albert Pinkham Ryder and Clyfford Still. But his legacy must also be evaluated in light of his own philosophy, sources, and intentions, which illuminate the evolution of his abstract style and the nature of his contribution to American painting. His rare blending of "abstract mysticism and technical innovation,"[2] his passion for color and decorative surface effects, his fascination with Asian art, and his organic sensitivity to the parallels between music and art helped to pave the way for Tack's abstraction. Though he shared many of the aims of American modernists such as Arthur Dove, John Marin, and Georgia O'Keeffe, his route to an abstract vocabulary based in nature was very much his own.

In many respects, Tack brought the nineteenth-century decorative tradition into the modern age, embodying in his mature work its most distinctive expressions: French symbolism, the academic practices of Beaux-Arts painting and their incarnation in the American Renaissance, and the formalism of the aesthetic movement. To these traditions he grafted an abstract vocabulary based on the "accidents of nature" observed in the landscape of the American West.[3] He adapted photographic effects in his fragmentation of form, and he drew further inspiration from twentieth-century design theory.

Tack's symbolist inheritance, evident in his postimpressionist painting style of the teens and his evocation of Charles Baudelaire and Maurice Denis in the 1920s, reverberates in the intimacy with which natural forms and sacred themes are linked in his work. The symbolist legacy is also apparent in his approach to form itself, which he renders in harmonious and decorative unities of color and elemental, repeating contours.[4] Tack's mature expression—the abstractions—contains vast spaces filled with arabesque designs distilled from fragmentary natural and human shapes.

Tack's abstract work has claimed attention from art historians since the early 1970s, after a period of neglect following his death in 1949. This resurgence of interest would not have surprised Tack, who made the prophetic claim that twenty years after his death a renewed appreciation of his work would arise. This late

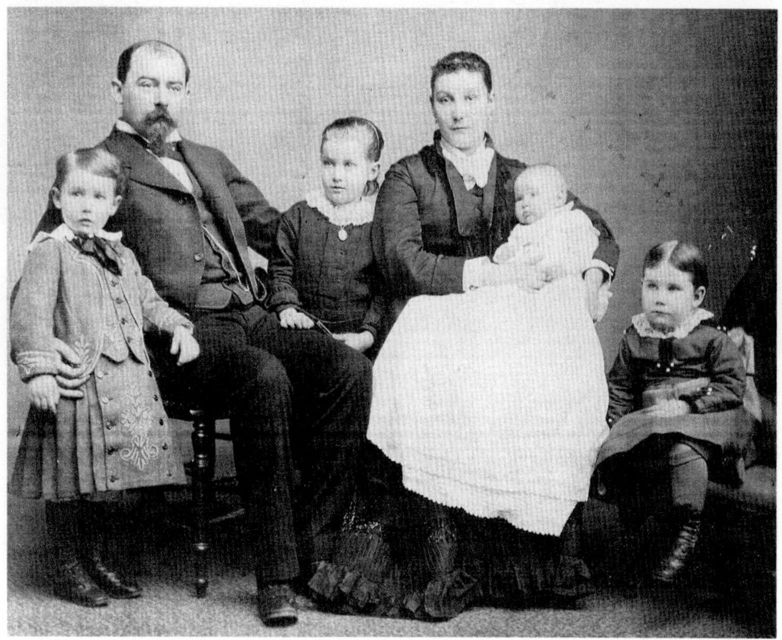

Fig. 1. Tack family, ca. 1875; from left, Augustus Vincent Tack, his father Theodore E. Tack, his sister Mary, his mother Mary Cosgrave Tack with his infant sister Julia, and his sister Elizabeth Tack. Collection of Mrs. Susan Tillman, Gulfport, Mississippi

recognition was also presaged by his foremost patron, Duncan Phillips, who contended in 1931, "This is an art not so much for today . . . as for tomorrow when science and mysticism meet . . . . Tack will be looked back upon as one of the major prophets of progress in painting."[5]

Tack's life and work elucidate the sometimes contradictory nature of the fin de siècle period and the first years of this century. The waxing and waning of his religious painting, the evolution of his mural work, and the development of his abstraction signal broader issues of cultural change. Reaching maturity in 1900, he had already witnessed the advent of Darwinian thought, the spread of scientific positivism, the rise of the machine, and the consequent subversion of spiritual certainties—in other words, the erosion of a traditional belief system. While the language of his abstract painting hints at this erosion through an employment of segmented forms, in fact Tack employed this language to convey his unrelenting belief in a pervasive divine order through his painting, a mystical vision at the core of his abstract expression. The vocabulary in which this expression occurred, highlighting increasingly immaterial imagery, is a striking embodiment of the sense of a world in flux.

A VICTORIAN CATHOLIC BOYHOOD

Augustus Vincent Tack was the second child and first-born son of Theodore Edward Tack and Mary Cosgrave Tack in a family that grew to fourteen children, seven of whom survived to adulthood (fig. 1). His mother was from an Irish Catholic Philadelphia merchant family, and his father served in the Civil War before entering the oil business in Pittsburgh during the industrial boom of the late 1870s. The Tacks lived in western Pennsylvania oil field towns until about 1883, when the success of the family business, the American Oil Development Company, enabled them to move to New York City.[6]

By all accounts a happy, close family, the Tacks were solidly associated with the pillars of Victorian society, the church, and the budding corporation. The parents engendered a love of the arts and literature, building a voluminous library and holding regular musical soirées. Their children shared a passion for art and music; several demonstrated talent in drawing, a skill that found its fullest expression in Augustus Tack. Family legend has it that his facility was first discovered by a priest who found himself caricatured in the margins of Tack's textbook.[7]

Tack had a rigorously classical Jesuit education that formed the intellectual and philosophical foundation for his life and work, informing his art from pure landscapes to church decorations and abstractions. At St. Francis Xavier College (now High School) on West 16th Street in Chelsea, lower Manhattan, he followed the prescribed Christian humanist curriculum; he progressed through grammar, rhetoric, belles-lettres, and philosophy and studied the classics within the framework of Christianity. The mythology of Homer, Aeschylus, Virgil, and Ovid, English-language classics such as Shakespeare and the romantic poets, and the natural sciences and mathematics completed his education.[8]

Tack undoubtedly received a potent introduction to religious art at St. Francis Xavier Church next door to the school. Completed in 1888, the church was adorned with monumental murals of the stations of the cross by the German artist William Lamprecht as well as with devotional statues of saints and the Virgin Mary. As a young man, Tack participated in the Sodality of the Immaculate Conception, an order of boys who performed and hosted special rites of worship of the Virgin. Strengthened by the glorification of women in the nineteenth century, this veneration remained a strong current in Tack's secular and religious painting, as, for example, in *Madonna of the Everlasting Hills* (cat. 13).

Tack distinguished himself as a young art student, though none of his pictures from his school years survive. The school was known for its strong music program, which no doubt stimulated Tack's early interest in music, his grasp of the analogous aims of music and art, and the significance of music in his later painting.[9]

AT HOME AND ABROAD: TRAINING AND FIRST SUCCESS

By the 1890s, the proliferation of new museums, art schools, and art periodicals—as well as the growing number of artists trained in Munich and Paris—was dramatically altering the American art scene. A new appreciation for native expression was apparent, as galleries devoted exclusively to American art opened, with William Macbeth taking the lead in 1892. The brightened palettes and broken brushwork of the impressionists were greeted with enthusiasm, and American impressionists and other innovators at last could compete in the art market.

In New York, these trends were intensified by the city's position as America's art center. In 1875, the Art Students League—the first independent art school in the country—was formed as a student-funded cooperative.[10] The league's free spirit and tolerance of various artistic directions attracted a gifted and diverse group of instructors, including James Carroll Beckwith, John Twachtman, William Merritt Chase, Willard Metcalf, and H. Siddons Mowbray. The classes ranged from conservative anatomy taught by Kenyon Cox to the more radical composition classes of Arthur Dow.

Tack began his formal studies at the league in 1890, probably as a student of John Twachtman. In Tack's later landscape painting, Twachtman's impact is clearly visible. Tack may also have taken advantage of William Merritt Chase's all-day painting classes. Tack's recollection of J. Alden Weir overseeing a *concours* (a ranking of student drawings) in which Tack participated bears out Weir's impact, both in landscape and portraiture, on Tack's work.[11]

Tack's studies from life began in Mowbray's classes in 1893 (fig. 2). The renowned muralist and figure painter was then at the height of his fame. His mural paintings were canonical examples of American Renaissance decoration, especially the French legacy, in their reliance on masterpieces of the Italian Renaissance and their poetic, allegorical tenor; he showed great sensitivity to the entire decorative ensemble of a setting (fig. 3). In particular, Tack's absorption of the latest mural techniques, including the use of projected images to enlarge drawings, was vital to his traditional mural painting and to his abstractions. Mowbray documented their ongoing friendship in his memoirs.[12]

In the 1890s more American artists visited

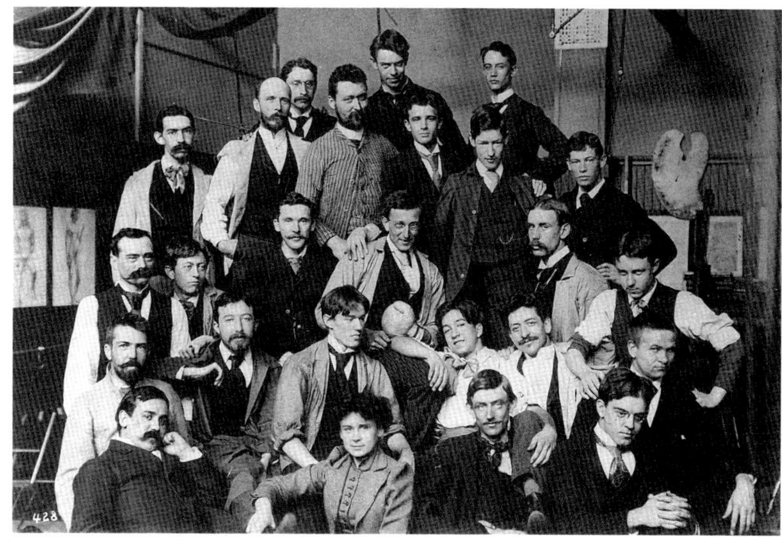

Fig. 2. H. Siddons Mowbray's life painting class at the Art Students League, New York, ca. 1893–95. Tack is seated behind the female model and is flanked by F. Luis Mora (right) and Thomas Fogarty (left), Archives, Art Students League

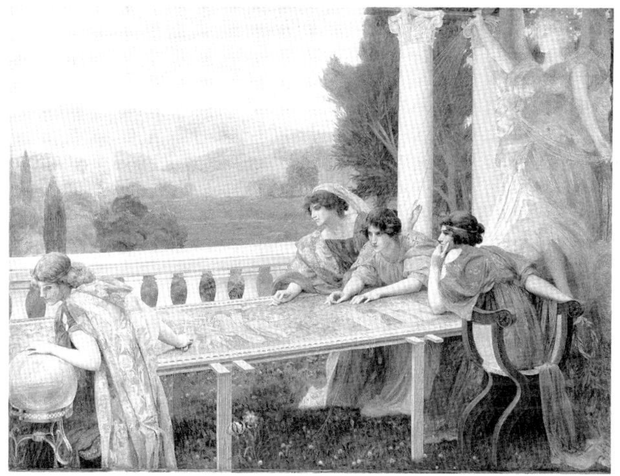

Fig. 3. H. Siddons Mowbray, *Le Destin*, 1896, courtesy, Museum of Fine Arts, Boston, Tompkins Collection

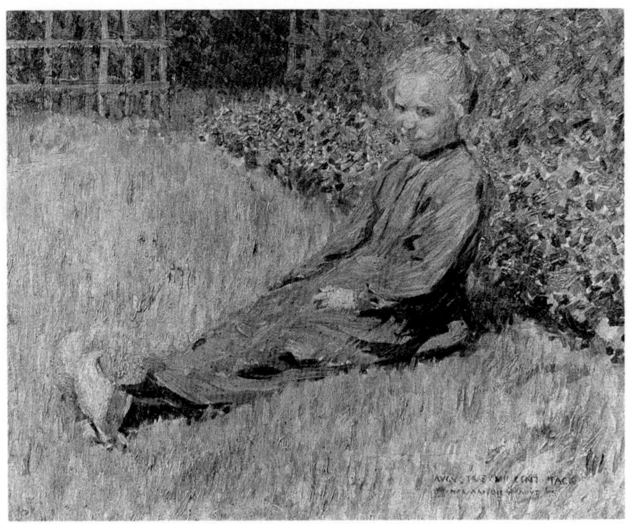

Fig. 4. Augustus Vincent Tack, *Girl in Sabots*, 1895, private collection, Chicago

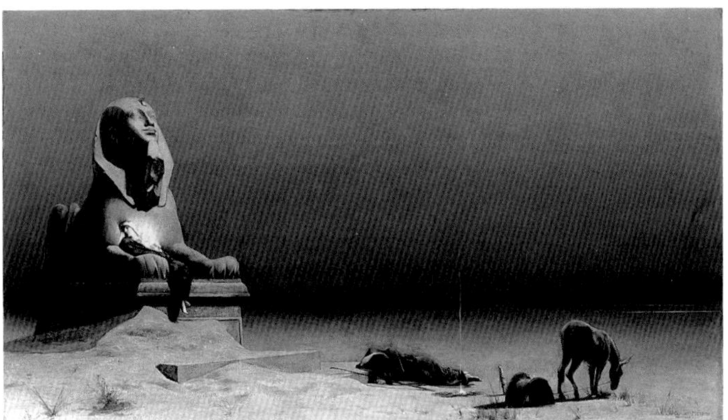

Fig. 5. Luc-Olivier Merson, *Rest on the Flight Into Egypt*, courtesy Museum of Fine Arts, Boston, Bequest of George Golding Kennedy

France than ever before. While many pursued academic training at the Ecole des Beaux-Arts or in the many private academies and ateliers in Paris, others traveled to Giverny, where Monet lived and worked, or to Brittany, in particular Pont-Aven. Bucolic motifs and peasant subjects in the French countryside also attracted artists from Paris during the summer months when the academies closed.[13]

Tack made his first journey abroad in 1890, traveling to the French Alps and the Basque region.[14] Two more trips followed, one in 1893, from which a painting of a Picardy landscape survives, and one in 1895. During the latter sojourn, Tack painted *Girl in Sabots* (1895, private collection, Chicago) in Normandy; the saturated colors, stippled brushwork, and volumetric form are a tangible record of his proximity to Monet and admiration of Theodore Robinson (fig. 4). Tack's European stays seem to have encouraged him to study impressionism and draftsmanship, the latter presumably with Luc-Olivier Merson (fig. 5).[15] Evidence of this association emerges in Tack's mature work, particularly in his keen understanding of atelier methods—such as pouncing, a means of transferring drawings that dates to the Renaissance or earlier—and in the linear severity of his preparatory studies for his murals.

Tack's approach to art is rooted in the pervasive influences of the last decades of the nineteenth century. He owes much to the ideology and diversity of the aesthetic movement, which permeated Anglo-American culture beginning in the 1870s (see Elizabeth V. Chew's essay, "Fenollosa, Dow, Tack, and Phillips: A Case for 'Subjective' Painting in America," in this catalogue). The movement was consolidating under the banner of art for the sake of beauty. It began largely in opposition to John Ruskin's moral imperative of an edifying art that, through imitation of nature, expressed the divine. With its emphasis on formal qualities, the aesthetic movement advocated music as the suitable analogue for painting: the harmonies of color and form gained primacy at the expense of narrative.[16] The movement was imported to America from England, primarily by its leading proponent, Whistler, whose writings and paintings were greeted with growing enthusiasm in the United States toward the end of the nineteenth century (fig. 23).

Although Tack came of age during the twilight of the aesthetic movement, the enduring reputation of Whistler and the new emphasis on the decorative in art contributed much to his vision. A craftsmanly approach, with an acute interest in and spontaneous response to the painting process, pervades Tack's work. In his attention to presentation, he continually acknowledged the work of art as a decorative object, an attitude he would never relinquish.

Coupled with the subjective tenets of the aesthetic movement, Tack's painting bore the idealistic naturalism of the American Renaissance movement, whose major exponents were John La Farge, Abbott Thayer, and John Singer Sargent. This style was expressed in numerous public and private decorative mural programs and sumptuous objects, conscious recollections of the Renaissance tradition. It never fully shed the moral underpinnings that were anathema to the "art for art's sake" philosophy of Whistler. Rather, from it flowered a selective revival of Greek, Asian, and Renaissance styles and subjects in the service of a new symbolic language to articulate America's golden age. The enduring monuments of the movement include ideologically ambitious and visually luxuriant mural programs informed by an idealized past: the Boston Public Library decorations by Puvis de Chavannes, Sargent, and Edwin Austin Abbey (completed 1895), Whistler's gilded, *japoniste* Peacock Room (1877, Freer Gallery of Art), and the decorative work and stained glass of La Farge, whose decorations for Trinity Church in Boston of 1876–77 earned him the accolade of "the father of American mural decoration."[17]

Tack applied methods gleaned from his exposure to highly trained and gifted decorators like Mowbray, Merson, and La Farge to his creation of many civic and religious mural decorations throughout his career. Further, like these artists, he was directly influenced by the Italian masters, in particular Giorgione and the Venetian painters.[18] After World War I, Tack was among those who resumed mural work in the tradition of the American Renaissance, particularly in nationalistic commemorations of the war effort. Even in Tack's evolution toward abstraction, when he omitted overt religious and allegorical subjects, he drew continually upon the methods and themes of this period. His career was thus a vivid example of the nineteenth century inheritance of American abstraction. The elegant accented and decorative borders with which Tack finished his work—abstract or conventional, easel or mural painting—are one of his strongest recollections of his classic training and aesthetic sensibility.[19]

In 1894, Tack launched his career in New York, taking a studio uptown on Eighth Avenue below Columbus Circle and listing himself in the city directory as a portrait painter. He exhibited regularly at the Society of American Artists, at the annual exhibitions of the Pennsylvania Academy of the Fine Arts and the National Academy of Design, and at the Carnegie International, where a portrait was considered for honors in 1898.[20]

In 1896, following his Paris sojourn of the previous year, Tack had his first solo exhibition at the gallery of Charles W. Kraushaar, later his dealer. The show included twenty-five paintings and drew critical notices highlighting Tack's strengths and weaknesses, many of which remained facets of his style. The *New York Times* critic, though faulting Tack for sloppiness in applying paint, proclaimed him a young artist of "considerable promise and no little feeling for color," praising particularly his direct, spontaneous manner, which was best expressed in the less elaborate canvases.[21]

From Tack's self-portrait of 1897, painted as a gift to his parents, peers a bespectacled young man, a naive, expectant youth at the dawn of his career (cat. 1). The broad brushwork suggesting the influence of Robert Henri or Chase carries through to the deep background tones and informs the pale, sketchy cast of the face, in which a single, fluid line defines the prominent chin.[22] But the personality these strokes capture conveys Tack's own gentle, tentative character. "I can imagine no life so full of possible beauty as an artist's," he wrote his wife Violet three years later. "It means the highest comprehension of life—the deepest faith in religion and is the very happiest existence."[23]

No other artist had as profound and pervasive an impact on Tack's life and work as the American painter La Farge. Well into Tack's seventies, he still referred to La Farge as "my master."[24] La Farge's prodigious talent as muralist, decorator, painter, illustrator, and creator of stained glass, his refined character, and his comprehensive mastery of several media made him the archetypal artistic persona for Tack and other artists coming of age at the turn of the century. With mentors who included the French painter Thomas Couture and the American William Morris Hunt, La Farge had a love of Asian art that would have affected Tack's own approach to painting. Although Tack's enthusiasm for non-Western art forms was inherited partly from Whistler, his early collection of Japanese prints undoubtedly reflects La Farge's influence. La Farge's study of the Old Masters, his use of photography, his belief in painting outdoors, and his acute interest in color all informed Tack's work. The two shared Catholic backgrounds, Jesuit educations, and patrician tastes, making the older artist an even more likely mentor.[25]

Tack's probing and sensitive portrait of La Farge is the first tangible record of the encounter between the two artists (1897–1900, Metropolitan Museum of Art; fig. 6). The portrait focuses on the hypnotic gaze of the artist, whose bespectacled visage emerges from a dusky, mysterious penumbra. The arabesque design of a Japanese screen is dimly contoured in the background, its spirals entwining with the curling smoke from La Farge's cigar. Tack imbued his subject with the mystic's vision and an Eastern inflection, aspects that Tack eagerly embraced.[26]

Tack probably initiated the portrait project,

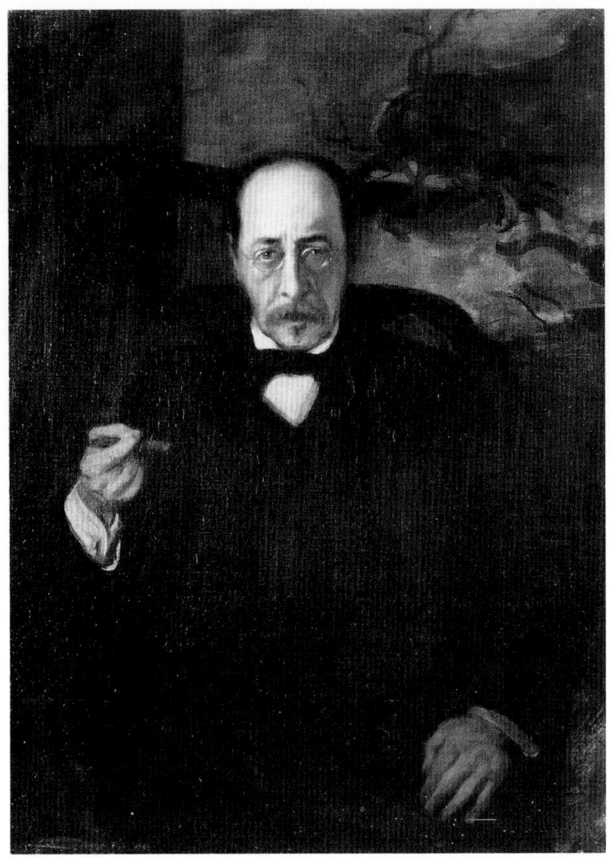

Fig. 6. *Portrait of John La Farge*, ca. 1897–1900, Metropolitan Museum of Art, New York, Arthur H. Hearn Fund, 1937

Fig. 7. John La Farge, *Rishi Calling Up A Storm, Japanese Folk Lore*, ca. 1897–98, The Cleveland Museum of Art, Purchase from the J.H. Wade Fund, 39.267, Cleveland, Ohio

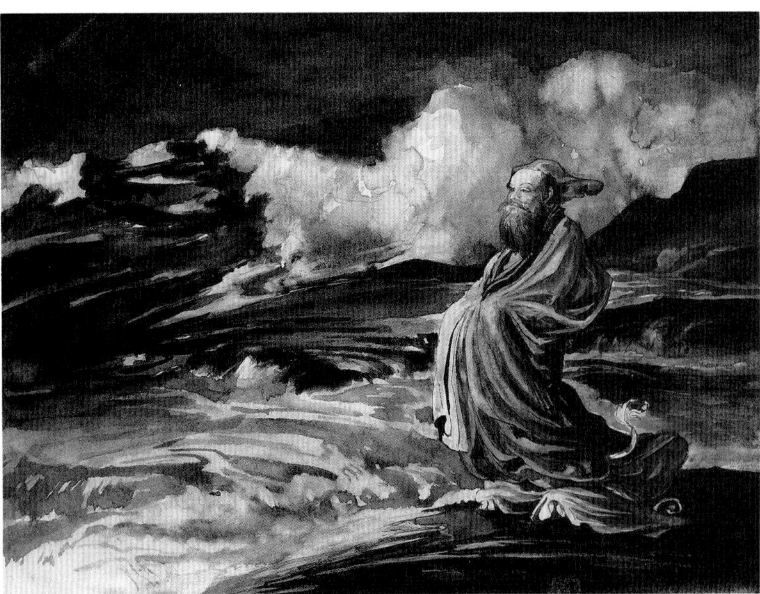

which spanned at least two years, with La Farge frequently deferring sittings due to ill health or absences from New York. The portrait occasioned the only surviving letter from La Farge to the younger artist. On November 14, 1899, he explained a recent lapse in sittings:

I don't know what to say about my portrait I fear that you may have thought me discourteous And that would be true, if I had been a well man; but I left New York hurriedly to get better and passed a whole month in bed in Newport.[27]

From that point, Tack worked from a photograph, a procedure that La Farge's son Bancel evidently recommended. Tack's greatest hope for the portrait—that it should some day be in the Metropolitan Museum—was ultimately realized.[28]

Despite La Farge's seminal influence, further details of contact between the two artists are few and the chronology problematic. For example, James Lane contends that La Farge was the first to recognize Tack's budding talent. At some point, seeing a portrait by the younger artist at the Society of American Artists, La Farge, then the society's president, gave it a place of honor and sent Tack a congratulatory letter.[29] According to James Yarnall, it is also possible that Tack frequented the Tenth Street Studio Building in the summers during the 1890s, gleaning what he could from watching the artist at work on mural and decorative projects. As late as 1936, the director of the Metropolitan Museum of Art invited Tack as one of four people to inform the selection and advise on the catalogue of the La Farge retrospective of that year, suggesting that the association between the two artists was acknowledged by others who knew La Farge well.[30]

Though their brief acquaintance was perhaps insignificant for La Farge, it was pivotal for Tack, paving the way for his highly original contribution to American decorative painting and providing a constant paradigm for Tack's experiments. Following his lead, Tack explored the abstract, decorative possibilities of Asian painting. In particular, his mural-like conceptions of *Storm* (cat. 25) and *The Voice of Many Waters* (cat. 27) are indebted to La Farge's hypnotic watercolors in which he comes closest to an Oriental, mystical expression, such as *A Rishi Calling Up a Storm, Japanese Folk Lore* (fig. 7). Tack's innovation is his eradication of the intermediary figures in favor of pure meditations on the landscapes in flat, patterned Asian idioms. Further, his *Rosa Mystica* (1922–23, Cleveland Museum of Art; fig. 18), in its mixture of borrowings from Asian,

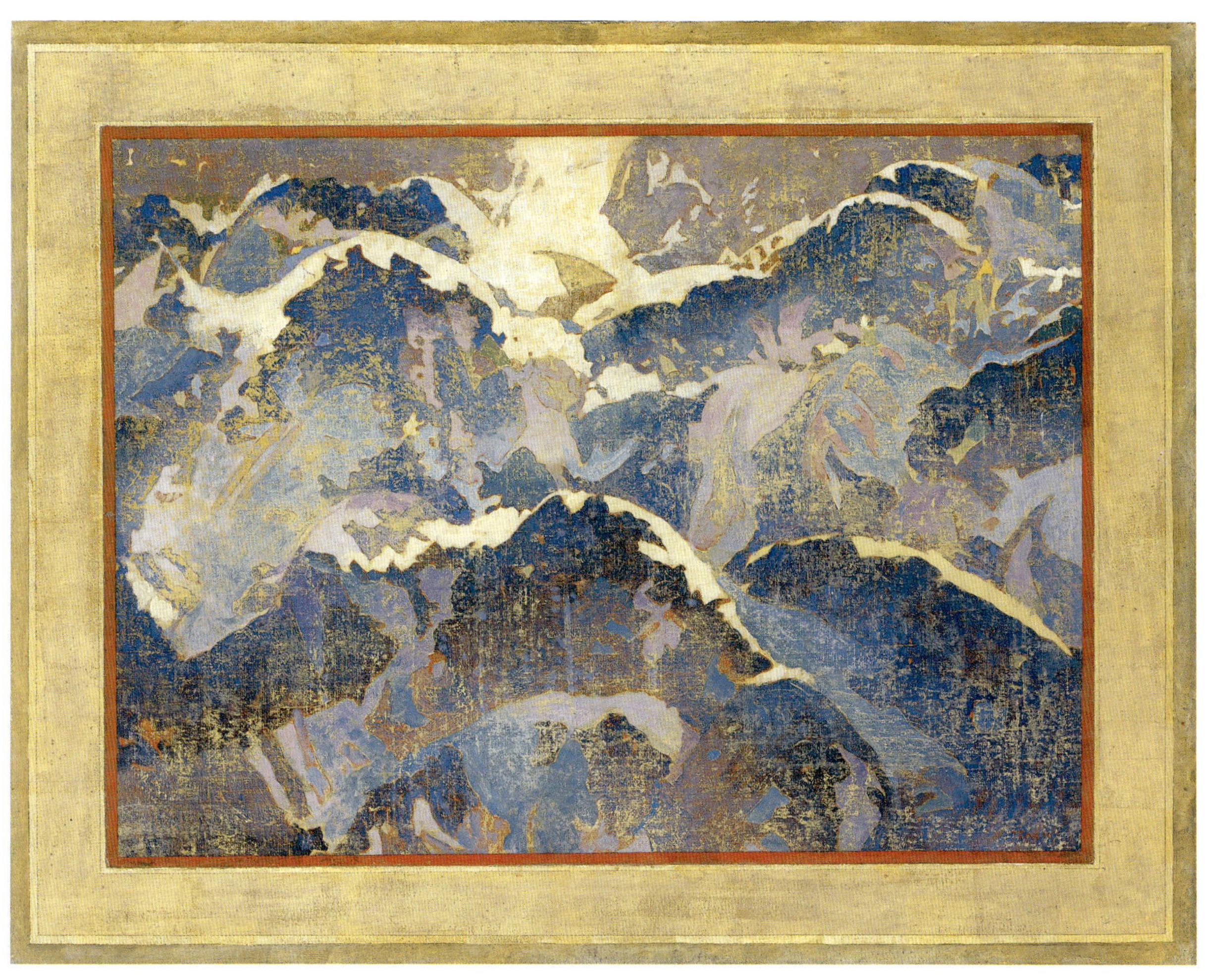

Cat. 25. *Storm*, ca. 1922–23, oil on canvas mounted on wallboard, 36 ⅞ x 48 1/16 in.

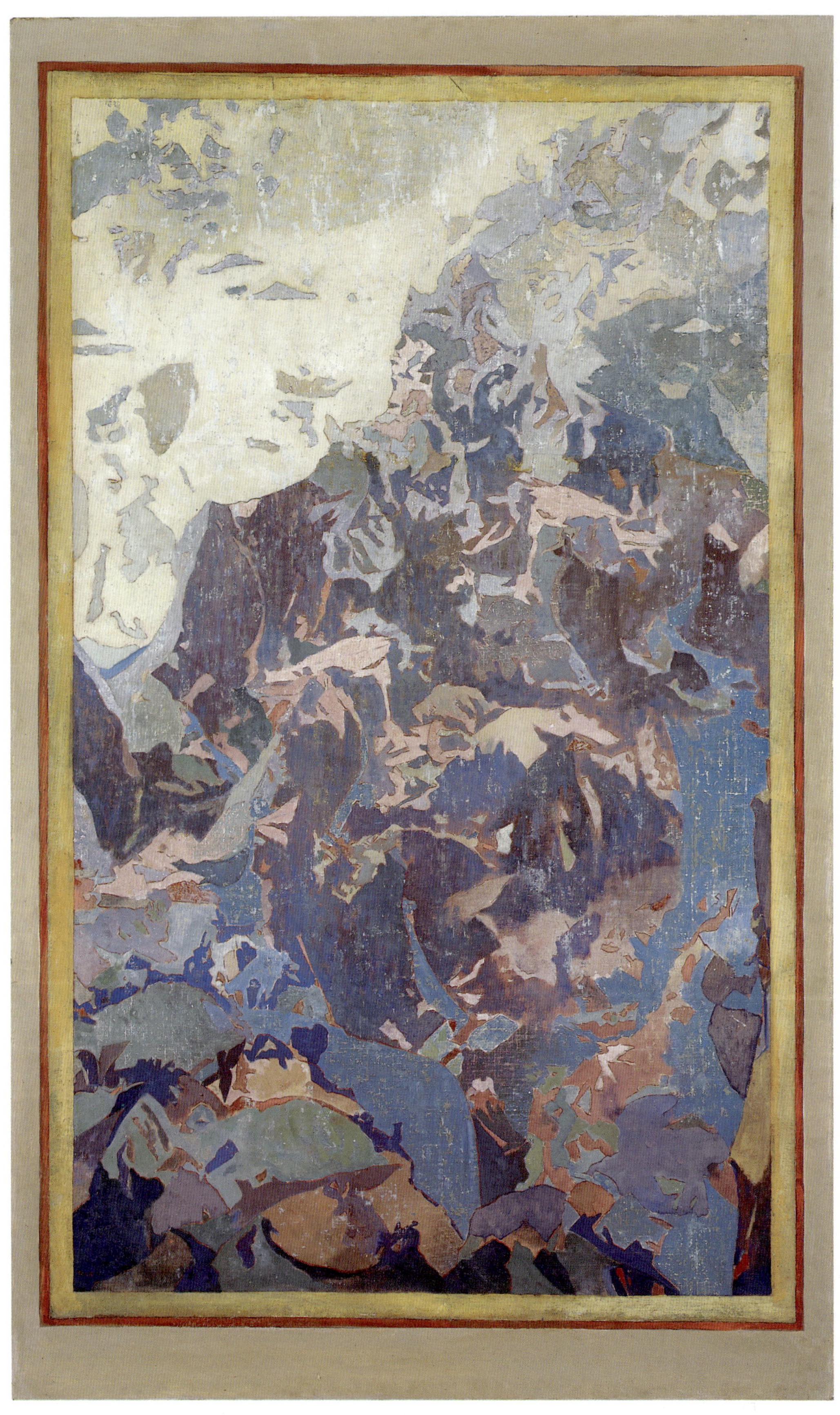

Cat. 27. *The Voice of Many Waters*, ca. 1923–24, oil on canvas mounted on wallboard, 77 ¾ x 47 ⅞ in.

Byzantine, and Italian painting, is a direct descendant of La Farge's *Ascension* for the Church of the Ascension, New York (1886–87; fig. 24). Tack's reliance on the deity Kuwannon for the figure of the Virgin, among other works, underscores the heritage of La Farge, who found inspiration in this figure.[31] Tack even carried La Farge's lessons into his own early decorative work for private homes in 1900, stating that he reveled in "playing real Michel Angelo" as he created a series of idealized figures across the walls of his brother-in-law's dining room.[32]

Duncan Phillips characterized Tack's art as "carry[ing] forward the La Farge tradition in American painting," imbuing the nineteenth-century tradition with his own modern search for "a new way to make the painter's raw materials serve the uses and ends of the spirit."[33] Yet ultimately it was La Farge's search for the ideal, for a new language of color, for art based in nature while preserving its decorative integrity that drew and held Tack's fascination in the first decade of his career and beyond.

DEERFIELD AND NEW YORK

Beginning in 1897, Tack divided his time between New York City and the village of Deerfield in western Massachusetts, a practice he maintained for the rest of his life. The rural retreat became his home as well as the focus of his landscape painting, until his discovery of the western landscape in the early 1920s. In contrast, New York, which he loathed, provided a living through the obligatory connections to galleries, portrait subjects, and decorative work. This divided life encouraged a duality in the artist, as the private and public self, the family man and the society joiner, the isolated mystic and the urban sophisticate flourished in contrasting milieus.[34]

Tack found community in the people and tenor of Deerfield, which was one of the first areas to recognize and preserve its eighteenth-century history, traditions, and architecture. When Tack arrived, a small-scale arts and crafts revival based on Ruskinian and transcendental notions of a community in harmony with nature was reaching its peak. A sense of continuity with the American past permeated the town, which seemed bypassed by the present.[35]

The Connecticut River Valley, with its quiet beauty and varied terrain, became the artist's constant reference for the forces of nature, which he recorded in winter, early spring, and autumn, at various times of day and night. Tack usually avoided settled areas, instead seeking motifs in the unpopulated slopes, such as Shelburne Hills, an area known as Wisdom Way, and Mount Tobey. His view of nature is similar to that of the tonalist painters and the American masters of impressionist landscape, John Twachtman and Willard Metcalf. Tonalism, a movement rooted in Barbizon painting that flourished from about 1880 to 1915, was practiced by artists who conveyed highly personal responses to nature and favored pictorial unity over detail in moody atmospheric landscapes. Like the tonalists, Tack focused on intimate, unpopulated scenes carrying romantic and poetic overtones, in the uncertain light of dawn or dusk and in seasonal transitions such as early spring or snowbound winter. His silvery hues and delicate brushwork also recall the work of such American painters as George Fuller and George Inness, forerunners of the tonalist movement.[36] In such landscapes as *Cloud Wrack* (cat. 5), Tack pays homage to Inness, treating the transitory effects of a storm advancing through the hills and conveying his awe before the power of nature.

An early work of great promise, *Windswept (Snow Picture, Leyden)* (cat. 8) is a powerful example of Tack's independent vision.[37] A snow-capped mountain looms, unattainable and remote, against a roseate sky, recalling the German romantic tradition that focuses on nature's grandeur and mystery. Tack's techniques and motifs are both subtle and daring: he mingled wet paint layers, favoring rose, yellow, white, and blue, to suggest the luminous effect of early morning. These tonal harmonies, laid in broad strokes, only obliquely distinguish sky from ground. The irregularly shaped patches of rock evolved from randomly placed bare spaces that Tack intentionally left in the hillside. These patches become the occasion for the abstracted pattern that appears suspended in the minimal composition. In their random disposition is an uncanny presaging of Tack's later abstractions. These arabesque patternings recall Twachtman's landscapes in their reliance on Japanese prints, an aesthetic of common interest (fig. 8).

Tack's paintings of the Deerfield landscape also include a suite of works that depict the countryside in different seasons; *Winter Landscape* (cat. 2), *Deerfield, Spring Landscape* (cat. 3), and *Twilight* (cat. 4) are representative examples. Despite their differing viewpoints—a meadow, a river valley, and a hilltop—they have a common structure of high horizons,

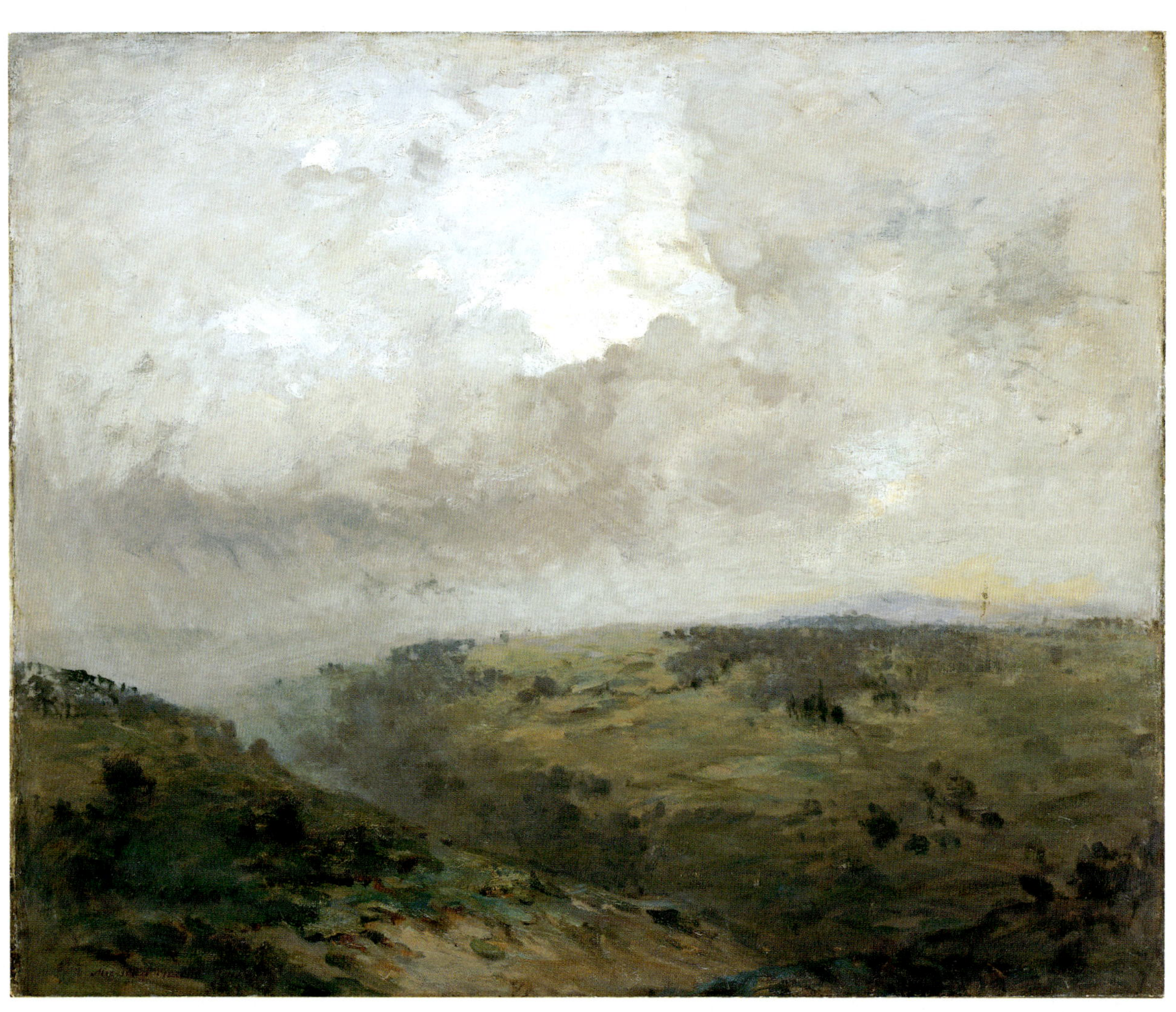

Cat. 5. *Cloud Wrack*, ca. 1900, oil on canvas, 29 ⅜ x 36 ⅛ in.

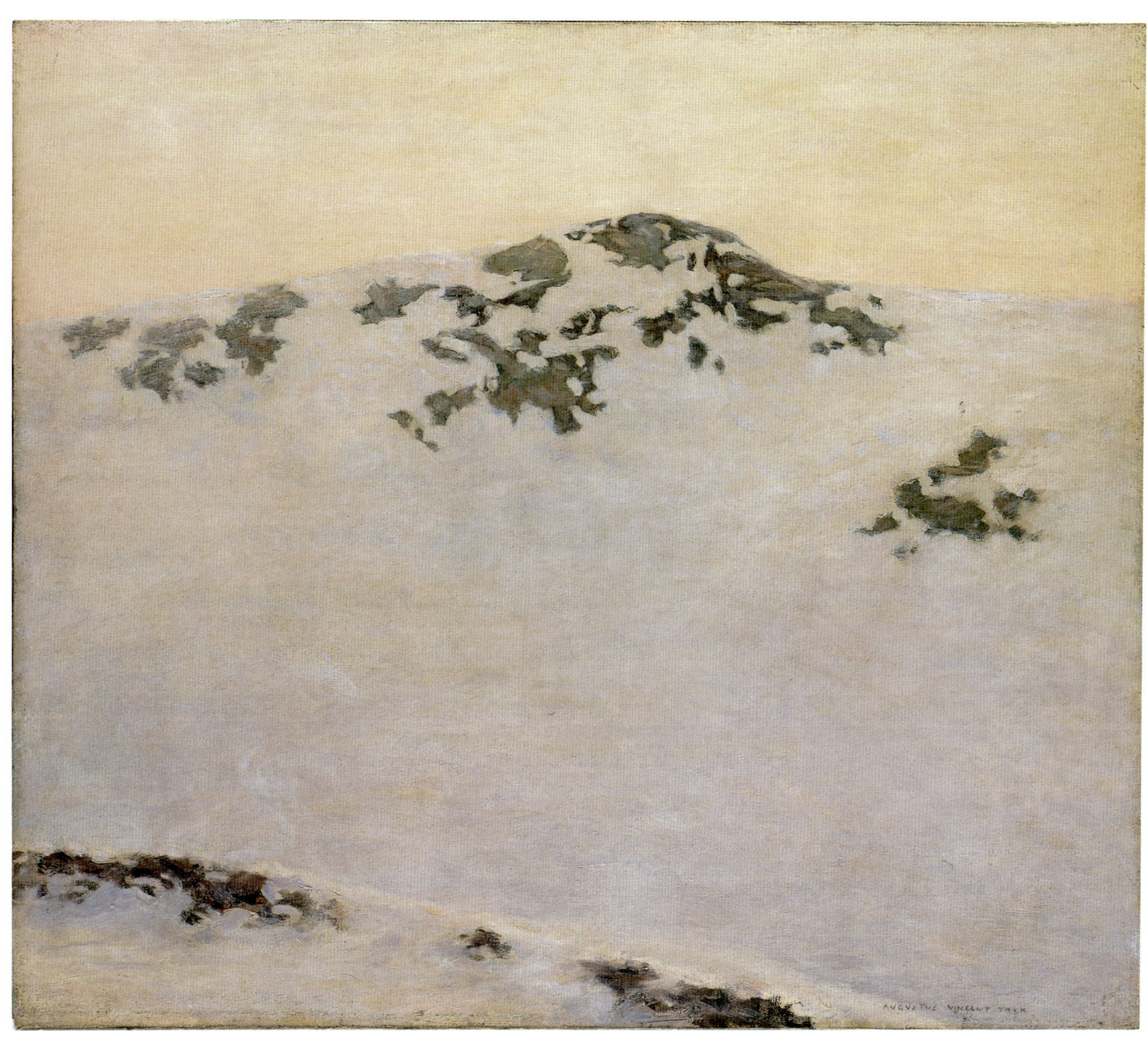

Cat. 8. *Windswept (Snow Picture, Leyden)*, ca. 1900–1902, oil on canvas, 31 x 36 3/16 in.

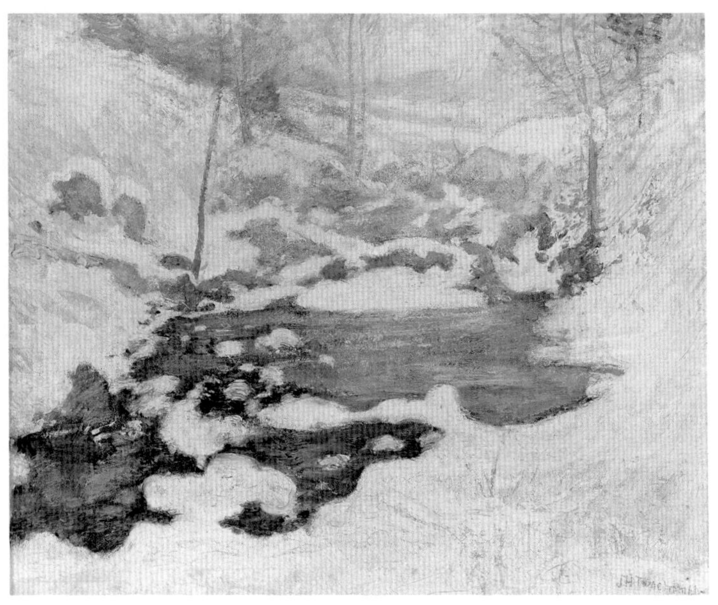

Fig. 8. John Twachtman, *Icebound,* Friends of American Art Collection, © 1993, The Art Institute of Chicago, all rights reserved

obscured or collapsed middle grounds, and views into luminous distances. They also share a tendency toward patterning in topographical generalities. For example, a foreground passage of grasses in *Twilight* recalls a similar design of shadows on the landscape in the far left of *Winter Landscape.*

Twilight, structured solidly in thick horizontal brush strokes, introduces aspects of Tack's landscapes that continue until his late painting. The traditional structure, with a pronounced contrast between an immediate foreground and a view into the distance, informed Tack's vision of landscape into the teens, in such pictures as *Canyon* (cat. 26), and even into the abstractions of the 1920s, such as *Largo* (cat. 29) and *Liberation* (cat. 33), which retain the contrapuntal design. An orange underpainting warming the canvas tones would also recur in his post-1930 painting.

Tack's most fruitful connection with Deerfield's artists and craftspeople was his contact with the photographers Mary and Frances Allen. Retired schoolteachers, the sisters took up photography at the turn of the century. They made sepia-toned photographs of Deerfield landscapes, people working in the fields, and domestic interiors, especially with mothers and children. Their photography owes much to the vision of the tonalists. An aesthetic exchange between Tack and the Allens is suggested by the correspondence and by several photographs of Tack's family, which bear close association with his portraits and figure pieces of the era (fig. 9). *Allegory—Love and Life* (*Mother and Child*) (cat. 9) echoes in theme and composition the graded contrasts of the Allen sisters' photographs. Their soft-focused, delicate landscapes must also have been a stimulus to Tack in his approach to the same scenery. A triptych depicting one continuous view may have found its source in the photographers' work.[38]

As Tack's painting unfolded against a rich background of colonial Americana, his landscapes took on a poetic quality, and his figure pieces echoed the idealism of the local legend George Fuller. The spell of Fuller's art, especially his depictions of the feminine ideal, found immediate form in the presence—and the astonishing beauty—of the artist's daughter Agnes, nicknamed Violet. Tack met Violet, also an aspiring painter, in his first summer in Deerfield.[39] They began an extended courtship with horseback rides through the Deerfield hills and painting expeditions. The relationship continued for three years while the pair, frequently apart, commuted between Cambridge, New York, and Deerfield. They were married in Deerfield on June 19, 1900.

Tack's idealistic quest for transcendence in

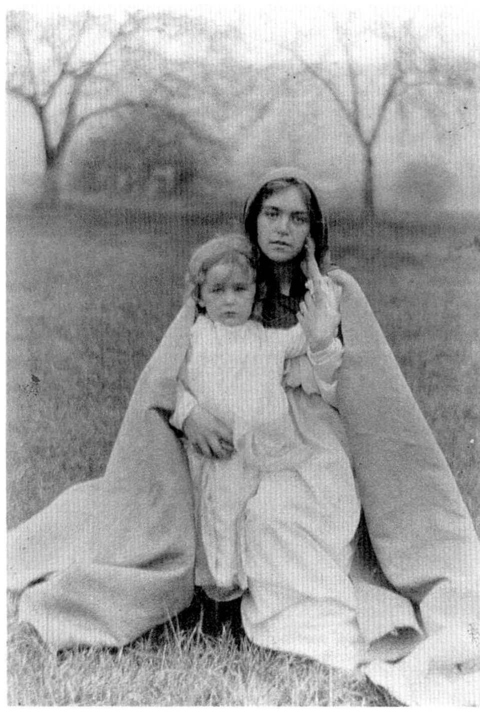

Fig. 9. Allen Sisters, *Agnes Tack and Her Niece, Elizabeth Fuller,* ca. 1899, from an original platinum print, private collection

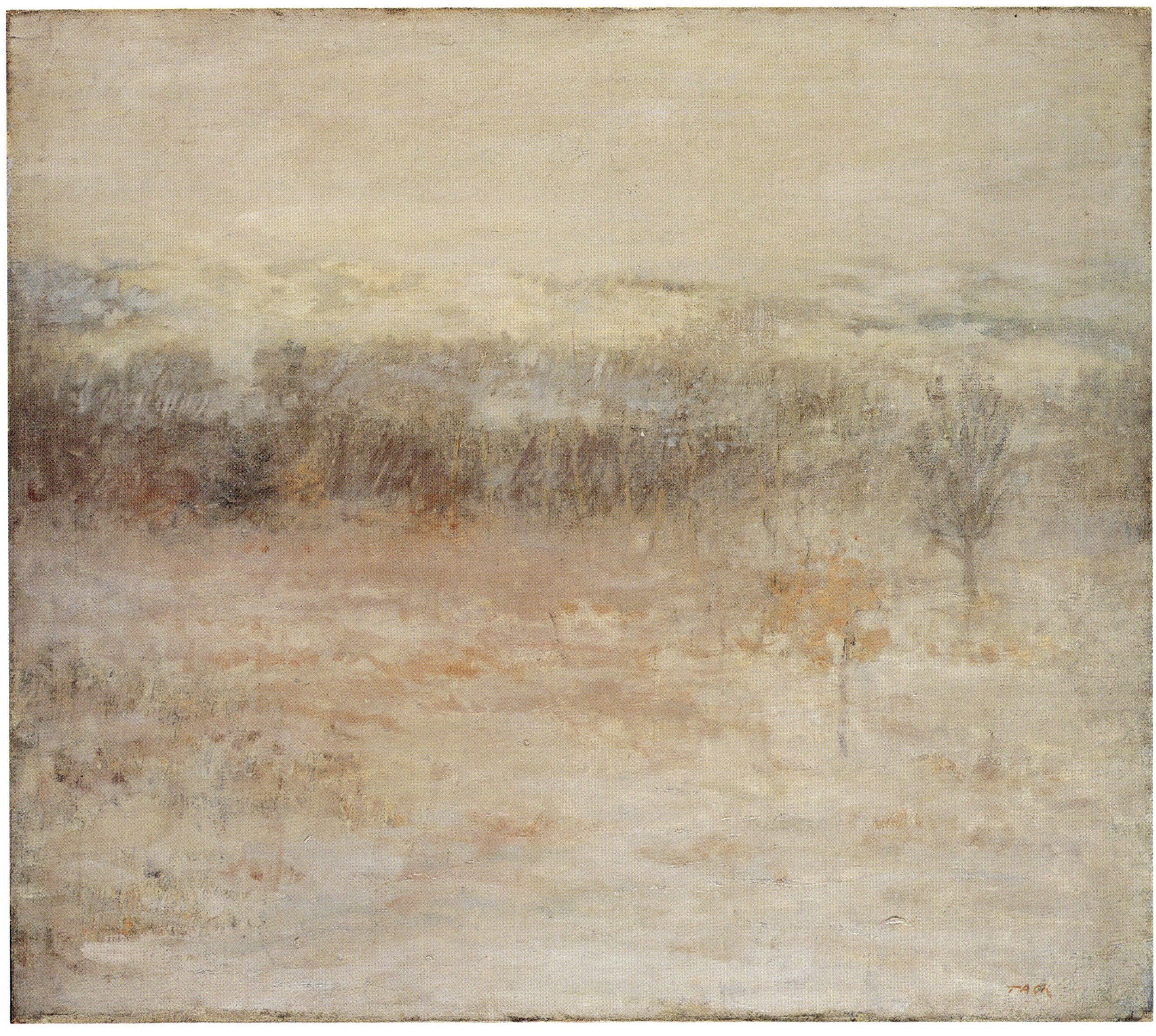

Cat. 2. *Winter Landscape*, ca. 1898–ca. 1902, oil on canvas, 24 x 28 in.

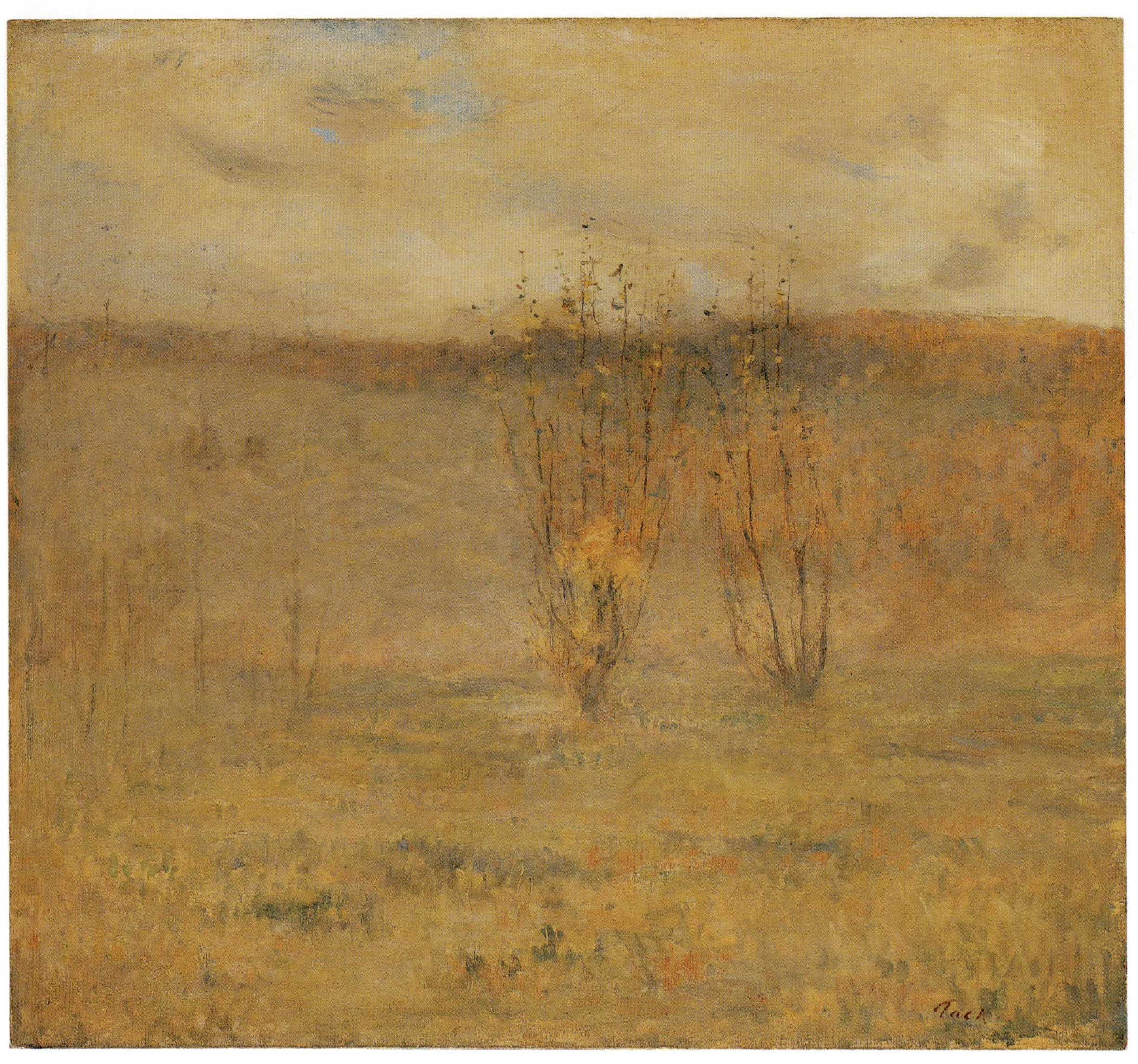

Cat. 3. *Deerfield, Spring Landscape*, ca. 1898–ca. 1902, oil on canvas, 25 x 28 in.

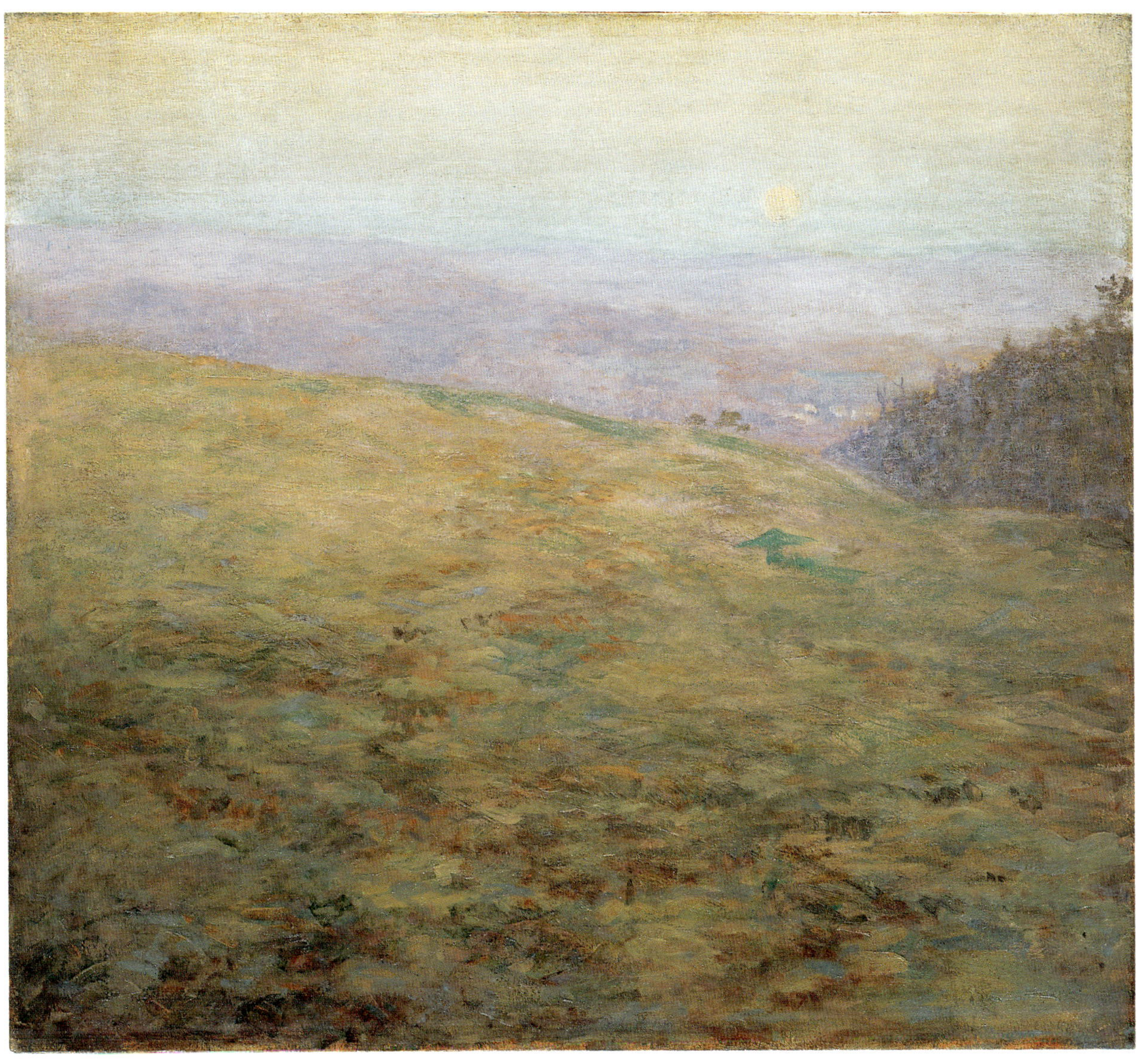

Cat. 4. *Twilight* , ca. 1898–ca. 1902, oil on canvas, 24 ¾ x 27 ¾ in.

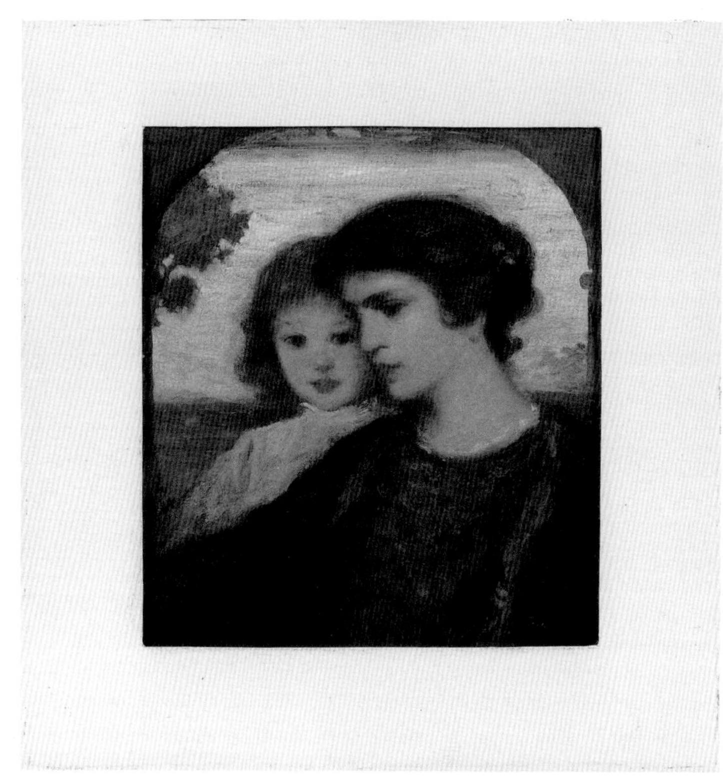

Cat. 9. *Allegory—Love and Life (Mother and Child),* ca. 1900–ca. 1907, oil on canvas mounted on hardboard, 25 x 24 in.

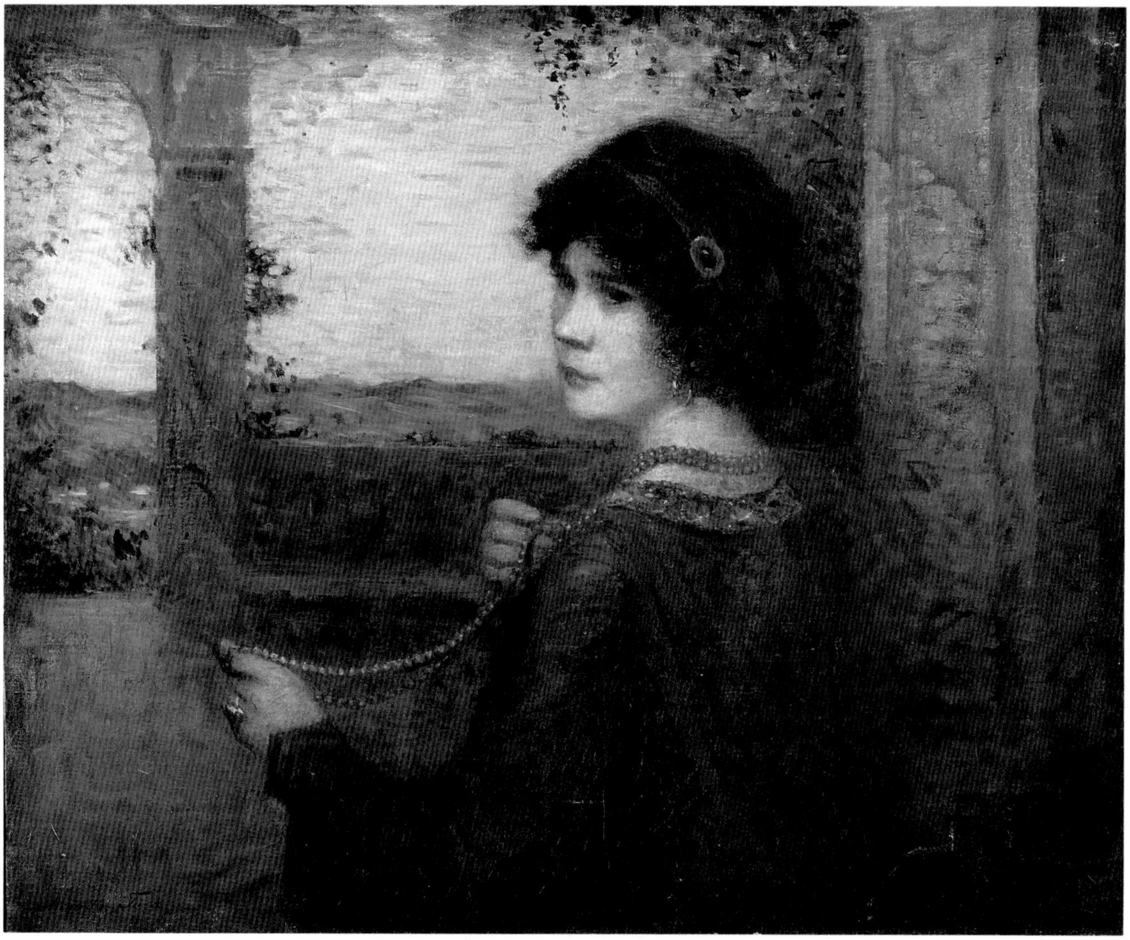

Cat. 6. *Figure in Red with Beads,* ca. 1900, oil on canvas, 29 ⅛ x 36 in.

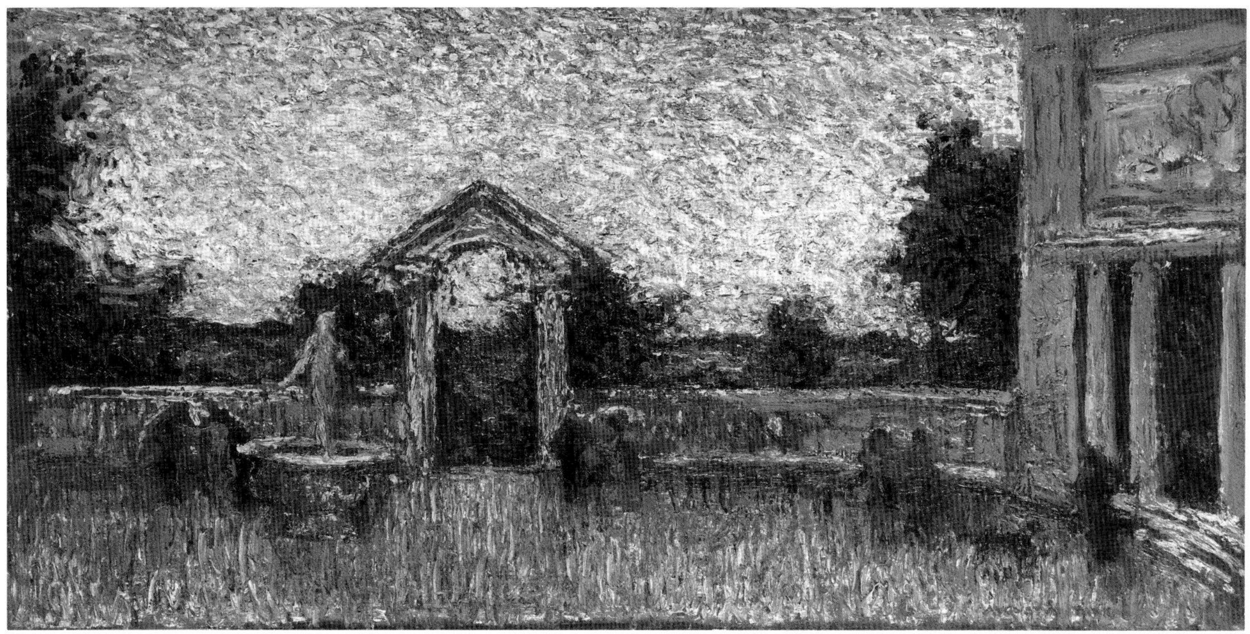

Cat. 14. *Court of Romance (Garden of Romance)*, ca. 1914, oil on canvas, 15 x 30 ¼ in.

his work and life, aspirations he expressed repeatedly in letters to Violet, disposed him toward George Fuller's vision. After one visit to Violet in Boston, he wrote:

I am back again at the studio all fired with enthusiasm having seen such fine pictures in Boston. The finest of all was the Winifred Dysart, it is the purest picture I have ever seen. . . . I think I shall never forget Duvenek's wife, also . . . do you know how much you have to do with both of these masterpieces? I felt my love for you in them both.[40]

Tack's portraits of his wife show a striking similarity to Fuller's approach, though Tack's painting is more sentimental.

Tack's first consistent subject matter was portraits and figure pieces. Particularly in his early years, he was preoccupied with the ideal figure in the landscape. *Figure in Red with Beads* (cat. 6) is a notable example. A woman poses before a medieval architectural setting, beyond which stretches the Deerfield landscape. Fingering a chain of red beads, she glances over her shoulder at the viewer.[41] The opulent tones reminiscent of the pre-Raphaelites and the rich coloration of Venetian painting, along with the delicate modeling of the face and hatched strokes reminiscent of traditional egg tempera techniques, are countered by a more impressionistic handling of the background. Her costume and the setting anticipate Tack's pointillist work of the teens, such as *Court of Romance* (*Garden of Romance*) (cat. 14). Yet the likeness clearly suggests an individual, perhaps a Deerfield model.[42]

The ebb and flow of Tack's activities as a portrait painter are the bellwether for his financial situation throughout his career. Despite the Tack family position and the Fuller inheritance, the marriage could not proceed without a show of material gain. This circumstance may have led Tack to attempt to establish himself in Boston as a portrait painter of local luminaries.[43] His portraits and, intermittently, his landscapes hung in a number of Boston Art Club exhibitions alongside the canvases of Childe Hassam, Inness, Chase, and Weir during the late 1890s and early 1900s. One of Boston's most prominent commercial galleries, Doll and Richards—perhaps not coincidentally, La Farge's primary dealer—gave Tack a solo exhibition in 1902.[44]

In the early 1900s Tack tried to make his fortune in the Deerfield region with portraits and landscape painting, renting a studio in the neighboring town of Greenfield and exhibiting locally with the Arts and Crafts Society and in his studio. The endeavor was short lived, and he again had a New York studio in 1908. Well into the teens, Tack continued to paint Deerfield scenes, such as *New England 1850* (*Ox Cart*) (cat. 12), the sole painting in which Tack includes a Deerfield landmark, the church tower. His focus on regional motifs and land-

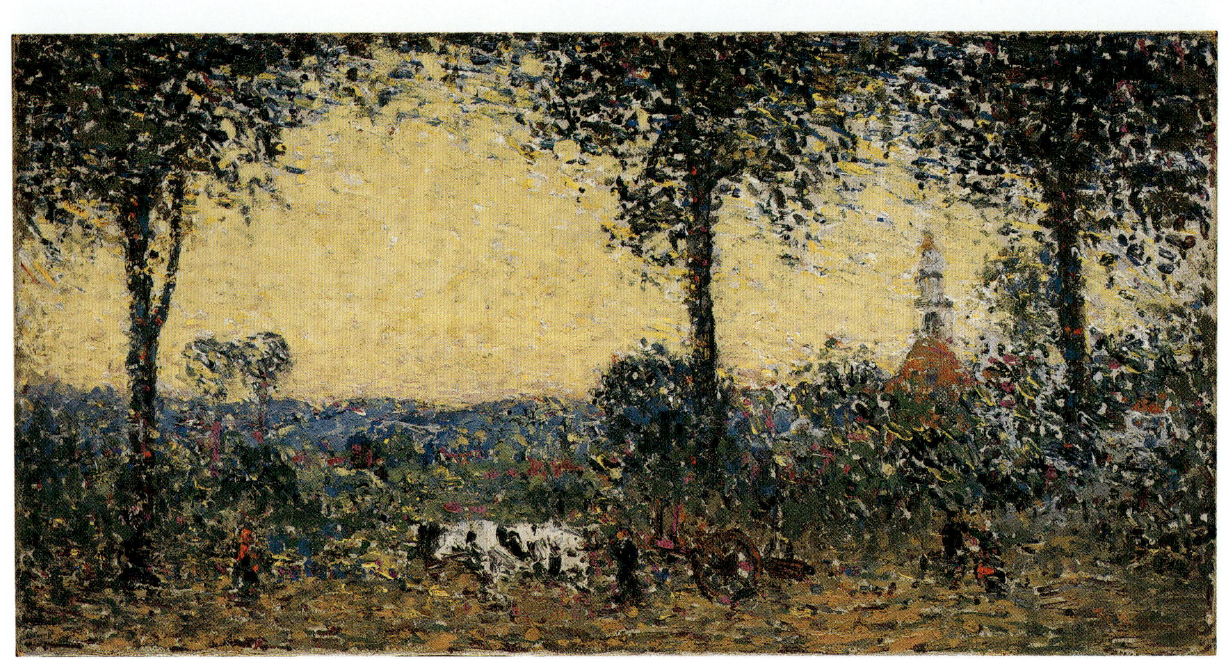

Cat. 12. *New England, 1850 (Ox Cart)*, early teens, oil on canvas, 15 x 30 in.

scapes, while perhaps reflecting the popularity of such subjects in the art market, was a sincere expression of his feeling for nature.

The Deerfield idyll was sadly interrupted in 1908, when Violet, always in delicate health, contracted tuberculosis. She sought treatment at the Trudeau sanatorium at Saranac Lake in the Adirondacks, where she remained almost full-time until 1913. Their two children were sent to live with relatives in Boston. The abrupt suspension of Tack's family life, along with the financial burden of daunting medical costs, was accompanied by a renewed struggle in his work, as the tonal impressionism of the early Deerfield landscapes gave way to more imaginary evocations.

NEW DIRECTIONS AND DENOUEMENT

Throughout the early years of his marriage, Tack struggled to establish a footing in the art world, with modest success. He joined the Architectural League and took a studio at 7 West 42nd Street in 1908. He solicited William Macbeth to visit him in Deerfield, eventually capturing the dealer's sustained interest with his fresh landscapes.[45] In November 1907 Macbeth hosted a one-person show of Tack's landscapes, the artist's most significant exhibition to that point. Although it was not a commercial success, the show drew acclaim from the press. Critics expressed surprise at the varied talents of the painter, best known as a portraitist. They commented on his genuine feeling for nature and his handling of color, though some suggested his form lacked conviction.[46] As if a swan song for Tack's early work, the exhibition showcased his tonal, impressionist vision of the 1890s and early 1900s.

Unlike artists of the Eight such as John Sloan and Robert Henri, Tack disliked the city. In his letters to Violet, he repeatedly expressed abhorrence for the noise, dirt, and crowds. Urban life found expression in only one known canvas: *Winter* (*New York in Snow*), a depiction of a Manhattan street transformed by a blizzard (cat. 7). Tack painted this view from a window, thought to be either his Eighth Street studio or his family's home on West 82nd Street.[47] The free brush strokes and decorative palette animate the surface in a dizzying mass, connoting the swirling snow and dense atmosphere enveloping the somber mass of buildings. Portents of Tack's pointillist period of the teens are seen in the cool range of blue and gray hues enlivened with lavender and in the tendril-like brush strokes, which recall Monet's late work. *Winter*, an anomaly, indicates the range of Tack's style and subject matter and invites comparison with American and French painters who explored urban themes in an impressionist idiom; its indigo hues and fading light bear special affinities with Childe Hassam's *Late Afternoon, Winter, New York* (1900, Brooklyn Museum) and coincide with an American revival of tonalism in the depiction of urban themes.[48]

In the teens, Tack was affiliated with some of the country's most orthodox art establishments: he taught at the Yale School of Fine Arts, became a member of the Century Association, and began a contract with Kraushaar Galleries. This conservative milieu might have secured his future as a muralist, society portrait painter, and landscapist in the enduring impressionist tradition. His sensitive portrayal of the social activist and art collector *Elizabeth Hudson*, a mutual friend of Tack and Phillips, shows his accomplished technique in the genre (cat. 17): the sitter's delicately modeled face and the bravura technique with which Tack brushed in her outfit and form rival the finest American portraiture of the period. Yet by the decade's end Tack was on the threshold of abstraction, moving from a predominantly perceptual observation of the landscape into more fanciful decorative evocations of nature and the human figure.

This gradual evolution testifies to Tack's desire for an art that would "eventually be able to exert a great power over the mind and the emotions without any resort to literary associations."[49] In the process, he was confronting new European and American developments in painting, including postimpressionism, symbolism, and, in particular, the decorative work of Arthur B. Davies and Maurice Prendergast (fig. 10). These artists, especially Davies, sought to recast the decorative symbolism of such masters as Puvis de Chavannes in a more modern idiom, an aspiration Tack shared.[50] Further, Tack's deepening interest in Asian art led him to new concepts of landscape painting. These influences spurred extremes: he experimented with orientalizing landscapes in lean washes and flattened, decorative form and with a highly expressive, original pointillism—two styles that he blended in a series of tonalist canvases of vaporous, thin paint, unexpectedly studded with concentrated areas of impasto. A vital impetus to Tack's progression toward

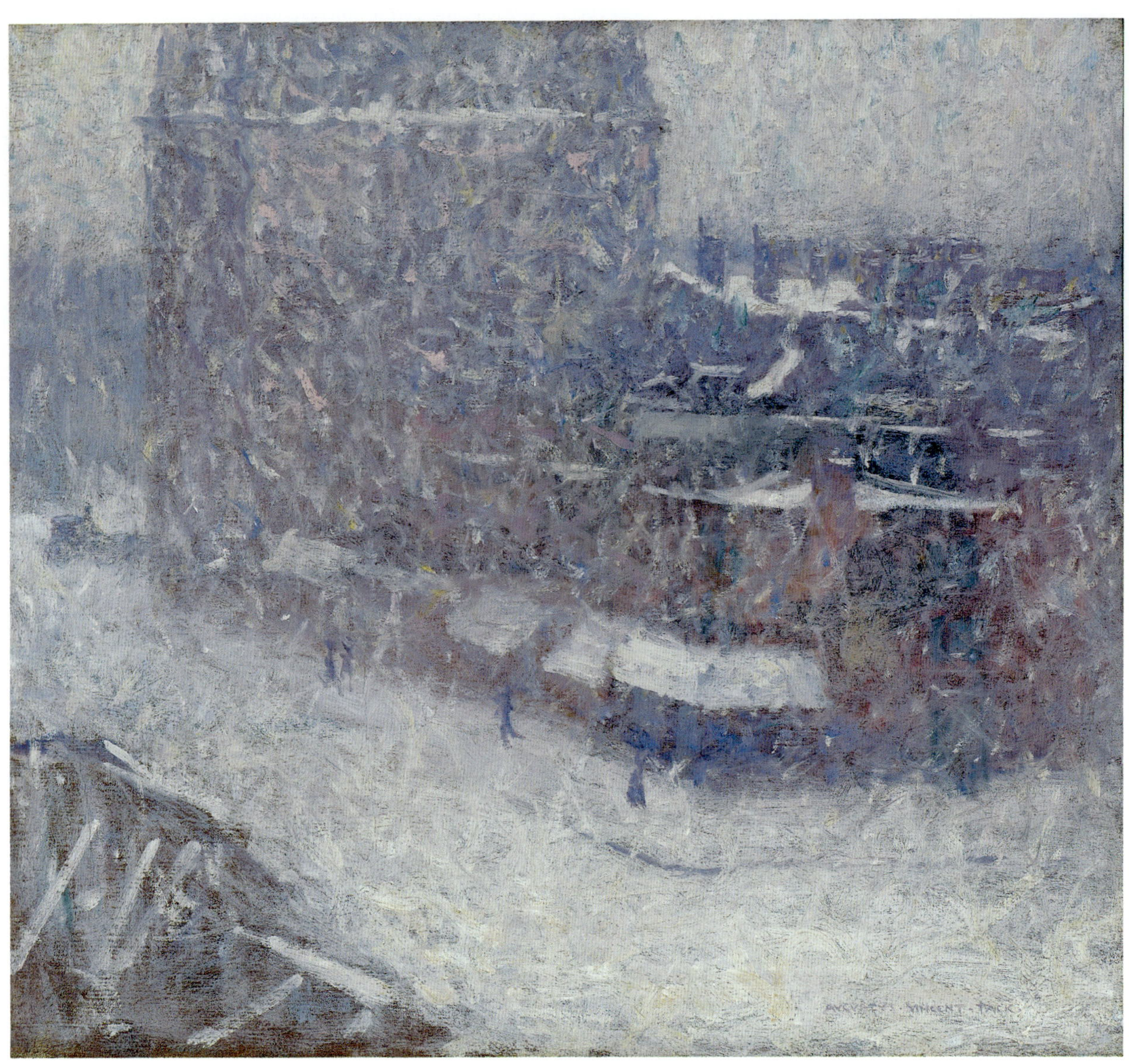

Cat. 7. *Winter (New York in Snow)*, ca. 1900, oil on canvas, 24 ⅞ x 27 ⅞ in.

abstraction during the teens was his encounter in 1914 with the young collector Duncan Phillips, who was drawn to the artist's latest work and would become his primary patron.[51]

A new emotional depth, heralded as early as 1908, developed fully in the works of the teens. Tack created his first truly symbolist works, which range from pastoral elegies conveying an ineffable joy to canvases rife with torment and loss. Notable among them are several monumental religious works of 1913–14, all relating to the Passion of Christ and possibly intended as a cycle for a church. The paintings ushered in a new gravity and a search for an original and potent expression. These works, his most significant of the decade, announce a vital shift to overtly spiritual themes. In them he married his new expressionistic style to a sustained exploration of religious subjects. By the beginning of the 1920s his landscape idylls and symbolist evocations of the divine were to be merged in a fresh, exciting abstract style.[52]

Among the landscapes of 1908–17 are buoyant paintings of idealized Deerfield vistas, including *Sunday Afternoon, Deerfield* (ca. 1911, The Phillips Collection) and *Deerfield in Twilight* (*The Dance*) (cat. 11). The element of fantasy and reverie in the scenes—one a pure landscape and the other a similar composition with a group of dancing figures in a twilight field—recalls the idyllic scenes of Davies and the tradition of Monticelli. The overmantel proportions, the sinuous filigree of trees framing the distant views, and the thick paint surfaces imbue the paintings with a decorative accent.

Deerfield in Twilight (*The Dance*) clearly shows the process and transformation of Tack's work. Three earlier conceptions reveal its origins. In two tiny drawings on the back of an envelope postmarked 1908 (private collection, Deerfield), Tack quickly sketched out the basic composition. The first drawing shows spherical, pictographic foliage, borrowed from Prendergast, and the second depicts trees with foliage signified by stippled dots closely resembling the painting. The third precursor, the initial rendering under the present surface of the work, was in a flat, smooth style. Sometime after 1911, Tack retouched the canvas in a playful stitching of thick impasto, laid on in staccato dashes.[53] The style, proportions, and subject—a dreamlike outdoor landscape—are reminiscent of Prendergast, although the gleaming light in the distant horizon bears spiritual and romantic overtones.

Like Prendergast and Prendergast's close

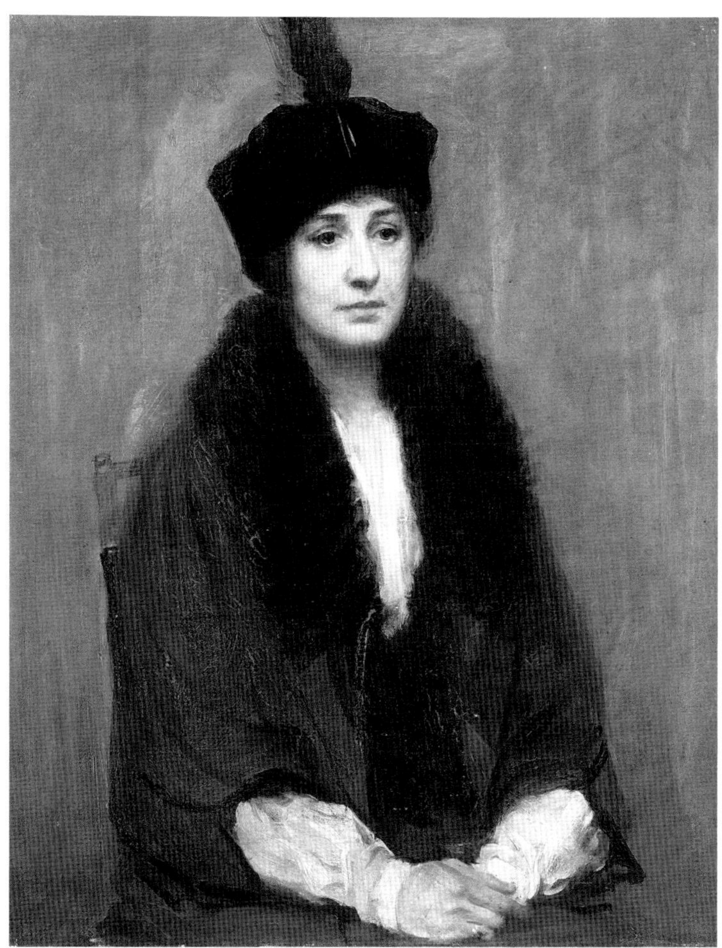

Cat. 17. *Elizabeth Hudson*, by 1914, oil on canvas, 36 x 29 ⅛ in.

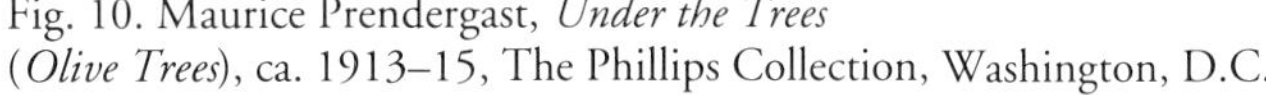

Fig. 10. Maurice Prendergast, *Under the Trees* (*Olive Trees*), ca. 1913–15, The Phillips Collection, Washington, D.C.

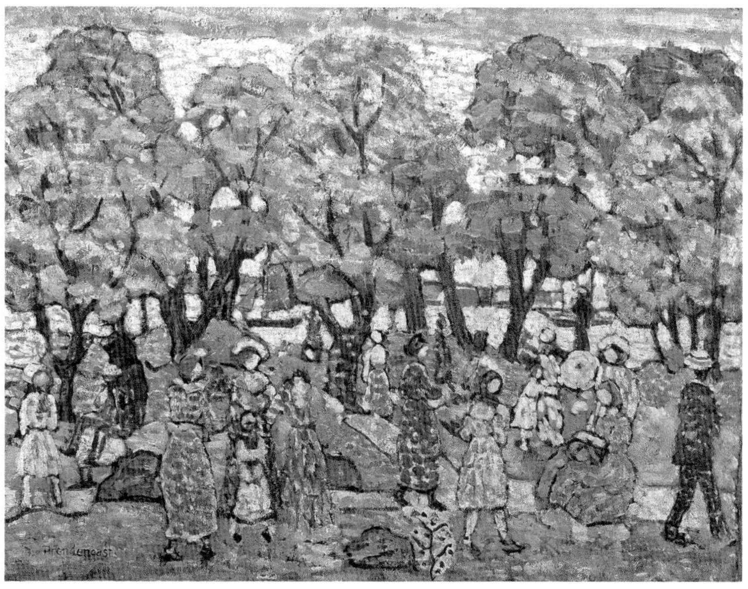

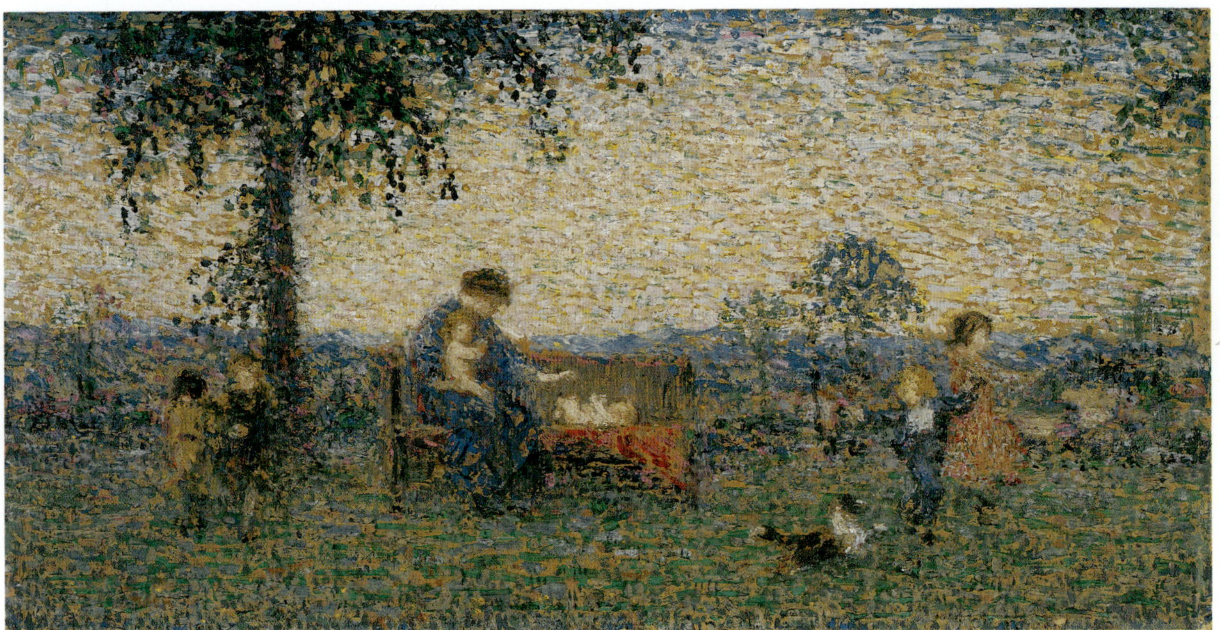

Cat. 18. *Allegro Giocoso*, by 1917, oil on cardboard mounted on plywood panel, 15 x 30 in.

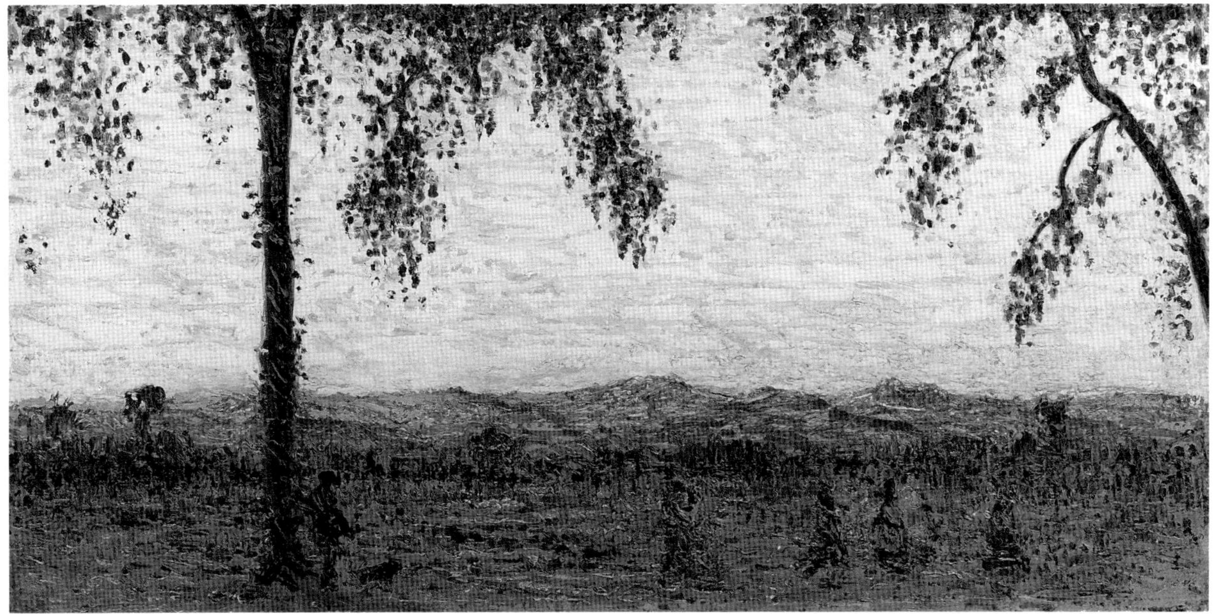

Cat. 11. *Deerfield in Twilight (The Dance)*, ca. 1908; retouched after 1911, oil on canvas, 14 ⅞ x 30 ⅛ in.

friend Hermann Dudley Murphy (an Art Students League classmate of Tack), Tack drew on Arthur Wesley Dow's influential treatise, *Composition*, in his search for formal harmony. Dow's cataloguing of essential elements of Japanese design and patterning were read and implemented by many artists who sought alternatives to narrative and imitative painting. His lessons about abstract harmonies, which he likened to musical arrangements, laid important groundwork for the pursuit of nonobjective painting in the United States.

Tack's shift in style during the teens required new techniques. He often worked with unblended pigments thickly laid in side by side in horizontal or radiating daubs. In *Allegro Giocoso* (cat. 18), he recorded his own renewed family life in Deerfield on his wife's return from Saranac in 1913; his children are at the right, and the family dog is even included. The pastoral mood and stippled technique—among Tack's freshest in tone and color—recall Prendergast and Ker Xavier Roussel. His use of heavy impasto worked in horizontal daubs creates a jewel-like surface. The twilight sky, milky white fading to gradations of pink, gives the work a soft tone, enhancing the intimate theme.

A brooding pessimism unexpectedly entered Tack's work for the first and only time beginning in about 1912, with paintings such as *Redemptor* (by 1912), *Prelude to a Lost Tragedy* (ca. 1910–19), and *Forgotten Poem* (by 1918). These paintings (all in The Phillips Collection), with their dark colors and tragic figures, convey a violent depth of emotion. Common themes—loss, shame, regret, and jealousy—infuse several of the works. The addition of the abstract quality of sound in *The Voice Crying in the Wilderness* (ca. 1914, unlocated) hints at a confluence of sensory experiences.[54]

Tack's series of Biblical scenes represent the apex of his new pointillist style. Phillips would later characterize these explorations: "After conservative beginnings with a lyrical romanticism which only half expressed him, [Tack] isolated himself to experiment with a semi-sculptural mosaic of pure pigments calculated to illuminate dark churches. The method was baffling in its difficulties." The style prompted comparisons with the work of Giovanni Segantini, Henri Martin, Henri Le Sidaner, and George Watts, and it clearly owes much to Seurat and Van Gogh.[55]

Tack underscored the neoimpressionist origins of his techniques: "Colors . . . placed in juxtaposition, pure and broken . . . at a certain focus . . . mix in the eye, giving a sensation of solidity and envelopment more vivid and vital than conventional painting."[56] He apparently traveled to France during this period to renew his acquaintance with early masters of religious and mural painting and absorb at first hand the more recent symbolist and pointillist works.[57]

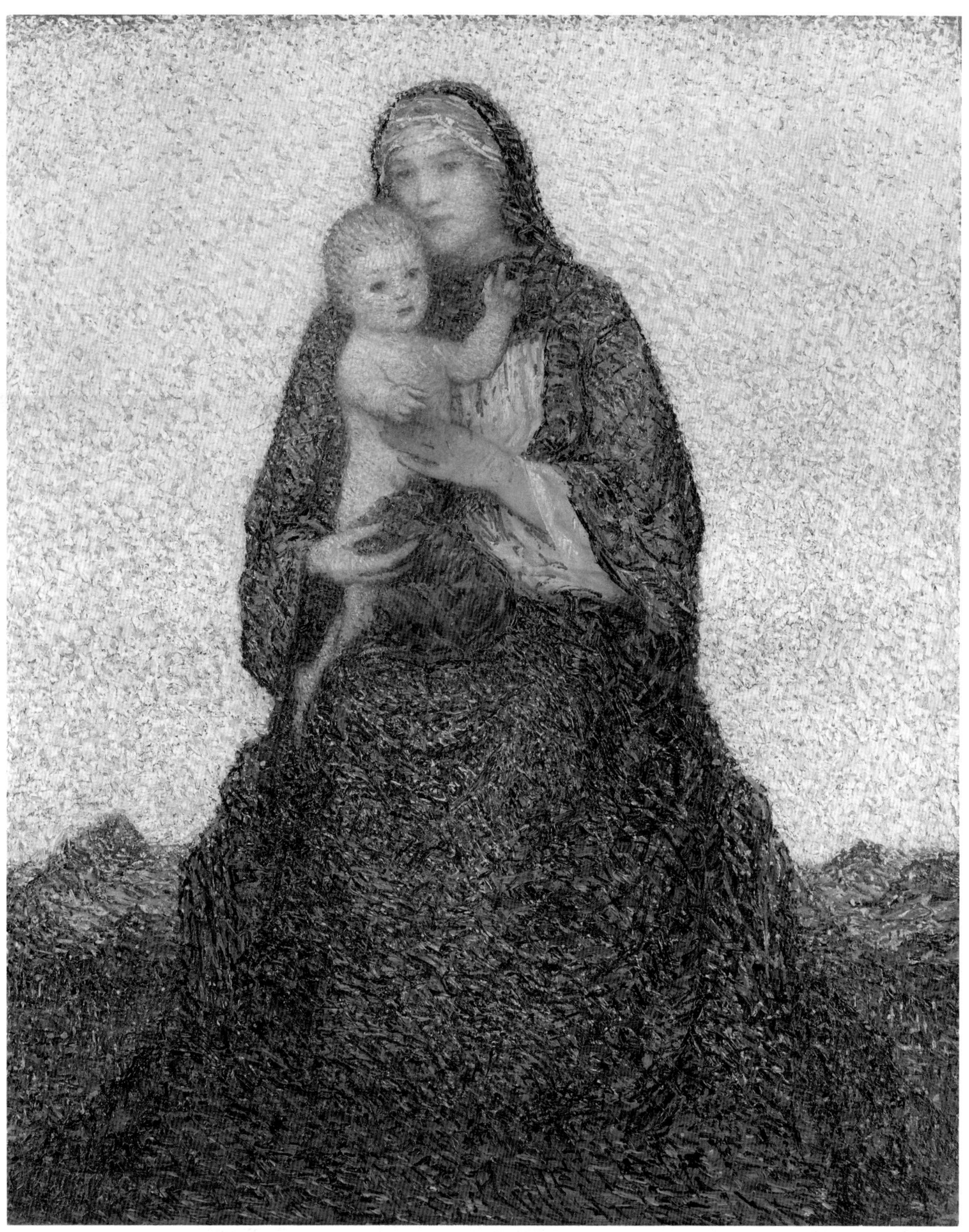

Cat. 13. *Madonna of the Everlasting Hills*, 1913–14, oil on canvas, 55 ¾ x 46 ⅛ in.

In *Madonna of the Everlasting Hills* (cat. 13), the Virgin's form is composed of slashing strokes of glossy, impastoed paint that appears to have been applied straight from the tube.[58] This frenzied treatment forms a network, the interstices revealing a neutral underpainting and offsetting the idealization and sentimentality of the image. Like some of his landscapes, such as *Deerfield in Twilight* (*The Dance*), this painting seems to have been reworked in an entirely new style. Careful examination reveals lunettes of gold leaf, later painted over, at the top corners and indications of a high horizon line, possibly of an earlier landscape. An abandoned composition—or perhaps a more conventional framework for this theme—lies beneath the present image.

The monolithic subjects of the Biblical paintings and Tack's passionate handling of them reflect his devout Catholicism. The works have in common a breaking light at their horizons, symbolic of the hope in redemption that runs through them. A merging of figures with earth recalls a contemporaneous symbolist preoccupation and suggests a harmonious, mystical union of man and his environment, a theme that concerned Tack throughout his career.[59]

The first showing of the religious panels in New York at Worch of Paris in 1915 brought Tack significant critical attention. The paintings were seen as Tack's most original and independent to date. "[Tack] has finally broken away from tradition and seeks only the fullest self-expression," one critic proclaimed. Like other American artists reckoning with the new movements, Tack believed that "new canons [of art] must be worked out if it is to continue to influence the minds of men."[60] Although treating Catholic themes, Tack attempted to universalize his message, characterizing the series as "a symphony in four movements with humanity for its theme." The works may have been prompted by the threat and onset of World War I or by the illness and death of his father in 1914. Whatever the immediate impetus, the paintings laid the foundation for Tack's pervading themes of human salvation and unity with the divine.

In several other canvases, Tack interprets the landscape in the same thick, tactile impasto as the Biblical paintings. *Canyon (The Valley)* (cat. 15) bears the symbolist nuances of the religious works in a stark foreground that opens into a light-filled valley. This composition also echoes the landscape conceptions of John La Farge, in particular recalling his *Landscape. Evening.*

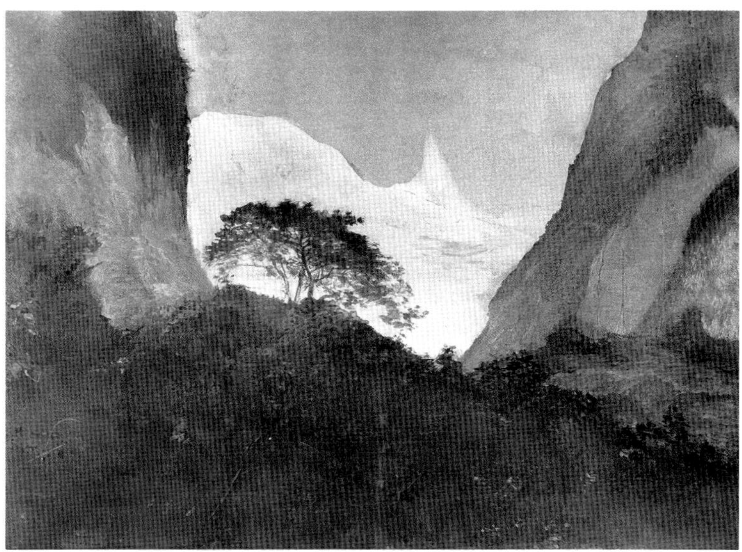

Fig. 11. John La Farge, *Landscape. Evening. Tahiti. Pass and Peak of Vaiaroa, Taiarapu*, 1891, private collection

Tahiti. Pass and Peak of Vaiaroa, Taiarapu (fig. 11). Phillips discerned in Tack's painting "that little space of sun and shade . . . between the mighty Silences of Birth and Death." The suggestion of a passage from a dark, foreboding region into a gentle, sunlit valley is symbolic of the interplay of Tack's themes and style. The painting's message is intensified by the contrasting techniques and hues: heavy, measured strokes in somber tones in the foreground and soft, stippled daubs of pastel colors in the valley.

Toward the end of the teens, Tack's intensified interest in Asian art emerged in a series of exotic landscapes that he termed "fantasies" and "chinoiseries."[61] His preoccupation with this art may owe something to his encounters through the Century Association with the historian and collector Vladimir Simkhovitch and the collector and diplomat John Ferguson.[62]

Simkhovitch was instrumental in securing Tack's first official public mural commission, in 1916–17. Mary Simkhovitch, his wife, was founder and director of Greenwich House, a settlement house in lower Manhattan. Vladimir Simkhovitch appealed to Delano and Aldrich, the architects of the institution's new building, to hire Tack to decorate the common rooms. Tack created two works, studies for which are in The Phillips Collection.[63]

The murals show Tack's inspiration in Chinese painting but also demonstrate a reliance on Watteau and recall the delicate figures of

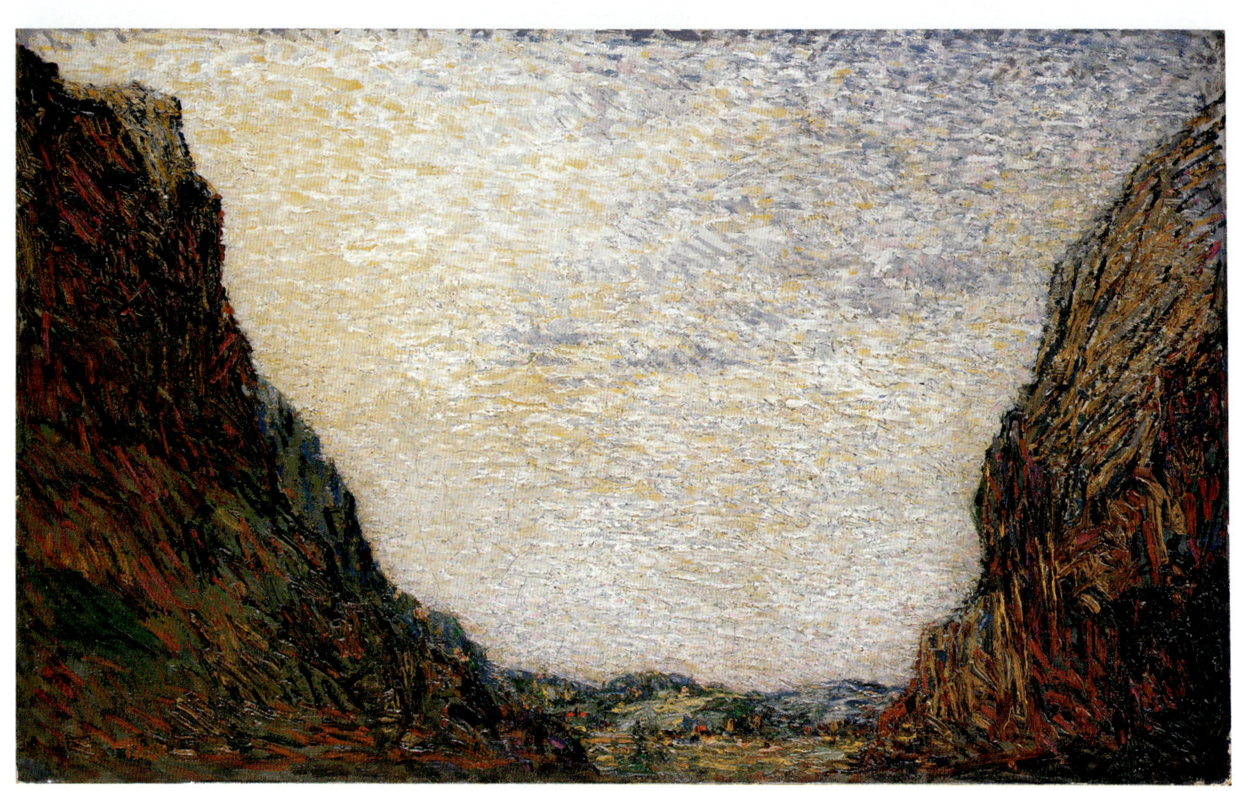

Cat. 15. *Canyon (The Valley)*, 1914, oil on canvas, 25 ⅛ x 41 ⅛ in.

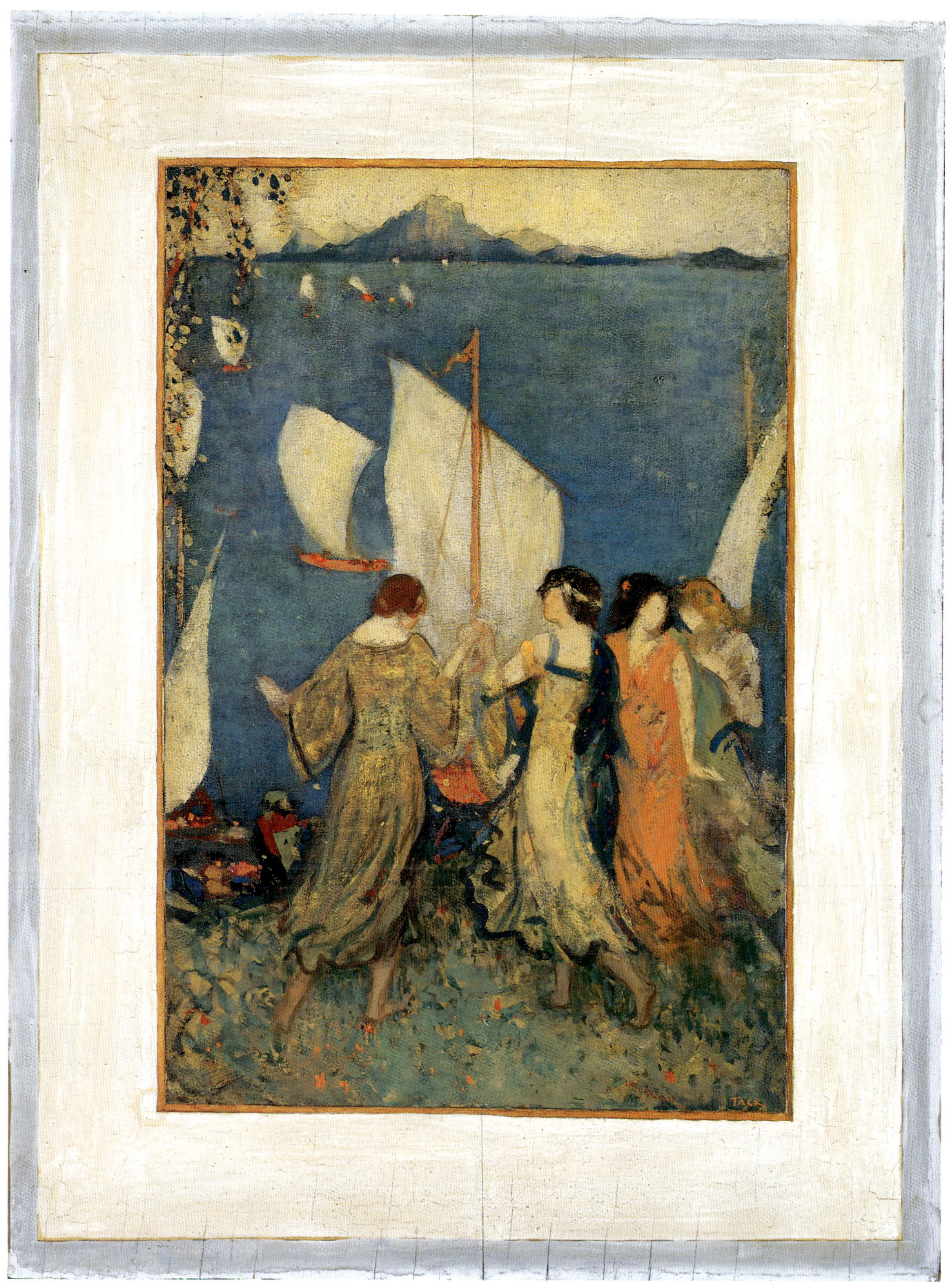

Cat. 19. *As the Ships Go Sailing By (Many Hopes)*, ca. 1917, oil on canvas mounted on plywood panel, 31 ½ x 24 in.

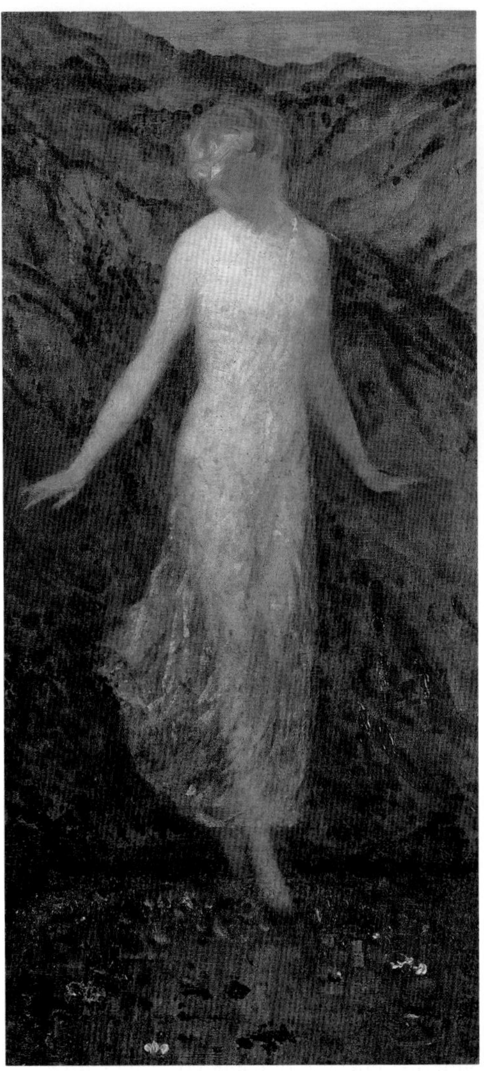

Fig. 12. Augustus Vincent Tack, *Lilith*, by 1917, collection of Saville Ryan, New York

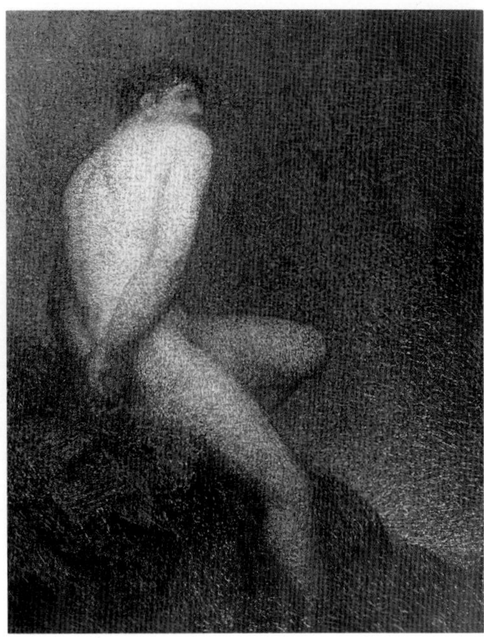

Fig. 13. Augustus Vincent Tack, *Earthbound*, by 1917, unlocated, archival photograph, The Phillips Collection Archives

the Renaissance painters. For example, the small sketch depicting the central figures of *As the Ships Go Sailing By* (*Many Hopes*) (cat. 19) is loosely based on the Florentine Renaissance painter Sandro Botticelli's figural groupings in *Primavera*, of which Tack owned several reproductions of details.[64] A luminous and richly colored painting, *Ships* bears an unexpectedly bright palette for the period. Tack's classical training is evident in the mural and its study in his reliance on pastoral, classical themes and traditional methods. For example, he carefully blocked in his figures in red for warmth of tone. The influence of Monet and Whistler's massed foliage, visible on the left, was echoed on the right in similar colored blotches, later removed. The small sketch, cut down from a

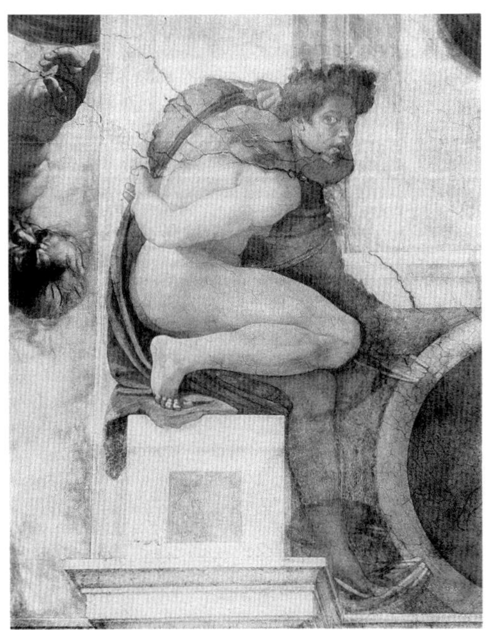

Fig. 14. Michelangelo, *Figure under Daniel*, detail of the Sistine Chapel Ceiling, 1508–12, The Vatican, Rome. From a reproduction in a scrapbook owned by Augustus Vincent Tack

larger composition, is an integral work in its own right.

Many of Tack's latest works were exhibited at Kraushaar's in 1917, his second annual solo show with his new dealer.[65] This exhibition featured idealized landscapes and figure paintings and was widely praised. It attracted the notice of the *New York Tribune* critic, Royal Cortissoz, a staunch advocate of expressionist painting. Cortissoz began to follow Tack's career, reviewing his work frequently, and the two became lifelong friends. Captivated by the artist's search for a personal style, enchanted by his pure, broken color—and lauding his rejection of cubism—Cortissoz was particularly struck by his "half observed and half invented" Chinese landscapes. At the same time, he lamented the "clogging earthiness" of the artist's mannerism which hampered some of the pictures. Tack's color rhythms and fanciful designs were widely admired. For his part, Phillips felt that these pointillist essays often "hindered the spiritual expression."[66]

In response to the exhibition, the critic Charles Caffin, an advocate of Matisse's painting and Stieglitz's photography, remained unconvinced of Tack's attempts to capture "life-rhythms," finding instead a superficial optic vibration as a result of the labored surfaces.[67] Tack, too, seems to have perceived the heavy technique as an obstruction to his increasingly abstract themes of rhythms and movement suggesting archetypal life forces. Possibly reacting to criticisms of his pointillist work, Tack devoted the latter teens to a series of paintings in scrubbed, lean surfaces and earthen tones contoured with accents of pure blue, purple, and deep gray, in sparse forms such as *Top of the Morning* (by 1921, The Phillips Collection). The romantic, dreamy quality, the pantheist's view that Phillips so cherished in Tack, remained one of the defining features of his art and was reflected in his later abstract imagery, which became more romantic and sublime, spiritual and monumental.

Some of the canvases in Kraushaar's exhibition recalled the exotic costume dramas of Edward Steichen's early photography and the pre-Raphaelite conceptions of Mowbray. *Lilith* (by 1917, Saville Ryan, New York; fig. 12), one of Tack's most original paintings, depicts the female demon of apocryphal legend, who appears not as the destructive tyrant of lore but as a beneficent, luminous apparition. The slim format of the canvas and the figure's graceful pose recall the allegorical figures of John La Farge as well as the symbolist women who float and hover in the canvases of Arthur B. Davies. The pigment, smoothly laid with brief passages of encrusted accumulations, heralds the approaching phase of flatter, more daring segmentation of forms through colored patches.

A pivotal example of Tack's borrowings from the antique is *Earthbound*, a monumental figure reinterpreted from Michelangelo's Sistine Ceiling mural cycle (figs. 13, 14). The painting, first shown in 1917, may have followed Tack's Biblical conceptions of the early teens and signaled his preoccupation with a theme he would explore for the next fifteen years.

As its title suggests, the nude shares with Tack's other allegorized Biblical figures a symbolic rootedness to a corporeal existence, a theme enhanced by the labored technique and thick paint. Tack observed:

> *This figure is a symbol of humanity with its earthly limitations, bound . . . but with aspirations and longings reaching to limitless spiritual heights. There is in the twisted action of the body the evidence of struggle, the effort . . . to rise above itself. This implies the idea of resurrection: "I shall not all die."*[68]

This figure's seminal importance is evident in its recurrence in Tack's work. The concept of enslavement to the earth recalls the Greek myth of Prometheus, a quasi-divine being who was chained to a rock and condemned to suffer eternally for bringing fire to earth. In his Christian incarnation, he symbolized both "the suffering liberator of mankind," prefiguring Christ, and the rebel against God, embodied in Satan.[69] Tack reused the figure as one of three at the far left of *Mystical Crucifixion* (ca. 1920–22, The Phillips Collection); the other two are the tyrannical, earthly ruler attempting to assume divine power and the crucified Christ. Fused force lines in the earth suggest that the figures represent various aspects of a single entity.[70] The Promethean figure appears again as the central form of the turmoil of humanity in *The Crowd* (cat. 21). In this incarnation the broader meaning of Tack's fascination with Prometheus is evident. In his Platonic guise, Prometheus embodies human enlightenment. Beginning with *The Crowd*, the rendering of order from chaos was a preoccupation that would drive Tack's creation of the Music Room panels commissioned by Duncan Phillips for his gallery.[71]

The desire to render transcendence in visual terms engendered an arresting convergence of archetypal form and meaning: In the evolution

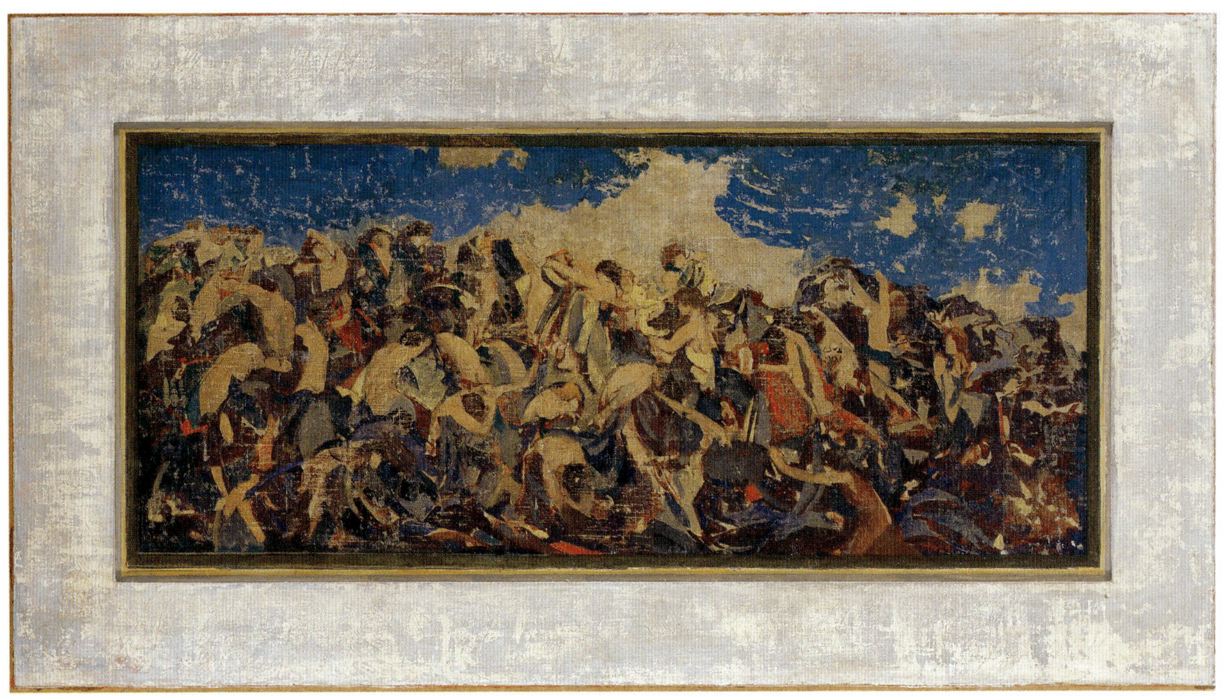

Cat. 21. *The Crowd,* 1921–22, oil on canvas mounted on wallboard, 25 x 45 ¾ in.

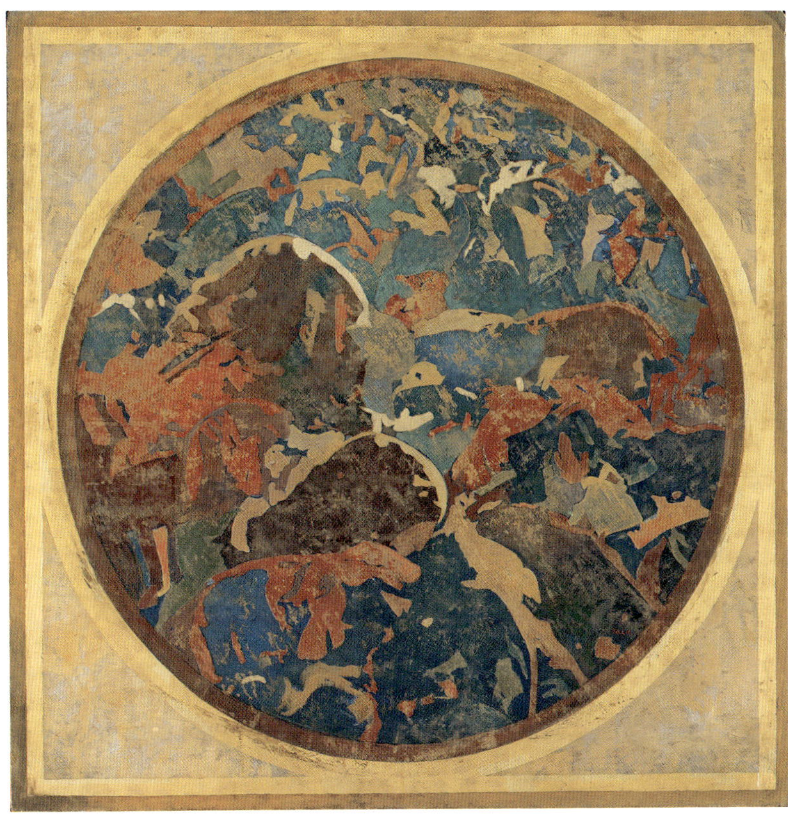

Cat. 24. *Magi's Journey*, 1922–23, oil on canvas mounted on wall-board, 48 x 47 ¾ in.

Cat. 22. *Entombment*, 1922, oil on canvas mounted on plywood panel, 29 x 40 in.

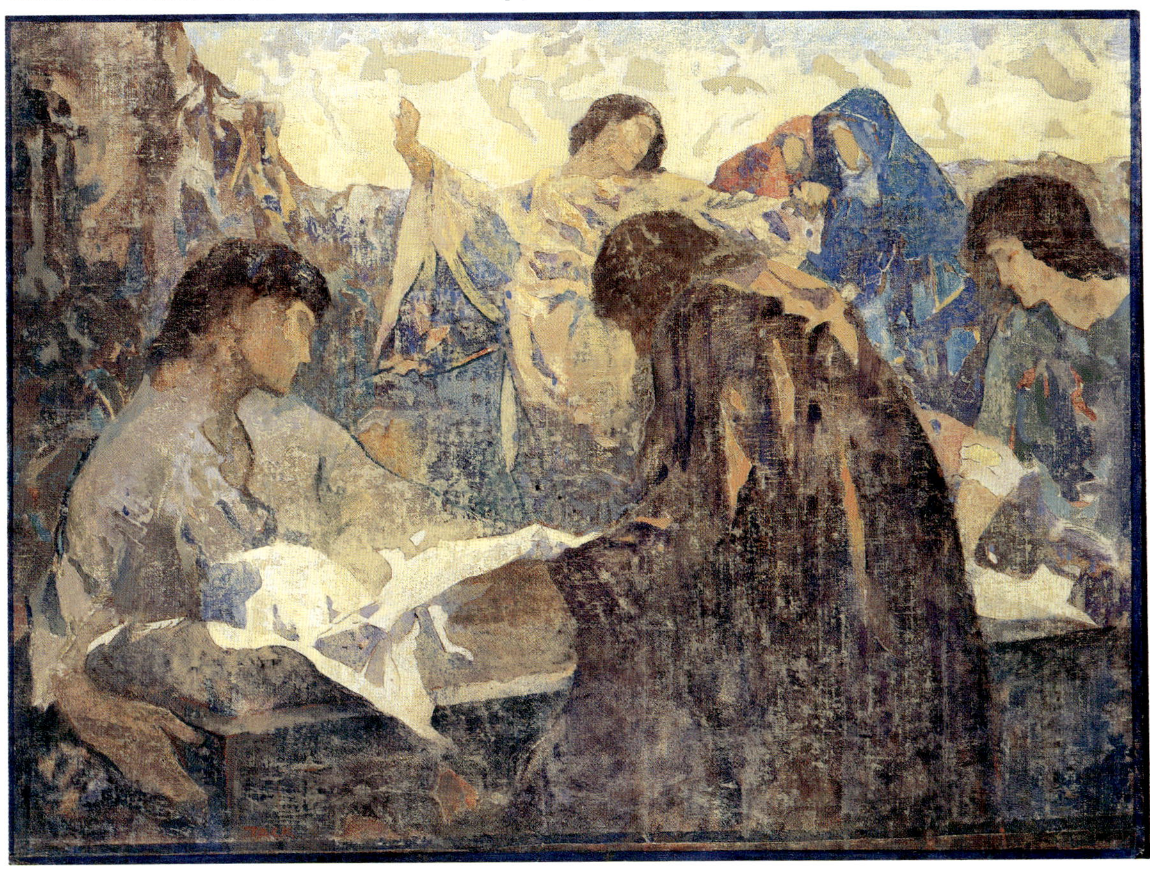

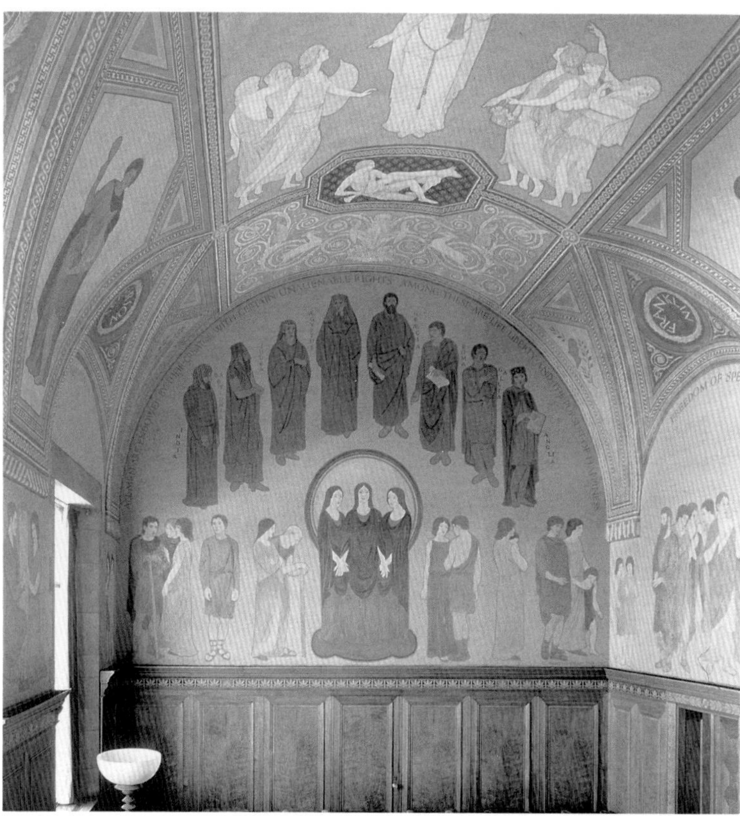

Fig. 15. East wall of the reception room, Governor's Suite, Nebraska State Capitol, Lincoln. Capitol Collections, Sidney Spelts Collection. Collection of Nebraska State Building Division

of Tack's imagery from sculptural, labored earth forms to floating, immaterial entities is a rare merging of form and content, paralleling themes of matter and spirit. Tack's path as a painter was to be defined hereafter by a single-minded search for visual terms in which to render the central spiritual dilemma: the human condition of a soul confined in a material existence, continually attempting union with the divine. Tack's exploration of these transcendent themes led him toward abstract expression.

THE MATURE WORK

For Tack, as for many American painters, the 1920s brought a conservative retrenchment. For a decade beginning in the late teens, his work for the war effort and a steady flow of civic and religious mural commissions occupied him. Yet between mural commissions for the Manitoba Legislative Building (1918–20) and the Nebraska State Capitol (1924–27; fig. 15), Tack began his most daring explorations in abstraction. While his mural work reinforced his American Renaissance and Beaux-Arts heritage, he consolidated methods and themes that contributed in unexpected ways to his development as an abstract painter.[72] His easel painting in an increasingly abstract vocabulary was constantly informed by traditional mural painting techniques, in the habitual outlining of forms, architectural approach to borders, and sensitivity to the wall plane. Most important, he increasingly employed transferral techniques for the bases of his designs, seeking to attain detachment from his forms and enhancing their synthetic, nonmimetic qualities. As Tack sought a truly abstract language of forms and the removal, or minimizing, of the artist's hand, he borrowed from traditional mural painting methods. He seemed aware that his abstractions never lose touch with nature and its suggestion of divine forces at work: he surely described his own dilemma when he observed in 1930 that some artists "would like to be abstract but . . . are pulled back by a hundred things—by memory, their training, custom—and they find it difficult to be wholly abstract."[73]

Tack continued to cast a wide net in his search for a meaningful new style, drawing on Renaissance, Asian, and nineteenth-century imagery and techniques. In highly original applications of ancient methods and disparate styles, he united tradition and modernism in a striking manner. Several trips to Europe in the 1920s awakened a deep interest in mosaics and the paintings of Giotto.[74] The splendor of gold leaf, saturated colors, linearity, and flattened forms of Byzantine painting as well as the eloquent gestures, luminous, rich hues, and expressive landscapes of Giotto informed Tack's figurative and abstract work. A Biblical symbolism, evoking in particular the Book of Revelation, was repeatedly expressed in his traditional mural work and formed the seminal themes of some of his abstract work.[75]

The artist's reuse of his own earlier imagery recalls the classical practice of creating a work of art in stages, from conception to preparatory sketches, and finally to a harmonious arrangement of the components into a whole. Employing this approach, the artist could easily reuse elements in various paintings. Thus Tack recycled imagery in his mural painting and later, even in his paintings of random, abstracted shapes from nature. To transfer his preliminary drawings to canvas, he sometimes used the pouncing technique. His early decorative abstractions began to bear evidence of such treatment in the 1920s. Tack may also have employed a type of transferral involving the stereopticon, a nineteenth-century ancestor of the overhead projector, in his traditional and abstract mural painting.[76]

These traditional methods were applied to an increasingly abstract language, principally derived from random natural forms, from 1921 on. Tack described his sources:

Who has not watched from the prow of a boat the white foam lying on black water, always changing, always following a law in its pattern, as beautiful as old lace? Who has not watched the rhythmical serrations of sand, or snow-drifts blown by the wind, or wind blown clouds, or the reflections of leaves in water, or patches of sweet fern growing on a hillside, or rain-stained walls or the foliage of thick growing crops?[77]

Tack professed that his inspiration from these "accidents of nature" had its source in the art theory of the Renaissance master Leonardo da Vinci. He also seems to have followed faithfully Leonardo's prescription for prompting fantasies of landscapes or scenes of human struggle:

If you look at stained or dirty walls . . . with the idea of imagining some scene, you will find analogies for landscapes with mountains, rivers, rocks, trees, plains, wide valleys and hills of all kinds. You will also see battles and figures with animated gestures and strange faces and costumes and an infinity of things.[78]

Leonardo might have been the source, too, for Tack's makeshift pinhole camera observations of nature, which he revealed in a 1931 lecture on abstraction at the Indianapolis Museum of Art:

Mr. Tack . . . gave away one of his secrets for working with design. . . . In a bit of cardboard a small hole not larger than a pinhole is made. . . . By looking through this while passing it back and forth before a mass of foliage or other collected forms in nature, the artist is enabled to concentrate in the finding of patterns. While not repeating natural forms line for line, Mr. Tack goes to nature for a suggestion of pattern in his work with abstract design.[79]

In addition to drawing on Renaissance sources, Tack seems to have returned to Dow's *Composition* in the early 1920s, as his painting *Glacier* suggests. It shows striking similarities to Dow's rendering of a detail from Puvis de Chavannes' *Hiver*, with which Dow illustrates the principle of "opposition and repetition (figs. 16, 17)."[80] Dow's canons—his reliance on Renaissance prototypes such as tondos, his experimental enlargement of imagery and sensitivity to secondary background patterns, and his use of mechanical means such as photography and stencils in design—were all part of his belief in the musical analogy. "Infinite possibilities of variation," in Dow's musically derived terms, were increasingly the leitmotifs in Tack's art, paralleling, if not directly derived from, Dow's principles. In color harmonies and subtle juxtapositions, however—so central to his abstract vision—Tack showed great imagination and independence.[81]

Tack made his own attempt to underscore the purpose of abstraction as the embodiment of an idea, relating it to symbolist and even allegorical thought:

These [abstractions] deal with the idea of things rather than with things themselves. They suggest subconscious moods, memories of experience, half-forgotten dreams, fragments of the mind . . . . They are composed of non-objective forms recalling through suggestion more definite points of departure. One looks not physically, but mentally,

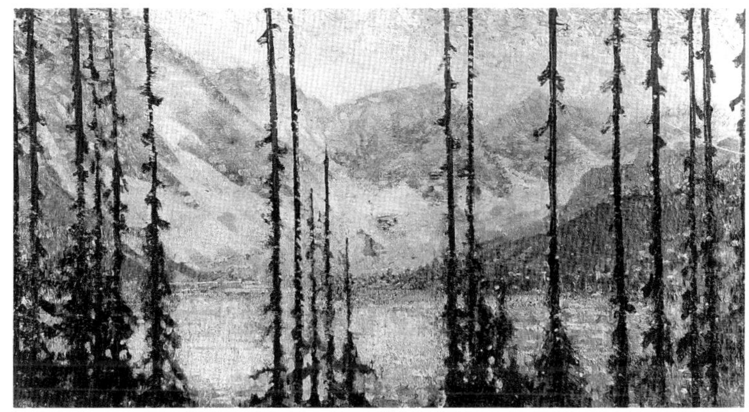

Fig. 16. Augustus Vincent Tack, *The Glacier*, by 1921, The Phillips Collection, Washington, D.C., archival photograph, Kraushaar Galleries, New York

Fig. 17. Arthur Wesley Dow, rendering of Puvis de Chavannes, *Hiver*, illustrated in *Composition*, 1931 edition

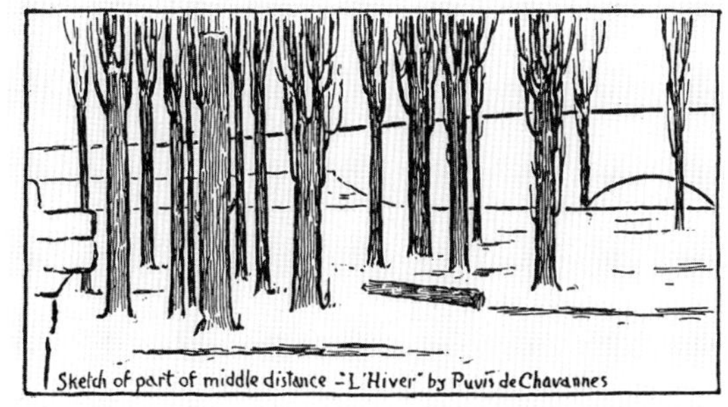

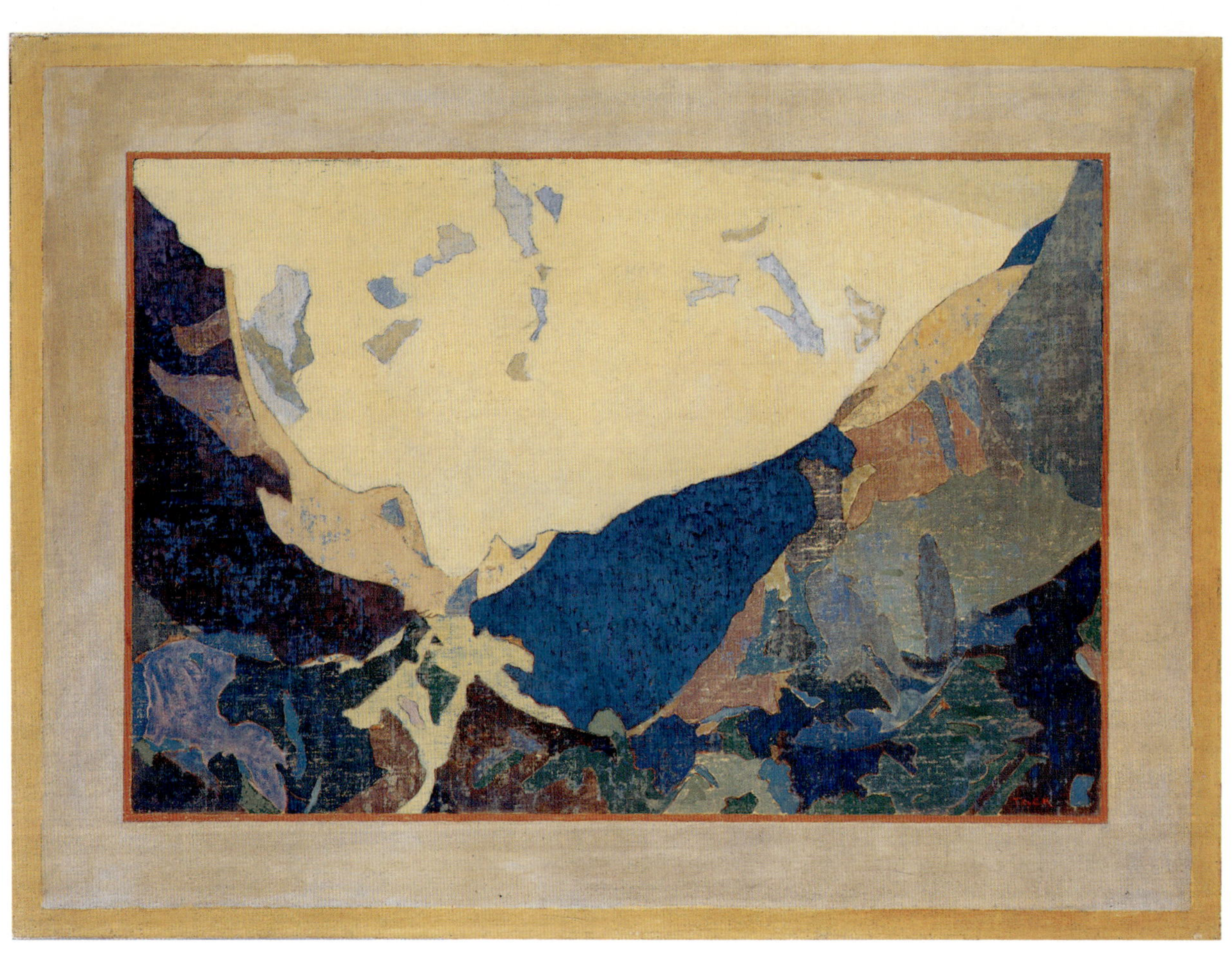

Cat. 26. *Canyon*, ca. 1923–24, oil on canvas mounted on plywood panel, 29 x 40 in.

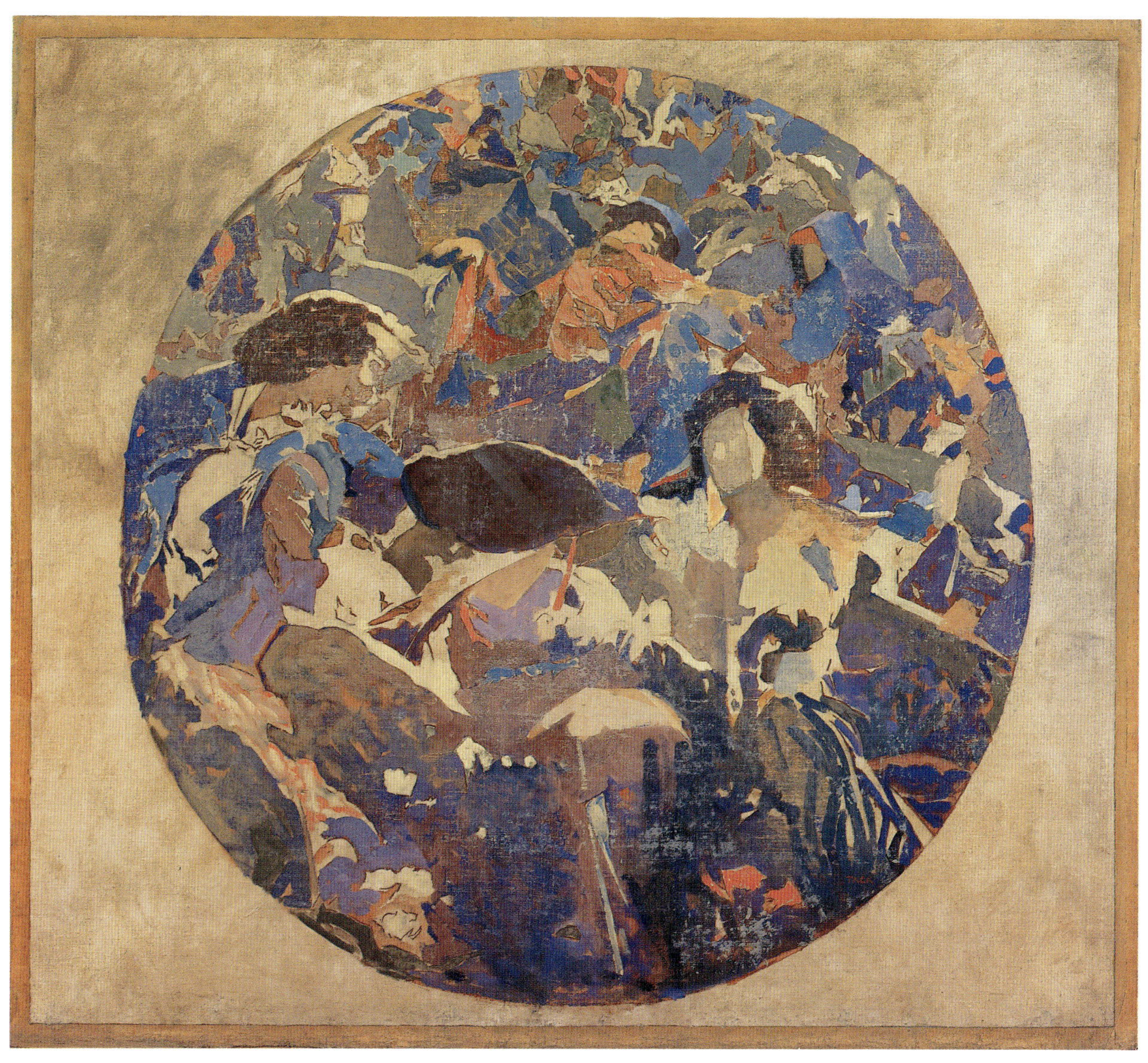

Cat. 23. *Passacaglia,* 1922–23, oil on canvas mounted on plywood panel, 43 ⅞ x 49 ¾ in.

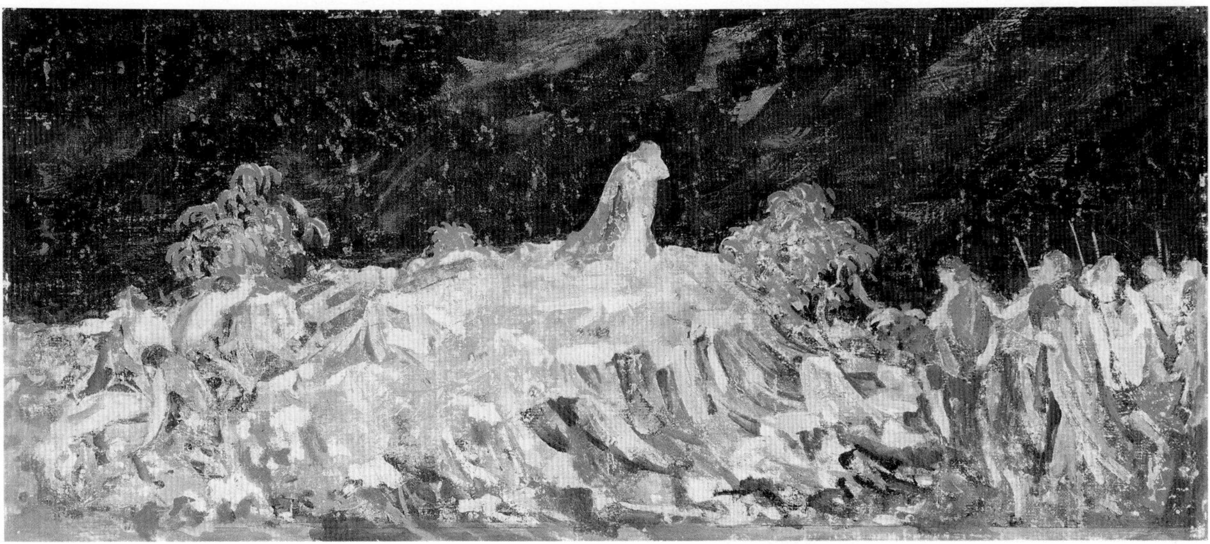

Cat. 20. *Gethsemane*, 1921–22, oil on canvas mounted on plywood panel, 16 x 37 1/16 in.

spiritually, emotionally. Perhaps this might be called the far side of painting.[82]

Around 1920–21, Tack executed two paintings of Biblical subjects that heralded his new style: *Gethsemane* (cat. 20) and *The Crowd* (cat. 21). *Gethsemane*, more tentative in style, was probably completed first.[83] The fourteenth-century Italian primitive painter Borgognona has been suggested as a source, and indeed the somewhat crude brushwork and elemental emotion support this supposition. Yet the construction of form through distinct color strokes recollects Cézanne and postimpressionism.[84]

The Crowd brought this rendering of form through color to a new stage of sophistication. It looks backward to Tack's reliance on the old masters and *japoniste* design and forward to his experiments with pure color, rhythmic formal harmonies, and fresh explorations of nature. One of Tack's most dynamic compositions, *The Crowd* conveys the sense of human and landscape forms inextricably linked in swirling movement and saturated color. The image forecasts the gradual sublimation of the figure in the landscape themes of Tack's later work. The painting served as the basis for much of the 1922–24 series as well as the Music Room series commissioned by Duncan Phillips for his museum in 1928.[85]

Writing in 1941, Tack discussed the Biblical theme of *The Crowd*:

The crowd preferred Barabbas to Christ. They shouted for him to be released and cried out that Christ be crucified, the choice of the mad world, and there is madness and confusion in this painting. There is the sense of turmoil and struggle. It is the world contending, and in its mad conflict, choosing wrongly.[86]

Tack claimed the forces of nature as his source for the image; according to Phillips, "the movement of this vast jostling crowd was inspired by wind over a tobacco field," a scene Tack could have encountered in Deerfield or in Tryon, North Carolina, where the Tacks owned a house.[87]

In *The Crowd*, Tack employed a nonhierarchical pictorial construction reminiscent of cubism, the unleashed energy in futurism, and the related American avant-garde movement of color rhythms, synchromism, which arose in the teens.[88] In a Biblical context, he created an image of anarchy and chaos with palpable moral undertones. The figures, posing in various attitudes of despair, worship, supplication, and fear, retain a heavily allegorical spirit; those on the right side appear in poses of prayer, while those on the left seem agitated and tormented.

Tack built up the picture with a collage-like combination of techniques, including stenciling, transferral of drawing or photographs, freehand painting, and the reserving of paint. The sky was painted first light blue and then beige with cerulean blue accents after the application of a coat of varnish. The entire work, including the aluminum-leafed frame, was dis-

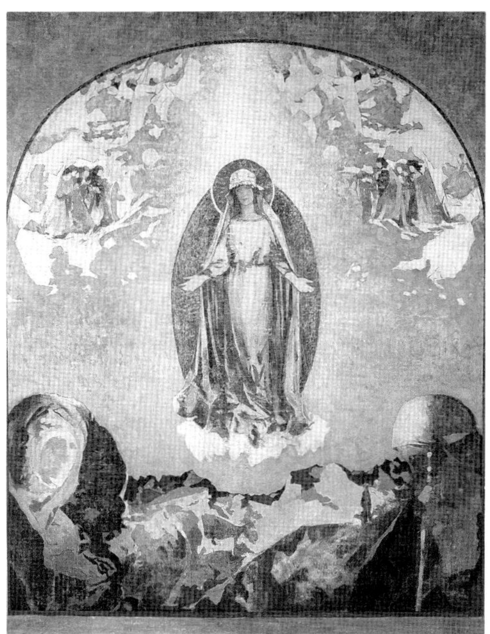

Fig. 18. Augustus Vincent Tack, *Rosa Mystica*, ca. 1922–23, Cleveland Museum of Art, Hinman B. Hurlbut Collection, 1340.23, Cleveland, Ohio

tressed with rollers and cloths, conveying the antique refinement characteristic of Tack's Beaux-Arts training and his love of texture.[89]

Tack used the directional lines, massing of forms, and random outcroppings of his abstracted underdrawing as the scaffolding for his seminal theme, the creation of order from chaos. The figures themselves appear to derive both from Tack's earlier paintings and perhaps from old master works of the Renaissance; the whole effect is undeniably reminiscent of the tangle of human limbs in such works as Signorelli's fresco, *The Damned Cast into Hell*.[90]

The *New York American*'s critic Peyton Boswell singled out *The Crowd* as "one of [Tack's] most colorful compositions . . . a vortex of reds and blues and whirling forms which epitomize the mob spirit." In a more conservative vein, the *New York Herald Tribune* critic praised the picture as "among [Tack's] best, although to some it may seem dangerously cubistic."[91]

Tack achieved a remarkable grandeur in the group of paintings produced between about 1922 and 1924.[92] Their formats draw on decorative and Renaissance sources: four are tondos; seven are "overmantels"; one, *The Voice of Many Waters*, is reminiscent of Asian scroll painting on a massive scale; and another, *Rosa Mystica* (fig. 18) is lunette shaped, intended for a private chapel. "They may be called," Tack wrote later, "forms of meditation through which the mind and the heart are uplifted." As their titles suggest, most of the paintings take Biblical themes: the ascension of the Virgin (*Rosa Mystica*), *Magi's Journey* (cat. 24), *Epiphany* (1922–23, formerly Everson Museum of Art, untraced), and *Entombment* (cat. 22). Even *Storm* and *The Voice of Many Waters* allude to scriptural events.[93]

In their focus on dynamism and movement, fragmentation of forms in space, and rhythmic repetitions, these paintings echo Tack's work of the early 1920s. Yet the saturated colors are toned and mannered, and the paint surfaces are delicately rendered, appearing burnished onto the canvas. Tack began with New Testament subjects and gradually turned to more universal evocations of matter and spirit.

"For his inspiration," wrote Phillips, "he has gone to two sources (1) the thought of the divine Nazarene, of the mighty spiritual forces created by Him to save the world from itself; (2) the majesty of high mountains in serenity and storm, the Elements which transcend time and place and speak with the voice of the Great Spirit."[94]

Tack's first view of the Rocky Mountains in the summer of 1920 permanently reoriented his approach to painting (fig. 19). In this imposing landscape he found a setting that would inspire his pictorial evocations of spiritual and elemental forces:

We took a horseback ride of sixteen miles over a trail which led to a wonderful valley. The ground was a carpet of flowers of every variety . . . . The

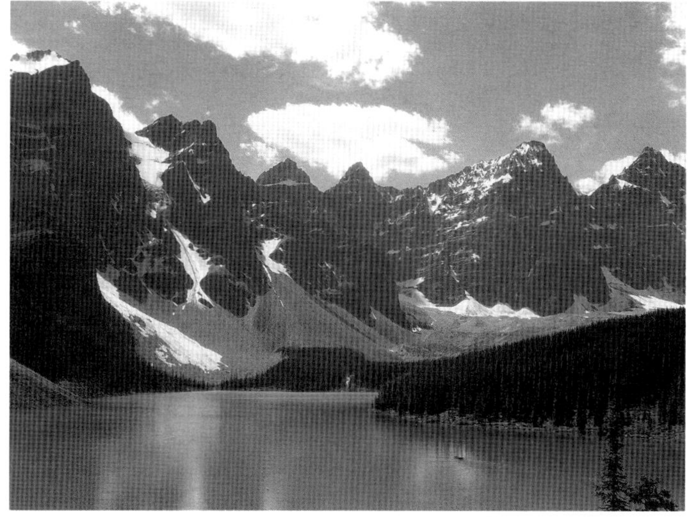

Fig. 19. Byron Harmon, *Moraine Lake in the Canadian Rockies*, ca. 1930, Whyte Museum of the Canadian Rockies, Banff, Alberta

valley was walled in by an amphitheater of mountains as colossal as to seem an adequate setting for The Last Judgement. Glacial lakes lay like jewels on the breast of the world—malachite and jade-greens of every variation. Battlements and pinnacles of rock rose to the clouds and on the mountain slopes great white glaciers seemed motionless and slumbering, but terrible in their potentialities.[95]

Nineteenth-century painters such as Albert Bierstadt and Thomas Moran had romanticized the western landscape; many later artists, including Childe Hassam, John Twachtman, and Arthur B. Davies, also sought to capture the majestic scenery of the West in highly personal, imaginative terms. In the West, the artist could infuse the natural grandeur with implications of a broader spiritual and philosophical meaning—an approach Tack adopted in the dematerialized shapes and fragmentary mountain forms of *Storm*, *The Voice of Many Waters*, and *Canyon* (cat. 26).[96]

The western terrain found its way into Tack's imagery in the 1922–24 series once removed. Rather than sketching or painting on site, he appears to have devised his grand, towering mountain forms and even his figural compositions such as *Passacaglia* (cat. 23) almost wholly from forms in *The Crowd* and *Entombment*. These two earlier conceptions, as well as the lower landscape of *Rosa Mystica* (possibly borrowed from the rocky forms underneath *The Crowd*), have been freely rearranged, enlarged, combined, and reconfigured to serve as the basis of a complex new series of images. For example, the gesticulating figure of St. Joseph in *Entombment* reappears in the center of *Passacaglia*, in the lost tondo *Epiphany*, and even in the suspended fragmentary forms of the "landscape" in *The Voice of Many Waters*. An area from *The Crowd* serves equally for the cresting waves in *Storm*, the craggy rocks in *The Voice of Many Waters*, the dancing figures in *Passacaglia*, the fantastic mountain silhouette of *Canyon*, and the heads of the magi in *Magi's Journey*.[97] The irregular, ragged forms suggest a photographic source for the imagery in light and shadow on the landscape, foreshadowing the use of photographs in several Phillips Music Room abstractions.[98] The images, thus fragmented and divorced from their previous functions and pictorial contexts, form new temporal and spatial relationships.

These startling innovations are balanced by the singular material richness and almost effete aestheticism of Tack's chromatic harmonies, surface treatment, mounting and framing. He achieved a gossamer delicacy in distressing his surfaces, scumbling them with a brush or roller, scraping back paint layers to reveal underpainting, and accenting the canvas texture. This burnishing and mechanical paint layering technique often extended to the frames.

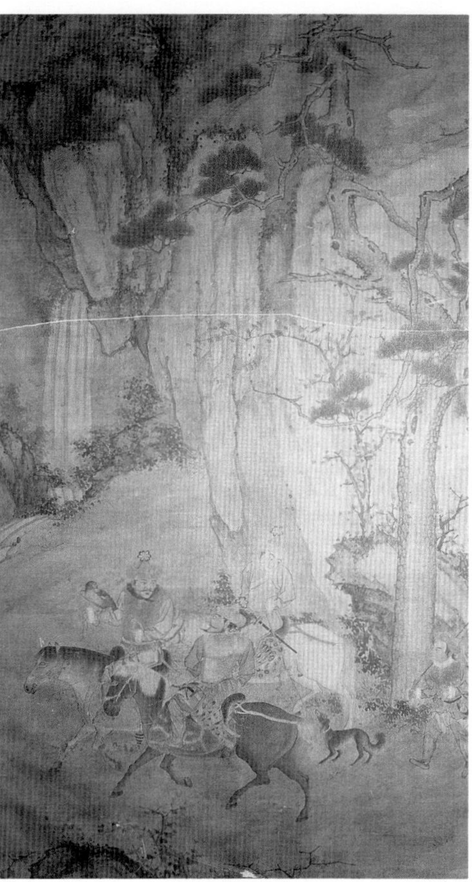

Fig. 20. *Horsemen*, Chinese, painter and date unknown, Washington County Museum of Fine Arts, Hagerstown, Maryland, Gift of Augustus Vincent Tack, 1945

In 1923, Tack described what he was attempting to his dealer:

I have been developing some compositions of form and colors based on essential rhythm and to my mind they are the most interesting things I have so far accomplished. They are abstractly decorative at the same time combining a deep mystical meaning which stimulates the imagination. It was given to the ancients to express the emotion of serenity—I sometimes think it may be given to our time to express the emotion of movement.[99]

Tack's fascination with timeless, elemental principles of art and his emphasis on abstract decorative form and mystical content recall symbolist and synthetist doctrine. His mention of the "ancients" probably referred to Byzantine, Asian, and Renaissance artists, who evoked a serene mood through formal harmony.

Entombment is the transitional work, combining a traditional sacred scene with landscape elements. The figures are almost an extension of the eerie desert landscape inspired by the western terrain. In lieu of a traditional rendering of the face and head of Christ, Tack used what appears to be one of his earliest inspirations from photographic effects, an orb of light translated into a silhouette of divinity.[100]

In *Passacaglia* Tack used the figural elements of *Entombment,* reiterating the shielding figure of St. John, Mary, the face of St. Joseph, and the shroud of Christ. One of his most complex, ambitious, and fresh creations, *Passacaglia* contains a few areas embellished with expressive brushwork apparently laid on freehand, reminiscent of *The Crowd.* The painting's pulsating, swirling movement, enhanced by the circular format, takes as its motif a medieval Italian street dance. "The interrelation of color and form," wrote the artist, "weaves an abstraction which may be felt subconsciously if we allow the painting to lead our imaginations, as in listening to music, and by not attempting to force the identity of objective realities."[101]

The ambitious scale of *The Voice of Many Waters* conveys Tack's great assurance with his subject and technique.[102] As in *Canyon,* the accretion of forms suggests a western panorama. A triangular grassy knoll fills the left foreground, as if extending the viewer's space into the picture—a *repoussoir* landscape construction seen frequently in Tack's previous painting. A waterfall cascades from a mountain face of peaks and crags, for Phillips a "vision of serenity, transcending time and change."[103] The drama of the painting is enhanced by its vertical dimensions (which Tack extended) and narrow format, which readily recall Asian art. The nuanced coloring, floating forms, and compressed space also reflect the Asian influence, notably recalling a painting from Tack's collection, *Horsemen* (fig. 20).[104]

The series inspired by the western landscape marks an important phase between the imagery of *The Crowd,* still reliant on the human form for its structure, and the radically abstracted natural forms of the Phillips Music Room paintings. Tack's progression from earthbound motifs and figures to ascendant forms seems to build toward ultimate resolution, approaching abstraction more closely than ever. In its monumentality and the interrelations of its forms

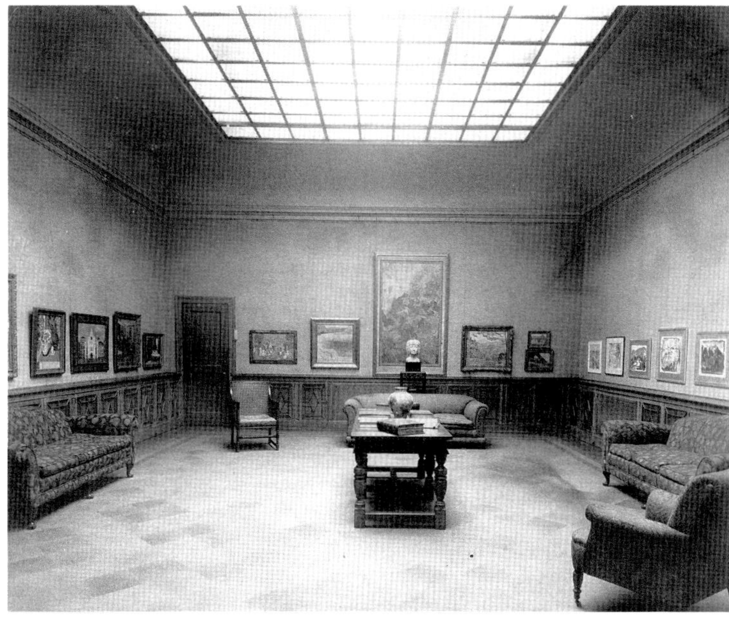

Fig. 21. Installation of the Main Gallery, Phillips Memorial Gallery, ca. 1930, with *The Voice of Many Waters* hung behind Egyptian head, The Phillips Collection Archives

and themes, the 1922–24 series is a direct forerunner of the Music Room panels.

The western paintings were the focus of Tack's first solo exhibition at Duncan Phillips's gallery in 1924, inaugurating the vast lower library (now the Music Room) for public exhibitions. Phillips pronounced the show "a howling success" with both press and public, and he acquired four of the new paintings immediately. Stating that the new panels showed the artist at his best, Phillips anticipated that with the new purchases his wish for a "Tack Room decorated solely by the artist would be practically an accomplished fact."[105]

The critical response to Tack's new works in New York and Washington in 1923–24, though generally laudatory, underscored his isolation: while the avant-garde largely ignored him because of his religious subject matter and aestheticism, his champions among the conservatives seemed to balk at his attempt at sacred themes in an abstract style. Many critics praised his new proficiency with color and design and saw the panels as pure abstraction.[106]

In later installations, one of Phillips's most prized arrangements was *The Voice of Many Waters* hung behind an ancient Egyptian head, a juxtaposition that he felt showed "the unity of the soul of man in art," relating Tack back to the first primitive impulse to artistic creation

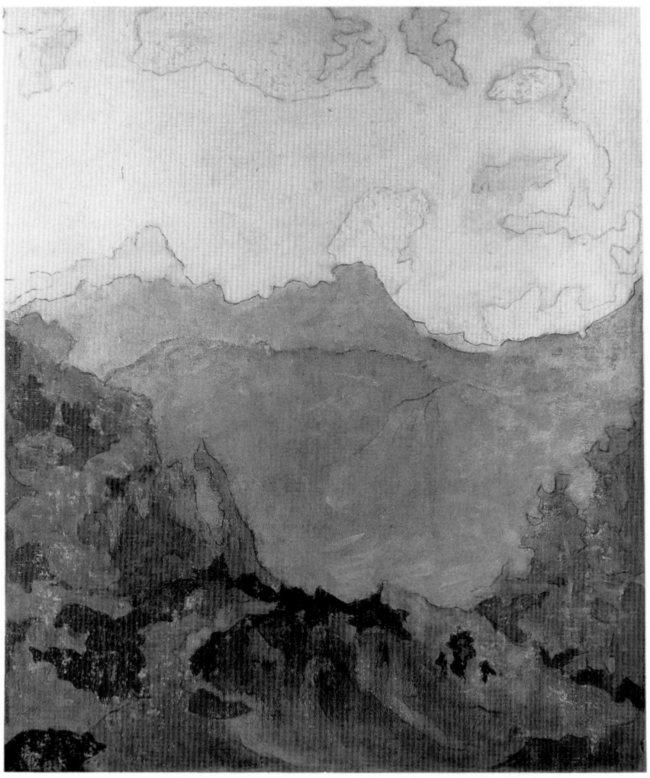

Fig. 22. Augustus Vincent Tack, *The Spirit of the Hills*, 1943–44, Gift of the Friends and Family of Henry Oliver, Jr., Carnegie Institute, Pittsburgh, Pennsylvania

(fig. 21).[107] Such a pairing also underscored Phillips's belief that Tack's mystical decorations anticipated the first true blending of Eastern and Western art in America.[108] "A room decorated by Tack," Phillips wrote in the 1924 exhibition catalogue, "is a place where the spirit and the senses are wonderfully reconciled, and where life takes on new meanings."[109]

The next ten years saw the most fruitful era of collaboration between the artist and his patron, who wrote about the singularity of Tack's vision:

His independence from the cliques and political organizations of painters both academic and modernistic makes his position one of inspiring dignity based as it is on the essential isolation of the true artist. . . .Soon he will stand revealed as an important pioneer into new fields of emotional expression in color and as the one creative mural painter since Puvis de Chavannes.[110]

Indeed, the jewel-like incrustations of Tack's work acquired an opalescent splendor, more removed from the requisites of representation.

By 1926, Phillips was weaving Tack into the fabric of American modernism as no other collector or critic was yet prepared to do. In that year, he exhibited *Storm*, one of Tack's new mystical panels based on natural forms, alongside the work of the Stieglitz circle, including Georgia O'Keeffe, Arthur Dove, and Max Weber. He exhibited the group with Odilon Redon, whom he felt to be a guiding spirit. Phillips must have delighted in the intriguing juxtaposition of Tack's *Storm* and Dove's *Golden Storm* (1925, The Phillips Collection), in which the artists' abstracted forces of nature and material richness of metallic paints strike a corresponding chord. Indeed, at one point he complained to Dove, asking him to do more work that was, implicitly, like that of Tack. Urging him to return to cosmic themes, he wrote: "Patterns are all very well and ingenious . . . but when there is a hint of great things going on in the mind of the artist and of his consciousness of the rhythm of the universe abstract art ceases to be an amusement for the aesthete and becomes a divine activity."[111] Phillips found the common ground of Tack and this younger generation of abstract painters to be the search "to link modernity to the infinite by their inventions of new or revitalized . . . plastic expression."[112] This expression was to take its most definitive form in the Music Room decorations for Phillips, which occupied Tack from 1928 until about 1931.

THE LATE WORK

Tack's entire career seemed to prepare him for the Phillips decorative panels. The series garnered him a modest reputation, which Phillips attempted ceaselessly to enhance. Indeed, in the 1930s, Tack had more solo exhibitions than ever, and several collectors—including Stephen Clark and the architects Chester Aldrich and Charles Downing Lay—acquired abstractions. Further, a few critics and art historians began to find a place for him in their surveys of the latest developments in American painting.[113]

Yet aside from Phillips, few private collectors and museums showed interest in acquiring Tack's abstract paintings. Those few who found his abstract work significant—such as Frederick Pratt, an important donor to the Brooklyn Museum, and Francis Henry Taylor, director of the Metropolitan Museum of Art—evidently could not persuade their institutions of the artist's contributions as an abstractionist.[114] Phillips's efforts to interest Paul Sachs of Harvard and the collectors Samuel Lewisohn and Mrs. Robert Woods

Bliss met with failure, Bliss claiming Tack's abstractions would clash with the rest of her collection.[115] Grenville Winthrop, though a dedicated collector of the academically rigorous drawings and religious paintings, never acquired Tack's abstractions.

After about 1932 or 1933, Tack's production of abstractions appears to have declined gradually. This change may be attributed to several factors, among them the prevailing regionalism and return to representational painting during the 1930s. A few late landscapes—for example, *The Spirit of the Hills* (fig. 22) and *Easter Morning*—manifest a return to representation, suggesting a compromise with Tack's more abstracted imagery of the late 1920s and early 1930s.

Within this unreceptive context, it was difficult for Tack to continue without the type of large-scale commission that Phillips had given him. Financial necessity impelled him to increase his production of portraits. But he did not give up abstraction altogether; rather, he continued to produce these works for Phillips and for himself alone.

The design for *Liberation* (cat. 30) served as a template for many of the abstract paintings that followed the cycle for the Music Room.[116] Tack continued to build selectively on the Music Room imagery until well into the 1930s and even returned to it in the mid-1940s for his last abstract mural projects.

A series of ovals in rectangular frames, set in painted or metal-leafed architectural borders, are among the most stunning in color and composition of Tack's career. They show a sophisticated mastery of materials and techniques and novel explorations in color, scale, and surface. Most were derived from enlarged segments of *Liberation*, but two works—one of which is *Blue Oval* (cat. 46)—draw on *The Crowd*, and one, *Night, Amargosa Desert* (cat. 53), has been found to quote *Ecstasy* (cat. 34).

By adapting preconceived designs, Tack sought to minimize the need to create abstract forms by his own hand. Instead, he sought nonliterary, nonnarrative designs of pure color and composition. By selecting segments of his original templates, manipulating negative and positive form, and above all, creating color harmonies, he could convey a particular mood. Tack's method of transferral eventually altered the original imagery. Through continual enlargement and tracing, the lines of the design lost their original crispness, becoming simpler and more rounded—effects Tack responded to and even emphasized with heavy outlining.

Among the most sumptuous of these oval paintings are *Christmas Night* (cat. 45), *Nocturne* (cat. 41), and *Untitled Oval (Golden Morning?)* (cat. 42). Tack painted *Christmas Night* on a ground of gold leaf, which gleams through the overpainting of deep blue, its luminous quality underscoring the theme.[117] In the horizontal oval *Nocturne*, he evoked a cloudy, moonlit sky. In a luxuriant union of impressionist broken brushwork and scattered light in the tradition of Monet, the painting conveys a moody romanticism. The oval becomes a window through which the viewer looks into a vast space. The range of sumptuous blue and purple hues create a dense, atmospheric effect. The impressionist palette, delicate, creamy brushwork, and allover treatment produce a serene effect. The elegant aluminum leaf, toned back with gray washes, imbues a refined, textural quality.[118]

Completely freed from a philosophical program, Tack returned to pantheistic themes conveyed in pure landscape. His description of the oval *Spring Night* (cat. 44) emphasizes these romantic leitmotifs:

> Spring Night *is a subconscious memory of a moonlit sky, of atmosphere filled with the perfume of ten thousand blossoms, of the awareness of awakening life—a Spring night in the South. There is a sense of mystery, of light, of earth fragrance, of night magic.*[119]

One of the most important abstractions Tack created after 1931, *Night, Amargosa Desert,* is the foremost example of an expressionist brushwork with which Tack experimented in several late abstractions. A cataclysmic grandeur exudes from this painting, probably inspired during Tack's trip to California in the summer of 1933. A sense of mystery and loneliness pervades the work, perhaps deriving from its somber colors and expansiveness.[120] The painting attracted Phillips, who offered to exchange the entire Music Room series for it.

An unexpected and refreshing new direction in Tack's painting emerged between 1934 and 1936. In December 1936, he wrote to Phillips, "I have some new panels I must have your opinion of."[121] When Tack showed at the Deerfield Valley Arts Association, he included works that signaled a marked departure from his large abstractions in both manner and size.[122] Their suggestive, romantic titles—such as *Dawn* (cat. 48), *Evening* (cat. 52), and *Cloud's Edge* (cat. 54)—and their softened infusions of Whistlerian tonal harmonies recall the impressionism of Tack's early Deerfield

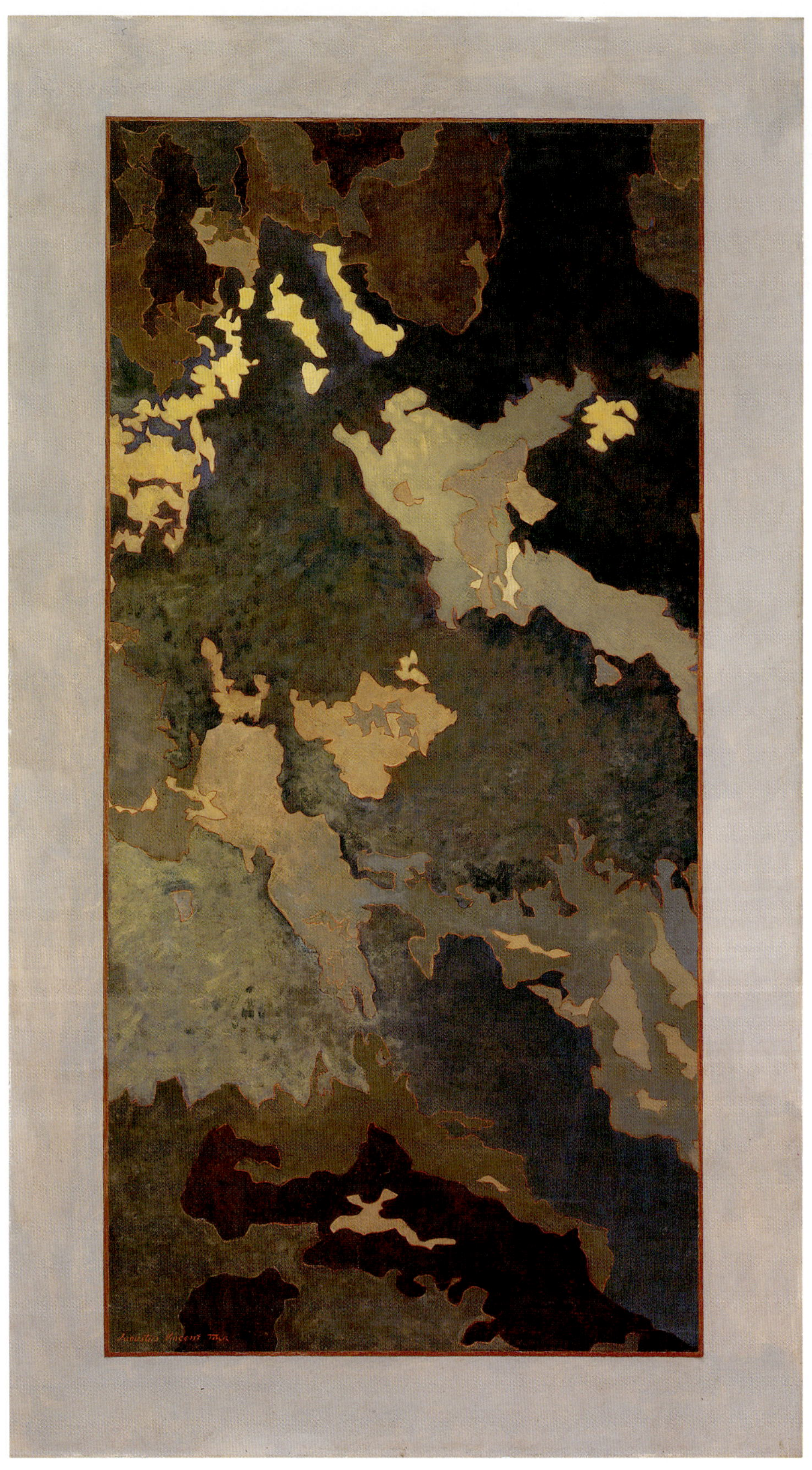

Cat. 53. *Night, Amargosa Desert*, 1935, oil on canvas mounted on plywood panel, 84 x 48 in.

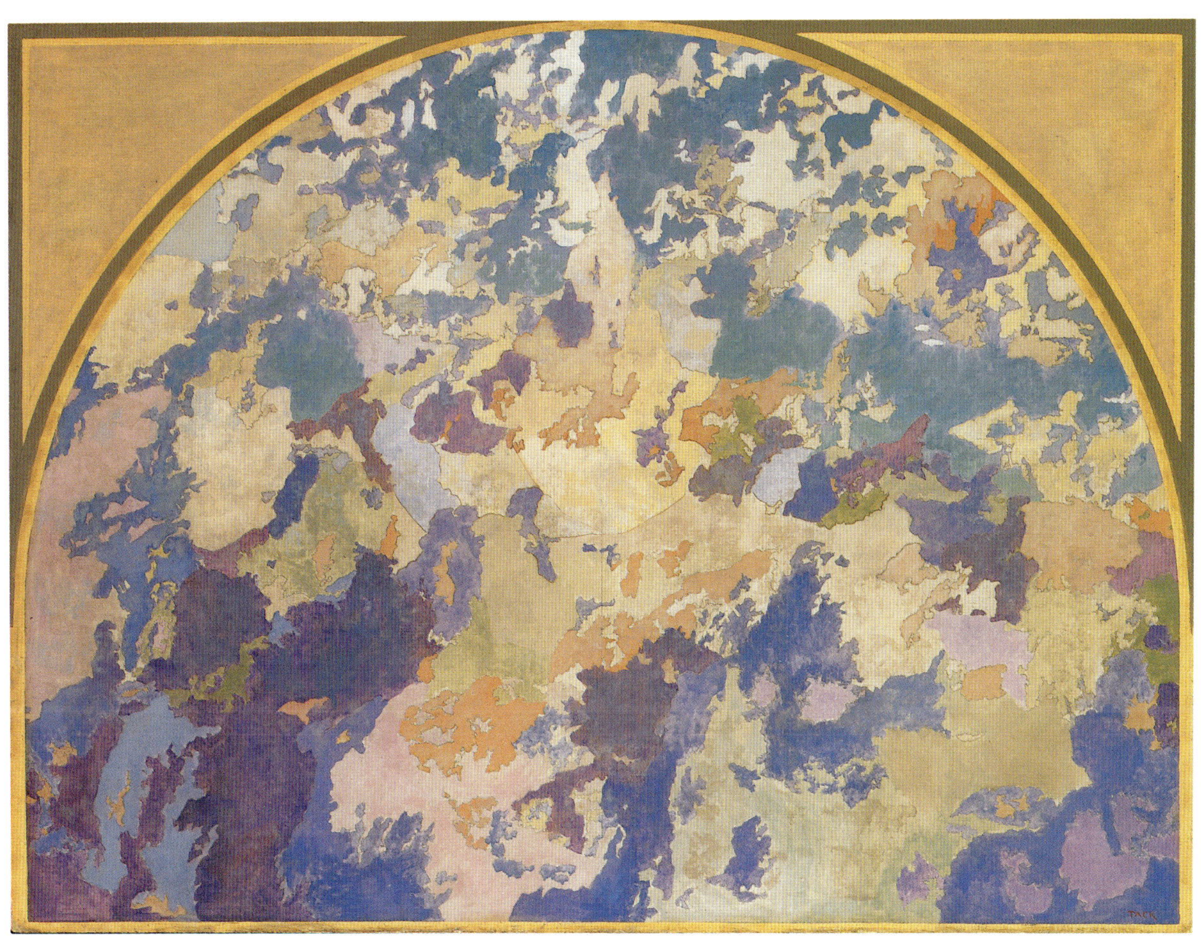

Cat. 34. *Ecstasy*, 1929, oil on canvas mounted on wallboard, 47 ¾ x 64 in.

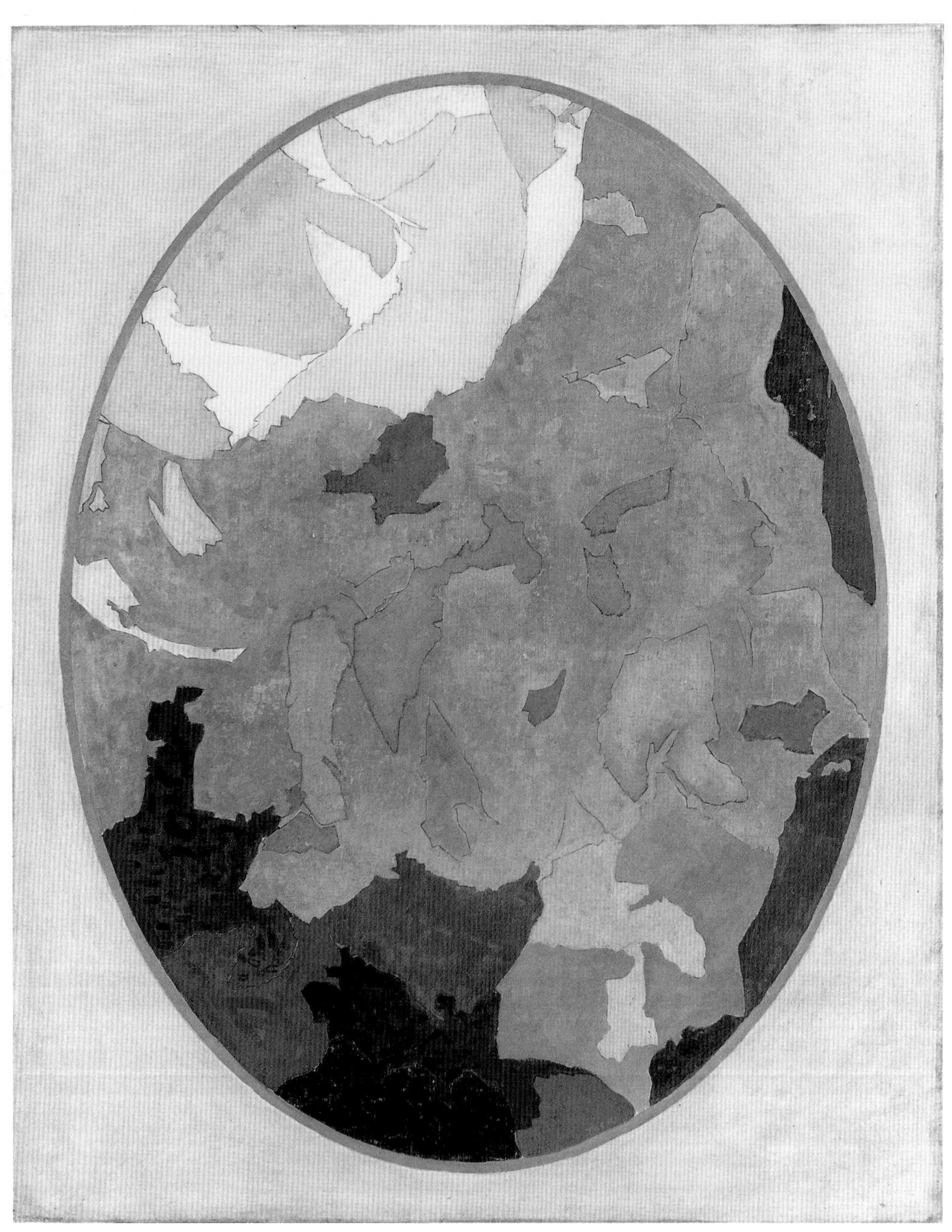

Cat. 46. *Blue Oval*, by 1933, oil on canvas mounted on wallboard, 42 ½ x 34 in.

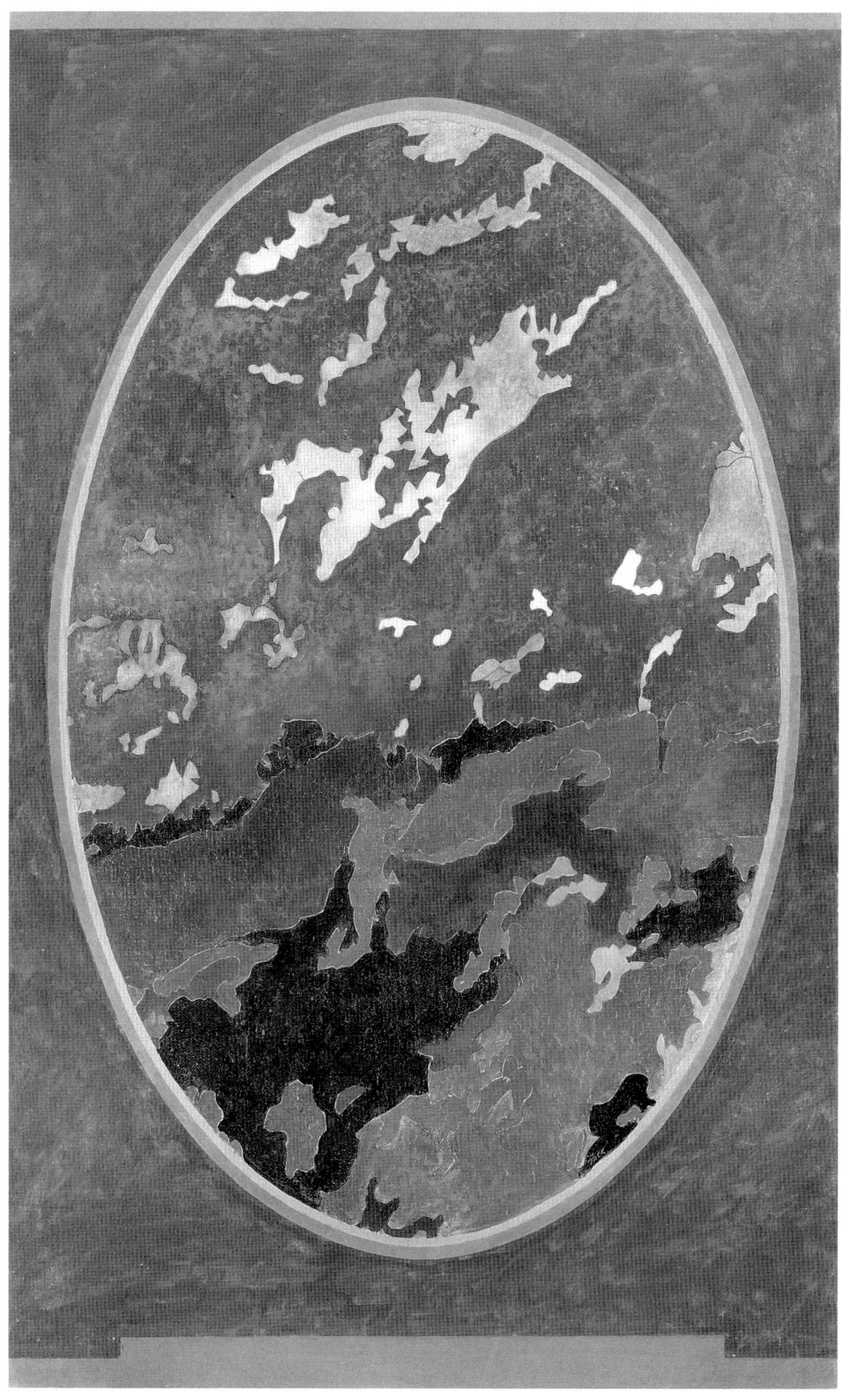

Cat. 45. *Christmas Night,* 1931, oil on canvas mounted on wallboard, 69 x 43 in.

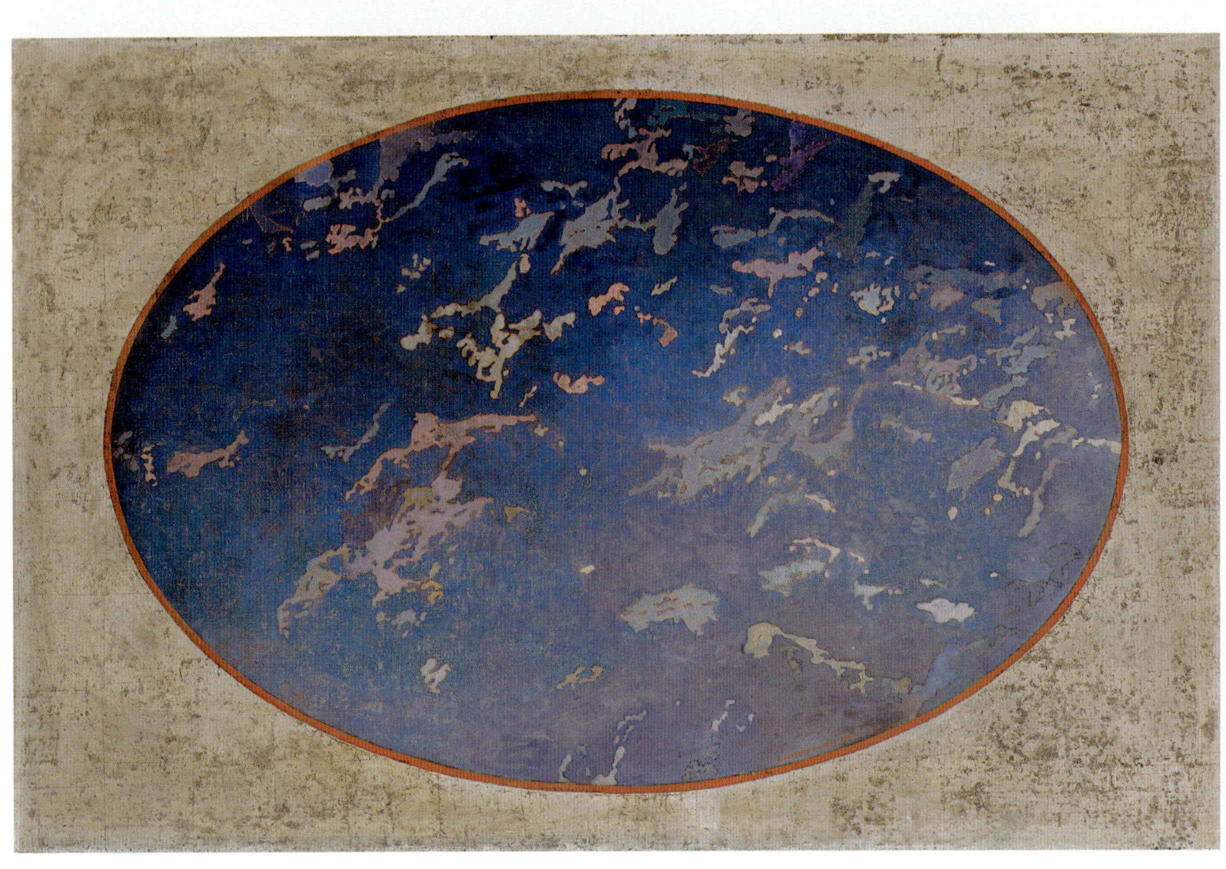

Cat. 41. *Nocturne*, 1930, oil on canvas mounted on wallboard, 43 ½ x 66 ⅝ in.

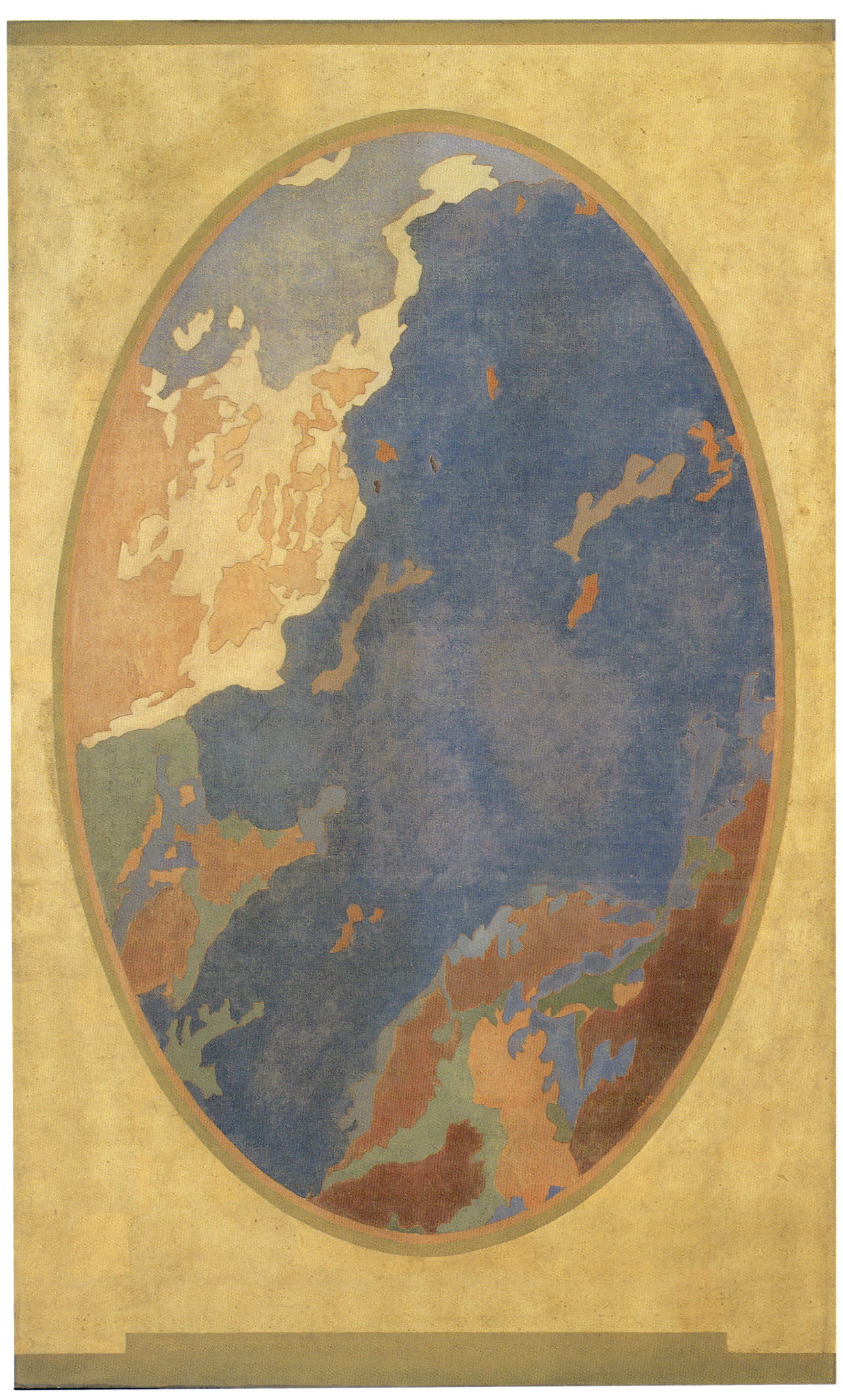

Cat. 42. *Untitled Oval (Golden Morning?)*, 1930, oil on canvas mounted on wallboard, 68 7/8 x 43 1/8 in.

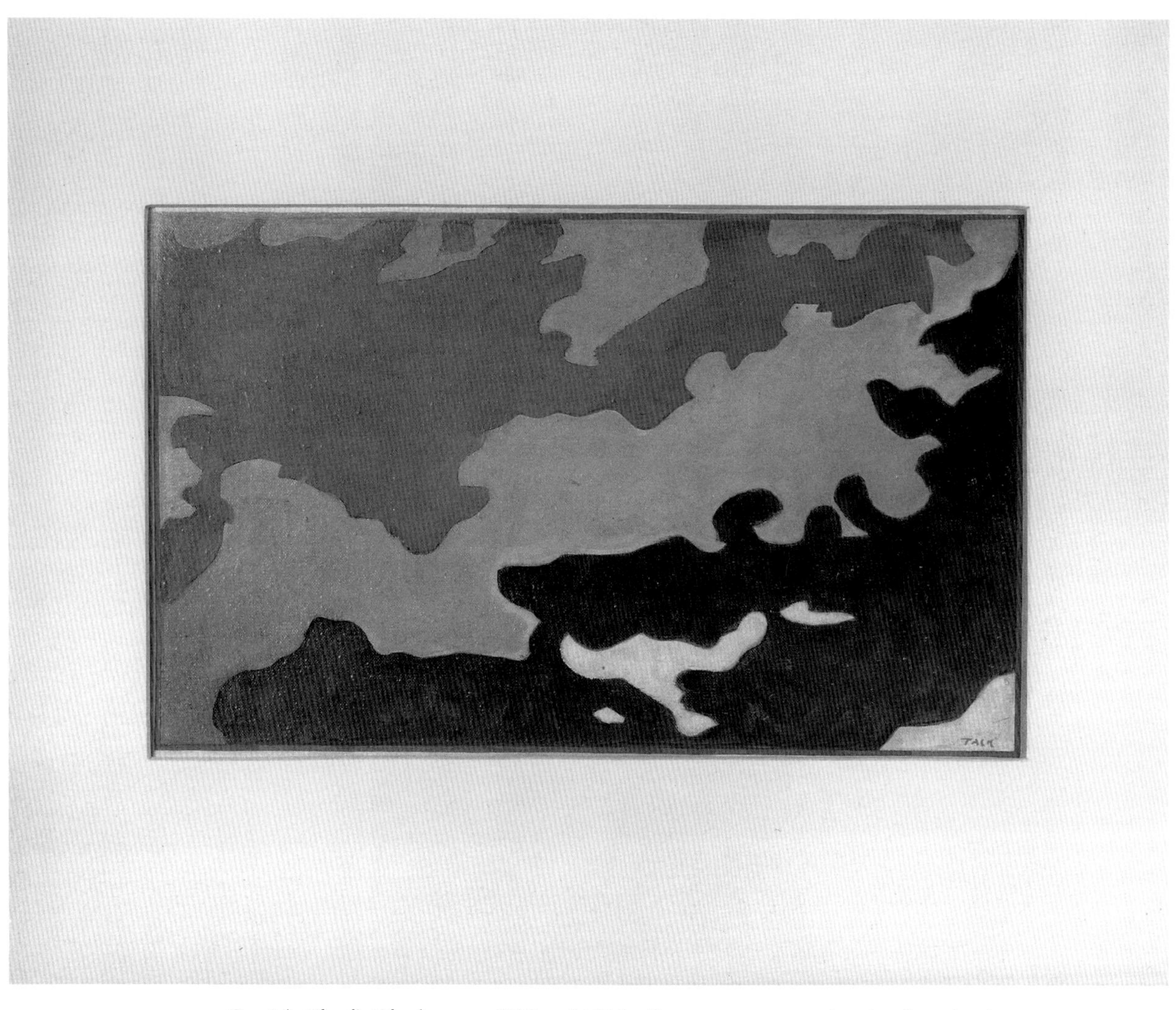

Cat. 54. *Cloud's Edge*, between 1935 and 1936, oil on canvas mounted on hardboard, 24 ¼ x 30 ⅛ in.

landscapes. This reminiscence is borne out in the elegance of the frames and gesso borders, honed by the artist to delicate hues of white and gray. Hand in hand with this seeming retrenchment, however, are the compositions themselves, whose shapes are the same scale as those of the monumentally proportioned abstractions of the late 1920s and early 1930s from which they derive.[123] But the drastically reduced dimensions permit a close focus on segments of nature that pushes to an extreme Tack's abstract vocabulary through a visual metonymy. The characteristic repertoire of forms—the oceanic swells and spray, the mountain peaks and cliffs—become radically fragmented, reduced to abbreviated telluric forms, vaporous clouds, and empty sky. In selecting segments of his cartoons, Tack sensitively composed new images, often with central voids suggesting space, sky, and abbreviated land forms, which he crafted into integral compositions.

Such amplification of selected designs from previous work led toward the most abstract expressions of his career—such as *Cloud's Edge*—in which form is emphasized over content. Reminiscent of the disorienting cloud studies of Alfred Stieglitz's *Equivalents*, the late work of Arthur Dove, and the photographs of Paul Strand abstracting fragments of nature, Tack's last era of abstraction shows his continuing flexibility and evolution. These small works intimate spatial dualities, alternately suggesting microscopic views of organic matter or views into vast skies. *Winter*'s shapes suggest simultaneously a cross-section of magnified

Cat. 52. *Evening*, between 1934 and 1936, oil on canvas mounted on hardboard, 23 ¾ x 23 ⅜ in.

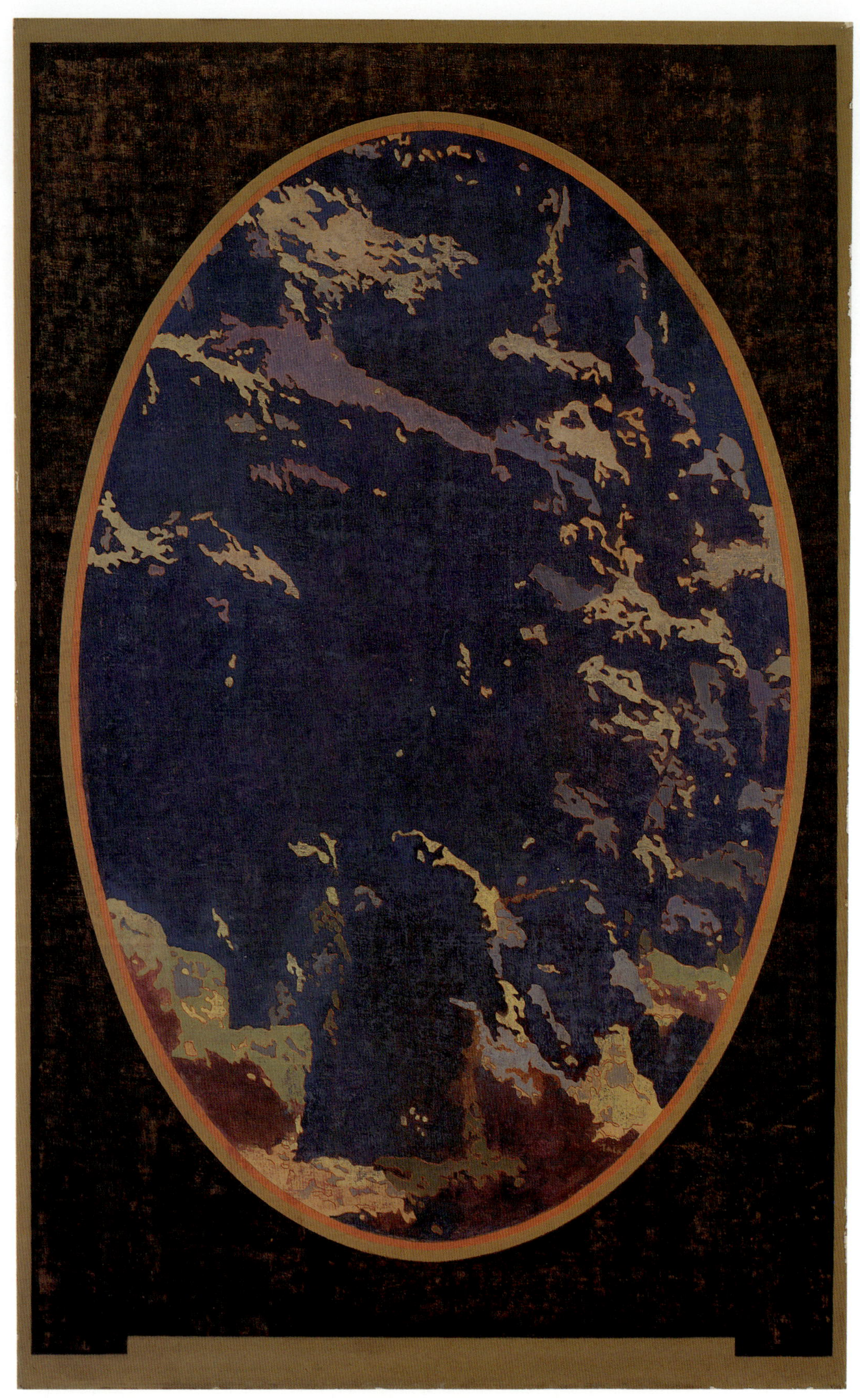

Cat. 44. *Spring Night*, 1931, oil on canvas mounted on wallboard, 68 ⅞ x 43 ½

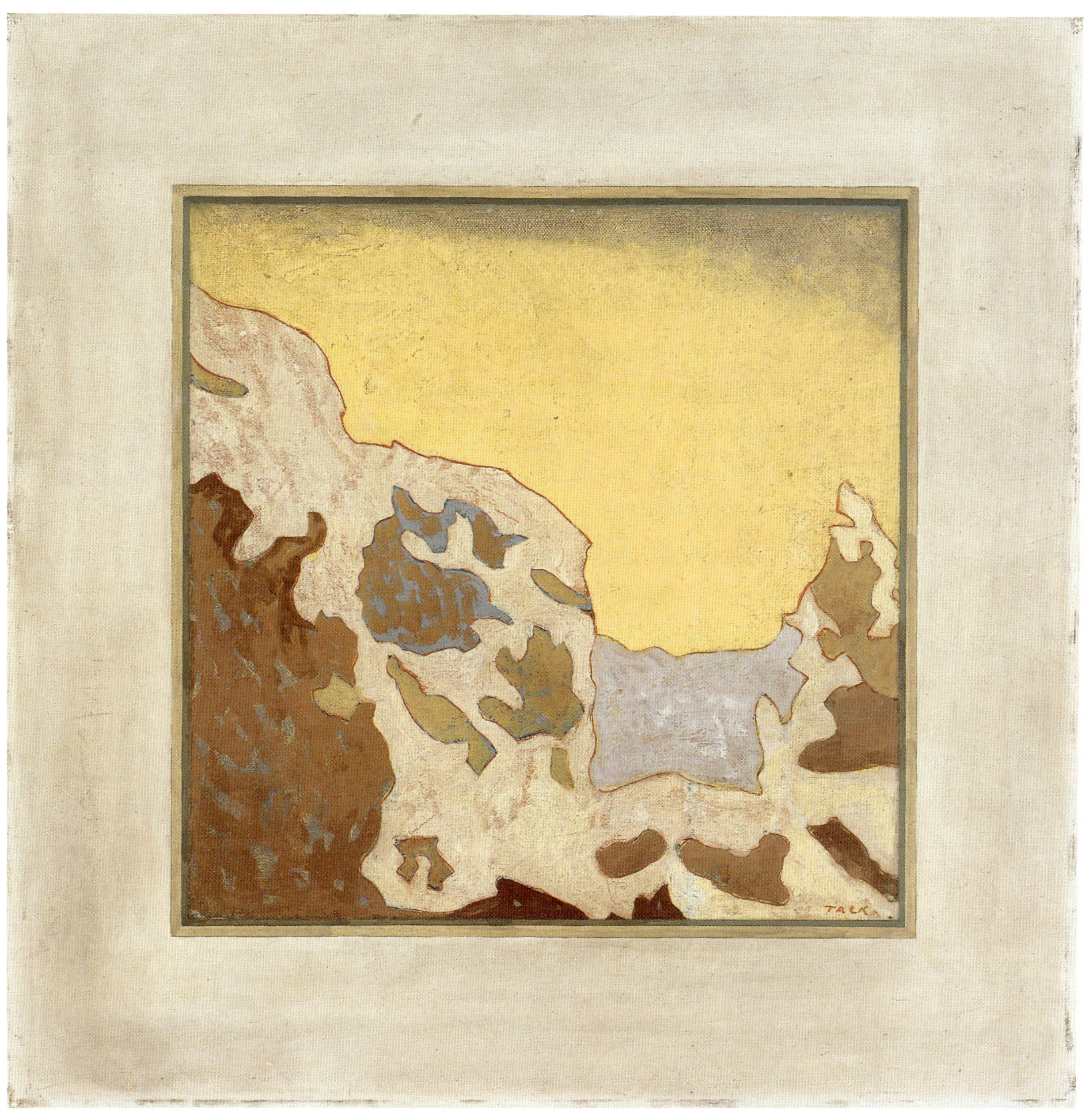

Cat. 47. *Winter*, 1934, oil on canvas mounted on hardboard, 23 3/8 x 23 9/16 in.

amoebic forms and Hiroshige's white-tipped waves (cat. 47). Often the canvases are starkly empty, as in the minimal *Evening*; they recall the compositions of Tack's earliest landscapes, infused with a twilight glow. They contrast deep space with an immediate foreground landscape or vegetal forms, as in *Hill and Sky* (*Hilltop*?) (cat. 49).[124] Tack might have felt that small-scale works would be more desirable to prospective collectors. He may also have observed the work of painters such as Dove and Stieglitz.

At some time, possibly for his solo exhibition at Karl Nierendorf's New York gallery in 1943, Tack inscribed many of these small abstractions with numbers, suggesting a sequence.[125] His treatment in *Evening*, the canvas numbered one, is of an arresting minimalism: the abbreviated earth forms at the base and the drifting clouds in the upper right subtly orient the viewer in an otherwise radically empty composition. The delicacy of the sky reinforces the romantic approach to nature that Tack perpetually selected, even in such severely composed paintings as *Evening*. A halo of pink around the contour of the hill suggests the lingering light of dusk, and evidence of thin veils of paint, worked wet into wet, suggest the atmospheric evanescence of early evening. The canvas numbered two (*Abstraction*; Telfair Academy; possibly exhibited as *Night* or *Moonlit* in 1934) shows the next temporal phase: a night sky of scattered stars and clouds edged with moonlight. Number three, *Winter*, however, bears no apparent temporal or compositional relation.

The sixth in the series, *Cloud's Edge*, forms the last in an intriguing dynasty of reincarnated forms. Tack enlarged a small section of *Ecstasy*, which reappears in *Night, Amargosa Desert*, and reversed the image laterally and turned it horizontally. As he did in all these works, he then reworked the painting, finishing it with two-toned borders in harmonious hues and brushing the simple square frame with gesso.

The Nierendorf exhibition in 1943 was Tack's most significant of the late era. The show followed a display of Kandinsky's work, prompting comparisons from critics, one of whom remarked upon "the thread of likeness." Nierendorf himself "told . . . Tack more than once how much he reminds me of Kandinsky—especially in his conception of life. They both have in common the serenity and profoundness, which is rare in the Western artist; it brings both close to Eastern culture." The critic Howard Devree, referring to Tack as "another veteran whose work has long 'gone modern,'" dubbed his recent work abstract impressionism. "You feel," wrote another critic, "that these are the vaguely ordered visions that registered in a sensitive soul at dawn or twilight . . . the color . . . modulated into visible music."[126]

The final monumental mural work of Tack's career was the fire curtain he created in 1944 for George Washington University's new Lisner Auditorium, designed by the Washington architects Faulkner and Kingsbury. With Phillips's help, he secured the commission from university president Cloyd Marvin. Marvin was intensely interested in art, and he aided Tack in developing the meaning and spirit of the painting. The work appears to recapitulate both Tack's formal preoccupations and his guiding philosophy of life. Drawn from the imagery of *Liberation*, its central themes were inspired by the Book of Genesis; by Henri Bergson's metaphors for life and human consciousness, notably *Creative Evolution*; and by natural forms, particularly the spiral.[127] Tack's explanation of his work on the mural provides significant insight into his creative process:

When President Marvin gave me the commission . . . my mind naturally turned to the meaning of a University. How could the Vital Principle or Soul of a University be expressed abstractly? A University—the center from which springs the expansion and development of human minds reaching out far into fields of astronomical proportions as well as into the infinitesimally small ranges of microscopic discovery. To find some symbol of Creation in Eternity—or of Time in Timelessness, and of the magnificent achievement of human intelligence, made in the image and likeness of God, was the purpose and the problem.

For the basic design of my composition I decided on the spiral, one of the fundamental forms in creation. Witness the spiral nebulae which lie out in space and through which the processes of evolutionary creation are going on. The whirlwind is a natural expression of the spiral, the whirlpool another. . . . where the spiral crosses itself in the center of the Design a form appears which has all the aspect of a WINGED VICTORY*—a triumphant and outspreading symbol of man's ever-growing achievement.*"[128]

Time and Timelessness (cat. 55), the sketch for the mural, was created in 1943–44. A one-to-one transferral of the center right portion of *Liberation*, both the painting and the finished mural contain much free, loose paint application in shades of blue and purple. A fanlike area of radiating lines at the central base in surprisingly soft, pearly tones is offset by the

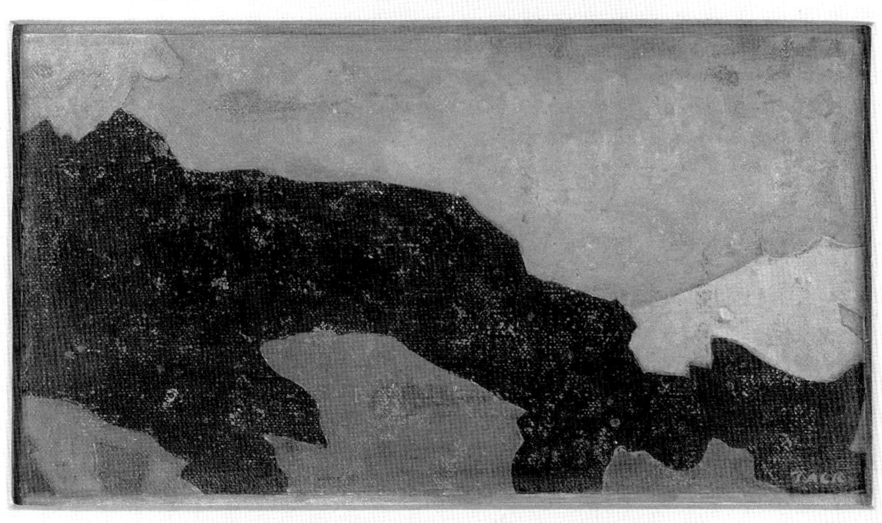

Cat. 49. *Hill and Sky* (*Hilltop?*), between 1934 and 1936, oil on canvas mounted on hardboard, 15 x 20 ⅛ in.

vibrant play of red outlines around the shapes. Pentimenti throughout the image show the removal of shapes laid in pounced lines from the cartoon. Numerous layers of paint in modulated tones are laid in with a large brush and in short daubs with a sponge.

Tack described to Phillips the daunting challenges of creating a work on so large a scale. "There were several moments in its genesis," he wrote, "when some obstacles seemed almost insurmountable": the location of a fireproof fabric; the decision to create the painting in fourteen separate panels; and the need for an assistant. The problem of applying a foundation of paint over such a vast area of canvas was accomplished with the novel use of a vacuum cleaner.[129]

In the midst of this project and on the eve of his first retrospective exhibition in Washington, Tack, seventy-four, suffered a near-fatal heart attack and was forced into convalescence in western Massachusetts, with only half the panels for the mural in place. He left the completion of the work to his longtime assistant, Carl Lella, whom he felt "is very well able to imitate my approach and intention." Tack approved and signed the final mural later that year before its inauguration.[130]

After his heart attack, Tack wrote to Phillips, "You know Hokusai's wish at ninety-five. 'If the fates will only give me five years more, I may do something.' I am always on the verge of that something and I suppose it will always be so."[131] From his hospital bed, the artist observed to Phillips, "The tempo of my life must now alter. The first movement having been allegro con brio, must now change to the second movement, andante sostenuto. I am not discouraged as I think of the most beautiful things in this mood. The second movement in most symphonies is often the best."[132]

In the 1930s, Phillips's steady collecting and Tack's production of abstractions both slowed. Yet Phillips still championed Tack, having

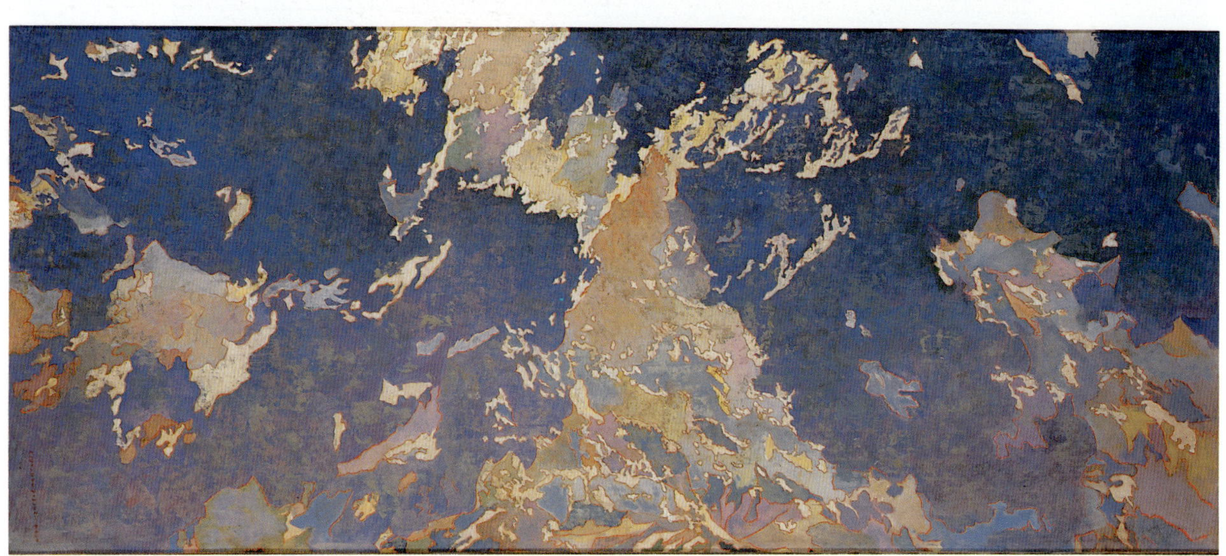

Cat. 55. *Time and Timelessness (The Spirit of Creation)*, 1943–44, oil on canvas, 39 3/16 x 85 ¼ in.

launched his effort with a gift of the religious painting, *In the House of Matthew* (by 1922), to the Metropolitan Museum of Art. Phillips's advocacy took its boldest and most forceful form when he threatened to resign from the board of trustees of the Museum of Modern Art if Tack's work were not represented in the 1930–31 exhibition of art by living Americans organized annually by Alfred Barr. Barr gracefully acquiesced, accepting three of Tack's Music Room decorations.[133]

Nevertheless, Phillips's attitude began to shift. In 1930 he had defended Tack as more "genuine" a modernist than Picasso, able to "move men to ecstasy and vision through [his] divine control of the emotional potentialities of light and color."[134] In 1932 he still saw Tack's art as the "portent of the coming of something epoch-making from the East . . . an acceptance of a Universe of unceasing flux."[135] Yet the next year Phillips published an ambiguous statement that contained a clear note of disappointment:

If Tack had been painting his unique maps of . . . color for the last twenty years he would now be reaping the reward in universal acclaim for having invented a new decorative language . . . his other researches of earlier years have not been so successful and his conservative portraits and traditional mural paintings have made him a limited reputation as an . . . eclectic painter . . . rather than as one of America's most original painters.[136]

Between 1933 and 1937, Tack had no solo exhibitions at the Phillips Memorial Gallery, although he had eleven at museums and galleries throughout the Northeast. Yet Tack's eagerness to have his foremost patron view his new works of 1936 gives evidence of Phillips's lasting power. Indeed, it was on Phillips's advice that Tack moved to Washington, D.C., and, with Phillips's fervent advocacy, secured several important official portrait commissions.

In the 1940s two main currents shaped Phillips's writings on and exhibitions of Tack. With the onset of World War II, the parallels between Tack's art and that of the East, and "all peoples of the world," were highlighted. In 1943, Phillips again exhibited Tack's Music Room series, writing in the catalogue: "In the midst of the most complete and terrible war of all time, at last Tack seems . . . of a prophetic timeliness," for "we have need for men who see their way around the globe and never forget the sky which arches over all men."[137] Also in the 1940s, probably through the influence of Law Watkins, Phillips sought to elucidate the functions of art and uncover the mysteries of emotional resonance of various shapes, forms, and colors. Tack's work figured in this context both in the "Functions in Color" exhibition and lectures and in the 1943 exhibition catalogue, where Phillips's first truly expository statements on Tack's sources and methods appear.

In 1949, Phillips hosted an exhibition of Tack's work. A few months before his death, the artist visited the exhibition, probably viewing his most important works for the last time. Afterward, he wrote Phillips: "I came away from your exhibition . . . in a state of fervor and exaltation . . . I can only make a feeble effort to express to you my appreciation of your recognition . . . You have been a very great friend."[138]

On his death, Tack bequeathed the paintings in his possession to Phillips, entrusting him with their distribution to various museums and galleries. Phillips duly made the rounds of galleries, museums, and collectors promoting Tack's painting and placed important abstractions in the Everson Museum of Art, the Brooklyn Museum, the Whitney Museum of American Art, and the Metropolitan Museum of Art. Two years before his death, Phillips wrote one of his last statements on Tack's career to Albert Ten Eyck Gardner, then curator of American painting at the Metropolitan:

The Abstractions are now in retrospect very important, and it is sad that they were not appreciated during the artist's lifetime . . . . As our Collection has grown into more modern idioms it has been possible to merge outstanding examples of Tack's abstract style with contemporary painting. Many admirers of the Abstract Expressionists of today have noted the resemblance to Clyfford Still, and it is obvious that he was feeling his way towards that large scale color symbolism. The surface however was much more emphasised than is the fashion today and the technique was magical.[139]

Phillips's qualified estimation of Tack as a precursor to the abstract expressionists has found resonance with recent scholars and critics.[140] As Phillips pointed out, however, Tack's aestheticism distinguished his work from that of the modern movement, whose tenets included a rejection of academicism and an eschewal of a decorative approach. These elements in Tack's work stigmatized him in the height of the modern era, occasioning the neglect of his painting in the years following his death. Not only Barr but American modernists like Dove and Stieglitz apparently had little use for Tack;

in 1937, Dove recounted to Stieglitz, with evident amusement, his son's reaction to Phillips: "He is quite a guy, very nice but still likes Tack."[141]

Although he continuously evolved toward abstraction, Tack never claimed to be a modernist. In fact, he was uncomfortable with the rhetoric of modernism. "I am somewhat out of patience with the word *modern* it is so much misused," he wrote Phillips in 1930, at the height of his abstract production.[142]

For Phillips, Tack's abstract style, which he had done much to foster, represented a desire to reconcile tradition and modernity, revitalizing both in novel yet nature-inspired art forms. Among the many roads to abstraction taken by American artists, Tack's was the constant pursuit of a language to express the underlying order in the universe, "the poetic world of spirit fringing on the world of fact."[143]

Elizabeth V. Chew

FENOLLOSA, DOW, TACK, AND PHILLIPS

A Case for "Subjective" Painting in America

AUGUSTUS VINCENT TACK has been recognized variously as a fashionable society portraitist, a painter of civic and religious murals, a mystical abstractionist, and a possible inspirational forefather of American color field painters of the mid-twentieth century. Considered in the context of aesthetic and artistic debate in fin de siècle America, he is ultimately a painter whose development and critical reception span the remarkable changes of that era and whose work embodies many of its inherent contradictions.

Throughout his career Tack pursued two different and seemingly mutually exclusive paths: that of portraiture and commissioned mural work—perhaps the most conservative, safe, and economically motivated kinds of artistic production—and that of a largely abstract, personal, and spiritual painted expression. His paintings can be placed in three major interrelated discourses: the use of music as an aesthetic model for painting, the influence of Asian art, and the relationship between the formal and the representational purposes of art.[1]

Tack received standard training for an American painter of his day: classes at the Art Students League in New York with H. Siddons Mowbray and probably also with John Twachtman, William Merritt Chase, and J. Alden Weir, the obligatory time in a Paris atelier (perhaps with Luc-Olivier Merson), and painting *en plein air* in Normandy and Picardy, all in the first half of the 1890s. He had an early facility for portraiture and for the impressionist-inspired landscape popular among art students abroad. He came of age as an artist during the American Renaissance, in the aftermath of the 1893 World's Columbian Exposition, the era of the apotheosis of American Beaux-Arts design and decoration and the celebration of materialistic values. Late nineteenth-century American art is characterized by the naturalism that this ideology fostered as well as by the subjective, introspective, and evocative visions of artists as diverse as James McNeill Whistler, Thomas Wilmer Dewing, and Elihu Vedder (fig. 23). Both characterizations—naturalistic and subjective—suit Tack.

Among the most influential artists and aestheticians of this time was John La Farge, a mentor of Tack, whose portrait the younger artist painted in 1897–1900. La Farge's well-documented, eclectic career, both progressive and conservative, sheds light on the dualistic nature of the period in which Tack matured as an artist. La Farge was an innovator of the first order; he was one of the first Western collectors of Japanese prints and among the first Western artists to apply Japanese principles of design to his own work, a painter who continually looked for new inspiration and avenues of expression.[2] He painted out of doors before American impressionists and visited Tahiti before Gauguin. He emerged by the 1870s as a leader among progressive artists, who recognized in his work the "aestheticism of James McNeill Whistler intermingled with the most venerable traditions of Western art."[3] Nevertheless, as Henry Adams pointed out, in La Farge's decorative and mural commissions, his religious paintings (fig. 24), and his efforts to

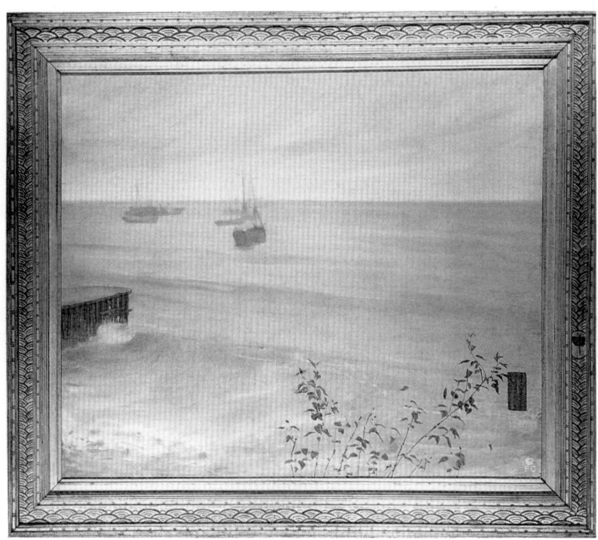

Fig. 23. James McNeill Whistler, *Symphony in Grey and Green: The Ocean*, with original frame, 1866, The Frick Collection, New York

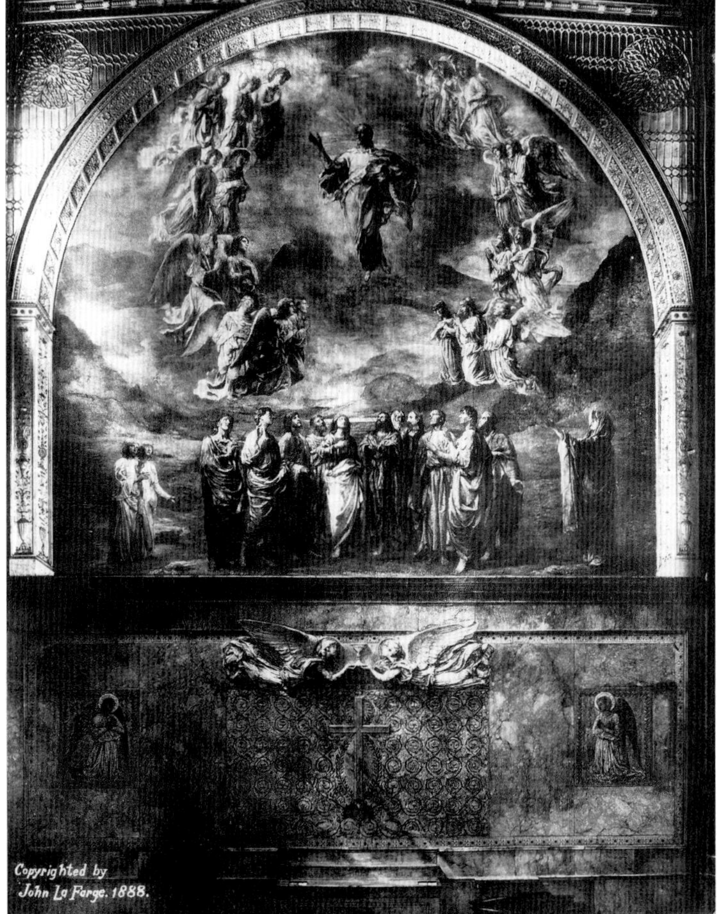

Fig. 24. John La Farge, *The Ascension*, mural in the Church of the Ascension, New York, 1886–87, photograph, Peter A. Juley and Son Collection, National Museum of American Art, Smithsonian Institution, Washington, D.C.

revive the moribund art of stained glass, his formal and technical advances remain connected to a conservative figural idiom.[4]

Russell Lynes called La Farge "an eccentric conformist,"[5] an appellation that elucidates the conundrum of Augustus Vincent Tack as well: an urbane gentleman of conservative society whose portraits graced the homes of America's wealthy and influential, who completed public and private mural commissions with social and religious themes, whose invalid wife enjoyed the life of the idle rich, but whose oeuvre increasingly included paintings that explored spiritual and mystical themes using color and form freed from representational ends. Duncan Phillips recognized the connection between Tack and La Farge, writing about Tack in 1926: "His culture and his intellect and his rare wisdom in selecting for himself the quality he needs from the best periods of Occidental and Oriental art enable him to carry forward the La Farge tradition in American painting with the initiative of new knowledge and with fresh symbols for his own age."[6]

In his earliest published writing about the work of his friend Tack, Phillips drew an analogy between painting and music. His continuing use of this musical correlation, his connection of Tack's work with that of La Farge, and his recognition in it of a synthesis between Western and Eastern concerns reveal his perspective on the artist and enable us to consider Tack's achievements through a mirror of the artist's own time.

In his first article on Tack, "The Romance of a Painter's Mind" (1916), Phillips discusses the heavily encrusted, jewel-like, pointillistic panels of the mid-teens, including *Court of Romance* (*Garden of Romance*) (cat. 14), in which Tack applied his pure pigments in "a rough-hewn sculpturesque art of color."[7] He presents the artist, in all his contradictory glory, as a mystic devoted to the "truth" of illusion and "the mind's dream of a world" and as a traditionalist who is "attentive to the most startling revolutionary disturbances in the realms of painting and music."[8] He asserts that Tack "feels that painting can come into great influence if it will enrich life with a decoration which will move men like music . . . . By studying the attractions and oppositions of color with the help of science and music, he believes that a painter will eventually be able to exert a great power over the mind and the emotions without any resort to literary associations."[9]

Eight years later, in 1924, the Phillips

Memorial Gallery exhibited Tack's "recent decorative work," including *Passacaglia* (cat. 23), *The Voice of Many Waters* (cat. 27), *Storm* (cat. 25), and other mosaiclike, nearly abstract works of the early 1920s. Writing in the brochure, Phillips again used music to explain the emotional effect of Tack's paintings:

In no other art has [the] identity of content and form seemed so inherent as in music, which is self-contained and self-sufficient. Yet painters, too, have dreamed of moving us like music, of giving painting the emotional potency and even the time element which music has hitherto monopolized. Augustus Vincent Tack is showing the way. . . . To his color-music we may go, either for rest and recreation, or for zest and stimulation; for seeing visions and for dreaming dreams.[10]

Phillips was not alone in his use of the musical analogy. The previous year Edwin Lefevre, the author of the catalogue foreword for Tack's exhibition at Kraushaar Galleries, had written:

There is nothing novel or revolutionary in the statement that the elements of form, of harmonious relations in sequence, of essential rhythm, exist in painting quite as definitely as in music. . . . We recognize the functions of music and its power to evoke emotions. . . . Since the essentials are the same it is a natural question to ask why the painter should not try to express through his medium what musicians have been expressing for ages. . . . Tack . . . has used his art to create moods which heretofore have been induced by music only.

Critic Jessie Lemont had referred in 1914 to a group of Tack's religious paintings as "a symphony in four movements."[11]

Phillips's use of the musical analogy to describe the emotional impact of Tack's art reflected a crucial theoretical discussion in early twentieth-century America. The correlation of color and music—and, more generally, the equivalence of different kinds of sensory experience, which dates to antiquity—became a useful tool with which artists and critics of the mid-nineteenth century described the effect produced on a viewer by the arrangement of forms and colors in a painting, removed from any narrative or subject matter. Music was a model for explaining abstract elements in paintings and for supporting the theory of art for art's sake. By the second decade of the twentieth century, the idea was closely associated with avant-garde art and literature, seemingly far removed from nineteenth-century sources. But it had firm roots in the symbolist and aesthetic movements in France and England in the 1860s. These nineteenth-century origins of the musical model, not its more progressive twentieth-century manifestations, led Phillips to connect these ideas to Tack's paintings.[12]

The music-painting discussion gained a particular foothold in the eighteenth century in the age of Bach, Haydn, Mozart, and early Beethoven, as aestheticians recognized the power of music to stir the emotions through sound alone, with no imitative or narrative purpose. During the romantic movement in the early nineteenth century in Germany, France, and the United States, artists as diverse as Delacroix and Thomas Cole articulated the notion that the abstract properties of music should serve as a model for those of painting.[13] In 1855, the poet and art critic Charles Baudelaire described Delacroix's painting *Lion Hunt* as "color that thinks for itself, independently of the objects which it clothes. . . . [T]hese wonderful chords of color often give one ideas of melody and harmony, and the impression that one takes away from his pictures is often, as it were, a musical one."[14] Two years later, in his poem "Correspondances" in *Les Fleurs du Mal*, Baudelaire evocatively expressed the relationship between odors, colors, and sounds.

Baudelaire was a key figure on both sides of the English Channel in propagating the idea of a communion of the senses. He particularly influenced his friend Whistler, who transmitted the discussion to the United States. Through Baudelaire and Theophile Gautier, ideas of beauty, musicality, art for art's sake, and correspondences among the senses also reached D. G. Rossetti, A. C. Swinburne, and Stéphane Mallarmé. Baudelaire's work provided important precedent through the concept of linking music and other arts to invoke the spiritual.[15] Swedenborgian mysticism, which infused physical existence with spiritual significance and had strongly influenced Baudelaire, fanned the interest among nineteenth-century artists and writers in synaesthesia, the name given to the equivalence among different modes of sensory perception.[16]

The best-known treatise on the correlation of sound, color, and abstraction—and the one that gained these ideas widespread acceptance in America—is Wassily Kandinsky's *Concerning the Spiritual in Art* (1912), first published in its entirety in English in 1914.[17] Americans were not, however, dependent on Kandinsky for the concept of synaesthesia. As early as 1903, in an appreciation of Whistler published at the time of his death, Arthur Jerome Eddy had quoted the painter's assertion from *The Gentle Art of Making Enemies* (1890):

As music is the poetry of sound, so is painting the poetry of sight, and the subject matter has nothing to do with the harmony of sound or color. . . . Art should be independent of all claptrap, should stand alone, and appeal to the artistic sense of eye or ear without confounding this with emotions entirely foreign to it, as devotion, pity, love, patriotism, and the like. All these have kind of concern with it; and that is why I insist on calling my works "arrangements" and "harmonies."[18]

Discussions of the music-painting analogy appeared frequently in Alfred Stieglitz's journal *Camera Work* from its inception in 1903, in articles by progressive writers such as Sadakichi Hartmann and Charles Caffin.[19] Caffin wrote in 1906:

If painting is to maintain a hold on the intelligence and imagination, as music does and possibly poetry, and to grow forward in touch with the growing needs of humanity it must find some fundamental motive other than the appearance of the world. . . . If [painting] . . . is to keep itself in living competition with the superior impressiveness of modern music. . . it must take on something of the quality which is the essence of music—the abstract. It is here that it may learn of the Oriental ideal, as exemplified in Japanese art. . . . [Whistler] realized that form, the concrete thing. . . draws off the mind of the spectator from the more abstract qualities of beauty; moreover, that music because of its appeal being uninterrupted by the concrete, is capable of deeper and farther reaching expression than painting, and that the nearest analogy to the harmony or sound within the scope of the painter, is the harmony of color.[20]

Caffin's and Eddy's discussions demonstrate their facility with these issues even before Kandinsky wrote about them. In and after 1914 the music-painting analogy received enormous attention as a result of Kandinsky in journals such as *291*, *The Seven Arts*, and *The Little Review*; in books on modern art, including Eddy's *Cubists and Post-Impressionism* (1914) and Willard Huntington Wright's *Modern Art* (1915); and even in such accessible publications as the *New York Times*, which reviewed Kandinsky's and Eddy's books.[21] The idea was so pervasive that even conservative critics such as Frank Jewett Mather, Jr., were prompted to comment. In "The New Painting and the Musical Fallacy" (1914), he wrote:

Kandinsky seeks his discipline in a kind of grammar of form and color which usurps the terms not of geometry but of music. An arrangement of simple forms is "Melodic" and arrangement of complex forms and colors "Symphonic". . . . The doctrine has manifest defects. . . . Music itself does not play with fixed abstract terms, such as Kandinsky wished the colors to be.[22]

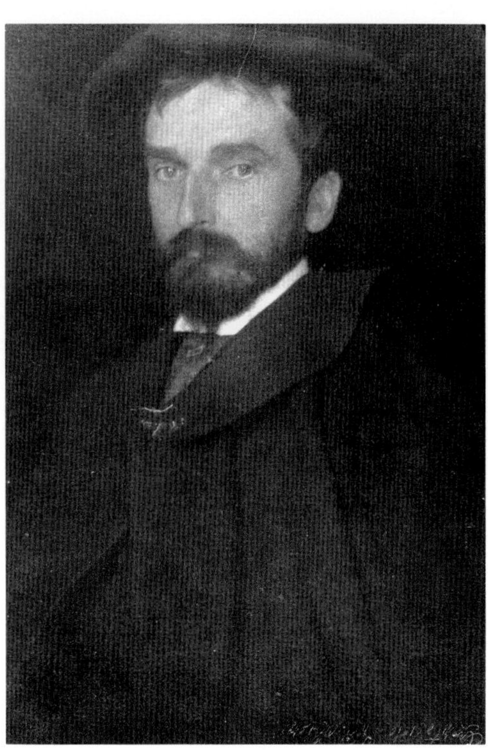

Fig. 25. Gertrude Kasebiër, *Arthur Wesley Dow*, ca. 1905, Arthur Wesley Dow Papers, Archives of American Art, Smithsonian Institution, Washington, D.C.

Despite their accessibility, avant-garde journals such as *Camera Work* and writers such as Kandinsky and Eddy would have been anathema to the young collector Duncan Phillips when he wrote his first article on Tack in 1916. Phillips may have known of Kandinsky in 1916, but only as one of the Armory Show artists whom he had characterized as "representatives of degeneracy in painting"[23] or through secondary sources such as Mather.

Phillips was not describing abstract painting in his article on Tack. It would be several years before the artist would paint pure abstraction or the collector would be comfortable with the idea. Phillips had not yet come to know Stieglitz and his coterie or Eddy, who were on the front line in the adoption of Kandinsky's theories and their avowal of the avant-garde.[24] Still, by the mid-teens, when he sought a metaphor to describe the work of his friend Tack, which had struck him so forcefully, he turned to music.

The use of the music-painting analogy by Ernest Fenollosa and Arthur Wesley Dow (fig. 25), two important American aestheticians and art educators at the turn of the century, provides a more compatible context for Tack and Phillips than do Kandinsky's concepts.[25] The work of Fenollosa and Dow forms the link between the theories of Whistler and his contemporaries and those of the more progressive Stieglitz circle, who may themselves have first recognized the importance of the musical analogy in discussions of the Fenollosa-Dow notion of synthesis.[26] Fenollosa's and Dow's ideas and their influence, on a number of levels, relate directly to Tack and the way in which Duncan Phillips apprehended his art.

Ernest Fenollosa (1853–1908), one of the first Americans to study systematically the art and culture of Japan, was professor of philosophy and political economy at the Imperial University, Tokyo; founder of the Tokyo Academy of Fine Arts; founder, donor, and curator of the department of Japanese art at the Museum of Fine Arts, Boston (1890–96); and author of seminal volumes on Asian art.[27] Fenollosa came to believe in the inevitability of a new American style of art fused from Eastern and Western traditions, based on harmonic relations of line, *notan* (the Japanese relational concept of light and dark), and color. He wrote of the "perfect marriage on equal terms between the beauty in the subject and the beauty in the pictorial form," which he found inherent in Chinese and Japanese painting. He called this relationship "synthesis, because every part and relation has been absorbed in the new organic product without a remainder."[28] Fenollosa's ideas profoundly influenced the compositional theories of his friend Arthur Wesley Dow (1857–1922), who in turn, through his teaching and art education manuals, stimulated a generation of American artists.

Dow and Fenollosa met in Boston at the Museum of Fine Arts in 1891, after Dow had been stunned by his discovery of Hokusai prints and sought out the Japanese collections at the museum. Dow, a landscape painter recently returned to Boston from study in Paris and Pont-Aven, had exhibited at the Salon and the 1889 Universal Exposition. Back in the United States, he had devoted himself to art education, teaching in Boston and founding a summer school in his native Ipswich, Massachusetts. In 1893 Fenollosa made him assistant curator in the department of Japanese art. Their close relationship and the confluence of their ideas would have a significant impact on the teaching of art.

In 1895 Dow and Fenollosa were jointly appointed instructors at the Pratt Institute in Brooklyn, where they applied their "progressive series of synthetic exercises,"[29] in which students started with the simplest of line arrangements. Fenollosa resigned after a year, but Dow continued to teach at Pratt and the Art Students League (1899–1903). From 1904 until 1922 he headed the art department at Columbia Teachers College, where his consid-

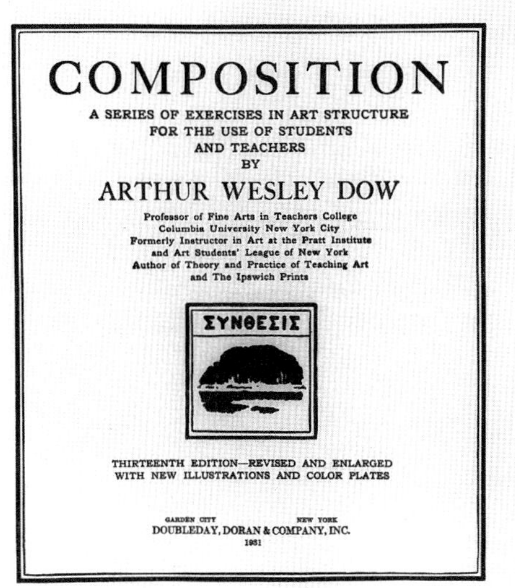

COMPOSITION

A SERIES OF EXERCISES IN ART STRUCTURE
FOR THE USE OF STUDENTS
AND TEACHERS
BY

ARTHUR WESLEY DOW

Professor of Fine Arts in Teachers College
Columbia University New York City
Formerly Instructor in Art at the Pratt Institute
and Art Students' League of New York
Author of Theory and Practice of Teaching Art
and The Ipswich Prints

ΣΥΝΘΕΣΙΣ

THIRTEENTH EDITION—REVISED AND ENLARGED
WITH NEW ILLUSTRATIONS AND COLOR PLATES

GARDEN CITY NEW YORK
DOUBLEDAY, DORAN & COMPANY, INC.
1931

Fig. 26. Title page, Arthur Wesley Dow, *Composition*, 1931 edition

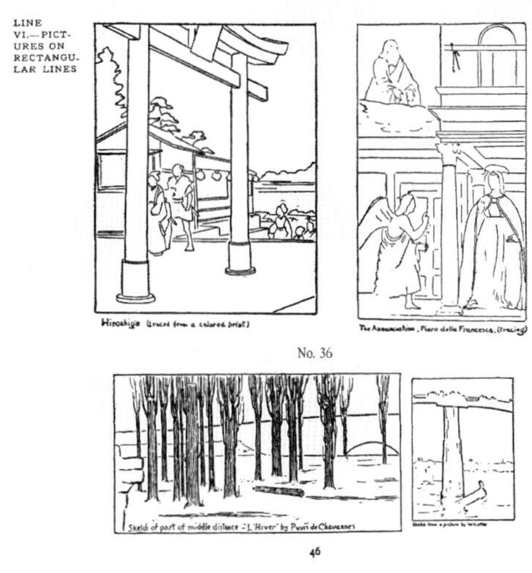

Fig. 27. Arthur Wesley Dow's rendering of various paintings to show linear design, in *Composition*, 1931 edition

erable influence on students, including Georgia O'Keeffe, has been well documented.[30]

In 1899 Dow published the first edition of *Composition*, which presented his and Fenollosa's philosophy of teaching art (fig. 26). They believed that art was construction, not imitation, and was based on an understanding of design (fig. 27). The method was founded on the "'putting together' of lines, masses, and colors to make a harmony."[31] This approach differed radically from the method of teaching art based on copying, which had held sway in the West since the Renaissance. "Painting what you see and as you see it is only studying; it is not creating; it is not composing," Dow had told the Boston Art Students' Association in 1894.[32]

In the introduction to *Composition*, Dow related the history of the academic style that his method refutes:

Soon after the time of Leonardo da Vinci, art education was classified into Representative (imitative), and Decorative, with separate schools for each—a serious mistake which has resulted in loss of public appreciation. Painting, which is essentially a rhythmic harmony of colored spaces, became sculptural, an imitation of modeling. Decoration became trivial, a lifeless copying of styles. The true relation between design and representation was lost.[33]

"Instead of setting up external nature as the standard," said Dow of his way of teaching, "the action of the human mind in harmony-building becomes the foundation for study."[34]

Central to Fenollosa's and Dow's discussion of the arrangement of line, *notan*, and color and the subordination of subject to form is the use of the musical analogy. Dow wrote of Fenollosa in his introduction to *Composition*, "He believed music to be, in a sense, the key to the other fine arts, since its essence is pure beauty; that space art may be called 'visual music,' and may be studied and criticized from this point of view."[35]

Dow believed that seeing visual relations was like hearing music. He proposed that a painter emulate the musical principles of subordination, repetition, harmony, and variation: "The great masters of music have shown the infinite possibilities of combination and varied expression. . . . Even so can lines, masses, and colors be wrought into musical forms and endlessly varied."[36]

In a 1917 article, Dow employed the musical analogy in a list of the objectives of modernist painters, stressing his belief in the importance of composition above subject, form above content. Fourth on his list was: "Less attention to subject, more to form. Line, Mass and color have pure aesthetic value whether they represent anything or not. . . . Ceasing to make representation a standard, but comparing the visual arts with music."[37]

Fenollosa had also expressed this idea of the subordination of content to form:

Representation is not art, it is literature. That a picture represents a man does not interest us . . . . It is a question of spacing, of how the pattern is worked out, that interests us . . .not the representational element but the structural element . . .not the realistic motive but the desire to find finer and finer space relations and line relations.[38]

The young collector Duncan Phillips traveled to Japan and China in 1910 and was keenly interested in the relationship between Eastern and Western art. In his essay "Nationality in Pictures" (1914), he referred to Fenollosa and his idea of synthesis: "It is to Japan that we must look for the universal art of the future, the art which will perfectly combine all that is best in the aesthetic self-expression of Orient and Occident."[39] He went on to discuss ideas of Japanese art that have affected the West: "the decorative technique: how to make effective patterns with the simplest means, emphasizing the numberless joys of color schemes, . . . the expressive possibilities of line and mass, and the value of surprises in picturesque invention."[40] His 1926 statement about Tack and La Farge similarly demonstrates an appreciation of Fenollosa's idea of fusion of East and West.

Phillips had in his library Fenollosa's monumental *Epochs of Chinese and Japanese Art* (published posthumously in 1911), Dow's *Composition*, and the work of another follower of Fenollosa, Denman Waldo Ross, who wrote in *A Theory of Pure Design: Harmony, Balance, Rhythm* (1907) that "Harmony, Balance, Rhythm . . . appeal to the eye just as absolute Music appeals to the ear."[41]

Fenollosa and Dow's belief that painting was fundamentally a harmonious arrangement of form and color analogous to a piece of music echoes earlier nineteenth-century theories, particularly the symbolists and Whistler. The language Phillips used to discuss Tack in the late teens and early 1920s recalls Fenollosa's and Dow's discussion of painting as formal relationships without regard to subject matter.

The French symbolist Maurice Denis's well-known statement of the movement's aesthetic was that "a painting, before being a war-horse, a nude, or some anecdote, is essentially a flat surface covered in color arranged in a certain order."[42] This description also bears close relationship to Whistler's definition, from the Ruskin trial, of a *Nocturne* as "an arrangement of line, form, and color first" or to his musical description from the Ten O'Clock Lectures of the artist as composer: "born to pick, and choose and group with science, these elements, that the result may be beautiful—as the musician gathers his notes, and forms his chords, until he brings forth from chaos glorious harmony."[43]

Symbolists divorced art from a dependence on nature, giving the artist the control over the design, and demanded that the result be subjective, evocative, mysterious, poetic, and musical. Symbolism represented all that was contrary to the prevailing materialism of fin de siècle culture. Whistler's work adheres to this description, although he may not be characterized precisely as a "symbolist." His acceptance by Fenollosa and Dow, particularly for the way in which he incorporated Japanese design, was complete. Both men saw Whistler as an ideal artist to demonstrate their principles. Fenollosa believed him "the nodule, the universaliser, the interpreter of East to West and West to East."[44] Dow used Whistler's work to amplify points in *Composition.*

Fenollosa and Dow codified the methods of Japanese design and the age-old relation of color to music as distilled by nineteenth-century theoreticians into what is essentially a how-to manual for art based on the harmonious arrangement of essential parts in which the subject has secondary importance. Tack created an art that adhered almost completely to Dow's criteria, and Phillips upheld it at every turn. Nowhere is this more clear than in a statement from Phillips's 1924 Tack catalogue:

People who will go to good music for spiritual nourishment and exaltation . . . will yet demand of painting that it be illustrative or imitative and will turn in bewilderment from paintings which seek only to speak to their souls in the same musical way, the way of pure design, the way of ordered and varied rhythms, with organizations of mass and color and line instead of movements of sound. [45]

In 1930 Phillips published an article by Tack in *Art and Understanding* to coincide with the inauguration of the artist's abstract mural series for the Phillips Memorial Gallery. In this "Note on Subjective Painting," Tack explicitly confirmed his connections to the idea of viability of art without subject and to the music analogy. "In painting, of whatever kind," he wrote, "that which eventually matters most is the filling of the space; in short, the design. After the subject has ceased to be considered . . . this conscious disposition of the colors and the shapes in space through rhythmical coordination remains the chief interest."[46] He then quoted Denis's famous definition and continued in a manner that could be a statement from Fenollosa or Dow: "It seems to be difficult for many to grasp that the essential qualities of painting should be sufficient in themselves, apart from all representation. . . . One does not copy nature. One is inspired by it to create on one's own account."[47] His statement about music was similarly clear, with extremely close correspondence to the writing of D. W. Ross: "Music has always been called the absolute art because it is free and in no way associated with natural sounds, nor in any sense ever a mere reproduction of them. Painting should be just as free. It too can be absolute. The pleasure inherent to it results from harmonious relations of color rhythmically progressive. Thus painting appeals to the eye exactly as music to the ear and both awaken emotions in the same absolute sense."[48]

At the time of his death in 1949, Tack was working on a group portrait of President Harry Truman and his chief advisers. Throughout his life, somewhat like Whistler, Tack was dependent on his income from portraiture. He nevertheless forayed into a seemingly antithetical mode of expression, in which he kept company with the likes of La Farge, Baudelaire, Whistler, Denis, and Dow. He is never connected with the most extreme abstract idiom in America; he remains rooted in the nineteenth century. Tack must ultimately be seen as an artist who felt the freedom to experiment amid the shifting tenor of his times and who found theoretical underpinnings in a variety of sources. In Duncan Phillips, he had a patron with the knowledge and sensitivity to connect his achievements to the larger stage of art in America.

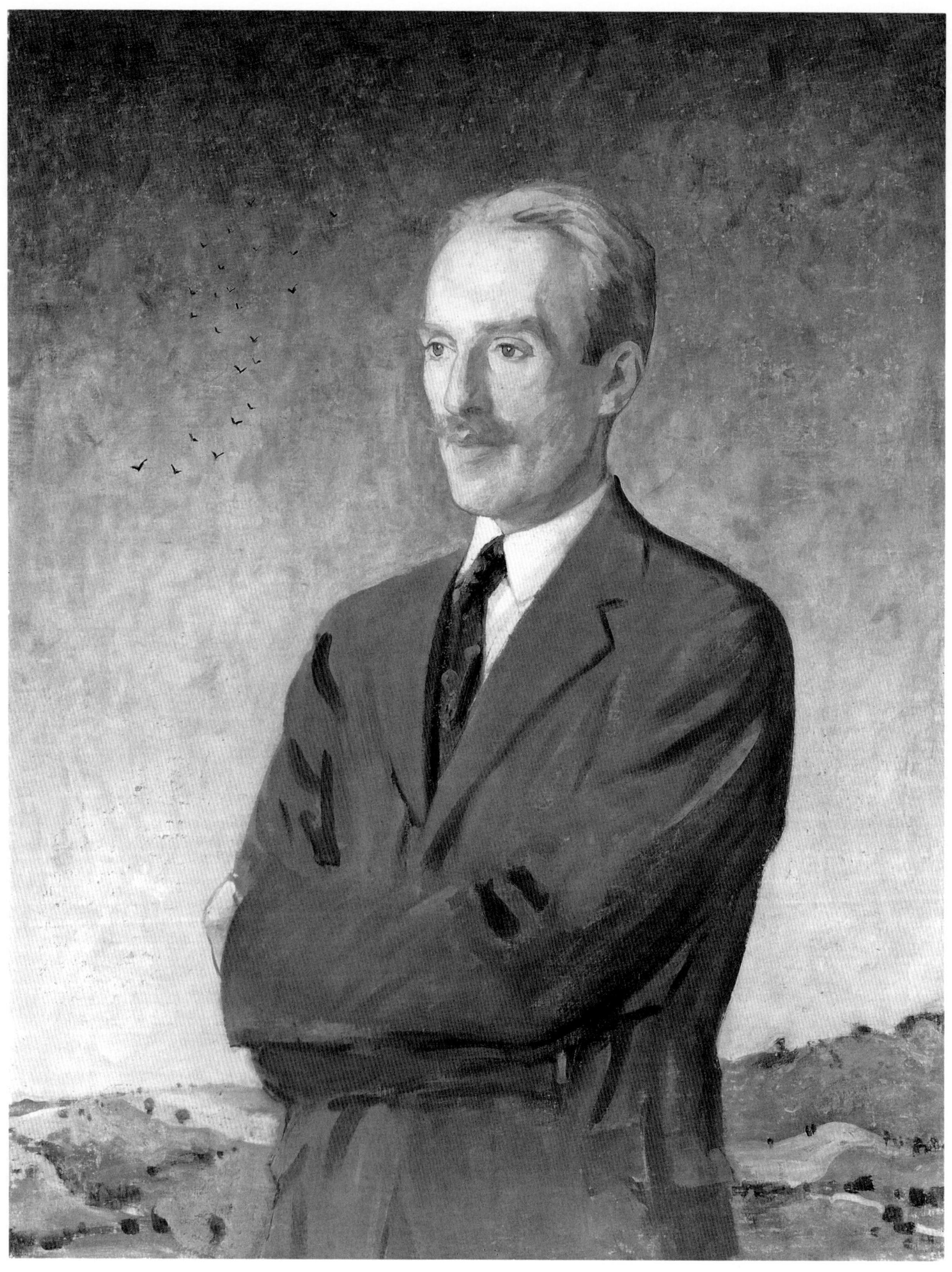

Cat. 28. *Portrait of Duncan Phillips*, completed 1926, oil on canvas mounted on plywood panel, 36 x 28 in.

David W. Scott

MUTUAL INFLUENCES

Augustus Vincent Tack and Duncan Phillips

ANY ACCOUNT OF THE LIFE and works of Augustus Vincent Tack would be incomplete without a consideration of his contributions to Duncan Phillips as a mentor in the arts and of Phillips's vital role as a patron-encourager of Tack's most significant paintings. The Phillips Memorial Gallery in its formative decade owed much to Tack, who in turn owed much to it (fig. 28).[1]

The two men were acquainted by 1914, and undoubtedly the mutual influences began by the time of Phillips's visits to Tack's studio in 1914–15, which resulted in his published appreciation of Tack's new paintings.[2] The visits took place some two years after the Armory Show, when the New York art scene was still polarized in reaction to that event. Duncan Phillips, who had considered himself an enlightened and liberal supporter of contemporary painters, had been stunned and shocked by the exhibition: on his recent trips abroad, he had not regarded the avant-garde works as worth serious consideration. In response to the Armory Show, he had written scathing condemnations of the modern movement from the postimpressionists to Matisse—and of Matisse in particular. Tack, on the other hand, left no explicit commentary, but his studio art apparently changed suddenly and radically, as if in response to a challenge. Beginning by 1914, he painted a series of larger, starkly powerful, boldly pigmented paintings based on a new, personal religious symbolism. Phillips saw paintings from this group at the time of his studio visits. The bold departures indicate that Tack was more venturesome than Phillips, although some fifteen years older and of a similar conservative cultural heritage. Indeed, the fundamental sympathies of the two men had much to do with the close friendship that they soon developed.

Their friendship was to have an intimacy unusual for the two customarily reserved men but which no doubt came from their shared background and temperament. Both came from families with money from Pittsburgh manufacturing; both had close associations with Yale University; by 1917, both were "Centurions."[3] Both had patrician tastes and manners, were highly literate, intensely fond of music. Both were idealists and romantics, conservative by background but committed to individual freedom and expression. Both looked to painting for beauty and life enhancement. Both sought imaginative escape and stimulation through "the dream" and symbolism. And each had contributions to make to the other: Tack as the experienced and creative professional artist, mentor to the younger writer and collector who was shortly to become involved in exhibiting art, Phillips as the sympathetic and supportive interpreter, patron, and promoter of the art of Tack and his friends.

There is no record of how the men first met, but a few pages in a Phillips journal of 1914 describe vividly the initial impact of Tack's landscapes on the young critic.[4] The journal entry was headed "Notes on the Art of Augustus Tack" and began:

My earliest acquaintance with the landscapes of Augustus Tack was one of those experiences which

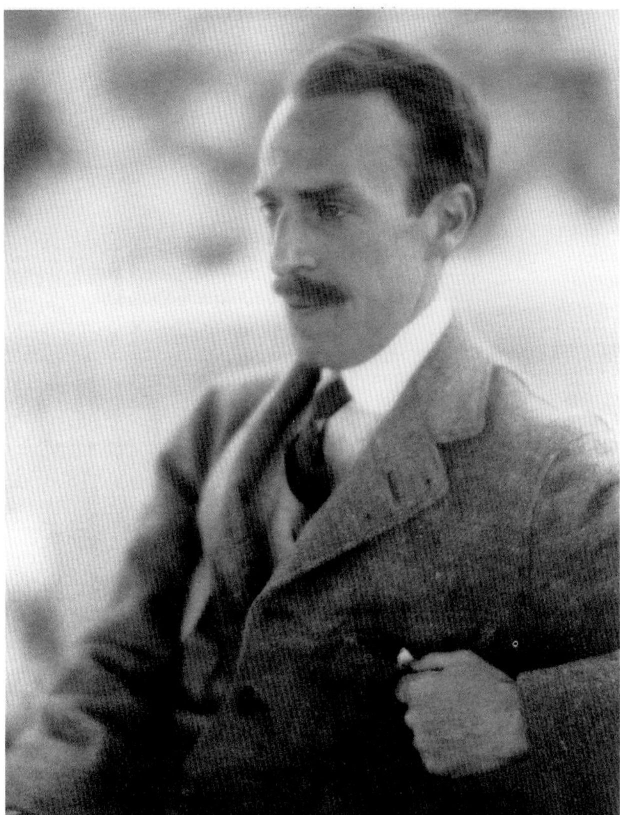

Fig. 28. Duncan Phillips, ca. 1921, The Phillips Collection Archives

mark an epoch in one's own mental development. Some small panel-shaped canvasses—quiet in color unobtrusive in form—made me none the less catch my breath with delight. Here was an artist who interpreted some individual moods which I had long known and cherished—Always the sense of quiet, mystery—and of "the big world"—even beyond the sunset.

Phillips continued to note his impressions of some nine landscapes, many of hills and clouds, writing, "And always, always the sky is exquisite and the cloud shadows are flying and we too want to fly with them over the hills and far away." Reading the journal, we can glimpse the direction that led to Tack's abstractions and Phillips's delight in them, but it is significant that Phillips makes no mention of the artist's then most recent and more experimental works: the large "pointillist" pictures and the chinoiseries, with which he was shortly to come to terms.

One can assume with confidence that Phillips read the lead article in the November 1914 *International Studio*, which must have stirred him again with the excitement of discovering a kindred spirit.[5] The article, by Jessie Lemont with an added note by Carroll Brown, discussed and reproduced four recent "pointillist" works by Tack: *The Remorse of Eve* (1913–14, National Shrine of the Immaculate Conception, Washington, D.C.), *Simon of Cyrene* (by 1914, National Shrine of the Immaculate Conception, Washington, D.C.), *The Pardon of Dismas* (by 1914, unlocated), and *Madonna of the Everlasting Hills* (cat. 13). The praise was unstinting and touched on just the qualities the young critic was seeking at the time. Lemont began by relating Tack's work to contemporary Europeans Phillips had admired on his travels abroad—Giovanni Segantini and Henri Le Sidaner, who "paints a world of dreams." The American, similar in "big, broad and unique brush handling, . . . reveals to us an originality and power both in conception and technique." The article continued:

Four large paintings recently completed by Augustus Tack might be called a symphony in four movements, with humanity for its theme. The force of the elemental flows through these paintings, each of which is complete in itself, yet is part of a great whole . . . . Each is dominated by a single human figure, Biblical in its bigness, symbolic of humanity's heights and depths.

Lemont found the works so unique in power and so original as to be comparable only to such masters as Auguste Rodin and George Frederick Watts. Watts's symbolism had appealed strongly to Phillips; such work as Lemont described would have evoked a similar response. Carroll Brown's note must have intrigued Phillips even more:

Mr. Tack's pictures strike a new note. In their unique commingling of method and idea they are distinctive of a new century, Impressionistic his technique certainly is in the employment of bold spots of pure color laid upon the canvas in the manner of a mosaic. But, unlike many of these latter-day adventurers into experimental regions, from his sound training and mental equipoise he never allows his method to master him.

Brown continued to discuss the paintings with a reference to works by "the loftiest geniuses." The article appeared in November, and it may not be mere coincidence that in late December Tack planned to take a "train to Washington to see Mr. Phillips," or that in 1915 Phillips paid several visits to Tack's studio.[6]

Duncan Phillips's first article on Tack, "The Romance of a Painter's Mind," appeared in the March 1916 issue of the International Studio.[7] It reveals much about their personal relationship. As a man, Phillips admired the painter greatly; as for the paintings, some he praised, others received a mixed review. The article began:

Painting for Augustus Tack is not merely a profession—it is an act of creation, a solemn and splendid miracle to be performed with reverence and joy . . . . He employs his remarkably diverse talent in the creation not of any one subject in any one style . . . but to the expression of his remarkably varied interest both in the visible world and the world of dreams. For Tack's conception of art is sincerely mystical, but his perception of life is spontaneously natural and his many-sided work reveals attractively a many-sided personality.

After praising Tack's "landscapes of the mind" with their romance and refreshing heights and distances, Phillips wrote of his several encounters with the painter—revealing of the man's profound knowledge of tradition, deep spirituality, love of romance and music, and inquiring youthful mind.

Phillips was particularly struck (and no doubt challenged) by finding Tack

curiously serious also over the sensational performances of Picasso. Although he deplores the hypocrisy and vulgarity which pervades so much of the modern movement, yet he sympathizes with the uncertain groping in the dark of some of the desperate pioneers who are so determined to escape from the tyranny of the past . . . . He feels that painting can come into great influence if it will enrich life with a decoration which will move men like music . . . . He believes that a painter will eventually be able to exert a great power over the mind and the emotions without any resort to literary associations.

Phillips concluded his article with comments on some of the paintings that were soon to appear in Tack's show at the Kraushaar Galleries. In the new, heavily pigmented manner, the monumental paintings were admirable in aim but not yet completely successful; he preferred the "little romantic panels which glow with jewelled colors" such as *Court of Romance* (cat. 17). But whatever his reservations about some of the paintings, Phillips cast the painter in a heroic mold: "Scorning the easy paths of small accomplishment, undaunted and splendidly serious, he strides forward."

The article clearly points the way each man was to follow for the next eight or ten years: Tack would create, and Phillips would learn to respond to, painting that through form, rhythm, and color could exert great power "over the mind and the emotions without any resort to literary associations." What degree of abstraction this implied to Tack, we cannot know. Phillips, in 1916, did not contemplate ever abandoning representational form. In an attack on modernism published in late 1917 and early 1918, he condemned "mere pattern making," which reduced art to "mere aesthetics unrelated to the emotions of life . . . . Representation is necessary to appeal to our emotion of recognition . . . thereby intensifying our joy in life itself."[8]

Tack's evolution toward abstraction, if we may judge by exhibition dates and titles (he did not put dates on the paintings themselves) took place deliberately over several years. Reviews of his 1917 Kraushaar exhibition commented on the variety of the works, including two "chinoiseries"—"half-observed, half invented" decorative landscapes, thinly pigmented. In 1918 his art and activity were involved with the war effort. In 1919 and 1920 he was engrossed in a government mural commission in Winnipeg, which was followed in 1920 by a painting trip to the Rockies. In the mountains he appears to have been again inspired to seek an art in which form and color, though springing from the subject, exercised a power over mind and emotions that transcended a conventional transcription.

If Tack's stylistic evolution was deliberate, Phillips's patronage of the more experimental works was even more so. Duncan's brother Jim purchased a portrait in 1916. Other paintings acquired between 1914 and 1919 included six landscapes and romantic subjects such as he had recorded in his 1914 notebook. In 1920 he first committed himself to some of Tack's less conventional works, notably *Madonna of the Everlasting Hills* and a "chinoiserie." Only in 1921, with the purchase of *Mountain Outposts* (by 1921, The Phillips Collection), did Phillips's acquisitions fall in line with the artist's current expressions.

Although the two men moved only slowly in the artistic direction glimpsed in 1916, their friendship grew rapidly. In 1917 Phillips joined the Century Association, which was frequently the mailing address for both men. In 1918 they were associated on the art front of the war effort: both were members of the Committee on Arrangements of the Allied War Salon, held in December at the American Art Galleries. At about this moment Duncan Phillips hit on the idea of creating an art gallery as a memorial to his father and brother. He was shortly to involve Tack in his planning.

In 1919 Phillips began forming his collection with the gallery in mind. He first exhibited as a collector at the Century Club, May 25–June 6, showing paintings by Fantin Latour, Eugène Louis Boudin, Claude Monet,

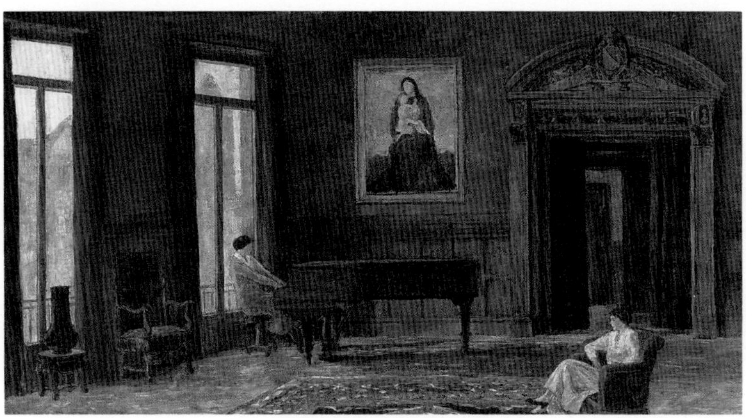

Fig. 29. Marjorie Phillips, *The North Library*, 1922, The Phillips Collection, Washington, D.C. Gift of the artist, 1984. In the background is Tack's painting, *Madonna of the Everlasting Hills*.

and several Americans, including Ernest Lawson, John Twachtman, and Tack (*Court of Romance*, a picture he had referred to as reminiscent of Monticelli).

Correspondence concerning the exhibition documents the close friendship between the artist and the collector. Phillips had been taken ill before the opening of the show and had gone to recuperate at a sanatorium in Kerhonkson, New York. Tack wrote him a warm letter on June 6 telling of the disposition made of the various works following the show, the success of the exhibition and the mark Phillips had made as a collector, and his intention to paint a larger version of *Court of Romance*, as Phillips had requested. The letter closed, after family references, with "Ever affectionately your Augustus," reflecting a degree of intimacy unusual among Duncan's friendships.

Phillips was extremely busy in 1920, selecting and collecting paintings, arranging trial showings of his growing collection, and planning and furthering his gallery project. On July 23 the Phillips Memorial Gallery was incorporated, with Phillips as president and Tack as vice-president. Tack, though hard-pressed by his Winnipeg mural commission, managed to keep in close touch through letters and meetings in both Washington and New York. He made special efforts to attend an exhibition of Phillips's collection at the Corcoran Gallery in March and took care of the disposition of his Century Club show in December.

The Corcoran show was Phillips's largest exhibition in 1920. It was significant in several ways. It consisted of sixty-two paintings, evidence of very rapid acquisitions. The pictures were arranged in groupings that emphasized affinities and contrasts—the collector's first chance to realize his exhibit philosophy on a large scale. The contemporary paintings, which represented his commitment to living American artists and were in preponderance, were shown in the context of what he considered to be the best traditional work. The examples of American "modernism" fell well short of any abstract idiom, but they appeared extreme to Washington in 1920. In a lengthy review, the critic of the *Star*, after wrestling with the problem of understanding the modernism of George Bellows, Jerome Myers, Arthur B. Davies, and Rockwell Kent, concluded by advising her readers that their pictures "cannot be explained and if one does not like them the wise thing to do is to pass them by."[9]

In the course of 1920 the projected gallery gradually came together, opening by the year's end. Tack and Phillips worked together closely. Phillips refined his statements of objectives and programs, and he must have worked on them with Tack, for at the first trustee meeting in February 1921, Tack helped him present his plans to the board. The minutes of the meeting were printed in a broad-ranging report that envisaged the presentation of "all kinds of exhibitions of contemporary art" within a very specially and harmoniously designed gallery-library-theater building. It was soon evident that Tack was intended to have a major role in the design of the harmonious setting.

Included in the minutes was a list of paintings in Phillips's collection as of June 1, 1921—an astonishing 237 works, most of them acquired within two and a half years. For the first time, Phillips listed a large unit by Tack—indeed, the largest by any artist: fourteen paintings representing a wide range of works, including his presumably very recent and expressive *Mountain Outposts*.[10]

Following the board meeting, Phillips wrote long and urgent letters to Tack requesting advice and assistance on a variety of matters—committee functions, paintings to see, a publication proposal—but above all, the finishing of the walls of "the new Gallery," for which he wanted Tack's sample to give to the architect. Then, on March 11, he told Tack, "I need you very much, Augustus, this coming week to advise me and help me with the hanging of the pictures. . . . It is again a matter of business and I enclose a check." Phillips was greatly concerned: "This hanging will be more or less permanent and open to the public." In fact, that month members of the College Art Association, meeting in Washington, were invited to view paintings at the Phillips home. By May both the Music Room and the new Main Gallery (recently built above the Music Room) held paintings (fig. 29). The gallery began quietly admitting the public by late fall, but the formal opening date was not announced until January 1922, when it was set for February 1.

Although the Phillips house was gradually to be turned, room by room, into a full-scale museum, this was not Duncan's original intention. The dream gallery building that he had described in longhand notes in 1920, in his published proposal for the Phillips Memorial Gallery in 1921, and again in instructions to the Committee on Style of Architecture in 1922, was eventually drawn in a very sketchy plan by the collector in a notebook datable to 1923 (fig. 30). Notations indicated a proposed location near the corner of Connecticut Avenue and Columbia Road. The scheme consisted of three main parts: a theater, a two-story block divided into twenty-four small galleries facing a central garden court, and a block containing two large library rooms separated by a monumental hallway. The theater was designated "Davies or Tack." One library was to show the work of Arthur B. Davies, the other that of Maurice Prendergast. The hallway was inscribed "Tack Hallway—large abstract mural paintings set in panelled walls—furniture—walls everything designed and colored by the artist."[11] (The surprising word "abstract" was inserted as an afterthought.)

The implications of these notations are indeed significant. The entire art content of the museum was to be framed in a permanent setting provided by three artists: Prendergast, Davies, and Tack. The great central hallway was to be completely the work of Tack, as designer, decorator, and muralist. And Phillips for the first time specified abstract art for his collection, associating it with Tack.

Phillips's desire for abstract murals traces directly to developments in Tack's paintings in 1920–23. The mountain landscapes of 1920 had shown a new freedom and breadth in handling. In his Kraushaar exhibition of February 1922, Tack displayed several canvases marked by a semicubist breaking of planes building to an expressive crescendo (*The Crowd* [cat. 21], *Gethsemane* [cat. 20]). During that year he took a further step: as he wrote to Kraushaar, "I have been developing some compositions of form and color based on essential rhythm . . . . They are abstractly decorative as the mystical meaning which stimulates the imagination."[12]

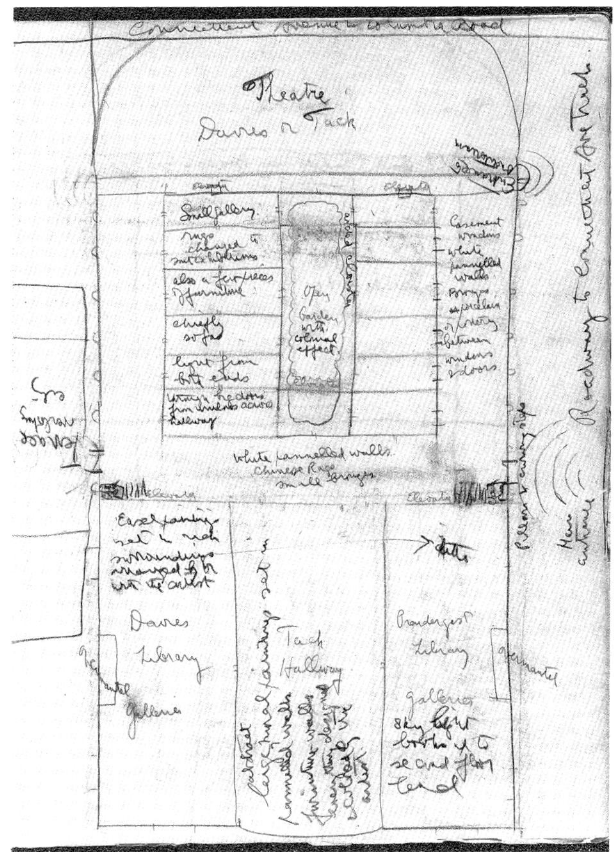

Fig. 30. Duncan Phillips, pencil sketch of his plan for a museum building with a theater and hallway decorated by Tack, from Journal B, ca. 1923, The Phillips Collection Archives

The results appeared in such works as *Storm* (cat. 25) and *Passacaglia* (cat. 23), shown in his February 1923 exhibition at Kraushaar's. Later that year the painter carried his expressive color and rhythm to a new effectiveness in *The Voice of Many Waters* (cat. 27), which may be regarded as a blending of impressions of mountain landscapes with a simile from the Book of Revelation.

Phillips followed this progression of Tack's closely and enthusiastically, proclaiming the artist "a star of the first magnitude."[13] He not only purchased works himself but gave a Tack painting to the Metropolitan Museum of Art and encouraged the Cleveland Museum of Art to buy another. In March 1924 he presented "Recent Decorative Paintings by Augustus Vincent Tack" in an exhibition in the Music Room, opened to the public for the first time. The exhibition consisted of some sixteen works, all belonging to the Phillips Gallery except the painting recently purchased by the

Cleveland Museum. It brought before the public a museum showing of Tack's most advanced works at the moment he attained fully his long-sought expression in an abstracted idiom. The accompanying catalogue by Phillips included his first public pleading for the cause of abstraction:

People who will go to good music for spiritual nourishment . . . will yet demand of painting that it be illustrative or imitative and will turn in bewilderment from paintings which seek only to speak to their souls in the same musical way, the way of pure design, the way of ordered and varied rhythms, with organizations of mass and color and line instead of movements of sound . . . . The greatest thing that art can suggest is the rhythm of life itself.

From this position Phillips took the logical next step when, early in 1926, he visited Alfred Steiglitz's gallery in New York, purchased two paintings by Arthur Dove, and initiated a broad patronage of American modernism.[14]

The 1924 exhibition prompted correspondence between Phillips and Tack about possible alterations to the Music Room to provide a permanent setting for work by Tack, the genesis of the mural project that was to result in a unique set of paintings some six years later. The 1924 exhibition appears to be reflected in Phillips's entry on Tack in his *Collection in the Making* (his first selective catalogue, published in 1926):

At last a great American mural decorator, great in visionary conception and in daring technical invention . . . . A room decorated by Tack is a place where the spirit and the senses are wonderfully reconciled, where we thrill to new sensations, and discover our own unsuspected capacities for make-believe and wonder and worship.[15]

By the mid-1920s Tack had made his essential contributions to Duncan Phillips. He had helped his friend come to terms with and develop a lively and deeply sympathetic interest in contemporary art, and he had helped him each step of the way as he created and took confident control of a unique museum. Duncan Phillips, in turn, had supported and encouraged Tack while the artist was making the most important conceptual and stylistic breakthrough of his career, creating a unique and personal art form. Their warm friendship was to continue for more than twenty years, until Tack's death in 1949, and Phillips remained the principal supporter and encourager of Tack's abstract painting. We owe entirely to Duncan Phillips's patronage the most important group of Tack's paintings, the Music Room series. Its history calls for an essay in itself and is provided in this catalogue by Leslie Furth. To Phillips also we owe the most sustained and widespread efforts to make Tack's work more widely understood and appreciated, through writings, exhibitions, and gifts of paintings. This is a continuing story beyond the scope of this essay, which is centered on the relationship of the two men from 1914 through 1924—the critical years of the birth of the gallery and of the most intensely creative transitions in the lives of both Duncan Phillips and Augustus Vincent Tack.

Leslie Furth

LANDSCAPES OF THE MIND

Augustus Vincent Tack's Decorations for the Phillips Memorial Gallery

"ONE LOOKS NOT PHYSICALLY," Tack had written in 1941, "but mentally, spiritually, emotionally. Perhaps this might be called 'the far side of painting.'"[1] Echoes of transcendentalist thought permeate Tack's observation, suggesting a similar intuitive and spiritual transport before nature and art. This mystical vision reached a culmination in a cycle of paintings that Tack painted between 1928 and 1931, which he esteemed the crowning achievement of his career. The paintings, created for the North Library of the Phillips Memorial Gallery, form an important chapter in the history of the museum as well as in the evolution of abstract painting in this country.[2]

Presented in arched lunettes with gilded borders, the works represent the final flowering of the Beaux-Arts tradition of the American Renaissance and reflect the legacy of American decorators such as John La Farge and James McNeill Whistler. The nineteenth-century decorative tradition also emerges in Tack's allegorical titles, the suggestive figural groupings of several paintings, and the overall program of the room. Further, the adornment of a library with murals had prominent antecedents in the decorated repositories of culture and learning conceived in the American Renaissance, such as the Boston Public Library and the more intimate Pierpont Morgan Library.[3] From the beginning of his career Tack worked as a muralist and decorator, creating murals for a private home as early as 1900 and joining the Architectural League around the same time. In the teens, he executed a monumental series of Biblical scenes with "high, vaulted, shadowy" spaces in mind, as if for "some great cathedral."[4] His murals of the 1920s, for the Manitoba Legislative Building (1918–20) and the Nebraska State Capitol (1924–27) further encouraged his muralist's conception of paintings on a monumental scale, unfolding through space and encompassing lofty themes. Tack brought this approach to his cycle for the Phillips Memorial Gallery. Yet he also desired a new vocabulary of abstraction, as expressed in his recent series of paintings based on the western landscape. A stark departure from the conventional symbolism of the American Renaissance, this syntax was inspired by his own devout spirituality and the scenery of the American West. From it, Tack forged a new abstract vocabulary in this series of paintings for his foremost patron's new museum.

THE EARLY HISTORY

The series includes twelve lunette-shaped paintings and a single monumental work, *Aspiration* (cat. 43), studies for murals that were never realized. The thematic plan seems to have originated in conversations between the artist and his patron.[5] According to Phillips, the room—which he referred to as "The Hall of Cosmic Conceptions"—invited the viewer to contemplate universal emotions and the underlying unity of life and art.[6] Elements of Catholic mysticism, neoplatonism, and aesthetic formalism are synthesized in an attempt to transcend the limits of painting and create a new symbolism. The titles outline a complex, interrelated program: *Rhythm, Order, Balance, Outposts of Time I* and *Outposts of Time II, Lib-*

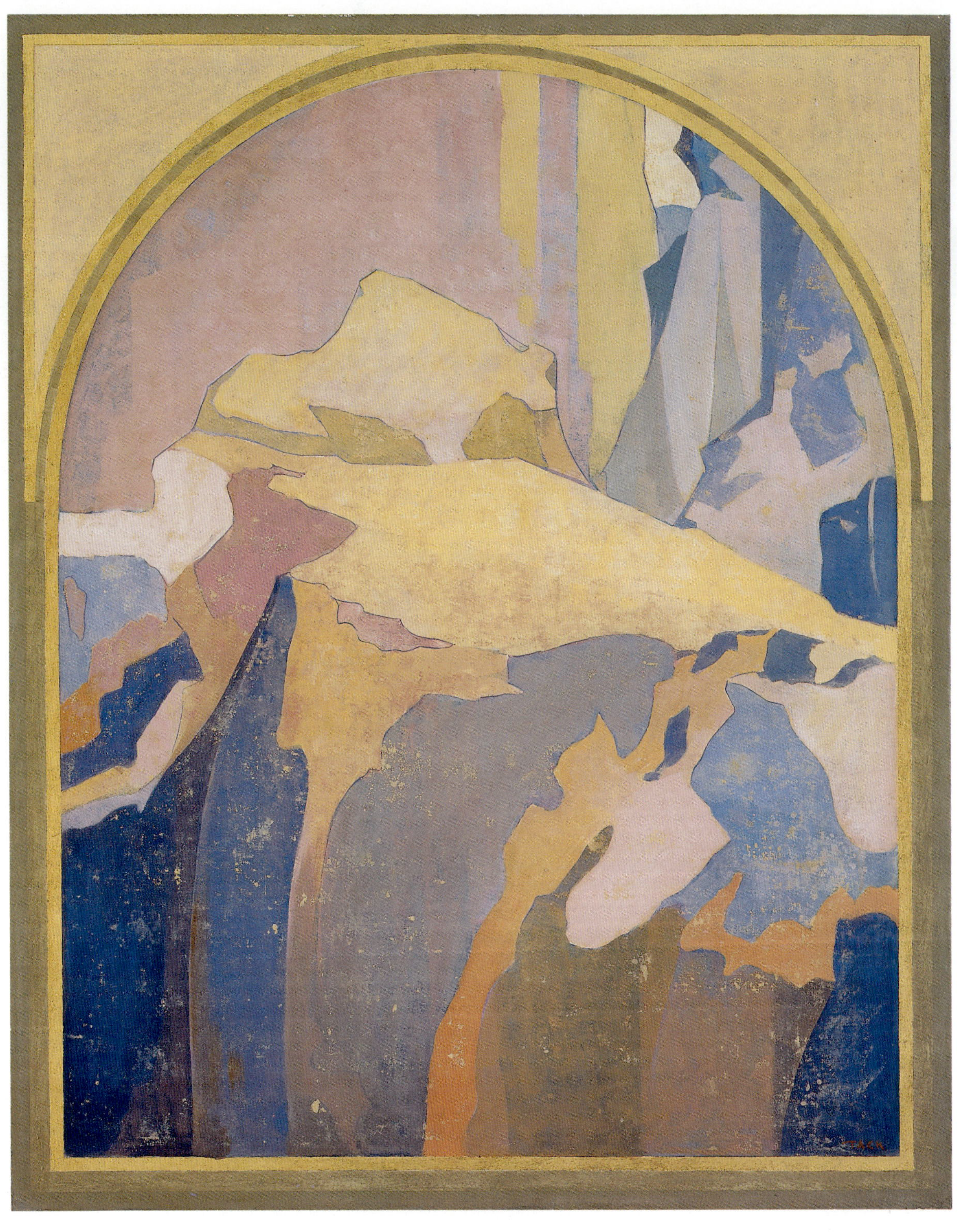

Cat. 37. *Outposts of Time I*, 1929, oil on canvas mounted on wallboard, 43 5/8 x 35 9/16 in.

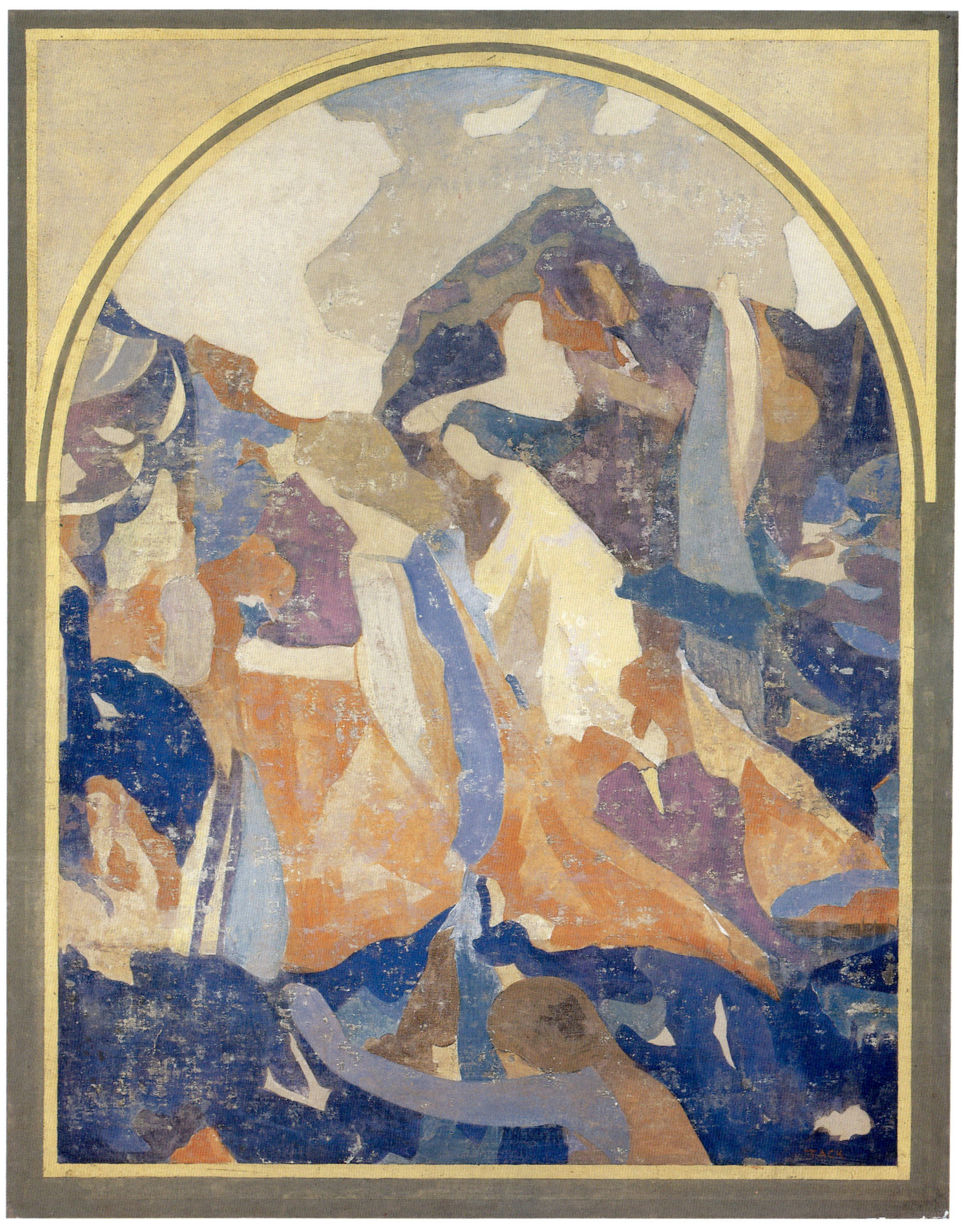

Cat. 32. *Rhythm*, 1929, oil on canvas mounted on wallboard, 43 ⅝ x 35 ½ in.

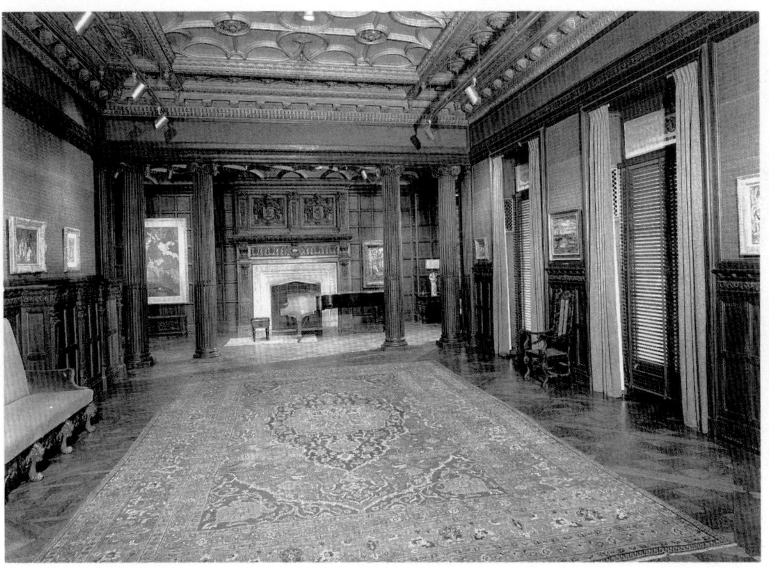

Fig. 31. The Music Room of The Phillips Collection, view toward the north wall and transept, 1950s or 1960s. Tack's *Night, Amargosa Desert* hangs on the wall at left, The Phillips Collection Archives

eration, Ecstasy, Andante, Allegro, Largo, Flight (Fugue), Far Reaches, and *Aspiration.*

Phillips's first recorded plans for a series of "abstract murals" by Tack date to about 1923, when he drew a freehand plan for a museum building that included a theater and hallway to be decorated with paintings by Tack (fig. 30).[7] Both patron and artist were keenly aware of precedents for such decorated environments. Phillips had taken a great interest in the opening of the Freer Gallery in 1923, inviting Tack to view it with him. There they would have seen Whistler's famous Peacock Room. Another inspiration may well have been Arthur B. Davies's cycle of paintings of 1914 for Lillie P. Bliss's music room in her New York home. When Phillips saw them in 1915–16, he was deeply impressed with their ambition and monumentality.[8]

The history of the room for which Tack's paintings were created bears on the series and its meaning. Now called the Music Room because concerts have been held there since 1931, it was built onto the original house as a library in 1907. At the time of Phillips's commission in 1928, the North Library, as it was then known, had not yet been continuously open to the public, save for an exhibition of Tack's painting in 1924 and for several hangings in 1927. The decorative series was part of the collector's plan to prepare the room for public use as an art library or reception room.

The room is a majestic space with irregular proportions, dark wainscoting, and a northeast window transept that made it a challenging setting for the painter to decorate (fig. 31). Probably because of the room's asymmetry—with a long narrow hall ending in pillars and a light-filled perpendicular space at its end—Phillips intended to alter it extensively to display a permanent installation of Tack's paintings. The works were to be scaled up to mural size, larger than the studies by one-quarter to one-third. A barrel-vaulted ceiling would accommodate the lunette-shaped panels, five on each side, to be placed in recessed areas of the wall, and one painting for each of the arched end-walls. Although these structural changes were never made, the works frequently have been hung together in the Music Room as a related series.[9]

The precise chronology of the paintings is uncertain.[10] Having completed his mural panels for the Nebraska State Capitol at the end of 1927, Tack might have created some panels in 1928 before the official commission in December. The conservative, figurative style of *Largo* (cat. 29) bears out its early dating of 1928 in the museum's records. By the time of their first public showing at Tack's New York dealer, Kraushaar Galleries, in November 1929, all but three of the panels were probably completed. *Flight (Fugue)* and *Far Reaches* (cats. 39, 40) followed in the spring of 1930, and *Aspiration* was completed, after a long interval, in 1931.[11]

Their exhibition at the Phillips Memorial Gallery in March 1930 marks the first time that the panels were hung in the space for which they were created. Yet then, as today, the work cannot be installed entirely as the artist intended in the absence of the planned architectural changes. Although Tack carefully dictated the order of the west wall, he did not record the proposed sequence for the opposite wall.[12]

The most carefully orchestrated interrelationship among the paintings is that of the earliest works: *Balance, Order,* and *Rhythm* (cats. 30–32), to be flanked with *Outposts of Time I* and *II* (cats. 37, 38). A diagram by Tack and Phillips's own description from late 1930 highlight this progression: "The static and architectonic grandeur and simplicity of the Outposts of Time function logically as the structure within which the swift rhythms of the three central panels live and move and have their being." Unified by complementary directional axes, the triad harmonizes in a sequence of rhythms across space.[13]

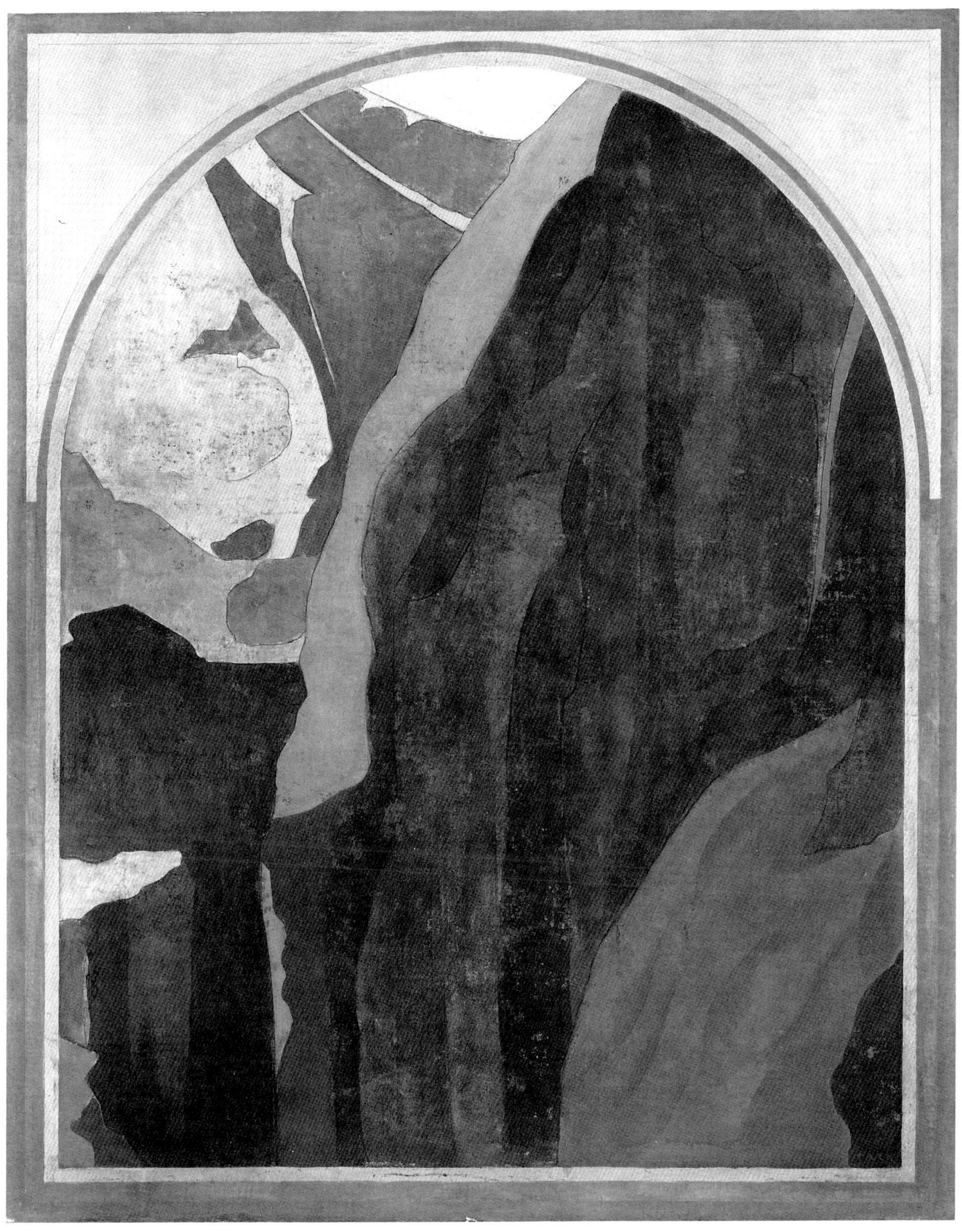

Cat. 29. *Largo*, 1928–29, oil on canvas mounted on wallboard, 43 ⅞ x 35 9/16 in.

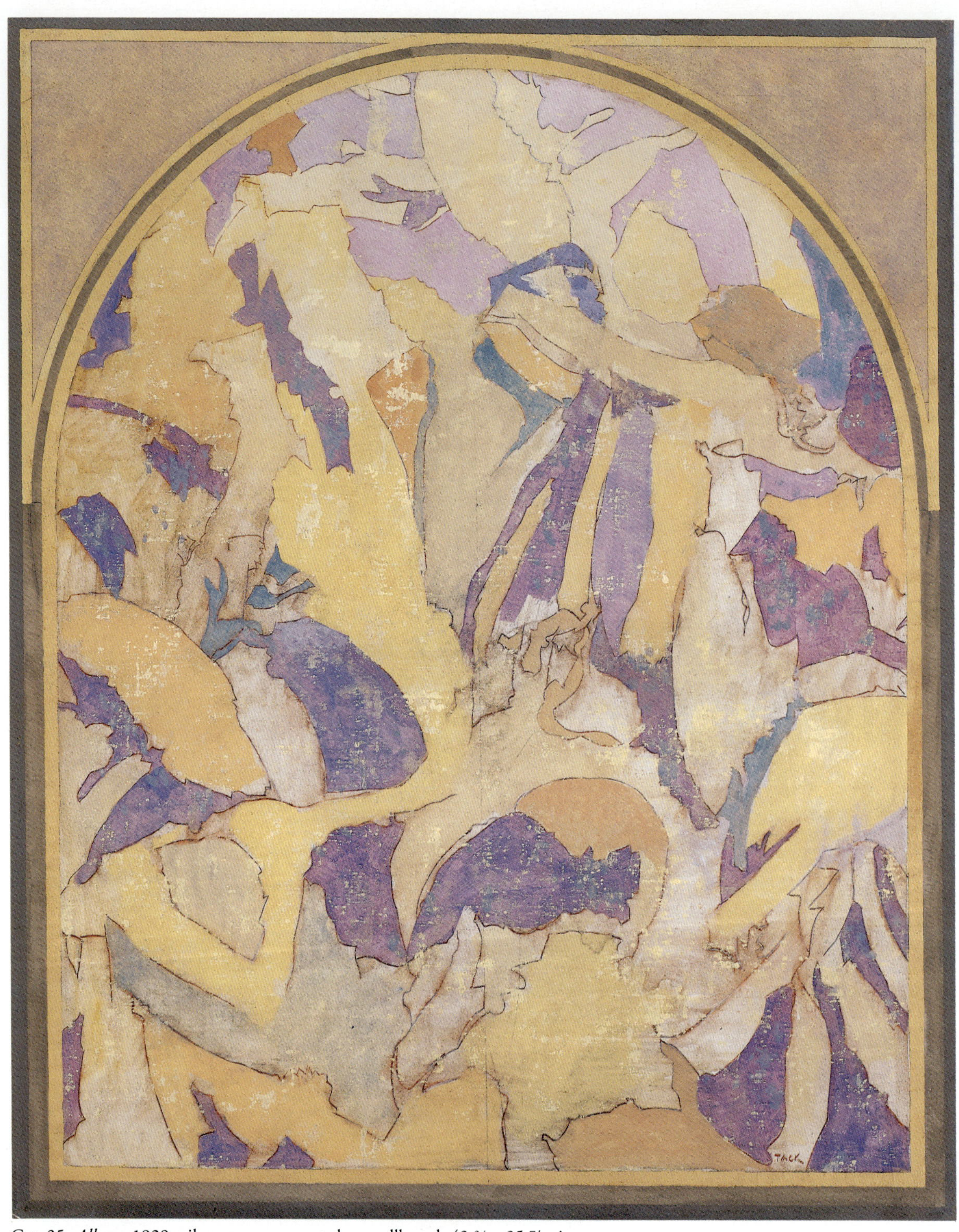

Cat. 35. *Allegro*, 1929, oil on canvas mounted on wallboard, 43 ¾ x 35 7/16 in.

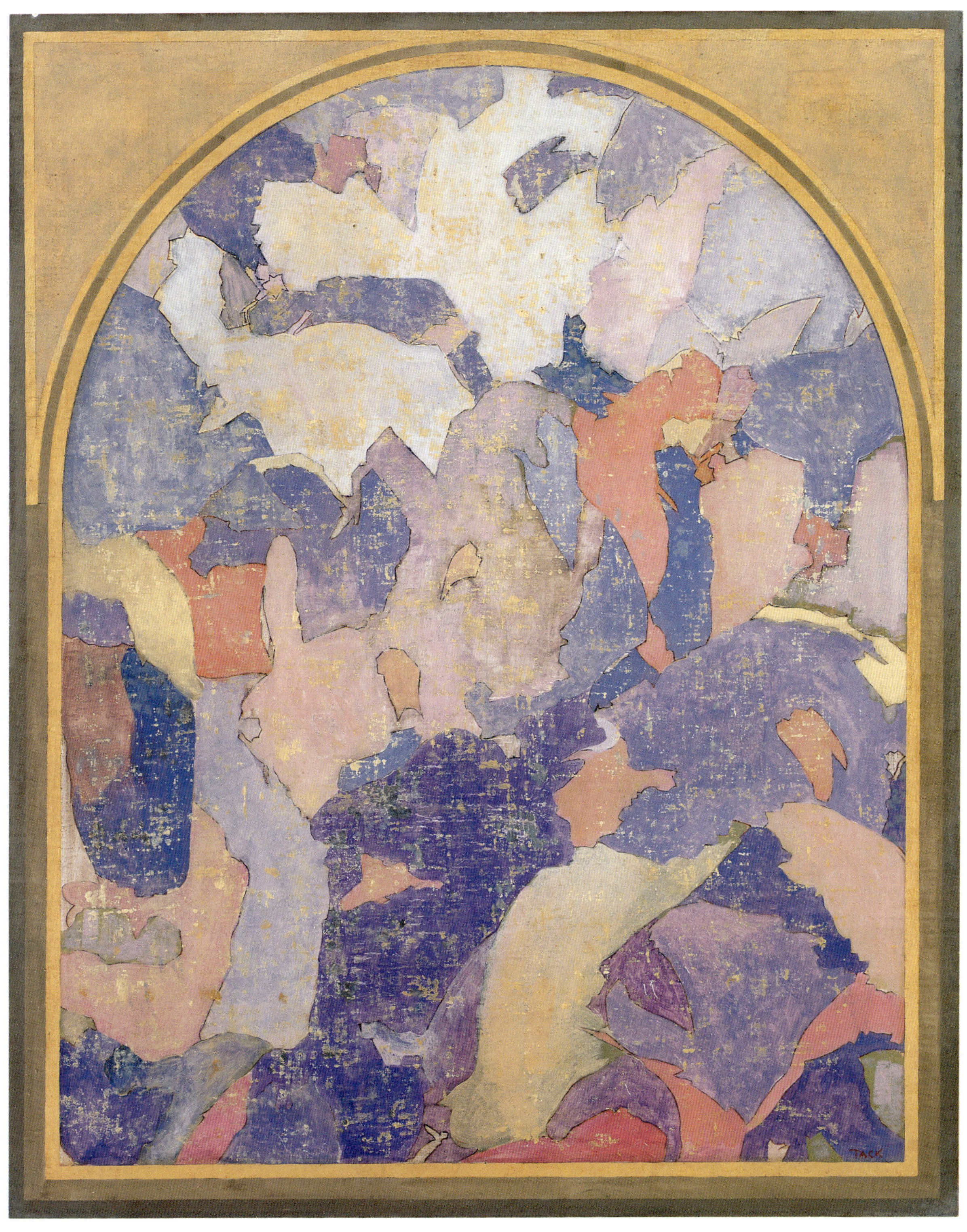

Cat. 36. *Andante*, 1929, oil on canvas mounted on wallboard, 43 ⅞ x 35 13/16 in.

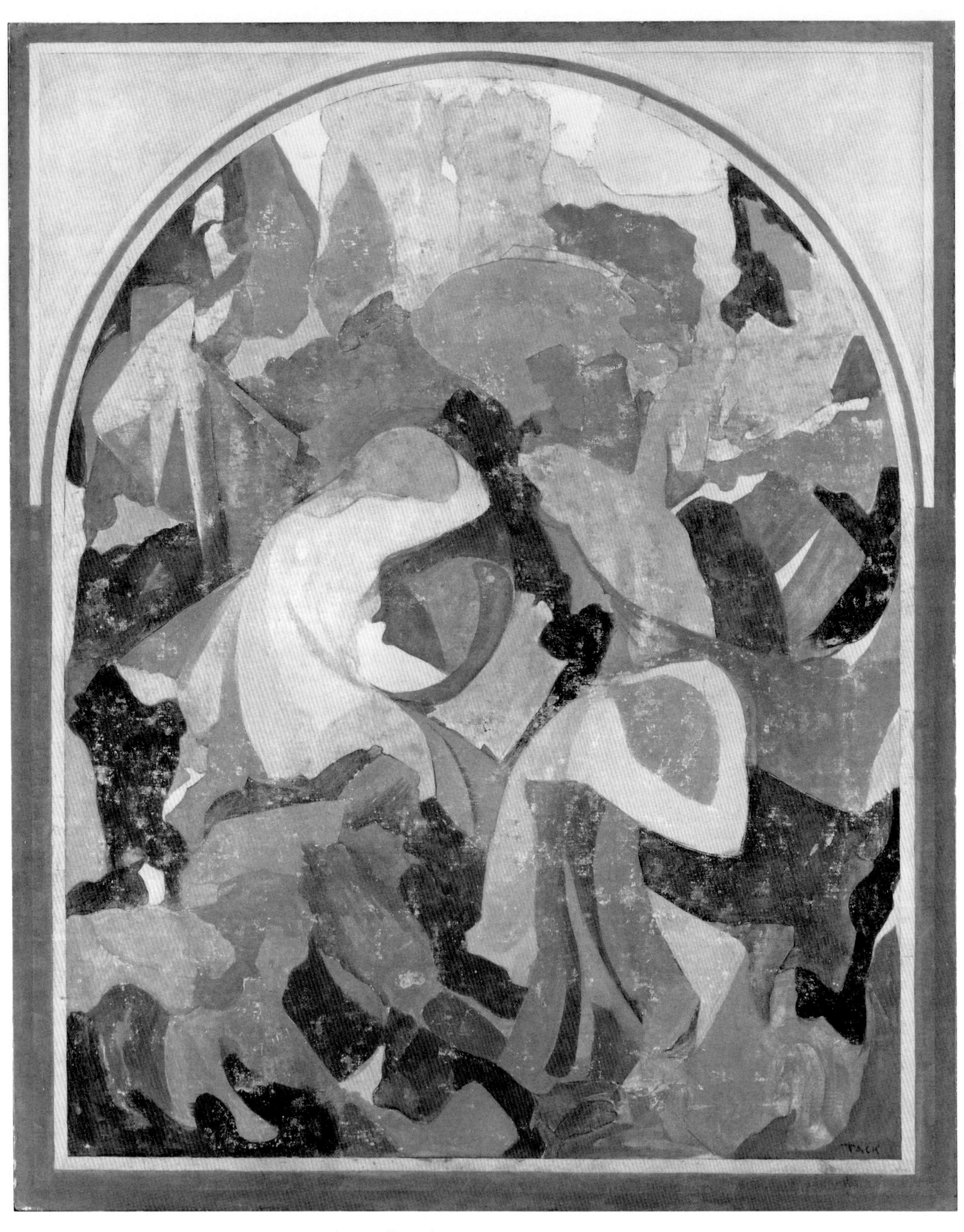

Cat. 30. *Balance*, 1929, oil on canvas mounted on wallboard, 43 5/8 x 35 9/16 in.

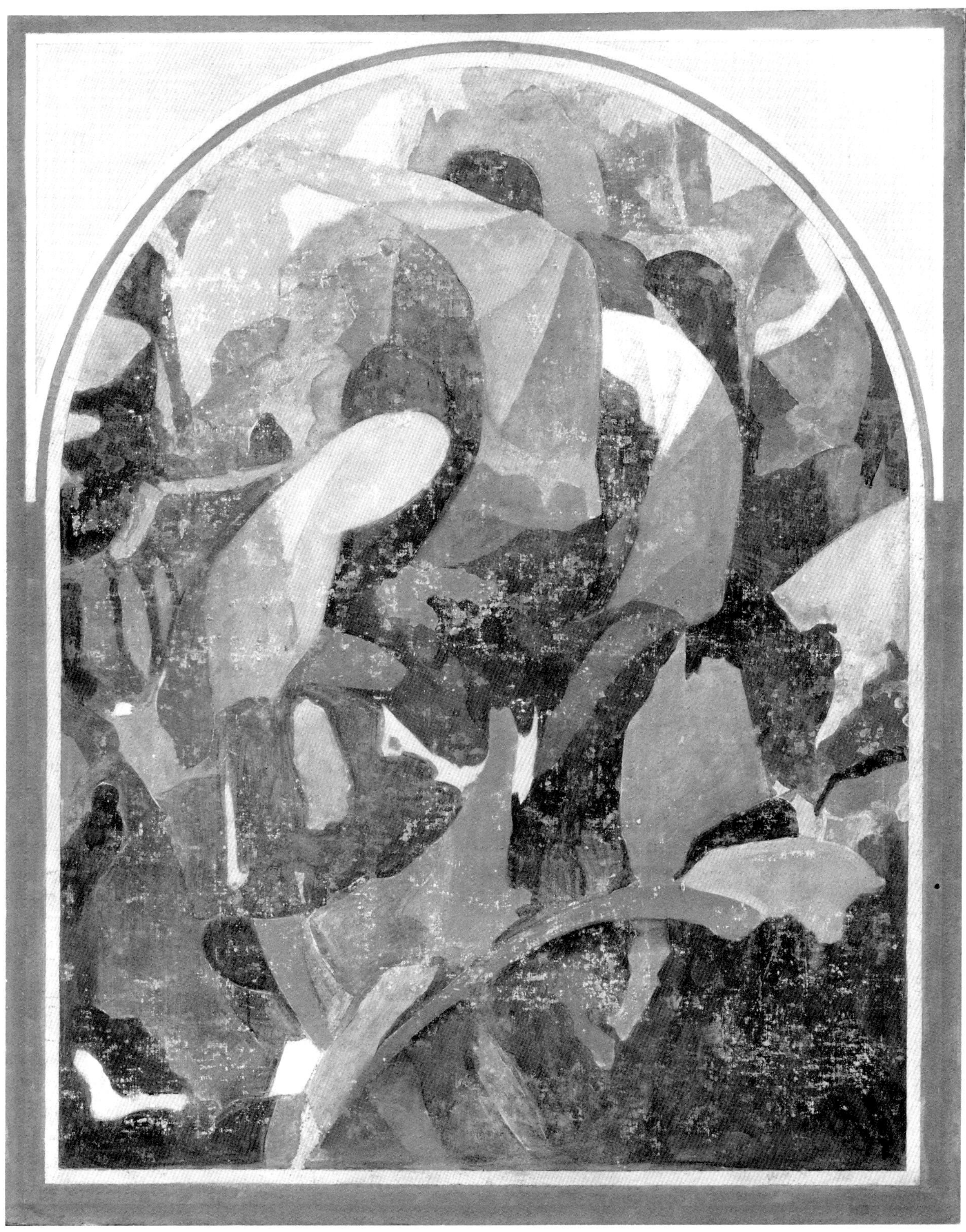

Cat. 31. *Order*, 1929, oil on canvas mounted on wallboard, 43 ⅞ x 35 ½ in.

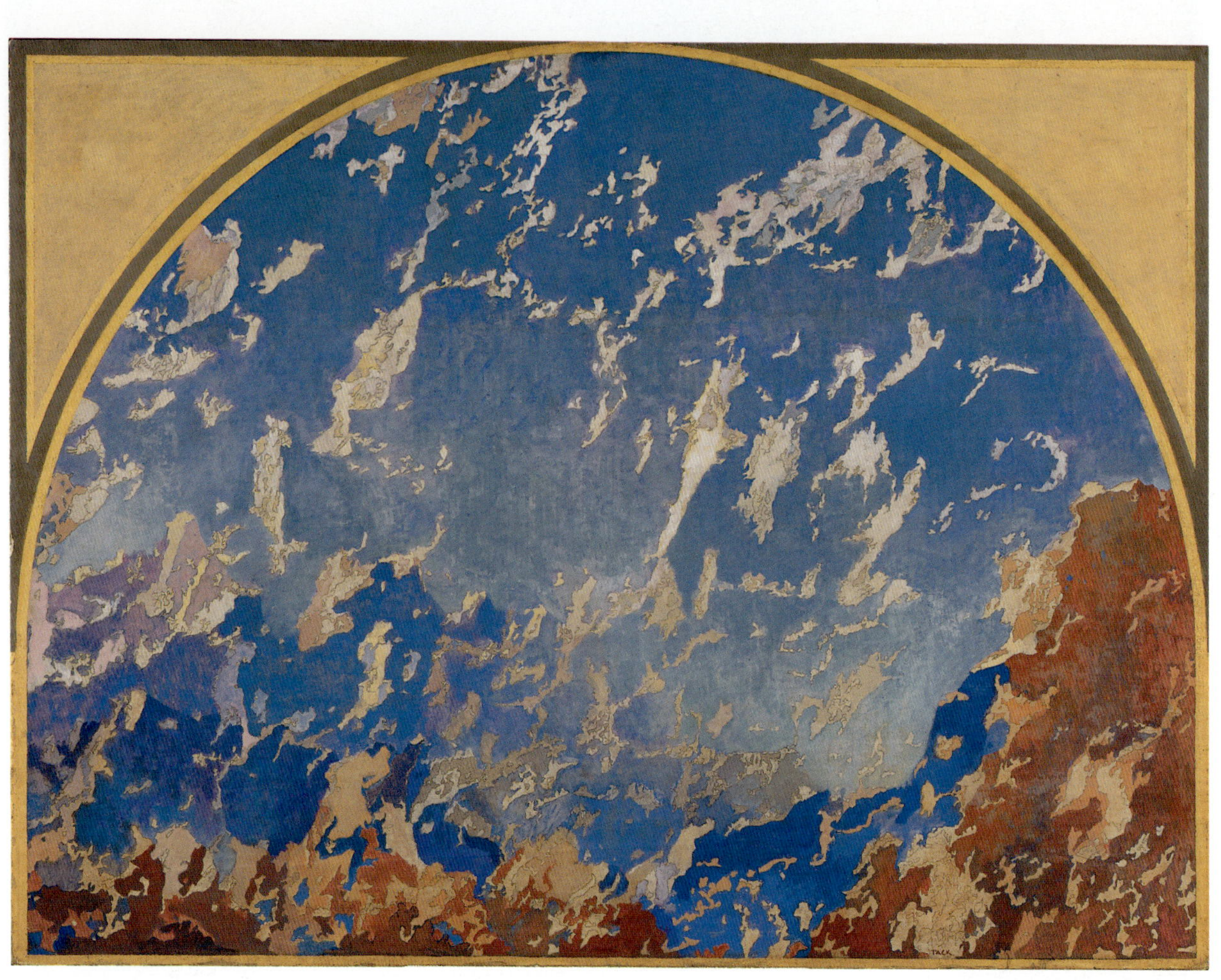

Cat. 33. *Liberation*, 1929, oil on canvas mounted on wallboard , 47 ⅞ x 64 ¼ in.

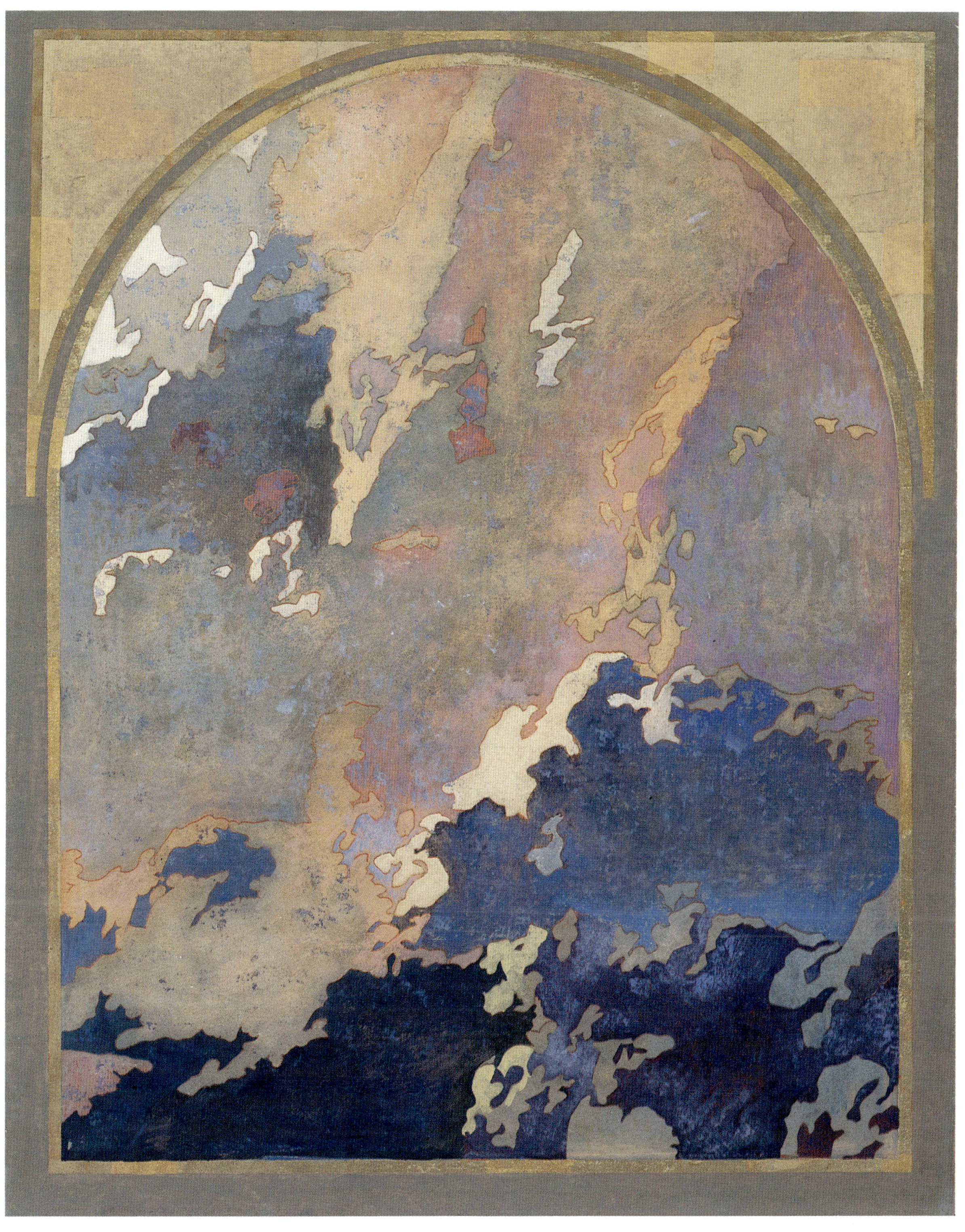

Cat. 40. *Far Reaches*, 1930, oil on canvas mounted on wallboard, 44 x 35 ¾ in.

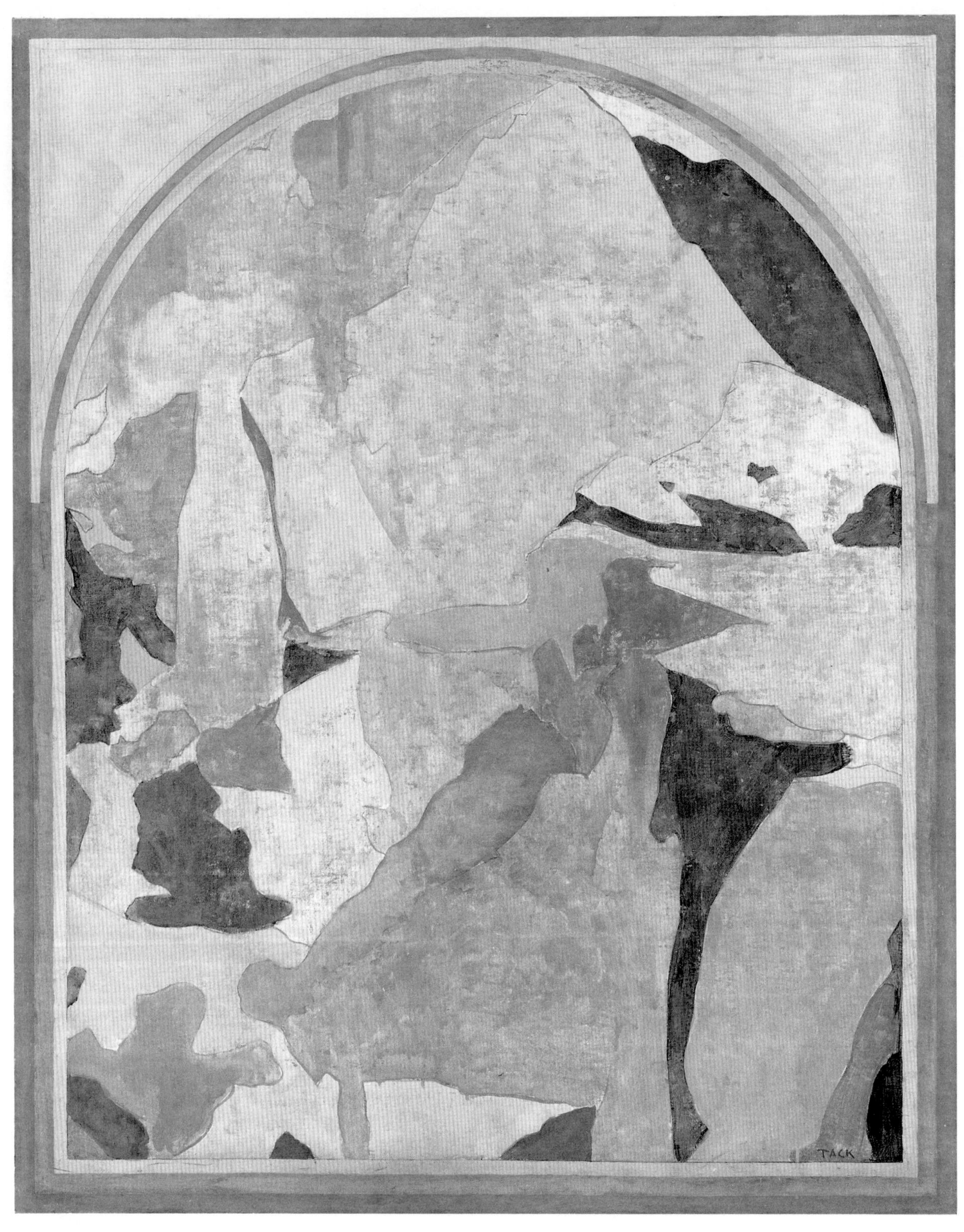

Cat. 38. *Outposts of Time II*, 1929, oil on canvas mounted on wallboard, 43 9/16 x 35 ½ in.

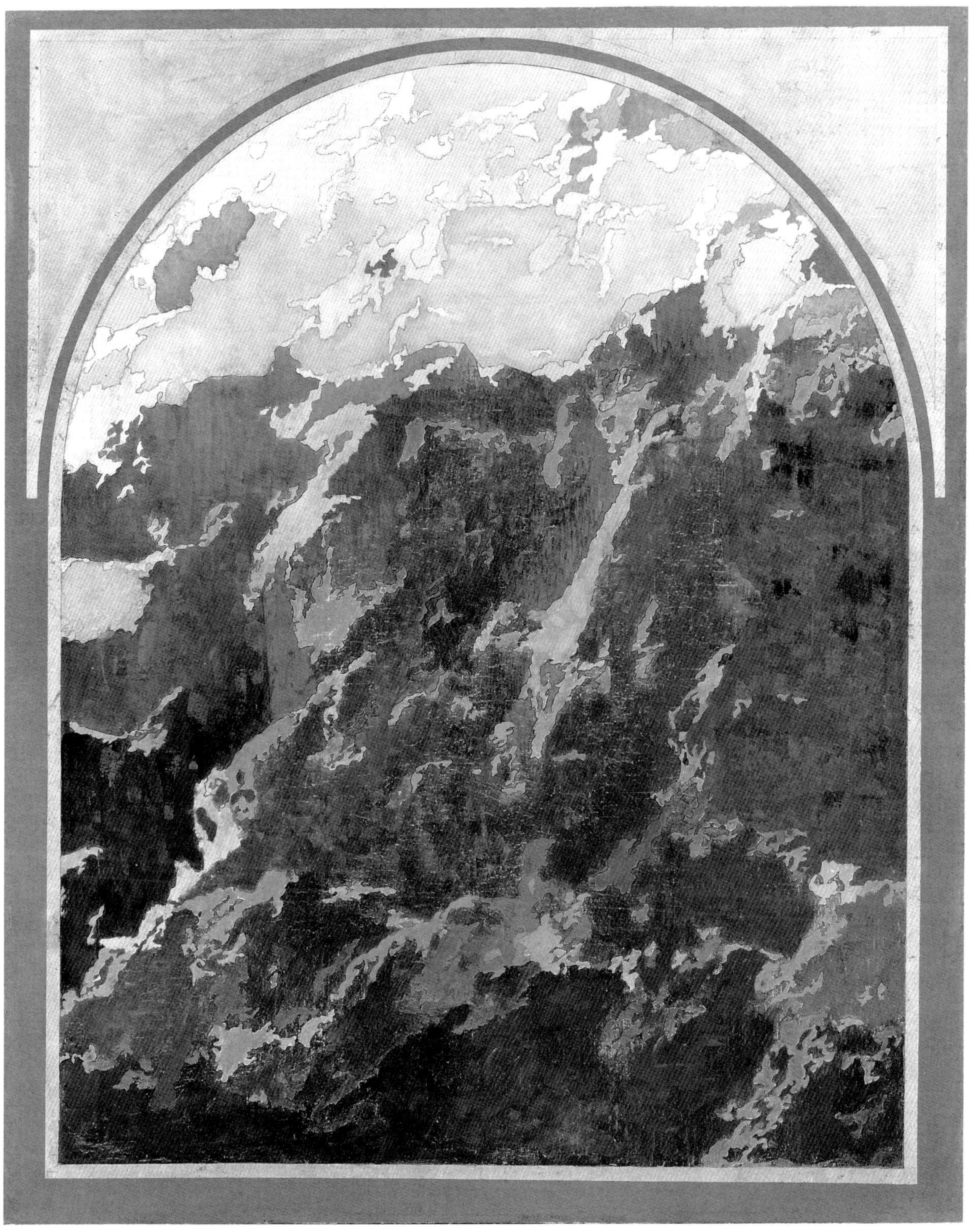

Cat. 39. *Flight* (*Fugue*), 1930, oil on canvas mounted on wallboard, 43 ⅞ x 35 ¾ in.

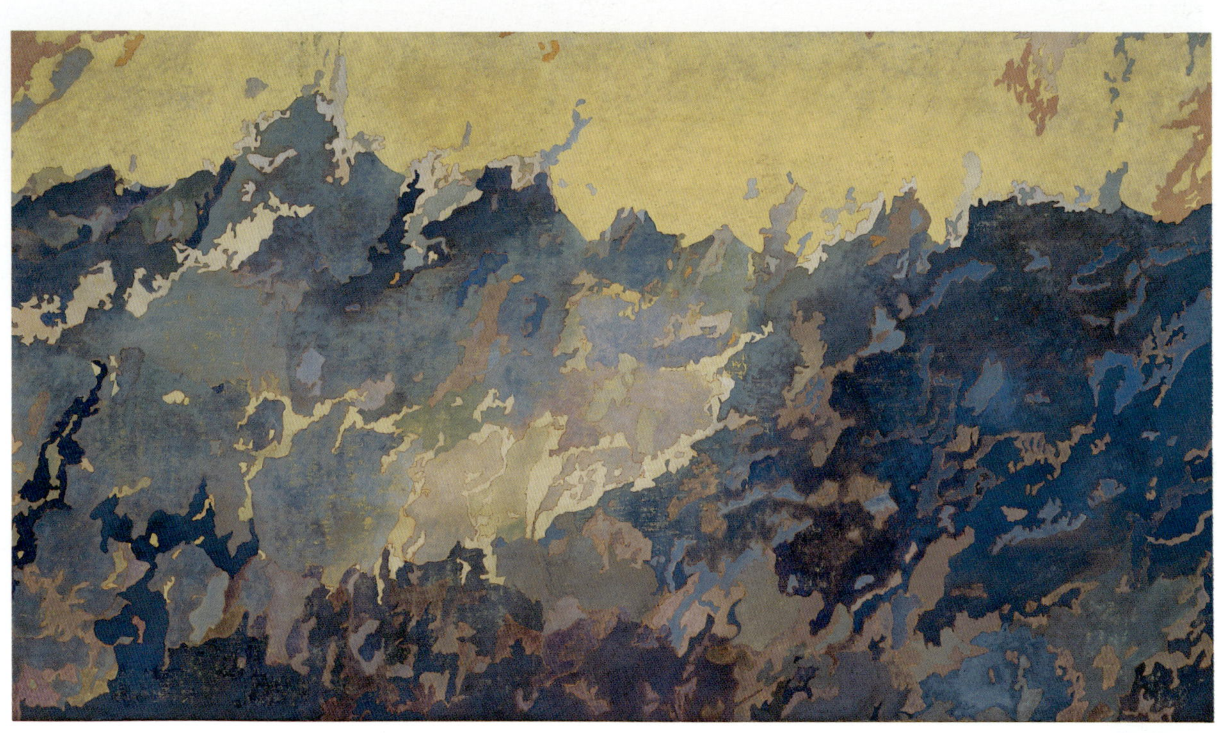

Cat. 43. *Aspiration*, 1931, oil on canvas, 76 ½ x 135 ½ in.

Tack probably conceived the sequence for the east wall as *Andante* (cat. 36), *Allegro* (cat. 35), *Largo* (or the original, *Orchid* [*Violet and Green ?*]; fig. 32)., *Flight* (*Fugue*), and *Far Reaches*; the latter two paintings were probably meant to be two "outposts of time." The third abstract panel—probably *Orchid* (*Violet and Green ?*)—would hang between them with *Andante* and *Allegro*, possibly leaving *Largo* as another "outpost" but without a formal function in the cycle. *Aspiration* was destined for a screen in the space across the windows at the room's north end.[14]

The formal treatment of these panels, radiant in color and luxuriantly finished, testifies to Tack's excitement in the orchestration of compositions in color and abstracted designs. The range of techniques he had learned over the course of his career informs the works. He adapted traditional mural techniques, creating forms from planned designs that he transferred to his canvases. Complementing this premeditated approach are his autonomous color choices, his spontaneous changes, and the loose and fluid brushwork with which he continually revised and embellished the compositions. His assurance with the materials and techniques of mural painting left him free to experiment with color and design.[15]

The lunette format flourished in Renaissance and nineteenth-century mural design. Tack prepared each arched canvas and then adhered it to board, an approach adapted from the traditional mural practice known as *marouflage*.[16] He visualized the shadowy heights of a barrel vault as the setting, as the matte surfaces, gold borders, and rich surface treatment with scattered highlights demonstrate. The decorated boards on which the panels are mounted imply and almost simulate the vaulted spaces. Decorative spandrels and borders of metal leaf confine each design.[17]

The finish of the canvases underscores their decorative function. Tack highlighted the texture with embellishments of scattered paint laid in with rollers, cloth, and sponges. The paint cleaved to the tops of the fabric threads, breaking up the surface with neutral highlights. His surface effects even extended to mixing sand or other granular particles with the paint, as, for example, in *Balance* and *Outposts of Time I*. These refined surfaces have an antique appearance reminiscent of medieval tapestries or Asian scroll paintings, an aesthetic countered by the contemporaneity of the abstract designs themselves. The duality of this expression conveys a timeless, universal quality central to Tack's spiritual themes.

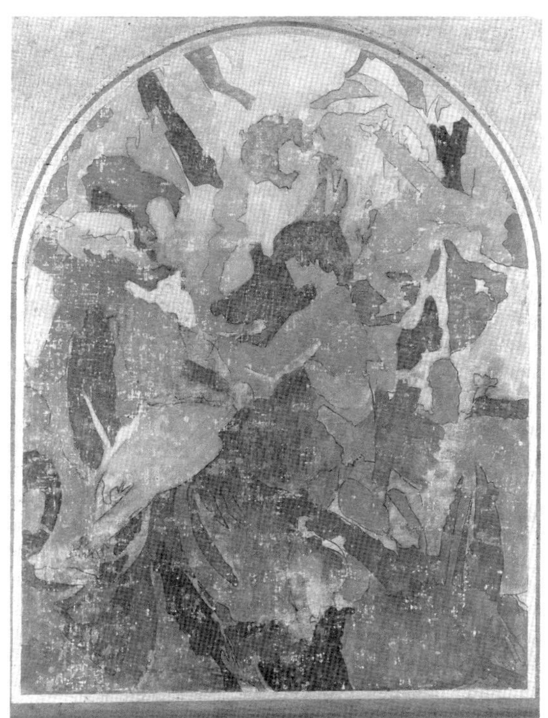

Fig. 32. Augustus Vincent Tack, *Orchid (Violet and Green ?)*, Sotheby's, New York

Although the designs were derived from secondary imagery, Tack worked spontaneously with his process, editing shapes or sometimes, as in *Ecstasy* (cat. 34), adding them freehand to break up forms. In some paintings, such as *Andante*, Tack shrouded the canvas in numerous thin glazes and scumbles and then scraped some of these areas back to reveal the multicolored layers. In *Allegro*, he allowed bare ground to show through the composition as breathing space for the assertive floral imagery. Modulated colors within the forms also render the space ambiguous. These modulations became more frequent as the work on the panels progressed, evolving from the tight, thinly washed surfaces of *Largo* and *Order* to the sparkling brushwork of *Flight* (*Fugue*). Similarly, the color combinations progress from the rich primary contrasts of *Order* and *Balance* through the subtle veiled infusions in *Andante* to the delicate gradations of related hues in *Liberation* (cat. 33), *Aspiration*, and *Flight*. In virtually all the paintings, the forms bear fluid red or blue outlines, which isolate shapes, reinforce the surface plane, and unify the compositions.

THE PHILOSOPHY OF THE MURAL PROGRAM

In their refined treatment, general sense of spirituality, and clear association with nature as an infinite source of beauty and pure visual delight, the works wear lightly a philosophical scheme that is nonetheless the most profound and personal of Tack's career. The cycle represents Tack's first opportunity to create a program of epic themes in a new symbolism of his own devising.[18]

Tack's classical and mystical education and world view deeply inform the philosophical program of these works. The paintings also reflect more modern investigations of artistic endeavor and creative process. In these works Tack approached ever more closely an abstracted, universalized vision of life with, in Phillips's words, "the mystic's sense of an all pervading God . . . seeking to create Cosmos out of Chaos."[19] Tack's transformation of nature and the human figure into a metaphysical domain for momentous spiritual events owes much to his devout Catholicism, to his classical Jesuit education, and to nineteenth-century romanticism and symbolism, and shared strong kinship with transcendentalism, propounded by Ralph Waldo Emerson and embraced by nineteenth-century American writers and artists.

The most important source for the panels is mysticism, which incorporates transcendental beliefs of neoplatonic philosophy. Tack drew on a dictum of the sixteenth-century Catholic mystic St. Ignatius of Loyola—art as an aid to meditation—to explain his own painting. Phillips referred to the paintings as "meditations," and the titles seem generally to correspond to St. Ignatius's belief in the phases of spiritual development leading to ecstasy and the union with God.[20]

The underlying precepts of a mystical notion of transcendence—its call for surpassing earthly limits through flight to a higher realm and its evocation of an infinite, nonmaterial, endlessly varied cosmos—reverberate in Tack's boundless spaces, which suggest divine realms. The notions of unity in diversity and of an underlying universal order also find expression in the commonality of shapes, spaces, and light. The luminous far distances in the works imply the perfect world beyond the earthly sphere.

Several documents support these interpretations of the room's philosophical themes. The most significant source is Tack's handwritten "Notes on Decorative Panels" of January 1930. Phillips's pamphlet, "Appreciations of the Decorative Panels of Augustus Vincent Tack," largely derived from Tack's notes, provides additional insight.[21]

The artist's 1930 notes outline the overriding concern in the central six panels with the ordering of the universe. *Balance, Order,* and *Rhythm* are the "three great abstractions which concern life and art."[22] The creative process, in which human beings order and harmonize inchoate matter, is a reflection of divinity. The dynamism of repeating curves—complementary rhythms linking the panels—seems to lie at the core of their meaning, the interrelationship of this universal code.

The three matching panels that were to go on the opposite wall describe the passages of life in allegorical terms: "Joyousness [*Allegro*], Contentment [*Andante*] and Sorrow [*Largo*] are the three emotional moods of human experience."[23] Also referred to as evoking the seasons, the paintings codify universal life experience in musical terms. They and the *Rhythm* triptych, which contains figures in allegorical postures, seem to echo the stages of a spiritual awakening as recorded by St. Ignatius, from despair and confusion to worship and prayer. This reading is supported by the visible horizon and greater clarity in *Rhythm* and the corresponding panel, *Orchid* (*Violet and Green ?*), both of which depict praying figures.

These six paintings evoking cosmic order are enclosed by the four "borderlands of Eternity": *Outposts of Time I* and *II*, *Flight* (*Fugue*), and *Far Reaches.* These four paintings, intended to be placed in the four corners, symbolize the delimitations of earthly time and space.[24] The pair entitled *Outposts of Time* are static, depicting remote mountaintops and suggesting vast, high realms beyond. *Largo*, bearing a similar structure, may once have been intended to function as an outpost. The other pair, *Flight* (*Fugue*) and *Far Reaches*, are freer in conception, more ethereal in their pictorialization of these limits; *Flight* even suggests, through its title and rising forms, a passage into eternity. These metaphysical boundaries are transcended in the panels meant for the end walls, *Ecstasy* and *Liberation*, just as in mystical thought, earthly limits are surpassed through intellectual and spiritual enrichment.

As its title *Aspiration* suggests, the last work, which was to be placed on the far east wall across the windows, conveys the human yearning for spiritual fulfillment, a concept borne out in its ascendant forms and progressively brightening hues. Shapes spiral upward, reminiscent of clouds, flames, or waves irresistibly rising in majestic rhythms. The painting's secondary title, *Cosmic Energy*, suggests an underlying generative force in which the rising forms signal the impulse toward the divine.

A further reverberation of Catholic mysticism occurs in the pair of end wall paintings, *Ecstasy* and *Liberation*, Tack's culminating statements on the attainment of spiritual fulfillment. Liberation, Tack suggested, was possible through "Spirituality and Religion." Ecstasy, he added, "expresses . . . Exaltation—the Victory of Life—The richness and exuberance of Nature." Liberation is attained through the renunciation of materialism and the search for moral and mental betterment in order to rise toward God. Ecstasy is attained in the final union with God. The paintings formally bear out their themes: *Liberation* has a sense of grandeur, uplift, and vast open space, and *Ecstasy*, a radiant patchwork of suspended colors. Phillips's special favorite, *Largo*, he found brooding and Dante-esque in mood, a consolidation of the cycle's "Far Eastern nature worship and philosophical revery upon time, space and infinity."[25]

RECAPITULATION AND CATHARSIS: THE CROWD REVISITED

Despite the striking variety of the forms of the paintings, careful analysis indicates that they derive from two sources: Tack's own earlier painting, *The Crowd* (cat. 21), and one or more enlarged photographs of a rocky desert landscape. One particular photographic source was used in several of the paintings. The hypothesis that *The Crowd* is also based on landscape forms from photographs or drawings creates yet another unifying thread in these disparate images—the exploitation of nature's random shapes in the creation of compositions conveying spiritual meanings. Tack's forms and techniques are inextricably related to these meanings.[26]

Phillips revealed the seminal importance of *The Crowd* to Tack's later oeuvre in 1943:

Starting with a low narrow panel [The Crowd], *symbolizing in its furious, frenzied lines and shapes the terrific clash of conflicting human passions, he made this the matrix for a series of noble answers to this agonizing problem of earth's turmoil and violence. In all the soaring waterfalls, mountains and skyscapes that followed, serenity and a steadfast faith in God were proclaimed in exultation.* [27]

The Crowd is known to be the basis of at least five of the Music Room panels and may be a partial source for the entire series.[28] The works that clearly derive from the painting are three with recognizable human forms—*Balance*, *Order*, and *Rhythm*—as well as two with concealed imagery—*Allegro* and *Andante*. A photograph clearly shows that the panel *Orchid* (*Violet and Green ?*) also originates in *The Crowd*.[29] *Allegro* recapitulates a central area of the painting; *Andante* quotes the far left area; and *Orchid* is taken from the central right figure. The images from Tack's earlier work have been scaled up with painstaking exactness, each pictorial element faithfully quoted. The transferral of the much smaller imagery from *The Crowd* was probably accomplished with some type of projection.[30]

The Crowd, an undulating pattern of human forms in chaos, draws on the Promethean theme of Tack's earlier work, in which man's materialism and neglect of spiritual growth condemns him to the earthly sphere. The themes of confinement and rootedness in the early work now appear as the starting point for Tack's evolving exploration of earthly existence, expressed in these forms, toward an expression of an immaterial, transcendent divine vision. The reiteration of segments from this painting in the decorative series conveys the same sense of confinement: in *Balance*, *Order*, and *Rhythm*, the horizon line and swirling composition engulf the figures, relenting only in the praying figure in *Rhythm*. The forms progress to a more ephemeral state in the paintings of moods and culminate in the weightless shapes of the end panels and the two last "outposts," *Flight* (*Fugue*) and *Far Reaches*, in which Tack ceased to rely on *The Crowd*. This sequence from grounded to gravity-defying forms, suspended in space and time, also symbolizes the progression from bondage toward freedom and ascent that courses through these paintings. The evolution from the first panel, *Largo*, to the final works, *Flight*, *Far Reaches*, and *Aspiration*, reinforces the suggestion of transcendence and catharsis for the artist through the creative act.

The imagery from *The Crowd* is most rigorously faithful in the first three panels, *Balance*, *Order*, and *Rhythm*—the only three in which human forms are prominent. Their female figures strongly resemble the fragmented shapes of Davies's panels for the Bliss music room, though Tack's figures are draped demurely in contrast to Davies's sensuous nudes. These panels also highlight the synchromist idiom from which their template, *The Crowd*, seems to draw inspiration.

A freer, more imaginative extrapolation from *The Crowd* exists in the paintings of moods or seasons, *Allegro, Andante,* and *Orchid* (*Violet and Green*). In *Allegro,* Tack deliberately distorted the image, creating a vibrating, jagged, expressive line and enhancing the degree of abstraction, as if seeking to free himself altogether from the recognizable forms of *The Crowd.* Thinly washed in bright complementary hues of lavender and yellow, the painting conveys a sense of joy and lightness in its chromatic scheme and floral shapes. *Andante,* a somewhat less resolved composition, bears the same ragged shapes and free adaptation of its source. *Orchid* appears to manifest the same irregular line and complex composition.

In *Allegro* and *Andante,* Tack sought more abstraction. He filled in the upper halves of the compositions with tracings of shapes from the lower halves, reversed to disguise the source. He then altered, highlighted, and distorted the shapes with color. The horizon line is thus eradicated, and the foreground shapes repeating at the top of the canvas create a sense of tension across the surface plane. The same treatment appears to have been used in *Orchid.*

TACK'S ABSTRACTIONS AND PHOTOGRAPHY

With their ragged cloud forms, dizzying panoramas of cliffs, and wave patterns suggestive of vast spaces and elemental forces, the decorative paintings are the true descendants of Tack's romantic early landscapes such as *Cloud Wrack* (cat. 5), *Windswept (Snow Picture, Leyden)* (cat. 8), and *Mountain Outposts* (by 1921, The Phillips Collection). The far western landscape provided Tack with the dramatic setting befitting the Biblical truths around which his art revolved. This landscape had transported him on first sight, and its cliffs, clouds, and peaks form the matrix of his imagery in many of the panels.

The representations that served as designs for these images were not painted or sketched before nature but recorded with the camera in the western desert and mountains, possibly on Tack's December 1928 journey to southern California with his family. Tack's photographic sources are readily discerned in *Liberation, Ecstasy, Flight* (*Fugue*), and *Far Reaches,* which are filled with traces of abstracted mountain forms, snow-capped peaks, and cloud patterns. According to his assistant, the Reverend William Wilfrid Bayne, "on a visit to Death Valley, in the far west, [Tack] had been fascinated by the interesting patterns of light and shadow made by the sunlight falling on the irregularities of the valley's alkaline soil. He had taken a number of snapshots of these "abstracts" fashioned by nature's artistry."[31]

The use of photography seems to embody Tack's concern with the paradox of earthly life defined and enriched by the spiritual and nonmaterial. The essential elements of his paintings—directional lines, the massing of shadows, and shapes randomly connected through the unifying glare of the sun—are the substrata for all these images. The positive forms—rocks, mountains, desert, valleys—are merely the occasion for the drama of animated, strange, eerie light and are left out of Tack's appropriations. Thus he was able to reuse these fragments endlessly as both negative and positive form. His inversion of the traditional focus on solid form to a focus on light, the incorporeal, echoes a mystical premise of the spiritual life as worthier and more "real" than that of matter and reinforces the artist's role as a visionary who created true "landscapes of the mind" from objective reality.

Bayne described in detail the manner in which landscape photographs were made to form the basis of the paintings:

He had taken a number of snapshots of these "abstracts [the patterns of light and shadow]" fashioned by nature's artistry, and had a professional photographer "blow them up" to ten or fifteen times their original size. These enlargements were now turned over to me, and I spent many monotonous hours making perforated replicas of them [for pouncing]. . . . These enlarged photographs were naturally somewhat vague in outline and to determine the contours I had to use my own initiative. When the perforated duplicates of the photographs had been laid upon the panels, and the clotted contours rubbed through, my next task was to strengthen them with a fine brush. At this point Mr. Tack took over, and . . . filled in the spaces indicated . . . with various colours.[32]

Liberation, a product of this technique, betrays pounce marks left clearly visible as part of the design.[33] As Bayne explained, while he performed the mechanical process, Tack made the color choices, sometimes disregarding the prescribed contours in favor of spontaneous enlargement of shapes, sudden transitions of color, and an occasional use of metallic paint within the image.

The compositions of *Liberation* and *Ecstasy* bear evidence of further manipulation of their initial source: both paintings subtly divide into several tiers with slightly different spatial and perspectival axes, either a result of combining different photographic sources or of projecting the same source at varying scales.[34] It is even possible that the very different paint application of *Ecstasy* and *Liberation* masks a source in the same photograph. Tack apparently wanted to create an illusion of land and sky and a clear progression from foreground to defined middle and backgrounds, distinctions evidently absent from the original photograph. Careful study of *Ecstasy* reveals that Tack attempted to suppress this subtle tiered effect by painting a play of forms across the divisions in the upper quarter of the canvas. Phillips was at first unenthusiastic about the complicated "agitato" of these shapes, feeling that it detracted from the painting, and encouraged Tack to edit them out.[35]

Liberation was a seminal work, its imagery becoming the template for virtually every important abstraction that Tack created from 1928 until the end of his life. The pounce marks, uniform in appearance due to the use of a perforated wheel to transfer the drawing, are visible in many areas and are an assertive part of the design. The painting thus has a slightly dry, formulaic quality befitting its function as a prototype. In keeping with this progression, Tack's manipulations of his materials seem to have become gradually more sophisticated and intuitive with the reprisal and enlargement of *Liberation* in the two last "outposts of time" paintings, *Flight* (*Fugue*) and *Far Reaches*. Just as he reused the figure groupings from *The Crowd*, he developed generation after generation of paintings, even beyond the imagery of the Phillips series, from the design for *Liberation*; in fact, it is doubtful that he created any new abstract imagery after 1928.

Tack's and Phillips's correspondence and published writings indicate that they shared an ambivalence about "explaining" these works of art. Tack chose not to give them titles when they were first exhibited in New York in 1929: indeed, in his "Note on Subjective Painting" of early 1930, he pleaded the case for pure painting whose meaning would be conveyed in formal terms alone. Phillips only "with extreme reluctance" published an interpretation of the series, insisting that "an artist can never communicate in words a symbolism which he has conceived . . . in color."[36] These attitudes arose in the dominant formalism of the late 1920s and early 1930s when critics and collectors overlooked content in favor of aesthetic qualities, prompting both Tack and Phillips to discount specific literary or allegorical associations for the series.

Overtones of the sublime in these arrangements of Rocky Mountain scenery carry forward Tack's neoclassical and transcendental view of nature as divinely created. As late as 1930, he would quote almost verbatim Inness's observations on the aims of art. In his romantic belief that "art is the awakening of the emotions" are echoes of Inness's conviction that "[art's] aim is not to instruct, not to edify, but to awaken an emotion. . . . Its real greatness consists in the quality and force of this emotion."[37]

THE DECORATIVE SERIES WITHIN THE AMERICAN TRADITION

Tack's attainment of a successful abstract style in the Phillips decorative paintings occurred more than ten years after painters among the American avant-garde such as Arthur Dove, John Marin, Georgia O'Keeffe, and Alfred Stieglitz began their pursuit of abstract painting or photography. Although he might have developed his abstract idiom in the early 1920s, the monumental civic mural projects of the late teens and mid-1920s occupied his time and energy in a more traditional vein.[38]

Many of the concepts in these panels relate to the aesthetic theory of early twentieth-century modernism. Notably, Tack's concern with the primal impetus of creation in art and life, as well as with the transcendent principles of all creative endeavor, finds parallels among the inquiries of many art theorists, writers, and artists of his era. A central precept of the avant-garde ideology of the teens was that abstract painters were visionaries and explorers of the cosmos, revealing through their art "universal order and harmony" in formal means. The writer and critic Willard Huntington Wright's equation of internal and external states such as human emotions and the seasons suggests ideas similar to those embodied in Tack's Music Room cycle. Tack's paintings also bear a clear relationship to Wright's more secular version of the ideology, in which attaining "emotional ecstasy" and "bringing order from chaos" are viewed as central to the creative endeavor. The Russian symbolist musician Alexander Scriabin was immersed in the same concerns.[39]

Music as the ultimate art and the archetypal transcendent aesthetic experience, a precept of the aesthetic movement, was a lifelong preoccupation for Tack. His correspondence is filled with references to the concerts he attended and the romantic music he loved, especially

Beethoven, Wagner, and Brahms; among his friends he counted many musicians, and he himself played the piano.[40] In his 1930 "Note on Subjective Painting," Tack described the "unavoidable analogies" between abstract art and music. Each medium was free from reproducing nature, he believed, and the "harmonious relations of color rhythmically progressive" in painting "awaken[ed] the emotions" as music could.[41] These analogies gained currency in the United States beginning in the 1890s and were galvanized in the early twentieth century by Kandinsky and his followers among the avant-garde. The concept of art seeking to express in color and form what music expresses through sound had long been organic to Tack's approach to art.[42] The rhythmic movement of the forms within the decorative panels and their unfolding over space and time parallel the structure of music. The recurrence of motifs, themes, and specific imagery liken the paintings to chords from an orchestral piece. Phillips invoked the musical metaphor frequently in describing Tack's paintings: "He knows the emotions that tones of color can produce, and he uses them as the composer uses tones of sound." Tack himself wrote that the works were intended as "painted symphonies"; he noted that *Flight* was his impression of a "fugue by Bach."[43]

Tack's reliance on chance imagery from nature in his exploitation of photographic effects and his often free and spontaneous use of color are the most arrestingly "modern" features of his work. His close-up focus parallels O'Keeffe's enlarged flower imagery, suggesting a common source in Arthur Dow's teachings and writings. His reiterated cloud forms find a striking correspondence in Stieglitz's series of photographs, *Equivalents*, which share the disorienting quality and the sustained concentration on sky, clouds, and horizon. Similarly, Dove's rhythmically dynamic paintings, such as *Golden Storm* (1925; The Phillips Collection) and *Waterfall* (1925; The Phillips Collection), address the same subjects as Tack's works, each artist creating an abstract vision through natural forms. Yet Dove's biomorphic style and his preoccupation with generative, sometimes sexual imagery make his interpretations strikingly different from Tack's work.

Phillips's comparison of Dove and Tack is telling: "Superficially," he wrote, "no two painters could be more unlike than the laconic Dove, who is concerned with the mere sight and touch of rugged, uncouth things for their own sake, and the romantic Tack, the material world well lost in celestial and spiritual meditations. And yet these two Independents are both intensely aware of the accidents of nature which can be developed, through their intervention, into an abstract art of ideas and essences."[44]

Steeped in mysticism, Tack used abstraction to reflect ancient truths rather than to spontaneously divulge his inner spirit or commune directly with nature. Unlike Kandinsky, Tack did not respond to an "inner need" before his canvas, painting in forms and colors corresponding to deeply personal emotions. The nineteenth-century aestheticism that permeates Tack's decorative series presents a visual context far removed from the raw, direct approach to painting sought by the American moderns. Tack's belief system, which originated from external, traditional sources, firmly separates him from the highly individual strivings of the avant-garde artists. It is revealing that while Dove and his contemporaries responded to the jazz age, painting to the rhythms of Gershwin and Stravinsky—and Marin to urban, architectonic rhythms—Tack's highest aim was to attain in paintings what Beethoven and Brahms had attained in symphonies. That Tack approached the Music Room series as a unified whole is borne out in the continuities of rhythm, line, imagery, and subject between the panels, which brings the compositions to life. This underlying continuity suggests harmonies in nature and life.[45]

In 1933, long after Phillips had come to accept modernism, he assessed Tack's achievement:

If Tack had been painting his unique maps of . . . color for the last twenty years he would now be reaping the reward in universal acclaim for having invented a new decorative language. . . . His other researches of earlier years have not been so successful and his conservative portraits and traditional mural paintings have made him a limited reputation as an . . . eclectic painter . . . rather than as one of America's most original painters."[46]

Yet in their abstract, evocative forms and their free and sumptuous range of colors, the Phillips decorative paintings find their place alongside the abstract explorations of Dove, Marin, O'Keeffe, and others of their generation.

THE LATER HISTORY OF THE DECORATIONS

The decorative paintings won Tack a recognition and visibility unprecedented in his career. Through Wilbur Peat, who had seen the panels in Tack's New York studio, a selection was shown at the John Herron Institute of Art in Indianapolis in 1931; Tack was invited to lecture on the meaning of abstraction. Frederick Pratt, an important donor to the Brooklyn Museum and husband of a trustee, had seen the paintings in Tack's studio and was ready to purchase an abstraction, awaiting only the board's approval, which never came. Through Phillips's efforts, three of the panels hung along with works by Dove, Marsden Hartley, and Charles Sheeler in the Museum of Modern Art's ninth loan exhibition, "Painting and Sculpture by Living Americans."[47]

The first New York showing of the panels in November 1929 at Kraushaar Galleries opened to mixed reviews. One critic found the suggestions of figures in some puzzling but the "spirit of stained glass and 'pure design'" quite satisfying. Royal Cortissoz, who had lamented the lack of visionary painting in America in the 1920s, found them perplexing and alluring. Their contribution to mural painting was repeatedly highlighted. These works formed the nucleus of an exhibition of twenty-four paintings at Karl Nierendorf's gallery in 1943. The display prompted the gallery director to write Phillips of Tack's affinities with Kandinsky "in his conception of life. They . . . have in common the serenity and profoundness . . . rare in Western artists." Many artists, including Marin and the French painter Dunoyer de Segonzac, praised Tack's color and originality.[48]

Public reception of the panels on their first Washington showing was overwhelmingly favorable. "I cannot tell you how many people have simply been made over by the experience of that room," Phillips wrote Tack. "Many people have spoken to me about the spiritual quality of your design and colors creating an atmosphere of a great church . . . . Your mystic and cosmic meditations are so sincere and profoundly affecting that it is wonderful the way visitors . . . become reverential and silent and happy under the influence of your art." Wrote Leila Mechlin of the *Sunday Star*, "This series is undoubtedly one of the most notable artistic achievements of the present day."[49]

Between 1923 and 1930, Phillips's concept of a museum as a static memorial with permanent decorations, reminiscent of Freer's museum, had shifted to a more dynamic notion with changing exhibitions, bringing it closer to Alfred Stieglitz's series of New York galleries. Further, with the depression, the idea of constructing a separate building was postponed indefinitely. To have a room decorated permanently by one artist in the existing building would mean there was less space for what was quickly becoming home to Phillips's growing collection. The plans for a permanent installation of Tack's murals, always chimerical, disintegrated altogether. "More and more I am coming to the opinion," Phillips wrote Tack in 1934, "that we must wait for better times to make a really satisfactory setting and lighting for your decorations."[50] This change of heart was, Phillips argued, in Tack's best interest: a group of easel pictures, as the panels now were, would allow continually changing juxtapositions of Tack's work with that of internationally known modernists, including Prendergast, Van Gogh, Rouault, Roussel, and Cézanne.[51] Hopeful that Tack would gain recognition in this grouping, Phillips must have felt that permanent mural decoration would solidify Tack's place in a nineteenth-century aestheticism rather than highlight his affinities with other abstract contemporary painters.

Three years later, Phillips proposed to the artist trades and sales of the mural works, writing that "the whole plan [of the Tack room] was a beautiful dream." This suggestion prompted a strong response from Tack, who replied immediately:

I am not happy in the idea of breaking up the decorative scheme, even if never accomplished on another scale, of the really heroic abstractions. I consider this conception my magnum opus. It may never be carried further, but it is complete. It is in a sense cosmic—a poem on Life itself.[52]

Tack's poem, set to rich, harmonious color chords, preserved as an integral set of moveable panels, remains richly evocative of both past art and contemporary innovation. Tack's deep spirituality and his ceaseless explorations of nature are the leitmotifs. He melded science and mysticism, employing photography to derive designs based in nature and imaginatively adapted to convey spiritual themes. Through this language, Tack conveyed the evolution from chaos to harmony, the central quest of his work. In these panels, with their transmutation of reality into vision and discord into unity, Tack's mystic aspirations are exquisitely fulfilled.

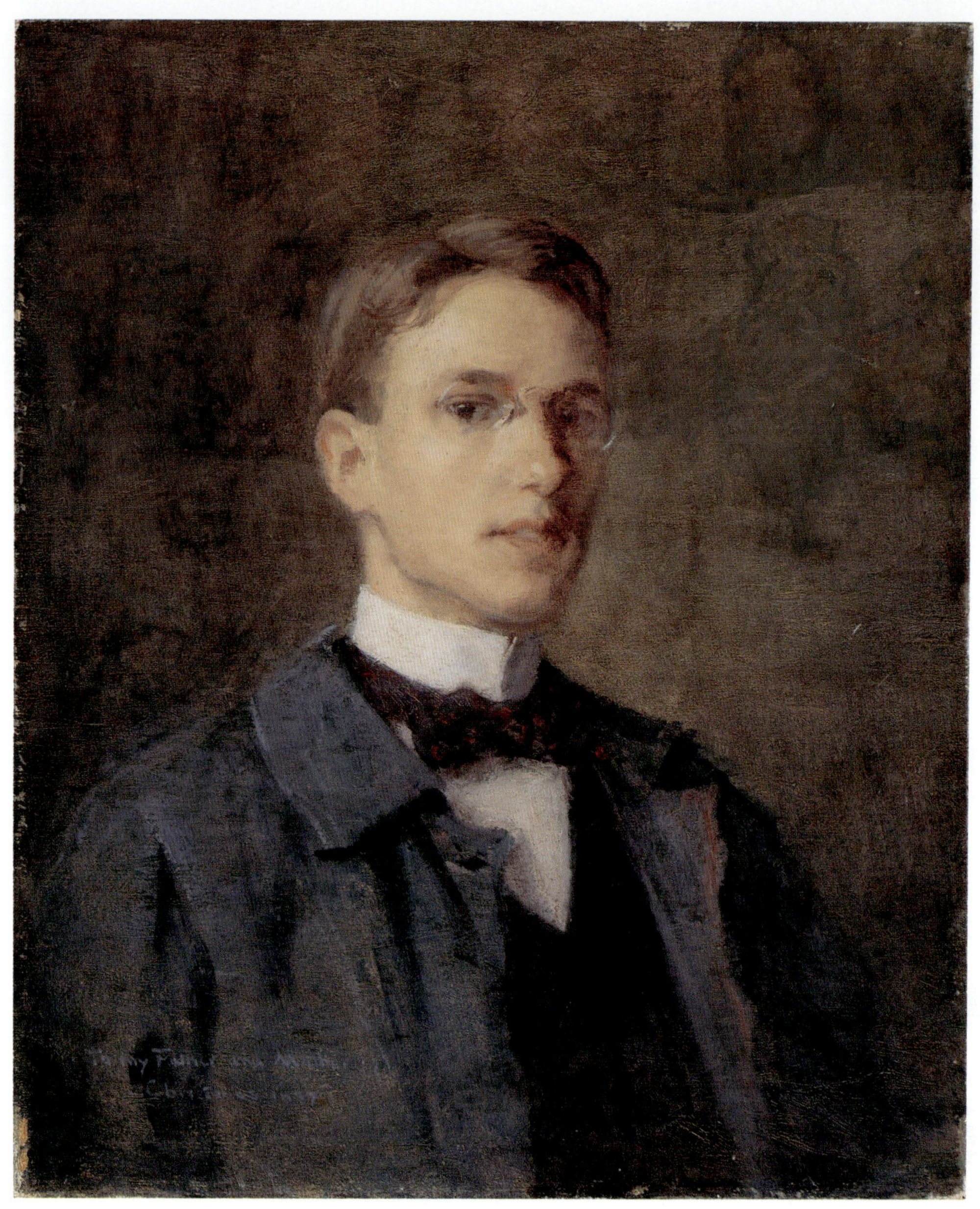

Cat. 1. *Self-Portrait*, 1897, oil on canvas, 24 x 20 in.

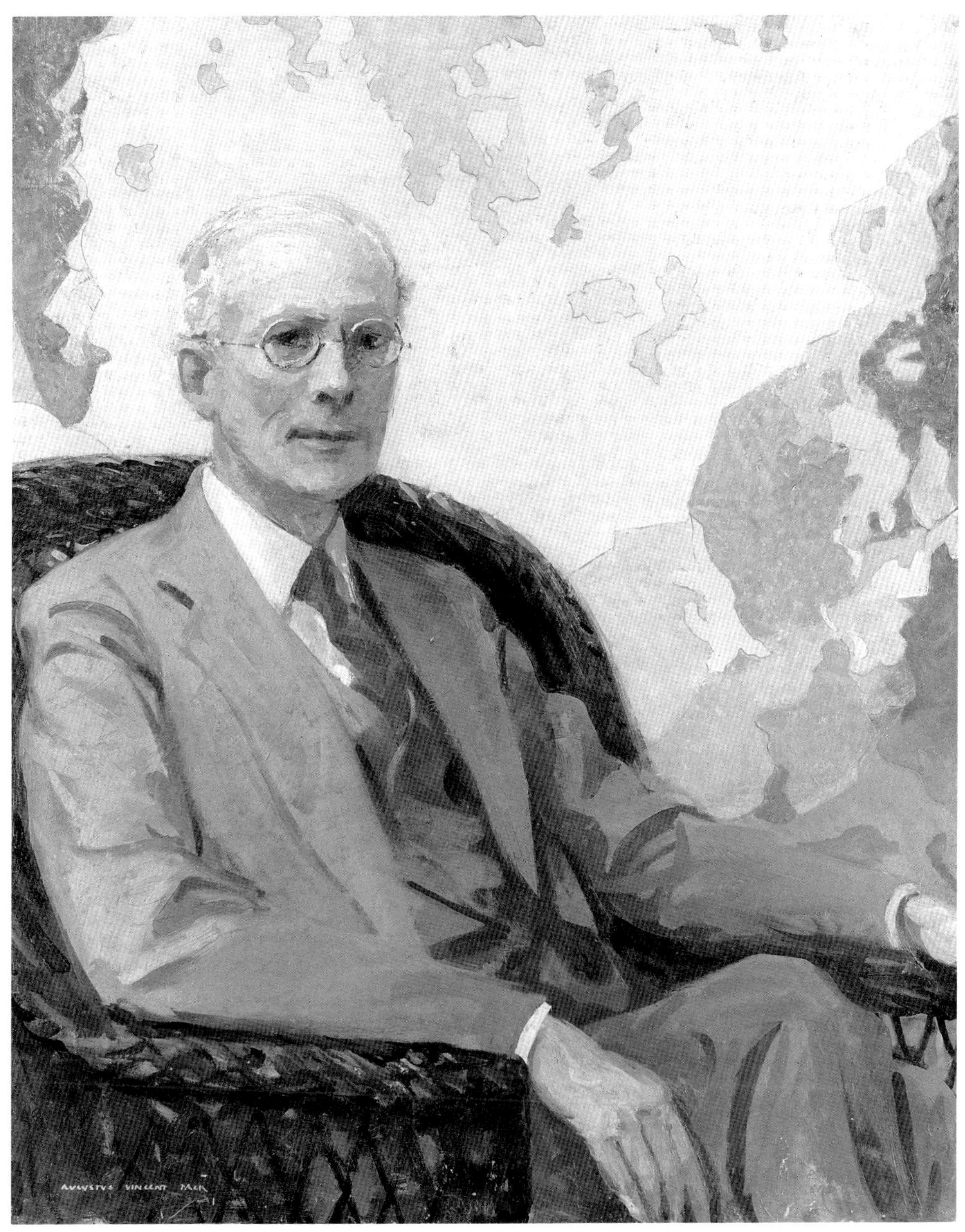

Cat. 56. *Self-Portrait*, 1940s, oil on hardboard, 39 ¾ x 32 ¼

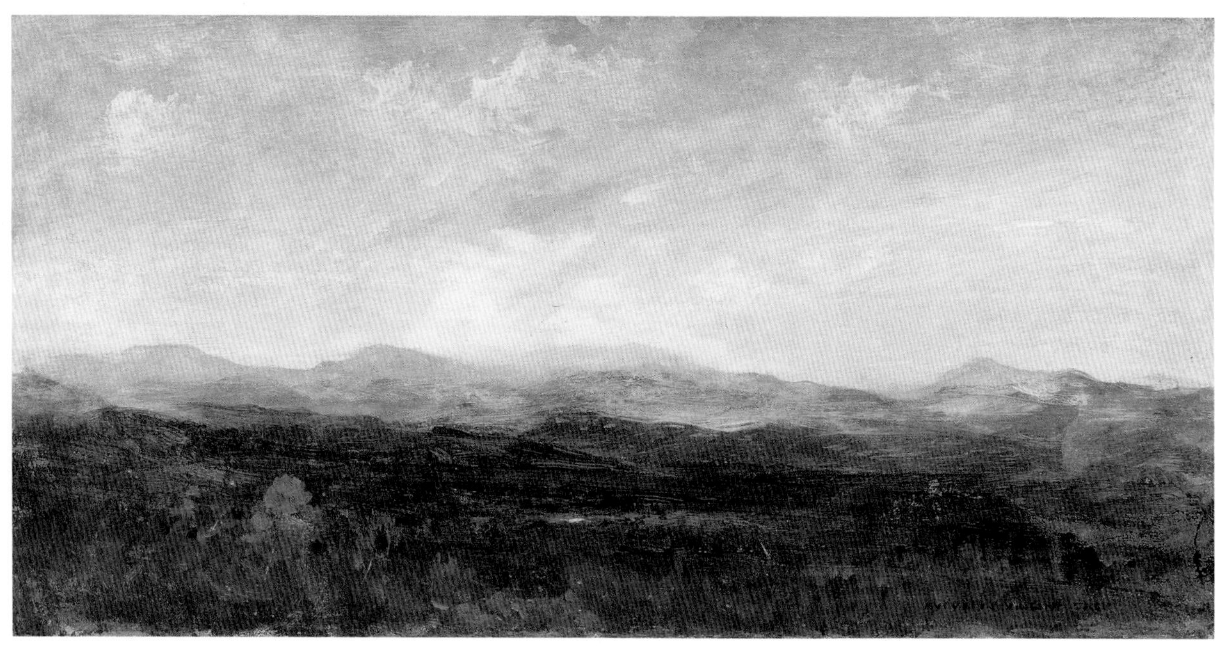

Cat. 10. *Sea of Hills*, ca. 1905–ca. 1910, oil on canvas mounted on panel, 15 x 30 ⅜ in.

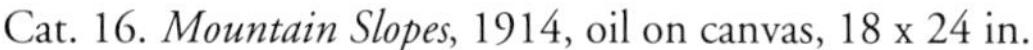

Cat. 16. *Mountain Slopes*, 1914, oil on canvas, 18 x 24 in.

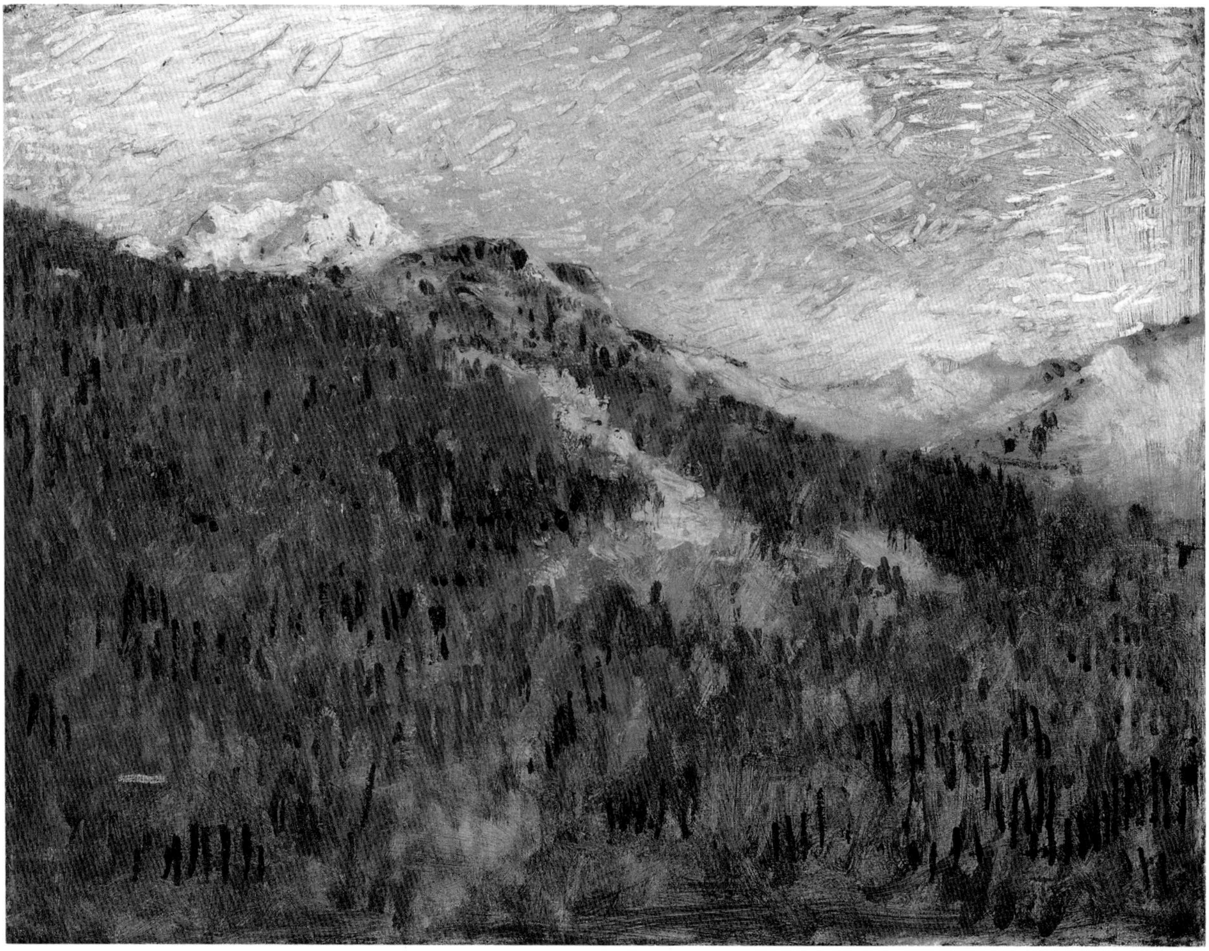

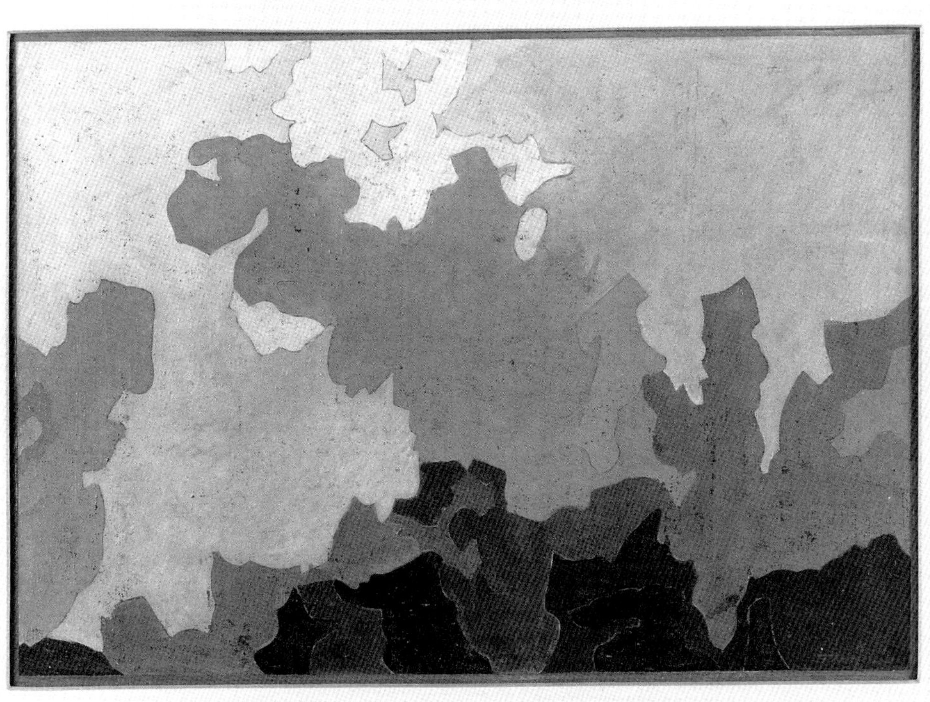

Cat. 50. *Daybreak,* between 1934 and 1936, oil on canvas mounted on hardboard, 26 x 33 ⅛ in.

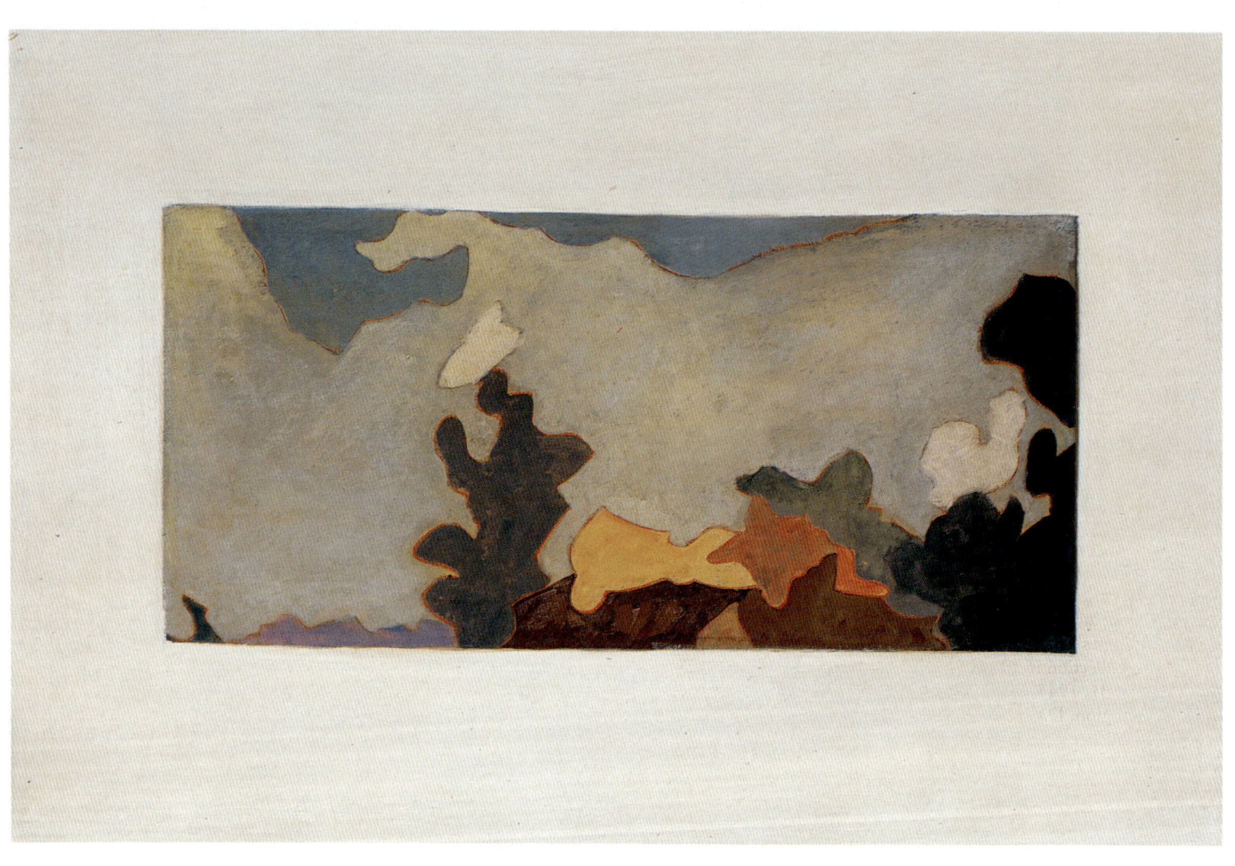

Cat. 51. *Above the Treetops*, between 1934 and 1936, oil on canvas mounted on hardboard, 20 ⅛ x 30 11/16 in.

NOTES

Augustus Vincent Tack: A Mystic's Journey to Abstraction

Leslie Furth

1. Tack made this statement in the checklist for his 1943 Karl Nierendorf Gallery exhibition, "Paintings by Augustus Vincent Tack."

2. Duncan Phillips, "American Old Masters," in *Artist Sees Differently*, 104.

3. Phillips, "Original American Painting of Today," *Formes* 21 (January 1932): 197.

4. Baudelaire and Denis are cited in Augustus Vincent Tack, "A Note on Subjective Painting," *Art and Understanding* 1, no. 2 (March 1930): 240–43.

5. Tack's prediction is cited in Mrs. Solton Engel, "Collection of Mrs. Zolton [*sic*] Engel," typescript, American Studies Group Papers, Deerfield Academy Archives, Deerfield, Massachusetts (hereafter ASG Papers). Phillips, "The Artist's Choice," *The Artist Sees Differently*, Phillips Publications, no. 6 (New York and Washington: E. Weyhe and Phillips Memorial Gallery, 1931), 134.

6. The family's movements are chronicled in an article (ca. 1911) on the Tacks from *Romance of American Petroleum and Gas*, 347–48, provided by Mrs. Theodore Robb, Philadelphia.

7. The family's interest in the arts and music is attested to by the artist's niece, Mrs. Susan Tillman (conversation with author, December 8, 1992). A textbook with Tack's drawings was still in existence in an unnamed collection in 1944 (Fra Salvatore to AVT, November 31, 1944, The Phillips Collection Archives, Washington, D.C.). Unless otherwise noted, correspondence cited is in The Phillips Collection Archives.

8. The young Tack distinguished himself academically, winning awards and honors throughout his school years (Fr. Vincent Butler, interview with author, August 24, 1992; Christine Ressmeyer Klein, *The Jesuits and Catholic Boyhood in Nineteenth-Century New York City: A Study of St. John's College and the College of St. Francis Xavier, 1846–1912* [Ph.D. diss., University of Pennsylvania, 1976]). Fr. Butler and Fr. William J. McGowan of St. Francis Xavier High School compiled Tack's academic record for me, answered my questions, provided photographs, and pointed me toward relevant literature.

9. Tack studied the piano as a boy. At age ten, he won prizes for copying from a print in crayon and for landscape drawing; at age eleven, he won prizes for crayon drawing and painting. Prizes were not awarded for older pupils in art, perhaps a measure of the lesser importance accorded art in the school's program.

10. See Ronald G. Pisano, "A Brief History of the Art Students League of New York," in *The Art Students League: Selections from the Permanent Collection* (Huntington, N.Y.: Heckscher Museum, 1987), 7–14, and Marchal Landgren, *Years of Art: The Story of the Art Students League in New York* (New York: Robert M. McBride, 1940).

11. James W. Lane attests to Tack's admiration: "Twachtman was also a master whom [Tack] early revered" ("Augustus Vincent Tack," *American Magazine of Art*, December 1935, 729). Marjorie Phillips recalls that Tack had "at one time studied with John Twachtman" (*Duncan Phillips and His Collection* [Washington: The Phillips Collection and W. W. Norton, 1982], 268). Tack remembered Weir's visit to a drawing class, certainly at the ASL, in "A Letter from Augustus Vincent Tack," in *Julian Alden Weir: An Appreciation of His Life and Works* (New York: E. P. Dutton, 1922), 99–100.

Tack's name, along with those of about seventy other students, appears on a petition to the Art Students League Board of Control to keep Chase on for the 1891–92 season (roll NY59–29, frame 232, Art Students League Papers, Archives of American Art, Smithsonian Institution, Washington, D.C. [hereafter ASL Papers]). Chase resigned from the league in 1896 to found his own school, believing students should begin painting directly without extensive drawing practice, and was replaced by Frank Vincent Du Mond. Chase returned in 1907.

12. Mowbray wrote, "I became . . . interested in many of my students, which developed into friendships that have continued ever since . . . such as [that with] . . . Tack." *H. Siddons Mowbray, Mural Painter, 1858–1928*, ed. Herbert F. Sherwood (privately printed, Florence Millard Mowbray, 1928), 48. Many of Tack's working methods were canons of Mowbray. Stephanie Wiles allowed me to see the galleys of her article and the text of her lecture on the analysis of Mowbray's mural technique; see Wiles, "The American Muralist H. Siddons Mowbray and His Drawings for the Larz Anderson House," *Master Drawings Quarterly* 31, no. 1 (Spring 1993): 21–34.

13. Many Americans seeking a traditional education in the Paris academies were drawn to the art colonies of Giverny and Pont-Aven. Theodore Robinson, John Leslie Breck, Robert Vonnoh, and Phillip Leslie Hale sojourned in Giverny; J. Alden Weir and, later, Arthur Wesley Dow frequented Pont-Aven.

Though family legend has it that Tack studied with Monet, no documentary evidence has been discovered. He may have made a brief pilgrimage to Giverny to join the American and European artists working there in the 1890s. William H. Gerdts, professor of art history, City University of New York, hypothesized that Tack was "among the dozens or hundreds of Americans" at Giverny "for the afternoon" (letter to author, July 2, 1986).

14. Tack's family believes that two watercolors from this trip are Tack's earliest surviving works. This belief is borne out by an inscription on one work: "Empress Eugenie's Villa - Biarritz, 1890." The second, undated, is inscribed, "from Splendido Hotel—Aix les Bains." Information provided by Mrs. Susan Tillman, Gulfport, Mississippi, and Mrs. Mary Ellis Carrere, New Orleans, Louisiana.

15. The landscape is *Picardie* (1893, Mr. and Mrs. Maxwell Solet, Cambridge, Mass.). No records of the trips before 1895 were located in the Passport Applications records, National Archives, Washington, D.C., or in the English-language newspaper published in France, the *American Register and Morning News*. See, for example, Florence Levy, "Who's Who in Art," in *American Art Annual* (Washington: American Federation of Arts, 1915), 483. No primary records linking Tack and Merson have been located, nor have formal studies or studio paintings from the French sojourns been located. Tack is not mentioned in the Ecole des Beaux Arts Archives; he is not listed as a student at the Académie Julian, where Merson also taught; and he did not register to make copies at the Louvre between 1890 and 1900 (Claude Laugier to author, January 25, 1993). Research in numerous Paris archives yielded no mention of Tack. However, according to leading Merson scholar Joël Perocheau, Merson had many private students.

Either directly or indirectly from Merson (1846–1920), a passionate reactionary and strict defender of academic methods, Tack absorbed the belief in clarity of line, integrity of draftsmanship, and concentration on classical subjects that Merson had obtained at the Ecole Nationale Supérieure des Beaux-Arts. A decorator, muralist, and professor in drawing at the Ecole from 1894 to 1905, when he replaced Bonnat as chef d'atelier, Merson worked in the linear tradition of Ingres and David. He studied with the religious painter Isidore Pils (1813–75) and underwent intensive study of classical subjects and draftsmanship at the Ecole and in Italy, where Florentine painting particularly captivated him. Merson's influence undoubtedly strengthened Tack's mastery of form and his technical approach. See Perocheau, *Autour de Luc Olivier Merson* (Paris: n.p., 1991). See also Léon Thévenin, "L'Art Chrétien chez Luc-Olivier Merson (Paris: Leon Vanier, 1897), and Charles Saunier, "L'oeuvre de Luc-Olivier Merson à l'Exposition de l'Ecole des Beaux-Arts," *Revue de l'Art* (May 1921): 303–10.

16. See David C. Huntington, "The Quest for Unity: American Art Between World's Fairs, 1876–1893," in *The Quest for Unity: America Between World's Fairs, 1876–1893*, 11–46 (Detroit: Detroit Institute of Arts, 1983), 27.

17. Robert Berkelman, "John La Farge, Leading American Decorator," *South Atlantic Quarterly* 56 (January 1957): 27–41, cited in Henry Adams, "The Mind of John La Farge," in James Yarnall et al., *John La Farge* (New York: Abbeville Press, 1987), 36.

18. Study of the masters would certainly have been encouraged at the Art Students League and during Tack's sojourns abroad. In a letter to Beatrice Winser (July 27, 1944, Archives, Newark Museum, Newark, N.J.), Tack cited the influence of Renaissance themes and styles on his painting *The Listeners* (*Momente Musicale*) (1899–1900, Newark Museum), inspired by a Robert Browning poem, "A Toccato of Galuppi." Tack gave the source as *The Concert*, formerly attributed to Giorgione, now given to Titian (ca. 1510, Palazzo Pitti, Florence).

19. Laughlin Phillips visited Tack's studio in the 1940s and remembers the artist's pride in his skill at techniques such as pouncing (interview with author, January 27, 1993). Merson's preparatory drawings for his Prix de Rome painting, *The Soldier of Marathon* (1869, Ecole des Beaux Arts), evince his diligent use of pouncing to transfer preparatory drawings to his canvas.

20. The work considered for honors was an unlocated portrait, *Portrait of Madame H.*

21. "Art Notes," *New York Times*, March 13, 1896, 4.

22. References to Tack's paintings in The Phillips Collection are based on extensive analysis of a number of paintings by Elizabeth Steele, paintings conservator, in meetings with the author. According to Steele, the hazy landscape in the background at right indicates an earlier composition.

23. AVT to Violet Tack (hereafter VT), April 5, 1901, Fuller-Higginson Family Papers, Pocumtuck Valley Memorial Association Library, Deerfield, Massachusetts (hereafter F-H Papers).

24. Engel, "Collection of Mrs. Zolton [*sic*] Engel."

25. According to James Yarnall, director of the La Farge catalogue raisonné, the artist—made vulnerable by a legal and financial debacle leading to his arrest in 1885—sought to restore his reputation in the late 1880s. Maintaining a high profile, he pursued decorative work, cultivating artists and New York society. During this period he was a likely mentor to a young, admiring artist. The claims in the literature of an 1889 meeting cannot be substantiated; rather, evidence points to a later meeting, around 1897 (see Chronology). However, La Farge is credited with encouraging Tack's studies with H. Siddons Mowbray at the Art Students League and with Luc-Olivier Merson in Paris (American Studies Group, *Augustus Vincent Tack: 1870–1949* [Deerfield, Mass.: Hilson Gallery, Deerfield Academy, 1968], 8 [hereafter ASG 1968]). It seems highly probable that La Farge fostered Tack's talent and even made introductions; conscious of his debt, Tack wrote, "he has been very good to me" (AVT to Violet Fuller [hereafter VF], November 16, 1899, F-H Papers). I am indebted to James Yarnall, who guided me to these aspects of the life and work of La Farge, which coincide with those of Tack.

26. The portrait is signed and dated 1899, but in 1937, at the time of its sale to the Metropolitan, Tack dated it to 1897–98 (Reproduction Form completed by the artist, May 10, 1937, Archives, Metropolitan Museum of Art, New York). The first indication that it was ready to exhibit occurs in a letter of March 3, 1900 (F-H Papers). It was first reproduced as the frontispiece in *Scribner's Magazine* 49, no. 2 (February 1911), in conjunction with an article by La Farge, "The Teaching of Art," 178–88.

27. La Farge to AVT, Thomas J. Watson Library, Metropolitan Museum of Art, New York. According to Tack's letters to Violet between November 1899 and 1900, he began the portrait at La Farge's studio in the Tenth Street Studio Building and completed it in his own studio, working from photographs provided by Bancel La Farge (AVT to VF, November 17, 1899, January 11 and 12, 1900, F-H Papers).

28. On January 12, 1900, Tack wrote Violet, "If it is a great success there is no telling what its future may be—perhaps the Metropolitan Museum" (AVT to VF, January 12, 1900, F-H Papers).

29. James W. Lane cites the date of this critical letter (unlocated) as 1889, probably based on Tack's own recollections (Lane, "Tack," 729). However, LaFarge was president of the Society of American Artists from 1897–1906, and Tack did not submit work to the 1889 SAA exhibition. It is possible that La Farge, as SAA vice-president, wrote Tack complimenting him on his submission to the 1896 SAA exhibition. In 1899, Tack exhibited a portrait and a genre scene there. Alternatively, the letter could have been prompted when La Farge viewed the 1898 Carnegie International and could have seen Tack's three portraits.

A further mystery in their affiliation is that although the literature on Tack consistently names La Farge as one of his teachers, La Farge taught only briefly at the Art Students League in the 1880s.

30. Herbert E. Winlock, director of the Metropolitan, wrote Tack on April 20, 1935: "It is my opinion that [a retrospective on La Farge] could be made a success only with the help of some of those who were close to La Farge . . . . I am writing also to Royal Cortissoz and Grant La Farge" (Archives, Metropolitan Museum of Art, New York). The retrospective, "An Exhibition of the Work of John La Farge," was held March 23–April 26, 1936.

31. See, for example, John La Farge, *Kuwannon Meditating on Human Life* (1887–1908, Butler Institute of American Art, Youngstown, Ohio). For a discussion of the influence on La Farge of Asian culture, particularly the Kuwannon deity, see James L. Yarnall, "John La Farge and Henry Adams in Japan," *American Art Journal* 21, no. 1 (1989): 40–77, esp. 69–72. Tack owned a T'ang dynasty painting, *Kuwannon (Kwan-Yin) Goddess of Mercy & Attendant*, attributed to Wu Tao-tzu, in the early 1920s, giving it to the Washington County Museum of Fine Arts, Hagerstown, Maryland, in 1945. He drew on this figure for his rendering of Saint Theresa for the Church of St. Paul the Apostle, New York, 1925.

32. AVT to VF, November 15, 1899, F-H Papers. The murals have not been located.

33. Phillips, *A Collection in the Making* (New York and Washington: E. Weyhe and Phillips Memorial Gallery, 1926), 56, and *The Abstract Decorations of Augustus Vincent Tack* (Washington, D.C: Phillips Memorial Gallery, 1943), n.p.

34. Tack first traveled to Deerfield in 1897 with his friends the artist Ruel Crompton Tuttle (1866–1940), a fellow student at the ASL, and Edward McDowell (active 1890s). Tack probably learned of Deerfield through his friend Tuttle, a resident of nearby Greenfield, or his teacher Mowbray, a native of North Adams. The region had received mention as early as the summer of 1890 in a *New York Tribune* article, "Seeking Rural Scenes: Where Artists Will Spend the Summer," suggesting a familiarity and appreciation of the area among artists in search of picturesque motifs (June 15, 1890, copy in scrapbook, roll NY59–Z4A, frame 00183, ASL Papers).

fUtopian vision, see Margaret Burnham Howe, *Deerfield Embroidery* (New York: Charles Scribner's Sons, 1976), 20, specifically her reference to the founding of the Blue and White Society, the needlework guild, in 1898. Joseph Peter Spang guided me to the pertinent literature on Deerfield and shared his broad knowledge of Historic Deerfield. The Summer School of History and Romance, flourishing between 1886 and 1891, attracted New England luminaries such as Charles Eliot Norton and the writer George W. Cable, who lectured on topics including New England history and literature, the functions of romance, transcendentalism, and theosophy. See Maxwell Grant, *Appropriating the Ideal: Myth, Community and The Deerfield Summer School of History and Romance, 1886–1891* (Deerfield: Pocumtuck Valley Memorial Association, 1991).

36. In his response to the 1900 exhibition of the predominantly tonalist works in the William T. Evans collection, Tack wrote of Inness: "He was a giant . . . broad and noble in his conception - full of wonderful simplicity and exquisite harmony and never stooping to little sentiment" (AVT to VF, January 26(?), 1900, F-H Papers). In the work of George Fuller, "with its realization of every inch of the atmosphere," Tack found "that freshness and truth of nature" (AVT to VF, January 30, 1900, F-H Papers).

37. Leyden is a small town north of Deerfield near the Vermont border.

38. Another parallel exists between Tack's *Ideal Figure in Rose* (ca. 1900, The Phillips Collection) and an Allen sisters' photograph of Elizabeth Fuller posing in classical garb. Tack wrote to Violet on January 4, 1900, "Yesterday the Allens sent me the enlarged photographs of my decoration and they are splendid - much better than the decoration itself" (F-H Papers). The Allen sisters' photography collection is preserved in the Pocumtuck Valley Memorial Association Library, Deerfield, Massachusetts

39. See Sarah Burns, "A Study of the Life and Poetic Vision of George Fuller (1822–1884)," *American Art Journal* 13, no. 4 (Autumn 1981): 11–37.

40. AVT to VF, December 8, 1899, F-H Papers.

41. Infrared photography by Elizabeth Steele, February 1993, reveals an earlier composition beneath the present painting; one or two figures may be present at the far right. The photograph also reveals the charcoal underdrawing for the present figure and the fact that the woman was originally holding a mirror or other object in her left hand.

42. Tack's approach to the human figure is evidenced in a letter to Violet: "Do your paintings and drawings at home and get some plaster full length figures and draw them in every light and paint everyone you can induce to sit for you " (AVT to VF, November 14, 1899, F-H Papers).

43. His subjects included Mrs. Gustave Schirmer, the wife of the music publisher (ca. 1907, Museum of Fine Arts, Boston), Thomas Wentworth Higginson (ca. 1903, The Phillips Collection), and the Massachusetts-based writer George Cable (late 1890s, unlocated).

44. Three-quarters of the paintings exhibited were portraits; the press particularly noted the maturity of his likenesses of Cable and LaFarge ("The Fine Arts: Portraits and Landscapes by Mr. Tack," *Boston Evening Transcript*, November 7, 1902, 9).

45. It is not known how long he leased his 1901 studio, Holbein Studios at 152 W. 55th Street; however, the Tacks lived almost exclusively in Deerfield between 1901 and 1908 (ASG 1968, 10). The first record of contact between Tack and Macbeth is in 1904 (see Chronology).

46. *New York Tribune*, November 20, 1907, n.p., clipping from scrapbook, roll Nmcy, frame 126, Macbeth Gallery Papers, Archives of American Art, Smithsonian Institution, Washington, D.C.

47. Patricia Paladines, Prints and Photographs Department, New-York Historical Society (letters to author, September 17 and October 2, 1987) pointed out that W. 82nd Street appears more likely as the site than the Eighth Street studio. Recent infrared photography by Elizabeth Steele reveals an unfinished portrait beneath the composition.

48. For the tonalist revival among painters and photographers, see Donaldson F. Hoopes, *Childe Hassam* (New York: Watson-Guptill Publications, 1979), 54.

49. Phillips, "The Romance of a Painter's Mind," *International Studio 58* (1916): 21, probably paraphrasing Tack.

50. For Tack's inspiration from Puvis de Chavannes, see Carolyn W. Delaney, *Puvis de Chavannes and American Mural Painters* (Ph.D. diss., New York University, 1939), 84–87, for which Delaney interviewed the artist. She highlighted Tack's search for the spiritual and the ideal more than any specific technical inspiration. Tack's own interest in Puvis and his familiarity with the Puvis mural sketches in Phillips's collection are evident in his foreword to the Century Association's exhibition catalogue, *Exhibition of French Masterpieces of the Nineteenth Century*, 1936.

51. Although it has been conjectured that Tack and Phillips met at the Century Association, an earlier encounter is documented in Phillips's handwritten draft of an essay in 1914 (Journal L, TPC Archives) and by mention of Phillips in Tack's correspondence. In 1917, Tack recommended Phillips for entry (Nominating Committee Minutes, Century Association, courtesy of W. Gregory Gallagher).

52. While there is no documentation that Tack saw the Armory Show, his work of the teens demonstrates some familiarity with and excitement about the continental developments represented there. The landmark exhibition was the first opportunity for many artists to view earlier movements such as symbolism and postimpressionism in the work of Van Gogh, Redon, and Matisse. Phillips had remarked on Tack's openness to various forms of art—his absorption in a "smoke-stained Japanese print . . . Chinese paintings and Gothic glass"—and "to the most startling revolutionary disturbances in the realms of painting," such as "the sensational performances of Picasso" ("Romance of a Painter's Mind," 20).

53. The painting appears in its first state as *The Dance* in the City Art Museum of St. Louis's 1911 exhibition catalogue, *A Collection of Paintings by Mr. Hermann Dudley Murphy, Mr. Augustus Vincent Tack, and Mr. William Baxter Closson*, n.p.

54. Whether or not Tack was exposed to Edvard Munch's work, it is striking that he created in this same period *The Voice Crying in the Wilderness* about which he wrote: "We naturally associate personality with a voice . . . . [It] becomes impersonal when it is heard only and its source is not seen. It then possesses an abstract quality conveying a sense of mystery." Tack, "Reflections on Pictures. Some Painted and Some Unpainted," typescript, 1941, collection of Joseph Peter Spang III, Deerfield, Massachusetts (hereafter Tack, "Reflections").

55. Phillips, *Collection in the Making*, 56. According to Tack's July 21, 1937, letter to Phillips, the series, now dispersed, comprised *Madonna of the Everlasting Hills*, *The Remorse of Eve* (1913–14, National Shrine of the Immaculate Conception, Washington, D.C.), *Simon of Cyrene* (by 1914, National Shrine of the Immaculate Conception), *The Voice Crying in the Wilderness*, *Earthbound* (by 1917, unlocated), and *The Pardon of Dismas* (by 1914, unlocated).

Jessie Lemont compares Tack's work to that of Segantini, Martin, Le Sidaner, and Watts ("Old Subjects in New Vestments" [with a note by Carroll Brown], *International Studio* 54, no. 213 [November 1914]: 3–10). Phillips, in "Art is Symbolic," *Artist Sees Differently*, 96, names Seurat at the source of Tack's color developments. Tack could have seen the work of Martin and Segantini in Paris in the 1890s.

56. Tack, "Some General Remarks about Paintings Called Abstractions," 1941–42, Phillips Academy Archives, Andover, Massachusetts. Written in conjunction with the 1942 exhibition at John-Esther Gallery, Abbott Academy, Andover. At his 1937 one-person Pittsfield exhibition, Tack also commented on the efficacy of this technique (AVT to DP, July 21, 1937).

57. Two months before the first exhibition of his new pointillist mural paintings of late 1913–14 in New York, Tack wrote his wife of plans to show "my Paris pictures" (AVT to VT, January 7, 1915, F-H Papers). Further, *Madonna of the Everlasting Hills* (cat. 13) is inscribed on the reverse with Tack's address, with the addition of "U.S.A." Mrs. Hotchkiss Ely, of whom Tack painted a portrait in late 1912, referred to Tack's bringing it to Paris for exhibition around that time.

58. Phillips, who undoubtedly had firsthand information on Tack's techniques, wrote: "At last he mastered the intricacies of applying the pure pigments from tube to canvas, until the method became a pliable medium for his self-expression" ("Romance of a Painter's Mind," 22).

59. See Charles C. Eldredge, "Visions of Life and Death," in *American Imagination and Symbolist Painting* (New York: Grey Art Gallery and Study Center, New York University, 1979), 94–103. Eldredge discusses Tack's *Madonna of the Everlasting Hills* in this context on p. 98.

60. "New Note in Art Struck by Painter of Highly Original Style" (review of March 1915 Worch Gallery exhibition), unidentified clipping, artist's file, Thomas J. Watson Library, Metropolitan Museum of Art, New York.

61. Phillips, "Romance," 24. La Farge entitled a segment of the New York Water Color Club's Eighth Annual Exhibition in 1897 devoted to his work, "Fantasies on Oriental Themes" (La Farge Family Papers, frames 1212-3–1216-3, Yale University Library, New Haven, Connecticut).

62. It is not known when Ferguson and Tack first met, but in 1921, Tack sent a letter of introduction to Phillips on Ferguson's behalf (AVT to DP, May 31, 1921). Simkhovitch's collection of Asian scroll paintings, known to Tack, may have helped to inspire Tack's own collection of Chinese paintings, which eventually numbered at least five.

63. In his endorsement of Tack, Simkhovitch wrote, "I have always thought of him as a portrait painter; not so. I have been amazed at his decorative work. He strikes me as one of the most interesting men of our times" (Simkhovitch to Aldrich, February 19, 1917, Greenwich House Collection, Tamiment Library, New York University Archives). The murals, still *in situ*, are both painted on canvas; one is adhered to the wall, a method known as *marouflage*, and the other is a framed canvas anchored to the wall.

64. A photograph album of reproductions that Tack collected, apparently in the late teens, includes the work of Michelangelo, Velasquez, Hals, and Leonardo da Vinci. The album is in the collection of Joseph Peter Spang III, Deerfield, Massachusetts.

65. The use of "earth colors," especially red ochre, to underlie figures in sketches was an academic approach described in detail by Alfred Boime in *The Academy and French Painting in The Nineteenth Century*, rev. ed. (New Haven: Yale University Press, 1986), 37–40. This technique carried into such abstracted conceptions as *The Crowd*, *Entombment*, and others of the 1922–24 series.

66. Upon Charles Kraushaar's death in 1917, John Kraushaar assumed the directorship of the gallery until his death in 1946.

Cortissoz, "American Art in Three Shows: Paintings by A. V. Tack, C. W. Hawthorne, and Robert Reid," *New York Tribune*, February 20, 1917, 11. According to the reviews Tack had reprinted some of Phillips's praise and criticism of his style: F. C. ("Mr. Tack's Pictures," *Boston Evening Transcript*, March 8, 1917, 19) observed that Tack "prints as a valuable interpretation of his work Duncan Phillips's declaration that Mr. Tack's 'paintings are not always entirely successful—we are often too conscious of the paint.'"

67. Charles Caffin, "Inventions Romantic by Tack," *New York American*, February 26, 1917, 7.

68. Tack, "Reflections," 35. This figure bears a strong resemblance to an allegorical nude that Tack used to portray "Courage and Vigilance" in the Manitoba Capitol's Legislative Chamber; see Marilyn Baker, *Manitoba's Third Legislative Building, Symbol in Stone: The Art and Politics of a Public Building* (Winnipeg, Man.: Hyperion Press, 1986), 114.

69. Cited in Richard Tarnas, *The Passion of the Western Mind* (New York: Crown Publishers, 1991), 110–11.

70. In a 1928 pamphlet on *Mystical Crucifixion,* Phillips gave the artist's scriptural source as John 12:32, Christ's vow, "And I, if I be lifted up from

the earth, will draw all men unto me" (TPC Archives, n.p.).

71. Tack's acquaintance with the Prometheus myth might have been reinforced in the teens when the Russian composer Alexander Scriabin's *Prometheus: Poem of Fire* had its world premiere at Carnegie Hall on March 20, 1915. Whether or not Tack attended the concert, he would certainly have been aware of it. Widely influential for American artists, the performance took visual form in colors in motion, their harmonies corresponding with those of the music. See James M. Baker, "Prometheus in America: The Significance of the World Premiere of Scriabin's Poem of Fire as Color-Music, New York, 20 March, 1915," in *Over Here! Modernism, The First Exile, 1914–1919* (Providence, R.I.: David Winton Bell Gallery, 1989), 90–111.

72. Tack's pointillist explorations informed his murals for Winnipeg, where he employed a leaner divisionist brushwork in the decorations for the three Legislative Chamber apses. In this, and in the rich color scheme of blues and reds, the works directly informed *The Crowd* and *Gethsemane.* For further information on the Winnipeg murals, see Baker, "Murals and Sculpture," in *Manitoba's Third Legislative Building,* 105–18. The Nebraska program encompassed universal themes that would continue in Tack's abstractions: the stages of life, the bounty of nature, the cycle of life and the seasons, and a symbol of Time in Eternity. Overall, the building and its decoration express "the aspirations and ideals of the citizens, reaching upward to the highest and noblest in civilization"—an ideal that contributed to Tack's conceptions for his Music Room panels, most directly *Aspiration.*

73. Augustus Vincent Tack [and Thornton Oakley], "Two Definitions of Art," *American Magazine of Art* 21 (October 1930): 576.

74. On the ship to Europe, Tack wrote that he had met "a great expert in the technique of mosaic and I have already learned a great deal about the practical side of that medium." From Venice he wrote, "I have seen the finest mosaics and studied them closely - I have also been deeply impressed by all the mural paintings of Giotto" (AVT to John Kraushaar, October 1, 1924 and November 7, 1924, Kraushaar Galleries Archives).

75. For example, the Winnipeg murals depicted the Tree of Life, drawn from the Book of Revelation; the Nebraska murals, for which Tack began preparing in the early to mid-1920s, evoked in allegorical terms the Revelation reference to the voice of God as the sound of many waters.

76. Tack's use of traditional Renaissance methods in his civic and religious murals is borne out by the many preparatory drawings for such projects that survive. For a description of the pouncing method, see Furth, "Landscapes of the Mind: Augustus Vincent Tack's Decorations for The Phillips Memorial Gallery," in this catalogue.

Stereopticon transfer was a standard tool of European and American mural painters in the nineteenth and early twentieth century; see Furth, "Landscapes," n. 30. Tack's abstract canvases that lack pouncing or other visible signs of transferral but are faithful copies of earlier pictures are likely to have been traced with this method. The advantage is that the scale of the projected imagery can be adjusted, while the pouncing technique is a one-to-one transfer. For the early history see "Enlarging Mural Decorations," *Harper's Weekly* 41 (November 13, 1897): 1122–23.

77. Tack, "Subjective Painting," 242.

78. Tack affirmed Leonardo as an inspiration in "Subjective Painting" and "Notes on Three Paintings," ca. 1944 (Special Collections, George Washington University, Washington, D.C.).

79. Lucille E. Morehouse, "Augustus Vincent Tack Tells Herron Audience Mysteries of Abstract Art," unidentified clipping, scrapbooks, Indianapolis Museum of Art, Indianapolis, Indiana.

80. Arthur Wesley Dow, *Composition,* 9th ed. (Garden City, N.Y.: Doubleday, Page & Co.: 1916), 45.

81. While Dow eschewed spontaneity in his premeditated designs, Tack constantly responded to his process and allowed it to lead him in new directions. In addition, Dow was more concerned with tonal effects of light and shadow—*notan*—than with pure color, which became the essential construct of Tack's compositions. An area requiring further research is Tack's work in camouflage in the late teens. The necessary distortion of shape, breaking up of form, and manipulation of abstract color may well have informed his abstract style.

82. Tack, "Some General Remarks about Paintings Called Abstractions," 1.

83. In the painting's original state, known from a black-and-white photograph, the sky was pale (photograph in Kraushaar Galleries Archives).

84. Borgognona is mentioned as a source by Lane, "Tack," 728. Tack might have been referring to *The Crowd* and other works in the style in a letter to John Kraushaar of September 2, 1921: "I have been working on six or more canvases and have had a most profitable summer in accomplishing certain qualities I have been long struggling to achieve. I hope you will like the results" (Kraushaar Galleries Archives). The reference to several works, as well as the exhibition history, indicate unlocated pictures in the style. The artist had also written to Phillips, "I have a number of canvases under way in the studio here I hope you will soon see" (AVT to DP, July 21, 1921).

85. For *The Crowd* Tack used the alternate title *Barabbas! Barabbas!* (Tack, "Reflections," 31, first exhibition at Kraushaar in 1922). *Turmoil,* probably Phillips's title, appears on the painting in Phillips's hand. *Gethsemane* is erroneously dated to 1918 in ASG 1968, 47, based on the incorrect assumption that it was included in Tack's Kraushaar exhibition in that year.

86. Tack, "Reflections," 31. In the catalogue for his 1941 Macbeth exhibition, the Biblical citation is given as Luke 23:18, "Away with this man and release unto us Barabbas."

87. DP to Bartlett Hayes, Addison Gallery, December 5, 1941. An examination of the Music Room panels derived from *The Crowd,* particularly *Allegro,* bears out this source: their forms are reminiscent of lush foliage. Other sources in Rocky Mountain landscape are suggested in several Music Room panels also derived from *The Crowd,* such as *Rhythm.*

88. For futurist theory, see F. T. Marinetti, "The Foundation and Manifesto of Futurism" (1908), in Herschel B. Chipp, *Theories of Modern Art: A Source Book by Artists and Critics* (Berkeley: University of California Press, 1968), 284–89. On synchromism, see Gail Levin, *Synchromism and American Color Abstraction 1910–1925* (New York: George Braziller and Whitney Museum of American Art, 1978). The relationship between the painting of Morgan Russell and Stanton MacDonald-Wright of the teens and Tack's early abstract work, notably *The Crowd,* requires further study. The parallels include inspiration from Michelangelo's sculpture. See also Willard Huntington-Wright, *Modern Painting: Its Tendency and Meaning* (New York: John Lane Co., 1915), for a discussion of "allegorical figures struggling against a toppling world" (297) and for Russell's theory of abstract formal construction (299).

89. See Elizabeth Steele, "Technical Notes," in this catalogue.

90. I am indebted to Elizabeth Steele for this comparison.

91. Boswell, " . . . Other Displays in New York's Art Galleries," *New York American,* February 12, 1922, 4; [Royal Cortissoz?], "Various Exhibitions in Many Galleries," *New York Herald Tribune,* February 19, 1922, 5.

92. In the summer of 1922, when Tack wrote Kraushaar of "six canvasses well under way, with four more planned," he probably referred to these conceptions (AVT to John Kraushaar, August 8, 1922, Kraushaar Galleries Archives); *Entombment* (cat. 22), a transitional work, was the first to be exhibited in December 1922. The other nine certainly would have included *Passacaglia, Rosa Mystica, Magi's Journey, Storm,* and *Epiphany,* all exhibited in February 1923 at Tack's annual Kraushaar show. The four "planned" works referred to in this letter probably included *The Voice of Many Waters, Canyon,* and possibly the tondo *Canyon* (ca. 1922–24, Brooklyn Museum). It seems likely that Tack began painting this series sometime after *The Crowd* and *Gethsemane,* probably in late 1921. In particular, a preliminary sketch for *Passacaglia* corresponds closely to the style and theme of *The Crowd,* suggesting that the drawing was contemporaneous while the painting followed early in the new series.

93. Tack related the scriptural source for *Storm* as "in St. Matthew: The Storm - 'Save us Lord we perish' and Christ's rebuke - 'Oh ye of little faith - did you not know that I was with you' " (AVT to DP, December 23, 1944). The phrase "the voice of God is like the sound of many waters" is from Revelation 1:12.

94. Phillips, "Exhibition of Recent Decorative Paintings by Augustus Vincent Tack" (Washington: Phillips Memorial Gallery, 1924), n.p. In 1926, he wrote "the subtle virtuoso with abstract patterns of color and form is at the service of the Christian disciple, telling New Testament tales again and grouping traditional figures with a backward glance at his revered ancestors of the age of faith . . . Giotto, Masaccio and Piero della Francesca" (*Collection in the Making,* 56).

95. Tack to Royal Cortissoz, August 2, 1920, Beinecke Rare Book and Manuscript Library, Yale University, New Haven, Connecticut; cited in Eleanor Green, *Augustus Vincent Tack 1870–1949: Twenty-Six Paintings from The Phillips Collection* (Austin: University of Texas, 1972), 17.

96. See Virginia Mecklenburg, *American Aesthetic Theory, 1908–1917: Issues in Conservative and Avant-Garde Thought* (Ph.D. diss., University of Maryland, 1983), 32, for a discussion of the roots of this approach to nature in the writings of John Ruskin, in particular *Modern Painters* (1847).

97. Analysis by Elizabeth Steele reveals the use of cartoons and perhaps stencils in transferring imagery to the canvas. In passages, the enlargements and distortions of earlier imagery suggest that Tack used a projection method. While Tack's use of photography as the foundation of his 1928 Music Room paintings was painstakingly described by his assistant, the Reverend William Wilfrid Bayne, no systematic study of the present series had been undertaken. Steele's "Technical Notes" in this catalogue inventory many of the techniques discussed here.

98. ASG 1968, 14–17. Green, *Tack*, 17, hypothesizes that Tack took his own photographs during the Rockies trip. There is no evidence that Tack himself owned or used a camera, but he mentions that his son Robert was "photographing the Indian country" in April of 1923; more probably, he recorded the western countryside for his father (AVT to John Kraushaar, April 30, 1923, Kraushaar Galleries Archives).

99. AVT to John Kraushaar, August 8, 1922, Kraushaar Galleries Archives.

100. This shape is used again in *Storm*. In a 1941 showing of the work, or a related sketch, the quotation from Mark 16:46 appears: "And laid him in a sepulchre which was hewed out of a rock" (Macbeth catalogue, 1941).

101. Tack , "Some General Remarks about Paintings Called Abstractions." This painting, along with the two *Canyon* paintings, is the only work devoid of overt religious content.

102. Correspondence between Tack and John Kraushaar documents the artist's progress on this painting. On July 22, 1923, he wrote from Deerfield: "I am working on a canvas now which interests me very much . . . — It is in the latest manner and I think more beautiful in color and feeling than any yet. I shall call it 'The Voice of Many Waters.' . . . I have three or four others in mind and hope to get underway soon so that I may have some things to show you when I return [to New York] in the fall" (Kraushaar Galleries Archives).

103. Phillips, "Augustus Vincent Tack," Journal GG, 1924, n. p., TPC Archives.

104. Undated, Washington County Museum of Fine Arts, Hagerstown, Maryland. *Voice of Many Waters* has been found to be an agglomeration of landscape elements from *Rosa Mystica* and figural elements from *The Crowd* and *Entombment.*

105. Phillips noted that about two hundred people came to see the exhibition, held in a room in the "lower gallery, not usually open to the public," on the opening day (DP to AVT, April 20, 1924). Phillips continued, "Your meaning baffles many in the symbolic pictures and it is significant that the Tondi are appreciated in the proper way whereas the compositions with figures . . . cause dissatisfaction because of their breaking away from the traditional treatment of such subjects."

106. For example, the *New York Tribune* critic ("Various Exhibitions in Many Galleries," February 19, 1923, 5) wrote that Tack "is one of the few American painters who dares attempt religious themes. Mr. Tack is somewhat of a pointillist and likes prismatic color, so his religious works must seem rather daring to those who seek them out . . . for the subjects." The *New York Herald* critic ("Tack Abstract Paintings Show Religious Subjects," February 11, 1923, 7) wrote: [Tack] has flirted with abstract art for a long time but now ventures deeper than ever before and with greater success. It seems the more daring as most of subjects are religious and it will be most interesting to see if the orthodox accept them."

The *New York Times* critic (February 11, 1923, 7) praised Tack's "harmonious pattern" and the color's "special sensitiveness and freshness," while Leila Mechlin ("Notes of Art and Artists," *Evening Star* [Washington, D.C.], April 6, 1924, 5), also lauded the color and their "strong appeal to the imagination."

107. Phillips, "Contemporary American Painting," February–May 1928, 49. Phillips also invoked Twachtman as an ancestor of Tack: "Had Twachtman lived on into this period it is probable that he would have carried [his] spiritualized naturalism into Tack's realm of abstract and technical innovation" (38–39).

108. Phillips, "Nationality in Pictures," *The Enchantment of Art* (Washington: Phillips Publications, 1927), 59, (note is dated 1926). Phillips drew on the theories of Ernest Fenollosa in his endorsement of this idea, quoting him in his notion of the Oriental composition as the art of the future (58).

109. Phillips, "Exhibition of Recent Decorative Paintings by Augustus Vincent Tack" (Washington: Phillips Memorial Gallery, 1924), n.p.

110. Phillips, "Augustus Vincent Tack," Journal GG, n.p.

111. DP to Arthur Dove, 1926, cited in Sasha Newman, *Arthur Dove and Duncan Phillips: Artist and Patron* (Washington: The Phillips Collection, 1981), 40–41.

112. Phillips, essay for Phillips Memorial Gallery, 1926, n.p.

113. Clark owned at least two Tack paintings for a period. According to Phillips, *Night, Amargosa Desert* "hung for some time in the . . . Collection of Stephen Clark but it finally gave it up as it took too much space on the already over crowded walls (DP to Powell Minnegorode, director, Corcoran Gallery of Art, February 27, 1937). Clark later owned a small abstraction (*Abstraction*, undated), which he gave to the Telfair Academy of Arts and Sciences, Savannah, Georgia, in 1943 (Beth Moore, Telfair Academy, letter to author, June 30, 1992).

Lorinda Munson Byrant, *American Pictures and Their Painters* (London and Toronto: John Lane Co., 1917), 272–73; Frank Jewett Mather, Jr., Charles Rufus Morey, and William James Henderson, "Recent Visionaries—The Modernists," in *The American Spirit in Art* (New Haven: Yale University Press, 1927), 160; Royal Cortissoz, "Further Steps in Mural Painting," in Samuel Isham, *The History of American Painting,* rev. ed. with supplemental chapters by Royal Cortissoz (New York: Macmillan, 1936), 583; Isham, *A Primer of Modern Art,* (New York: Tudor Publishing Co., 1939), 171; Homer Saint-Gaudens, *The American Artist and His Times* (New York: Dodd, Mead & Co., 1941), 247–48; and John I. H. Baur, *Revolution and Tradition in Modern American Art* (Cambridge: Harvard University Press, 1951), 116.

114. According to Phillips, Taylor tried to secure the abstraction *Time and Timelessness* for the Metropolitan in 1944 (November 3, 1944; December 23, 1944; November 21, 1945; December 10, 1945).

115. For Sachs, Lewisohn, Bliss, and Clark, see DP to Sachs, November 21, 1932; DP to AVT, June 3, 1930; DP to AVT, May 26, 1937; DP to AVT, May 24, 1934. For Clark, see n. 113 above.

116. Some of the works may have originated as the designs for the large-scale panels before the idea of the completed project on a larger scale disintegrated. Tack may have then adapted his designs, already prepared on canvases.

117. Although *Christmas Night* is not formally part of the Music Room, the former is referred to in Phillips's pamphlet on the Music Room cycle, *Appreciations by Duncan Phillips of the Decorative Panels by Augustus Vincent Tack* (Washington: Phillips Memorial Gallery, 1932). The spiritual themes of the room would culminate in *Christmas Night*, suggesting the decisive moment of Christianity.

118. *Ad Astra* (by 1931, private collection), a painting from the same area of *Liberation* as that used for *Nocturne*, employs the design in a vertical oval. *Ad Astra* suggests the contour of a solid form resembling a wave or mountain peak.

119. Tack, "Some General Remarks about Paintings Called Abstractions." With the disintegration of Tack's theological statements in abstraction, he returned to traditional religious painting. By the early 1940s several were exhibited in a retrospective at the Macbeth Gallery. For a prospective mural for a chapel in the Cathedral of Saint John the Divine, New York, at the invitation of the architect Ralph Adams Cram, Tack executed a preparatory study. A quiet, somber, and deeply mystical painting, *All Souls* depicts Christ's descent into Limbo (1933, Fogg Art Museum).

120. The forms at the base of this painting are an enlargement and reversal of the lower left corner of *Ecstasy.*

121. AVT to DP, December 23, 1936.

122. In 1934 the New York gallery, Wildenstein & Co., held a retrospective of Tack's work, showing the small-scale abstractions for the first time. It has recently been discovered that *Winter* and *Cloud's Edge* are enlarged segments of *Liberation* and *Ecstasy,* respectively. The fact that each segment had already figured in the enlargements of *Spring Night* and *Night, Amargosa Desert* indicates

that Tack's reuse of imagery depended in part on expediency: he employed existing enlargements of works, or segments of works, rather than beginning fresh.

123. For example, *Winter* is a one-to-one transferral from *Spring Night* and *Cloud's Edge* from *Night, Amargosa Desert.*

124. These small works may have been part of a large canvas and a single composition that Tack cut into pieces and mounted individually. Evidence of this includes traces of broad, sweeping brushwork in the ground layers, the absence of tacking margins, and small paint losses on the edges. *Night, Amargosa Desert,* created around the same time, bears the same ground treatment and fabric.

125. Numbers in Tack's hand appear in red paint on the backs of *Evening* (no. 1); *Abstraction* (no. 2; ca. 1934–1936, Telfair Academy of Arts and Sciences, Inc. [Beth Moore, letter to author, June 30, 1992]); *Winter* (no. 3); *Above the Treetops* (no. 4), and *Cloud's Edge* (no. 6). The largest known number is no. 12. The three works in TPC that are titled by the artist on the reverse on exhibition labels are *Evening, Winter,* and *Cloud's Edge.* TPC also has four small abstractions that the artist did not number: *Untitled Abstraction, Hill and Sky, Dawn,* and *Daybreak,* while the Whitney Museum of American Art's *Before Egypt* also does not bear a number. Many disparities in size and presentation of the numbered series exist.

126. Nierendorf to DP, December 18, 1943; Devree, *New York Times,* January 24, 1943, and Melville Upton, "One-Man Shows of Interest," unidentified clipping; both in scrapbook remnants, Nierendorf Gallery Papers, Solomon R. Guggenheim Museum Archives, New York.

127. Cloyd Marvin, in an undated letter to Nathaniel Sims of the Deerfield American Studies Group, wrote that he and Tack "ended our several meetings with [Henri] Bergson's *Creative Evolution*" (1907; first English edition, 1911) (ASG Papers).

128. "Notes on Three Paintings," exhibition checklist, ca. 1944, Special Collections, George Washington University, Washington, D.C.

129. AVT to DP, July 21, 1944. Use of the vacuum cleaner is cited by Mrs. Solton Engel, "Collection of Mrs. Zolton (*sic*) Engel," ASG Papers.

130. AVT to DP, June 26, 1944. On June 14, 1944, Marvin wrote Tack, "M. Lella and I have the understanding that we shall not varnish the work nor sign it until you join with us for the ceremony [in the fall]. That will give you the chance to go over the glorious creation . . . when you are able." Carl Lella (1899–?) is listed as having studied with Tack in *Who Was Who in American Art,* ed. Peter Hastings Falk (Madison, Conn.: Sound View Press, 1985), 366.

131. AVT to DP, July 21, 1944.

132. AVT to DP, June 5, 1944.

133. DP to Alfred Barr, November 10, 1930. Barr hastily telegraphed back with apologies that Tack's name had simply not arisen in the planning meetings, but that "I am most happy to include Mr. Tack" (November 11, 1930).

134. DP, "Modern Art, 1930," *Art and Understanding,* 144.

135. DP, *Artist Sees Differently,* 17.

136. DP, "Original American Painting of Today," *Formes* 21, no. 21 (January 1932): 197.

137. Phillips, "The Decorative Panels of Augustus Vincent Tack," n.p.

138. AVT to DP, February 9, 1949.

139. Phillips to Gardner, July 22, 1964.

140. Eleanor Green (*Tack,* 26–30) discusses Tack as a precursor to the abstract expressionists and Washington color field painters. This discussion is taken up by Robert Rosenblum, "The Primal American Scene," in *The Natural Paradise: Painting in America 1800–1950* (New York: Museum of Modern Art, 1976), 14–37, and reevaluated in his essay, "Resurrecting Augustus Vincent Tack," in *The Abstractions of Augustus Vincent Tack* (New York: M. Knoedler and Co., 1986).

141. Dove quoted his son William to Alfred Stieglitz, 2/4 July 1937, in *Dear Stieglitz, Dear Dove,* ed. Ann Lee Morgan (Newark: University of Delaware, 1988), 386 (signed "Reds and Dove").

142. AVT to DP, January 22, 1930, referring to his notes for the decorative panels he created for the Phillips Memorial Gallery.

143. AVT to DP, February 9, 1949.

Fenollosa, Dow, Tack, and Phillips: A Case for "Subjective" Painting in America

Elizabeth V. Chew

1. I am dependent on the exhaustive research done on Tack by Leslie Furth and presented in this catalogue.

2. See Henry Adams, "John La Farge and Japan" *Apollo* 119 (February 1984): 120–29; Adams, "John La Farge's Discovery of Japanese Art: A New Perspective on the Origins of Japonisme," *Art Bulletin* 67 (September 1985): 449–85; and James Yarnall et al., *John La Farge* (New York: Abbeville Press, 1987).

3. Kathleen A. Foster, "John La Farge and the American Watercolor Movement: Art for the 'Decorative Age,'" in Yarnall et al., *John La Farge,* 136.

4. "The Mind of John La Farge," in Yarnall et al., *John La Farge,* 71.

5. Quoted in ibid., 71.

6. Phillips, *A Collection in the Making* (New York and Washington: E. Weyhe and Phillips Memorial Gallery, 1926): 56.

7. Phillips, "The Romance of a Painter's Mind," *International Studio* 58 (March 1916): 22.

8. Ibid., 20.

9. Ibid., 21.

10. Phillips, *Exhibition of Recent Decorative Paintings by Augustus Vincent Tack* (Washington: Phillips Memorial Gallery, 1924), n.p.

11. Lefevre, "Paintings and Decorative Panels by Augustus Vincent Tack" (New York: C. W. Kraushaar Art Galleries, 1923), n.p.; Lemont, "Old Subjects in New Vestments," *International Studio* 54, no. 213 (November 1914): 3.

12. For a history of the music-painting analogy, see Andrew Kagan, "Ut Pictura Musica, I: To 1860," *Arts Magazine* 66 (May 1986): 86–91. For a discussion of the analogy as it relates to modernism, see Judith Katy Zilczer, "The Aesthetic Struggle in America, 1913–1918: Abstract Art and Theory in the Stieglitz Circle" (Ph.D. diss., University of Delaware, 1975), 43–110; Howard Risatti, "Music and the Development of Abstraction in America," *Art Journal* 39 (Fall 1979): 8–13; Ron Johnson, "Whistler's Musical Modes: Symbolist Symphonies/Numinous Nocturnes," *Arts Magazine* 55 (April 1981): 164–76; Eliza Rathbone, "The Role of Music in the Development of Mark Tobey's Abstract Style," *Arts Magazine* 58 (December 1983): 94–100; and Donna M. Cassidy, "The Painted Music of America in the Works of Arthur G. Dove, John Marin, and Joseph Stella: An Aspect of Cultural Nationalism" (Ph.D. diss., Boston University, 1988), 2–59.

13. See Cassidy, "Painted Music of America," 3–6.

14. Baudelaire, "L'Exposition Universelle" (1855), quoted in Cassidy, "Painted Music of America," 5.

15. See Johnson, "Whistler's Musical Modes," 172.

16. Judith Zilczer and Ron Johnson both connect the ideas of Whistler and his contemporaries with Swedenborgian mysticism.

17. Kandinsky's basic assertion was that "color is the keyboard, the eyes are the hammers, the soul the piano with many strings. The artist is the hand which plays, touching one key or another to cause vibrations in the soul." *Concerning the Spiritual in Art,* intro. and trans. M.T.H. Sadler (1914; New York: Dover Publications, 1977).

18. *Recollections and Impressions of James McNeill Whistler,* quoted in Risatti, "Music and the Development of Abstraction in America," 9.

19. For a list of early twentieth-century writings on the music-painting analogy, see Cassidy, "Painted Music of America," 379–88.

20. Quoted in ibid., 23–24.

21. See Gail Levin's discussion in "Kandinsky's Debut in America," in Levin and Marianne Lorenz, *Theme and Improvisation: Kandinsky and the American Avant-Garde, 1912–1950* (Boston: Bulfinch Press, 1992), 10–19.

22. *The Nation,* November 12, 1914; quoted in ibid., 17.

23. Phillips, "Revolutions and Reactions in Painting," in *The Enchantment of Art,* 54. For discussion of Phillips's development as a collector and an advocate of modernism at this time, see Eliza E. Rathbone, *Duncan Phillips: Centennial Exhibition* (Washington: The Phillips Collection, 1986) and Elizabeth Hutton Turner, *Men of the Rebellion: The*

Eight and their Associates at The Phillips Collection (Washington: The Phillips Collection, 1990).

24. Phillips did not begin his association with Stieglitz until the mid-1920s. His library contained a 1914 edition of A. J. Eddy's *Cubists and Post-Impressionism*, but it is difficult to believe that he would have been sympathetic to Eddy at this time.

25. Robert Rosenblum made a formal connection between the work of Dow and Tack in "Resurrecting Augustus Vincent Tack," in *The Abstractions of Augustus Vincent Tack (1870–1949)* (New York: M. Knoedler & Co., 1986), 15. The genesis of my thinking about the connection of Tack and Phillips with Fenollosa and Dow, however, was the discussion of the latter pair in Marianne W. Martin, "Some American Contributions to Early Twentieth-Century Abstraction," *Arts Magazine* 54 (June 1980): 158–65.

26. Judith Zilczer suggests the debt owed by Caffin, Hartmann, and Eddy to the Fenollosa-Dow theory ("Aesthetic Struggle in America," 52).

27. The two major published sources on Fenollosa are Lawrence W. Chisholm, *Fenollosa: The Far East and American Culture* (New Haven: Yale University Press, 1963) and Van Wyck Brooks, *Fenollosa and His Circle* (New York: E. P. Dutton, 1962). It is interesting to note that Fenollosa welcomed John La Farge and his traveling companion Henry Adams to Japan in 1886.

28. Fenollosa, "The Significance of Oriental Art," *The Knight Errant* 1 (1892): 65, quoted in Clay Lancaster, "Synthesis: The Artistic Theory of Fenollosa and Dow," *Art Journal* 28 (Spring 1969): 287.

29. Arthur Wesley Dow, introduction (1912) to 1931 edition of *Composition* (1899; Garden City, N.Y.: Doubleday, 1931), 5.

30. See Frederick C. Moffatt, *Arthur Wesley Dow* (Washington: Smithsonian Institution Press, 1977) and Nancy E. Green, *Arthur Wesley Dow and His Influence* (Ithaca, N.Y.: Herbert F. Johnson Museum of Art, 1990).

31. Dow, *Composition*, 3.

32. Quoted in Chisholm, *Fenollosa*, 184.

33. Dow, *Composition*, 4.

34. Quoted in Chisholm, *Fenollosa*, 194.

35. Dow, *Composition*, 5.

36. Dow, *Composition* (1899), 18, quoted in Cassidy, "Painted Music of America," 10.

37. Quoted in Zilczer, "Aesthetic Struggle in America," 33.

38. Brooks, *Fenollosa and His Circle*, 49. No date or source for this quote is given.

39. Phillips, *Enchantment of Art*, 82

40. Ibid., 84

41. Ross, *A Theory of Pure Design: Harmony, Balance, Rhythm* (New York: P. Smith, 1933).

42. Denis's "Definition du neotraditionnisme" was first published in *Art et Critique* (23 August and 30 August 1890), and was later incorporated into *Theories: 1890-1910, Du Symbolisme et du Gauguin vers un nouvel ordre classique* (1913). I am grateful to Charles Eldredge, *American Imagination and Symbolist Painting* (New York: Grey Art Gallery and Study Center, New York University, 1979), 50, for the citation for this often-repeated Denis quote. The translation is mine.

43. Johnson, "Whistler's Musical Modes," 175, 173.

44. Chisholm, *Fenollosa*, 174.

45. Phillips, *Exhibition of Recent Decorative Paintings*, n.p.

46. Tack, "A Note on Subjective Painting," *Art and Understanding* 1, no. 2 (March 1930): 240.

47. Ibid

48. Ibid., 242.

Mutual Influences: Augustus Vincent Tack and Duncan Phillips

David W. Scott

1. The gallery was incorporated as the Phillips Memorial Art Gallery but was usually referred to as the Phillips Memorial Gallery from 1923 until the 1940s; it became The Phillips Collection in the 1950s.

2. The documents that provided most of the dates and other data on which this essay is based were made available by the Research Office of The Phillips Collection, directed by Erika Passantino. Principal credit for exhaustive research on Tack is due Leslie Furth.

3. Members of the Century Association, a New York social club for men of distinguished cultural standing, were termed "Centurions." (The stationery heading read "Century Club.")

4. The account appears in Journal L in The Phillips Collection Archives (hereafter TPC Archives) and is dated by internal evidence to 1914. It appears to have been written after a studio visit, with possible publication in mind; it was revised with numerous deletions and later insertions.

5. Lemont (with a note by Carroll Brown), "Old Subjects in New Vestments," *International Studio* 54, no. 213 (November 1914): 3–10.

6. Tack to Violet Tack, December 31, 1914, Fuller-Higginson Papers, Pocumtuck Valley Memorial Association Library, Deerfield, Massachusetts.

7. *International Studio* 58 (March 1916): 19–24.

8. Phillips, "Fallacies of a New Dogmatism in Art," pt. 1, *American Magazine of Art*, December 1917, 43.

9. *Sunday Star* (Washington), March 7, 1920, 11. The author was probably Leila Mechlin, the paper's art critic.

10. The next largest groups were by Arthur B. Davies and Ernest Lawson, at thirteen each.

11. Phillips, Journal B, 1923–29, TPC Archives.

12. AVT to John Kraushaar, August 8, 1922, Kraushaar Galleries Archives, New York

13. DP to F. A. Whiting, director, Cleveland Museum of Art, March 31, 1924, TPC Archives.

14. This account of Phillips's conversion to modernism is by no means intended to imply that he was not responding to many influences—those of artist friends such as Arthur B. Davies and Maurice Prendergast, of critics such as Clive Bell and Roger Fry, and of his intense exposure to the New York art and gallery scene. However, the influence of Tack as friend, aesthetician, and painter was undoubtedly the most pervasive and persuasive.

15. Phillips, *A Collection in the Making* (New York and Washington: E. Weyhe and Phillips Memorial Gallery, 1926), 55–56.

Landscapes of the Mind: Augustus Vincent Tack's Decorations for the Phillips Memorial Gallery

Leslie Furth

1. Augustus Vincent Tack, "Some General Remarks about Paintings Called Abstractions," typescript, 1941-42, 1, Phillips Academy Archives, Andover, Massachusetts. Written in conjunction with the 1942 exhibition at John-Esther Gallery, Abbott Academy, Andover.

2. Various records and inventories conflict on the works officially included in the series, probably in part due to Phillips's ambivalence toward the permanent installation of the works; the series became amorphous as the plan disintegrated. *Christmas Night* and *Aspiration* were included in Phillips's revised essay in the pamphlet on the series, *Appreciations by Duncan Phillips of the Decorative Panels by Augustus Vincent Tack* (Washington: Phillips Memorial Gallery, 1932, n.p.). No other corroboration of *Christmas Night*'s role in the cycle is given in hanging records or correspondence. *Aspiration*, completed in 1931, was intended to "go in the space in the North Library transept across the windows," according to Tack (August 20, 1931), but it was seldom hung in the room as part of the cycle. In addition to these works, a painting known in the correspondence as *Orchid (Violet and Green)*, one of the "decorations of seasons" was apparently traded back to the artist (Duncan Phillips to Augustus Vincent Tack, October 29, 1930). The painting similar to *Andante* and *Allegro*, with imagery derived from the right center of *The Crowd*, surfaced at Sotheby's, New York; it may be *Orchid*, from the original series.

Unless otherwise indicated, all correspondence cited in this essay is part of The Phillips Collection Archives (hereafter TPC Archives).

3. See Richard N. Murray, "Painting and Sculpture," in *The American Renaissance 1876–1917* (Brooklyn, N.Y.: Brooklyn Museum, 1979), 185–87.

4. These observations appear in "The Romance of a Painter's Mind," *International Studio* 58 (March 1916): 22.

5. Phillips wrote Tack: "I did want your written exposition of your philosophical thought, what you have so often told me in words" (January 23, 1930). Phillips was emphatic that the significance of the paintings be outlined for the public and pressed Tack for notes. The artist's handwritten "Notes on Decorative Panels," which formed the basis of Phillips's writings on the series, were sent with a letter to Phillips on January 31, 1930.

6. In *Appreciations by Duncan Phillips of the Decorative Panels by Augustus Vincent Tack*, essentially a reprint of his 1930 flyer for the first exhibition of the library panels, Phillips called the room the "Hall of Cosmic Conceptions," adding "as it has been called," suggesting that he was quoting someone else.

7. These plans were drawn on the first pages of a diary begun in 1923. Phillips drew two floors, including a theater by Tack or Davies, libraries by Prendergast and Davies, and a Tack hallway. The emphasis on libraries is striking in light of the fact that the museum on 21st Street lacked even one library for a significant period of its history (Phillips, Journal B, 1923–29, TPC Archives).

8. Phillips wrote to Tack (May 3, 1923), "Do come for a brief visit. . . . You will have a chance to see the Freer Museum." Although there is no proof, it is difficult to imagine that the visit did not take place, especially given Tack's and Phillips's keen interest in the progress on the decoration of the Freer Gallery in 1921, before its opening.

Phillips's writings on Davies underscore the early importance of the artist to his vision. They include "The American Painter, Arthur B. Davies," *Art and Archeology* 4 (September 1916): 169–77, and "Arthur B. Davies: Designer of Dreams," in *Arthur B. Davies: Essays on the Man and His Art* (Washington: Phillips Memorial Gallery, 1924), 3–22.

9. According to the correspondence, Tack, along with the architect Charles Downing Lay and the gallery's treasurer, Dwight Clark, made tentative plans for the architectural renovation to present to Phillips. In letters to Tack (October 30 and November 2, 1929), Clark wrote of sealing off the windows permanently to screen out the daylight and use the recessed areas of the upper windows to accommodate Tack's panels. In December 1929, Phillips tried to organize a meeting to discuss the plans, but it is not known whether it took place (DP to Charles Lay, December 3, 1929).

No architectural plans for these alterations survive, so it is difficult to project how the necessary vertical expansion would have affected the main gallery just above the room. The ornate suspended ceiling, then out of fashion, would presumably have been sacrificed. The present panels, intended as preparatory studies, were to be traded back to the artist when the finished murals were created. Tack advertised panels for purchase "on completion of the full size paintings" in their first showing, "An Exhibition of Decorative Inventions for The Phillips Memorial Gallery," at Kraushaar Galleries, November 19–December 3, 1929.

10. In his letter of commission (December 28, 1928), Phillips referred to "the panels on which you are working," implying that Tack was already at work on the cycle. Further, he enclosed a payment for two panels, possibly the number Tack had produced at that point. Tack wrote of his keen desire to have Phillips see the progress on the decorations (March 7, 1929). After a spring 1929 visit to the studio, Phillips wrote Tack of his favorable impressions of the "new decorations" and sent payment for two more works (June 4, 1929).

11. *Largo* probably predated the official commission by several months. Certainly most of the panels were completed for the Kraushaar showing in November–December 1929, in which the works were given numbers rather than titles. On March 2, 1930, Tack notified Phillips that two large lunettes and nine smaller panels were being shipped for their first showing at the museum. The two large lunettes would have been *Liberation* and *Ecstasy*, and the nine smaller panels would have included *Balance, Order*, and *Rhythm* (to which Tack refers by title), and some combination of *Allegro, Andante, Largo*, possibly the panel *Orchid (Violet and Green ?)*, and either *Outposts of Time I* or *II*. Although Tack had written Phillips on January 31, 1930, that he was just finishing "the last panel of your series . . . the fourth of the end paintings . . . expressing the borderlands of Eternity," in his March 2 letter he explained that he did not send "the new panel," the last outpost of time, because it was out of scale and needed repainting. The constant alterations of the titles, as well as their frequent designation by colors in the correspondence, prevents a definitive identification of each panel in the original scheme. For example, Tack and Phillips referred to *Allegro* and *Andante* as *Orange and Yellow* and *Blue Violet and Red Violet* well into the 1930s, designating other works by colors. On October 10, 1930, Phillips wrote Tack that he planned to come to his New York studio to view the new decorations; on October 22, 1930, Phillips wrote Tack, "You are to send at once the two new lunettes, the blue one and the red one [*Flight* and *Far Reaches*] . . . . we agree that they complete both the symbolism and the decoration of the library." Tack was at work on *Aspiration* by March 8, 1931, per correspondence, and had completed it by August, when it was sent to an exhibition in Indianapolis (AVT to DP, August 20, 1931).

12. The architectural setting is described in Tack's handwritten "Notes on Decorative Panels" and in Phillips's essay, "Decorative Panels by Augustus Vincent Tack," in the flyer for the 1929–30 exhibition, "The Second Tri-Unit Exhibition of the Season of 1929–30 of The Phillips Memorial Gallery," apparently published mid-March 1930 (DP to Aida Rainey, March 12, 1930). The essay is reprinted in two subsequent pamphlets, *Decorative Panels by Augustus Vincent Tack* (1930) and *Appreciations by Duncan Phillips of the Decorative Panels by Augustus Vincent Tack* (1932). The text also appears in "Our Exhibitions: Decorative Panels of Augustus Vincent Tack," *Art and Understanding* 1, no. 2 (March 1930): 244–49.

13. Tack sketched a diagram showing the sequence of *Balance, Order*, and *Rhythm* in a letter of January 9, 1930. Later that year, Phillips wrote Tack that he had hung the pictures "exactly as you planned the scheme" with "the two primeval Out-posts at the ends," flanking the above pictures (October 29, 1930). The east wall, with its windows, would not accommodate an installation, while the west wall afforded the space for a nearly complete hanging. As the scheme for permanent decoration became uncertain, the artist may have been discouraged from prescribing a specific plan. In his October 29 letter, Phillips wrote Tack that he had "hung [*Flight* (*Fugue*) and *Far Reaches*] in the two spaces between the window where they lead up to the grand climax of *Liberation*," a tradition that has continued to the present.

14. *Largo* may have been intended as one of the four corner paintings symbolizing the "borderlands of eternity." Phillips observed that *Largo* "has no mate among the other panels and stands outside of the decoration of the lower gallery"(DP to AVT, October 29, 1930). *Aspiration* was intended for "the space in the North Library transept across the windows" (AVT to DP, August 20, 1931).

15. The formal analyses in this essay are based on extensive consultation with Elizabeth Steele, painting conservator at The Phillips Collection, who conducted an exhaustive evaluation of the artist's methods and materials. See her "Technical Notes," in this catalogue.

16. *Marouflage* involved preparing the canvas on an auxiliary support and gluing it directly to the wall. Tack frequently used the process in his civic and religious murals.

17. *Aspiration* is the only work not canvas mounted on board. Once it became clear that the lunettes would hang not in a high, dark, vaulted ceiling but on the walls of the existing room in daylight, Phillips asked Tack to remove the golden spandrels (DP to AVT, January 24, 1930). Tack complied, covering the gold with flesh-colored paint on all but *Flight* and *Far Reaches* (AVT to DP, January 26, 1930). He perhaps anticipated that they would hang alongside the windows and would not be seen in direct natural light.

18. Tack brought to the mural cycle something of the pedagogical idealism of earlier civic projects, in particular the plan for the Nebraska State Capitol building, completed in 1927, with a philosophical program created by Hartley Burr Alexander. It, too, encompassed a universal theme exalting life and art, the stages of life, and the passage of time. Its structure—barrel-vaulted with lunettes—was similar to the plan for the gallery, and it was completed with an abstraction entitled *Cosmic Energy*.

19. Phillips, "The Artist Sees Differently," Trowbridge lecture delivered at Yale University, New Haven, Connecticut, March 20, 1931, 13.

20. Neoplatonic philosophy, which originated in the third century, merges the rational ideology of Plato with Christian mysticism. It saw a full-scale revival in the Renaissance and again in the nineteenth century.

Loyola's quotation appears in the front of Tack's typescript of 1941, "Reflections on Pictures. Some Painted and Some Unpainted," collection of Joseph Peter Spang III, Deerfield, Massachusetts.

21. Phillips's several amplifications on "Notes on Decorative Panels" are enumerated above. Tack provides a more general exegesis on his approach to abstract painting in "A Note on Subjective Painting," *Art and Understanding* 1, no. 2 (March

1930): 240–43 and "Two Definitions of Art," *American Magazine of Art* 21 (October 1930): 576–78. Tack and the artist Thornton Oakley delivered the latter as an address to the American Federation of Arts, Washington, D.C., May 16, 1930.

22. Tack, "Notes on Decorative Panels."

23. Ibid.

24. AVT to DP, June 22, 1937, in a reprise of his outline of the cycle's philosophical significance.

25. Phillips, "The Modern Argument in Art and Its Answer," *A Bulletin of the Phillips Memorial Gallery*, October 1931–January 1932, 49. Both *Outposts of Time I* and *II* have as their source the landscape of Tack's 1922–23 painting, *Rosa Mystica* (Cleveland Museum of Art), possibly itself a quotation from *The Crowd*. The forms recur throughout the 1922–23 series, never with the monolithic stature they attain here.

26. *Liberation* was derived from a photographic source, and the same source was enlarged for *Aspiration*, which corresponds to the lower left area of *Liberation*. *Flight* (*Fugue*), in turn, derives from a segment of *Liberation* blown up and turned upside down, while *Far Reaches* repeats and enlarges this latter motif. Examination by Elizabeth Steele (September 27, 1992) reveals that beneath the freely created figures of *The Crowd* lies an underpainting of abstracted forms, a scaffolding visible on the far right of the composition. Pinholes throughout the canvas may indicate the transferral of imagery.

27. Phillips, "The Abstract Decorations of Tack," in the catalogue for The Phillips Memorial Gallery's 1943 exhibition, "The Abstract Decorations of Augustus Vincent Tack," n.p.

28. The same drawing or photograph Tack used for *The Crowd* may have served as the substructure for such Music Room panels as *Liberation* and *Ecstasy*. The general drift and sweep of forms in *The Crowd* corresponds to those in the large panels, notably the left sides of *Liberation* and *Ecstasy*. Tack had also employed sections of *The Crowd* in the 1922–24 series, including *The Voice of Many Waters* (cat. 27) and *Storm* (cat. 25).

29. A source for *Largo* has not been determined but may also be *The Crowd*. *Blue Oval* (cat. 46) and *Pink Oval* (by 1933, private collection) appear to be Tack's last works deriving from *The Crowd*.

30. A tracing or drawing from the painting (or from preparatory sketches) would be projected onto a wall, where an attached canvas or tracing paper could serve as a guide to the artist in filling in forms for the painting. This method was common, but not exclusive, to muralists; Arthur Dove is said to have used pantograph or slide projection to enlarge his sketches of nature into painting. See Sasha Newman, *Arthur Dove and Duncan Phillips: Artist and Patron* (Washington and New York: The Phillips Collection and George Braziller, 1981), 27, n. 64.

31. Tack's response to the western landscape is recorded in a letter to Royal Cortissoz of August 2, 1920, cited in Eleanor Green, *Augustus Vincent Tack 1870–1949: Twenty-Six Paintings from The Phillips Collection* (Austin: University of Texas, 1972), 17. Tack's assistant of four years (1925–29), William Wilfrid Bayne, sent a typescript (finished by hand), "My Association with Augustus Vincent Tack," to the American Studies Group in 1967 (American Studies Group Archives, Deerfield Academy, Deerfield, Massachusetts; quotation from p. 5). The memoir is extensively quoted in the academy students' American Studies Group exhibition catalogue, *Augustus Vincent Tack: 1870–1949* (Deerfield, Mass.: Hilson Gallery, Deerfield Academy, 1968), 14–17.

The snapshots may have been taken by Tack's son Robert rather than by the artist himself. The "professional" photographer who blew the photographs up was probably Louis Dreyer, a New York commercial photographer whom Tack used throughout the 1920s.

32. Bayne, "My Association with Augustus Vincent Tack," 5–6.

33. For *Aspiration*, Tack apparently relied on projection, as there is no sign of pouncing. Pounce marks are visible on both *Far Reaches* and *Flight* (*Fugue*).

34. Study of the "cloud" shapes would seem to indicate that these forms were adapted from light on the land masses, the masses themselves edited out. This argues for several sources for the tiered segments of these paintings.

35. DP to AVT, January 23, 1930. Phillips later changed his mind, writing to Tack, "This decoration is my special favorite of them all" (January 24, 1930). The reproduction of *Ecstasy* appearing in *Art and Understanding* shows the painting in an earlier state, before, for example, painted lines were added in the center of the panel (*Art and Understanding* 1, no. 2 [March 1930]: opp. 244.

36. Phillips, *Decorative Panels by Augustus Vincent Tack*, n.p. He continued, "although without any literary allusions, and without any program notes at all," a later alteration of the actual facts due to the unfashionably "literary" and allegorical nature of these notes.

37. Inness, quoted in "A Painter on Painting," *Harper's New Monthly Magazine* 56 (February 1878): 458, cited in Michael Quick, "The Late Style in Context," in *George Inness* (Los Angeles: Los Angeles County Museum of Art, 1985), 47.

38. In 1931, Phillips noted in "The Artist's Choice" that Tack's murals for Winnipeg and Nebraska and numerous churches "interrupted the artist's daring inventions of ten years ago" (*The Artist Sees Differently* [New York and Washington: E. Weyhe and Phillips Memorial Gallery, 1931]), 134.

39. See Mecklenburg, "Issues in Avant-Garde Aesthetics," in *American Aesthetic Theory*, 117; Wright's observation—"the every-day action of our lives, the ability to perceive order in the seasons, is only a reflection in man of his own organization and unity"—from "The Forum Exhibition," *Forum* 55 (April 1916): 469, is cited in Mecklenburg, *American Aesthetic Theory*, 129. The citations from Wright on ecstasy and order from chaos are from Wright, *Modern Painting* (New York: John Lane Company, 1915), 10, 278. For Scriabin, see Leonid Sabaneiev, "Scriabin's 'Prometheus,'" in *The Blaue Reiter Almanac*, ed. Wassily Kandinsky and Franz Marc (new documentary edition ed. Klaus Lankheit) (New York: Da Capo Press, 1989), 127–40.

40. Tack's association with musicians in Deerfield and his piano playing are recorded by Margaretta B. Sander in an interview with Elizabeth Fuller, a descendant of Violet Fuller, for the exhibition catalogue *Augustus Vincent Tack 1870–1949: Loan Exhibition of Seventeen Abstract Paintings From The Phillips Collection* (Kingston, R.I.: University of Rhode Island Fine Arts Center Main Gallery, 1973).

41. Tack, "Subjective Painting," 242. Phillips had referred to rhythm as the "origins of emotion, and of the arts" ("Rhythm and the Arts," MS 74 [1915], TPC Archives). At the time, Phillips was reading Charles Caffin on Matisse; he writes on page 2, "Rhythm is Balance." Tack's titles *Rhythm*, *Order*, and *Balance* correspond closely with the painter and theorist Denman Ross's title for his 1907 treatise, *A Theory of Pure Design: Harmony, Balance, Rhythm*. Phillips owned the 1933 edition of Ross's book (New York: P. Smith). Tack's first remark on "essential rhythm" is found in an August 8, 1922, letter to Kraushaar (Kraushaar Galleries Archives).

42. An article on an address Tack gave at the John Herron Institute of Art in late October 1931 reported: "As a young man . . . he resented the smug feeling that music was the only absolute art, and dreamed of being able to present absolute and pure art in terms of color and canvas" (". . . Describes Expression of Musical Ideas in Art," *Indianapolis News*, scrapbooks, Indianapolis Museum of Art). Another early record of his strong feeling for music is found in his painting, *The Listeners, (Momente Musicale)* (1899–1900, Newark Museum), in which three people listening to music each experience a different level of emotional "awakening." This painting illustrates Tack's preoccupation with the power of art "to move men like music."

43. Journal L, 1914, n.p. Tack's comments are from ". . .Describes Expression of Musical Ideas in Art."

44. Phillips, "A Collection Still in the Making," in *Artist Sees Differently*, 18.

45. The program harkens back to a nineteenth-century impulse toward a unity of all the arts in the synesthetic urges of symbolism. The German romantic composer Wagner strove to eradicate the boundaries of art, drama, and music as embodied in the concept of *gesmentheswerke*— a "total work of art."

46. Phillips, "Original American Painting of Today," *Formes* 21 (January 1932): 197.

47. On Pratt, see AVT to DP, September 4, 1930. For Phillips's efforts on Tack's behalf at the Museum of Modern Art, see Furth, "Augustus Vincent Tack: A Mystic's Journey to Abstraction," n. 133, in this catalogue.

48. *Art News* 28 (November 23, 1929), 13; Cortissoz, "A Landscape Painter with a New Vision: Two Able Artists; Recent Works by Edward and Augus-

tus V. Tack," *New York Herald Tribune*, November 24, 1929, 10; Karl Nierendorf to DP, December 18, 1943. For Marin, see DP to Edward Alden Jewell, April 4, 1930; Phillips cited de Segonzac's impressions of Tack's panels in the flyer (and pamphlets reprinted from it) for "The Second Tri-Unit Exhibition of the Season of 1929–1930, of The Phillips Memorial Gallery," n.p.

49. DP to AVT, April 15, 1930; Mechlin, "Notes of Art and Artists: Tack Panels at Phillips Memorial Gallery," *Sunday Star*, (Washington), November 16, 1930, sec. 7, 19.

50. DP to AVT, May 24, 1934. I would like to thank David Scott for sharing his keen understanding of Phillips's evolution as a museum director and a collector with me.

51. Throughout the correspondence of the early 1930s he encourages the mixed hangings, referring to these and other modern painters. The hanging records reflect similar groups.

52. DP to AVT, June 18, 1937; AVT to DP, June 22, 1937.

Leslie Furth with Vivien Greene

Chronology

1870

November 9: Augustus Vincent Tack is born to Theodore Edward Tack and Mary Cosgrave Tack in Pittsburgh, one of fourteen children. His father is a founder and director of the American Oil Development Company.

1883

The Tack family moves to New York City, to 118 W. 82nd Street. The family firm is expanded and renamed Tack Brothers Oil Company.

Autumn: Augustus Vincent Tack, whose family is Catholic, is enrolled in the Jesuit school, St. Francis Xavier College, in Chelsea, New York, where he studies until 1890.

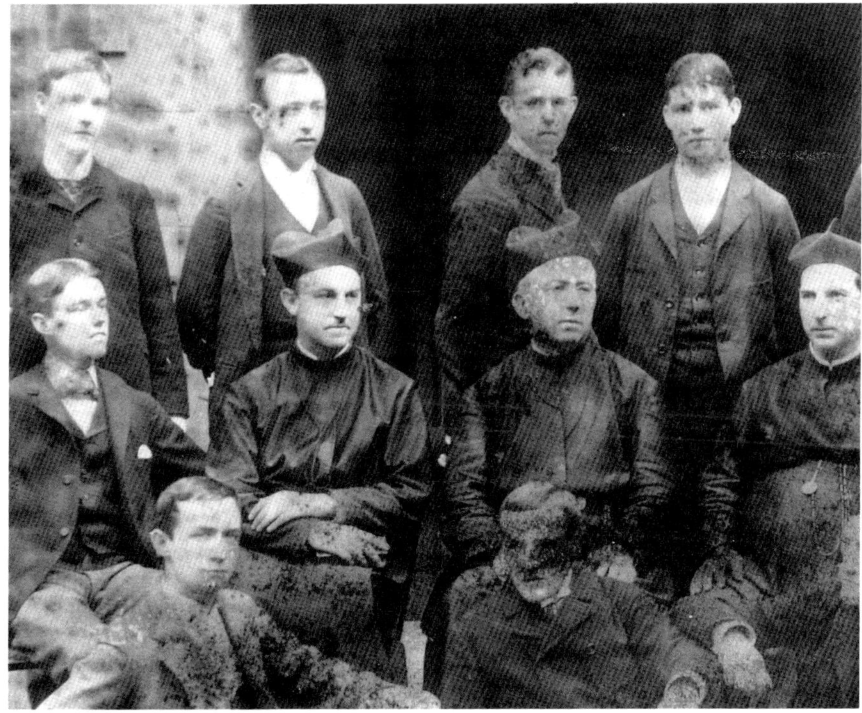

Augustus Vincent Tack with Jesuit instructors, late 1880s, Saint Francis Xavier High School, New York

1890

Spring: He graduates from St. Francis Xavier College with a bachelor of arts degree.

Summer: Tack visits France, traveling to the Basque region and to the French Alps.

Autumn: Tack's name first appears on the student register of the Art Students League in New York, where he studies until 1895, probably beginning as a student in John Twachtman's antique class.[1]

1893

April: Tack exhibits for the first time, submitting a painting, *Day Dreams*, to New York's Society of American Artists' fifteenth annual exhibition.

Summer: He travels again to France where he paints a landscape and several watercolors.

Autumn: Tack spends the next two years studying from life in the ASL class of figure painter and muralist H. Siddons Mowbray (1858–1928).

1894

Tack establishes a studio in New York City at Van Dyck Studios, 939 8th Avenue, where he works until 1901. He lists himself in the city directory as a portrait painter.

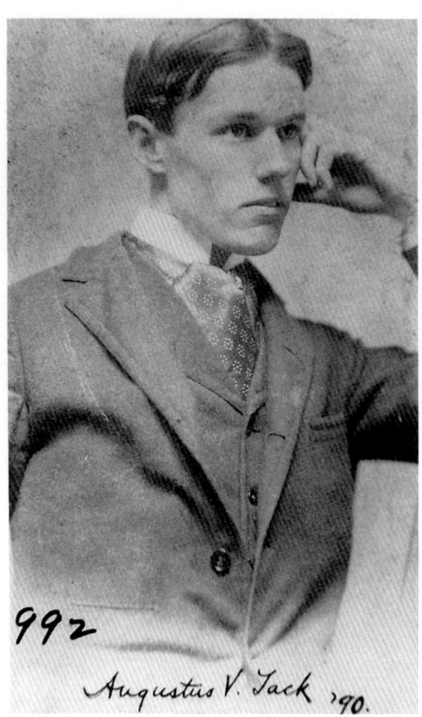

Tack at twenty, school photograph, 1890, Saint Francis Xavier High School, New York

1895

April: Tack departs for Europe and arrives in Paris on April 25. He applies for a passport at the French embassy, along with fellow ASL student Bryson Burroughs. His temporary address is 24 rue Cassette, in the sixth arrondissement, Saint Germain.[2]

April–May: He exhibits at the National Academy of Design.

Summer: In Normandy, he paints *Woman Sitting at Window* and *Girl in Sabots.* By August, he is back in New England.

December: The Pennsylvania Academy of the Fine Arts accepts one of his portraits.

1896

Tack submits a painting to the Carnegie Institute's annual exhibition, which is rejected; this is the first of many such submissions with some twenty rejections and nine acceptances between 1896 and 1913.

March: Kraushaar Galleries gives Tack his first one-person show, including portraits, landscapes and compositions. Charles Kraushaar was later to become Tack's dealer.

1897

Summer: Tack and fellow artists Ruel Crompton Tuttle and Edward McDowell sojourn in Deerfield, Massachusetts, where an artist's colony grew around the legacy of the painter George Fuller. There Tack meets Agnes (Violet) Gordon Fuller, an artist and Fuller's daughter , whom he begins courting.[3] He may begin John La Farge's portrait as early as this year, finishing it in 1900 with the aid of sittings and a photograph.[4]

1898

January–February: Tack is represented in the Boston Arts Club exhibition, showing there every two years until 1905, and submitting in 1906 for the last time.

Tack has three paintings, *Maid Marion, Master Frank* and *Portrait of Madame H(igginson?),* accepted at the Carnegie Institute, juried that year by J. Alden Weir, John Twachtman, and William M. Chase, among others. The latter portrait, probably of Violet's mother, is considered for honors.

1899

ca. 1899: Tack probably receives a letter from John La Farge in this period, announcing that the painting he sent to the Society of American Artists, of which La Farge was the president, was conferred a "Number One rating," earning the place of honor.[5]

October: In Deerfield, Tack has contact with the Allen sisters, photographers of landscape and figures, an encounter that may have borne fruit in his later uses of photography.

November: The painting he submits for the Paris exhibition passes the first jury but is rejected by a second, a disappointment eased by his first mural commission, to decorate a private home.[6] Two works by Tack are included in a group show at the Art Institute of Chicago.

December: Tack's admiration for Fuller and for Duvenek's portraiture is strengthened by a Boston exhibition.

1900

Tack establishes a studio in Greenfield, Massachusetts, which he maintains until 1907.

January: At Chase's Gallery, Boston, Tack's portrait, *Maid Marion,* draws favorable notice in the press. Tack completes a portrait of an old priest, reputedly a cousin of James McNeill Whistler. Tack writes to Violet that his *Portrait of George Washington Cable in His Study* receives the place of honor in the Pennsylvania Academy of Fine Arts exhibition in Philadelphia.[7]

March: Tack submits portraits to the Society of American Artists which are all "more ambitious than anything I have hitherto sent." One is rejected because it is "too flat and not modelled solidly"—a struggle with form that marked Tack's early career.

April 19: Tack is nominated for membership in the Architectural League by Bryson Burroughs. He is listed as a decorator in the Architectural League Annual from 1900 through 1908.[8]

May: Tack mentions his private art collection, which includes a number of Japanese prints, the first evidence of his lifelong passion for Asian art.

June 19: Fuller and Tack are married in Deerfield. The Tacks subsequently set up house there, and Tack divides his time between this home and New York.

1901

Spring: Tack moves his New York studio to the Holbein Studios, 152 W. 55th Street.

June 3: The Tacks' first child, Agnes, is born, while Tack undergoes an appendectomy.

July: In Deerfield, Tack hosts a successful studio show.

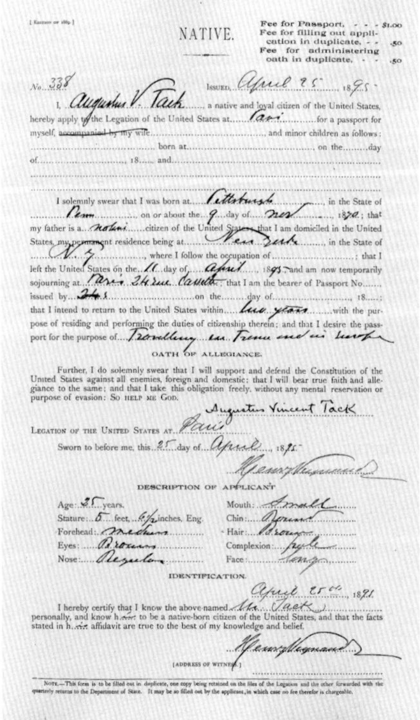

NATIVE.

Fee for Passport, - - - $1.00
Fee for filling out application in duplicate, - - .50
Fee for administering oath in duplicate, - - .50

No. 338 Issued, April 25 1895.

I, Augustus V. Tack, a native and loyal citizen of the United States, hereby apply to the Legation of the United States at Paris for a passport for myself, ~~accompanied by my wife~~ .... and minor children as follows: .... born at ...., on the .... day of ...., 18.... and ....

I solemnly swear that I was born at Pittsburgh, in the State of Penn on or about the 9 day of Nov, 1870; that my father is a native citizen of the United States; that I am domiciled in the United States, my permanent residence being at New York, in the State of N.Y., where I follow the occupation of ....; that I left the United States on the 11 day of April, 1895, and am now temporarily sojourning at Paris 24 rue Cassette; that I am the bearer of Passport No. .... issued by .... on the .... day of ...., 18....; that I intend to return to the United States within two years with the purpose of residing and performing the duties of citizenship therein; and that I desire the passport for the purpose of Travelling in France and in Europe

OATH OF ALLEGIANCE.

Further, I do solemnly swear that I will support and defend the Constitution of the United States against all enemies, foreign and domestic; that I will bear true faith and allegiance to the same; and that I take this obligation freely, without any mental reservation or purpose of evasion: So help me God.

Augustus Vincent Tack

Legation of the United States at Paris

Sworn to before me, this 25 day of April, 1895.

[signature]

DESCRIPTION OF APPLICANT

Age: 25 years.	Mouth: Small
Stature: 5 feet, 6½ inches, Eng.	Chin: Round
Forehead: Medium	Hair: Brown
Eyes: Brown	Complexion: Pale
Nose: Regular	Face: Long

IDENTIFICATION.

April 25th, 1895

I hereby certify that I know the above named Mr. Tack personally, and know him to be a native-born citizen of the United States, and that the facts stated in his affidavit are true to the best of my knowledge and belief.

[signature]

(Address of witness.)

Note.—This form is to be filled out in duplicate, one copy being retained on the files of the Legation and the other forwarded with the quarterly returns to the Department of State. It may be so filled out by the applicant, in which case no fee therefor is chargeable.

Tack's emergency passport application made in Paris, April 1895, National Archives, Washington, D.C.

1902

The Art Students League votes Tack a life member.

November: The Doll and Richards gallery of Boston holds a one-person show of Tack's portraits and landscapes.

1903

January: Tack completes a portrait of Thomas Wentworth Higginson of Cambridge, Violet Tack's uncle. This is one of the many commissions Tack would receive through the connection established by his marriage to Violet.

Winter: The Worcester Art Museum hosts an exhibition of Tack's portraits, giving them prominent gallery space.

1904

ca. 1904: Tack begins a relationship with the prominent American art gallery of William Macbeth that continues intermittently throughout his life.[9]

March 2: Robert Tack is born.

1905

August: Tack travels with his family to Cohasset, Massachusetts, where he paints outdoors.

1906

Autumn: Tack begins teaching a portrait class at the Art Students League and continues there until 1910.[10]

1907

November: William Macbeth hosts a one-person exhibition of Tack's landscapes in New York.

1908

Tack takes a new New York studio, at 7 W. 42nd Street, Room 33.

Violet Tack enters a sanatorium in Saranac Lake, New York, for treatment of tuberculosis and remains until 1913. Tack visits her frequently, painting the surrounding landscape and portraits of Saranac society.

December: Tack exhibits for the first time at the Corcoran Gallery of Art's annual American paintings exhibition, showing there again in 1910.

1909

May: He paints the artist and critic Arthur Hoeber's (1854–1915) portrait upon the latter's acceptance into the National Academy.

Summer: Tack visits the Adirondacks, where the scenery provides inspiration for his landscape painting.

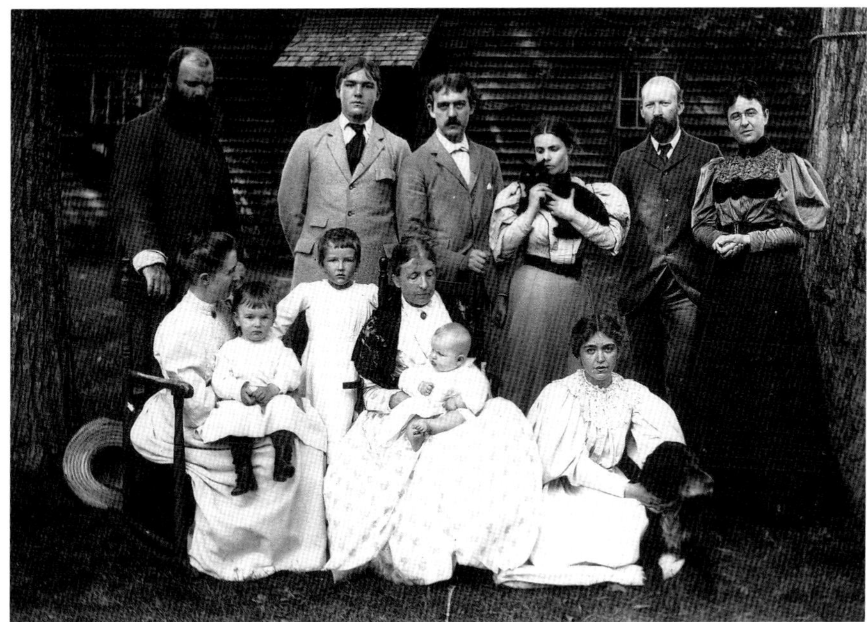

The Fuller family outside George Fuller's studio at The Bars, Deerfield, 1895. Violet is seated at right with the dog. Fuller-Arms Photograph Collection, Pocumtuck Valley Memorial Association, Deerfield, Mass.

1910

May 28: Tack attends a dinner in honor of the artist James Carroll Beckwith (1852–1917) at the Players Club, given by former students and friends.[11]

Autumn: Tack joins the faculty of the Yale School of Fine Arts as instructor in painting. He teaches there until 1913 and is awarded an honorary bachelor of fine arts degree at the age of forty-two.

1911

February: The Connecticut Academy of Fine Arts organizes a three-person exhibition of Tack, Hermann Dudley Murphy, and William Baxter Closson; the show travels to St. Louis and Detroit.

1912

Tack joins the Connecticut Academy of Fine Arts, retaining his membership until about 1919.

April: Tack exhibits for the first time at the New Haven Paint and Clay Club, becoming an active member and serving occasionally on the jury.

October: The society magazine *Delineator* publishes Tack's portrait of Mrs. Hotchkiss Ely of Saranac on its cover.

1913

January: The collector and wine merchant Alexander Morten and his wife visit Tack's studio, possibly seeing *Eve's Remorse*, which they later purchase. Tack executes a portrait of Mrs. Morten for her family in England.

Autumn: Tack teaches an extramural color class under the auspices of New York University, resuming the position the following season.[12]

November: Championed by the artist James Carroll Beckwith, Tack becomes a member of the Century Association. He is active on numerous committees and as a contributor to exhibitions until the end of his life.[13]

1914

Duncan Phillips's first impressions of Tack's painting are recorded in a handwritten essay, indicating that the young collector made a studio visit as early as 1914.[14]

November: Jessie Lemont writes "Old Subjects in New Vestments," which appears in *International Studio*, highlighting Tack's recent cycle of religious paintings.

December: Tack's first mention of Duncan Phillips occurs in his correspondence; Tack visits him in Washington, D.C., for the first time.

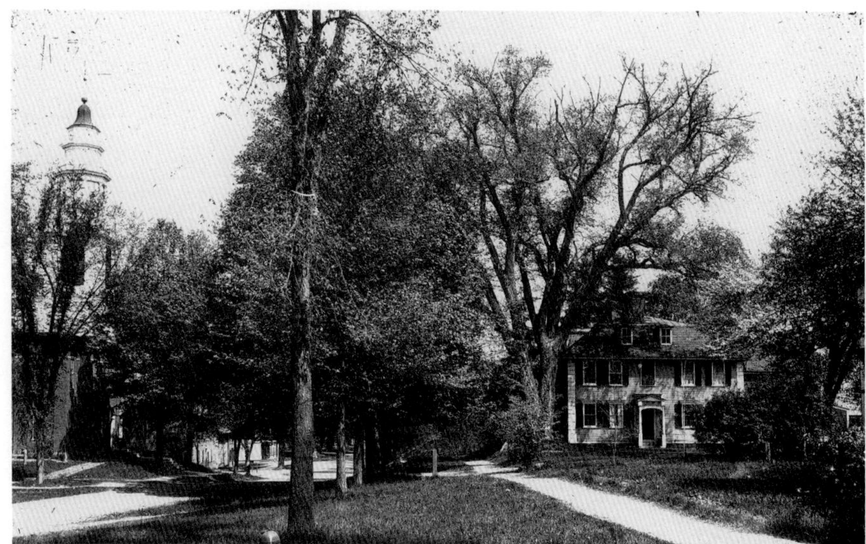

Allen Sisters, *The Street, Deerfield*, from an original platinum print, collection of Pocumtuck Valley Memorial Association Library, Deerfield, Mass.

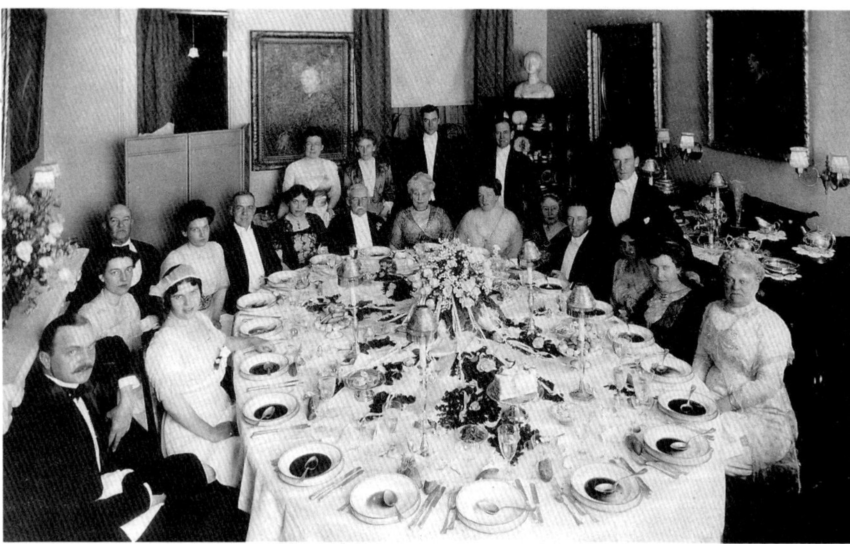

A Tack family celebration, ca. 1914, The Phillips Collection Archives

1915

February–March: Edgar Worch's New York gallery exhibits Tack's recent work which draws his first significant critical attention. The press notes his pointillist technique and the work's religious and mystical content.

Summer: Tack's *Portrait of John La Farge*, on tour with the American Federation of Arts exhibition of American portrait painters, draws public notice.

1916

March: Duncan Phillips publishes "The Romance of a Painter's Mind" in *International Studio* and becomes a champion of the artist. An intimate friendship begins that would prove vital to Tack's sustenance and artistic evolution throughout his life.

An exhibition of Tack's works opens at Kraushaar, marking the commencement of a fruitful association. Tack would show new works here every year into the early 1920s.

April: Phillips commissions Tack to paint his brother, James Laughlin Phillips.

1917

February–March: Tack sells six paintings from his annual show at Kraushaar Galleries, several to Phillips. *New York Tribune* critic Royal Cortissoz notes in a February 20 article that he is "feeling his way toward a really personal means of expression."

April: Championed by fellow Centurion Vladimir Simkhovitch, a connoisseur of Asian art and a prominent historian, Tack creates his first public mural decorations, for Greenwich House, the settlement house in lower Manhattan founded by Simkhovitch's wife, Mary.

December: Tack participates in the war effort by painting camouflage for the government on battleships and fabric and donating work to Art War Relief.

1918

Tack becomes a member of The Coffee House, an informal group of "painters, writers, sculptors, architects, actors and members of other professions" in New York, whose members include Childe Hassam, Herbert Hoover, Charles Dana Gibson, Cole Porter, and P. G. Wodehouse.

February: The annual Kraushaar exhibition of Tack's work again attracts notice, and critics observe the influence of "chinoiserie" on his work. Tack receives his first commission for a large secular mural project for the walls of the Legislative Chamber at the Manitoba state capitol in Winnipeg, Canada. The design for the cycle is a collaborative effort, with architect Frank W. Simon's original 1913 program serving as a basis.

December: Together with Duncan Phillips and the collector Albert Gallatin, Tack organizes "The Allied War Salon," in support of artists abroad, shown at Madison Square Garden and then at the Carnegie Institute. Tack contributes several works. His further efforts for the war include the mounting of the Fifth Avenue Shop Window Display of paintings for the Fourth Liberty Loan Drive.

1919

February: Royal Cortissoz reviews Tack's Kraushaar show in the February 2 *New York Tribune*. He finds him "in splendid form" and compares his decorative conceptions with Arthur Davies and Arnold Böecklin. He faults only the pointillist method as "too assertive."

May: The first mention of Tryon, North Carolina, occurs. There, on the South Carolina border, not far from Asheville, the Tacks purchase a horse ranch where they spend many summers, occasionally with the Phillipses as their guests.

June: Tack repaints *Court of Romance* on a larger scale for Phillips.

1920

March: Tack organizes the Julian Alden Weir exhibition at the Century Association. He visits Duncan Phillips in Washington, D.C.; as the friendship develops, his visits become more frequent. He attends shows of both Twachtman and Kent in New York, the latter perhaps at Phillips's behest. He finds Kent's work "full of imagination and much beauty."

April: Tack installs the finished panels in the Legislative Chamber in the capitol at Winnipeg to critical acclaim. The Winnipeg *Free Press* devotes several pages to the new capitol and its decoration, and Royal Cortissoz pronounces Tack "an artist of originality and power who is breaking new ground."

July: At the first meeting to incorporate the Phillips Memorial Art Gallery, Tack is invited to serve as vice-president and trustee and is elected to membership in the corporation.

August: Tack and his family travel through the Rockies, from Winnipeg to Banff and Lake Louise, and from Revelstoke to the Arrow Lakes and through the Kootenay Pass into Montana.

December: Phillips negotiates for Tack to paint the statesman Elihu Root's portrait.

1921

Tack rents studio space in the southwest corner of Grand Central Station, sharing an expansive, light-filled room in the attic with the muralist Ezra Winter, with mural commissions in mind. "He would often retreat [there] when he sought to escape Deerfield and dedicate himself wholeheartedly to his work."

ca. 1921: John B. Ferguson, a trustee of the Hagerstown Museum of Fine Arts in Maryland, meets Tack and they become friends. Ferguson introduces him to Hagerstown society, and Tack paints numerous portraits there.

February: He is elected vice-chairman of the Phillips Memorial Art Gallery's "Committee on Scope & Plan" for one year, and his role soon expands to other committees, including those for publications, interior decoration, drama, music, and lectures, and financial resources.

March: His role as advisor to Duncan Phillips on the purchase of new works strengthens, and Phillips writes Tack on March 11: "I need you very much . . . to advise me and help me with the hanging of the pictures . . . .[This] needs to be done with that unfailing sense of the ensemble which you have always shown."

May: Tack receives his first significant religious mural commission, to decorate the Church of the Paulist Fathers in New York. The church's walls are already adorned with the murals of John La Farge.

June: Phillips publishes an "Inventory of the Phillips Memorial Art Gallery" that includes fourteen Tack works, more than any other artist.[15]

1922

Tack helps Phillips to compile material for *An Appreciation of the Life and Works of J. Alden Weir*, contributing a letter in which he reminisces about his brief contact with Weir when the older artist oversaw a ranking of student drawings at the ASL.

Marjorie and Duncan Phillips commission Tack to paint their portraits, while his earlier *Portrait of James L. Phillips* is accepted by the Phillips Memorial Gallery as a gift.

March: To enhance Tack's reputation, Phillips purchases his religious painting *In the House of Matthew* from the Kraushaar exhibition and donates it to the Metropolitan Museum of Art.

April: The Tacks travel to northern California for Easter.

August: Tack writes to his dealer from Deerfield, "I have been having a quiet summer here painting everyday. . . . I have been developing some compositions of form and color based on essential rhythm and to my mind they are the most interesting things I have so far accomplished. They are abstractly decorative . . . combining a deep mystical meaning which stimulates the imagination."

December: Tack returns to California, spending the holidays in Santa Barbara.

1923

February: Tack contributes an essay for the "Centennial Exhibition of the Works of George Fuller" for the Metropolitan Museum of Art.[16] Press coverage of Tack's annual Kraushaar exhibition highlights his increasingly abstract imagery. Kraushaar writes Phillips of the exhibition's success, "Mr. Tack's pictures are attracting a great deal of attention."

May: Encouraged by Duncan Phillips, the director of the Cleveland Museum of Art purchases Tack's recent canvas, *Rosa Mystica.*

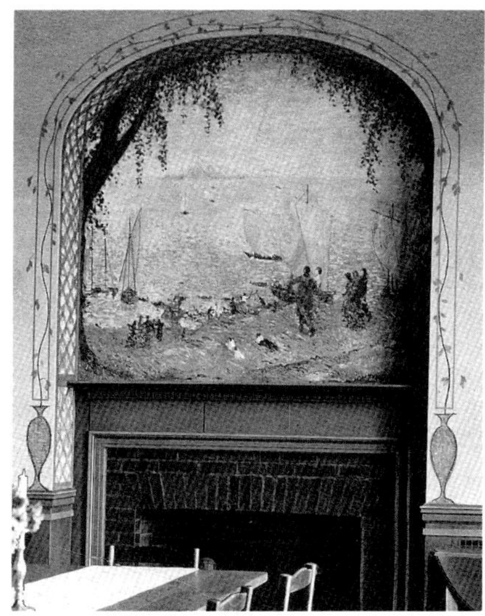

The common room of Greenwich House, New York City, with Tack's mural in place, ca. 1917 Tamiment Institute Library. New York University: Greenwich House Collection

August: Tack sets sail on the *President Van Buren* for Europe, embarking on a tour with his son Robert for "study and recreation," planning to visit England, France, the Netherlands, Switzerland, and Italy.[17] In Paris, he visits the sculptor and painter Antoine Bourdelle, whose work and charm impress him. He writes Kraushaar from Europe, "We are having a wonderful trip. . . . it would require a volume to write about . . . This trip should do great things to my painting—It has certainly been inspiring."

Late 1923: Phillips draws plans for a museum intended for a site on Connecticut Avenue and asks Tack to compose a series of paintings for it. Phillips's plans are never realized, but Tack's program for the new building would evolve five years later into the paintings that often adorn the Music Room.

1924

On Mrs. Fuller's death, Violet Tack inherits George Fuller's studio known as The Bars, in Deerfield's South Meadows, where Tack often worked.

February: Tack writes Phillips on February 5 of his shock at the death of Maurice Prendergast. "I was away . . . or I should have gone to his funeral. A very distinguished and individual painter—one of the few." He visits Arthur B. Davies on Phillips's behalf concerning the mono-

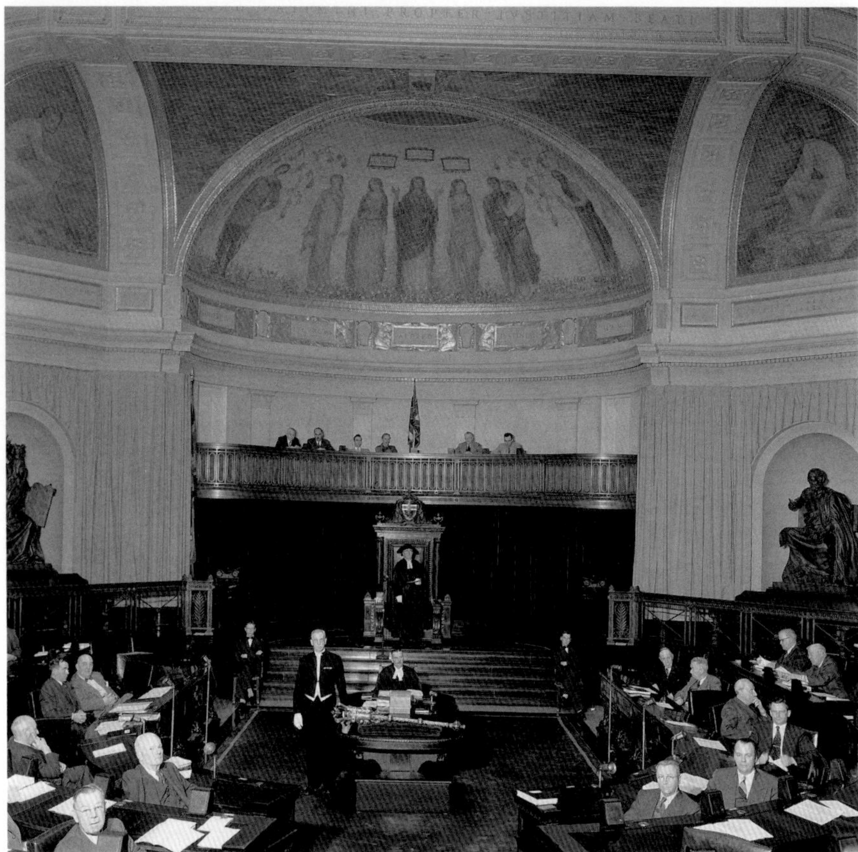

Legislative Chamber, Manitoba Legislative Building, Winnipeg, 1953, with Tack's murals, executed in 1918–19, Provincial Archives, Manitoba

graph the museum director is preparing.

March–April: Phillips hosts Tack's first one-person show at the gallery, opening the lower gallery to the public for the first time. The "Exhibition of Recent Decorative Paintings by Augustus Vincent Tack" would in Phillips's words "give [us] a clear idea of that phase of Tack's art which is most original and stimulating."

April–May: Largely through Phillips's efforts, Tack's work is shown at the Corcoran Gallery of Art.[18]

Late summer: Tack secures his second major secular mural commission, a series of decorations for the Governor's Reception Room at the state capitol in Lincoln, Nebraska.

Autumn: The Tacks travel to Italy in the autumn, where Tack makes special studies in Siena and Perugia with the Nebraska commission in mind.[19] Tack writes to Kraushaar from Venice of his enthusiasm for Giotto and for the mosaics he sees. He also mentions special trips to Siena, Perugia, Rome, and Lisieux, France.

1925

William Wilfrid Bayne, a monk from Portsmouth Priory, Rhode Island, begins as Tack's assistant, a position he holds until late 1929.

August: Tack studies blueprints of the architect's drawings for the North Library (now called the Music Room) of the Phillips Memorial Gallery in preparation for his designs for the museum's mural decorations.

Autumn: Tack travels to England. Back in America, his murals of St. Thérèse, Little Flower of Jesus, for the Church of the Paulist Fathers in New York, are unveiled.

1926

February 18: Tack is reelected vice-president of the Phillips Memorial Gallery and continues as primary advisor to Phillips. Phillips includes him in a show of modernists who were associated with Alfred Stieglitz, such as Georgia O'Keeffe, Arthur Dove, John Marin, and Marsden Hartley.

May 2: The first record of a visit between Tack and the New York collector Grenville Winthrop (1865–1943) appears in Winthrop's social calendar.[20] Winthrop later became an ardent admirer of his graphic work and traditional religious painting and saw Tack more than any other artist throughout the late 1920s and 1930s. His collection of pre-Raphaelite and European academic and romantic painting now forms the basis of the Fogg Art Museum. He entertained Tack both in his Lenox, Massachusetts, country home and in his New York townhouse, where Tack would have become acquainted with his extensive art collection.

May–June: In Newport, Tack oversees the installation of murals he created for the Chapel of the Convent of the Cenacle.

1927

Frank Jewett Mather, Jr., includes Tack in his survey, *The American Spirit in Art*, placing him in the "Recent Visionaries—The Modernists" section where he writes: "An entirely lucid mysticism gives him a place apart among contemporary painters.[21]

Plans for the new decorations of the North Library at the Phillips Memorial Gallery continue to develop.

February: Tack is awarded the Courier and Louisville Times Purchase Prize for his religious panel, *The Arrival at the Inn.*

1928

January: The mural decorations for the capitol at Lincoln are dedicated and receive an enthusiastic response from the press and public.

September: Phillips publishes an essay on the symbolism of *Mystical Crucifixion*, a painting he asks Tack to rework the same year.

December: Plans for the decoration of the library in the Phillips Memorial Gallery are solidified as Phillips sends Tack the "first payment for the work you are doing in preparation for the ultimate decoration of the Phillips Memorial Gallery's art library."

1929

January: Phillips places Tack at the top of his list of the twenty-five most important American painters.

Spring: Tack works on the preparatory panels for the library project.

October: Alfred Barr, director of the Museum of Modern Art, sees Tack's works for the first time at the Phillips Memorial Gallery and is impressed, as is the French artist de Segonzac.

November: An exhibition of the finished panels for the library opens to generally favorable reviews at Kraushaar Galleries in New York before their first showing in Washington in 1930.

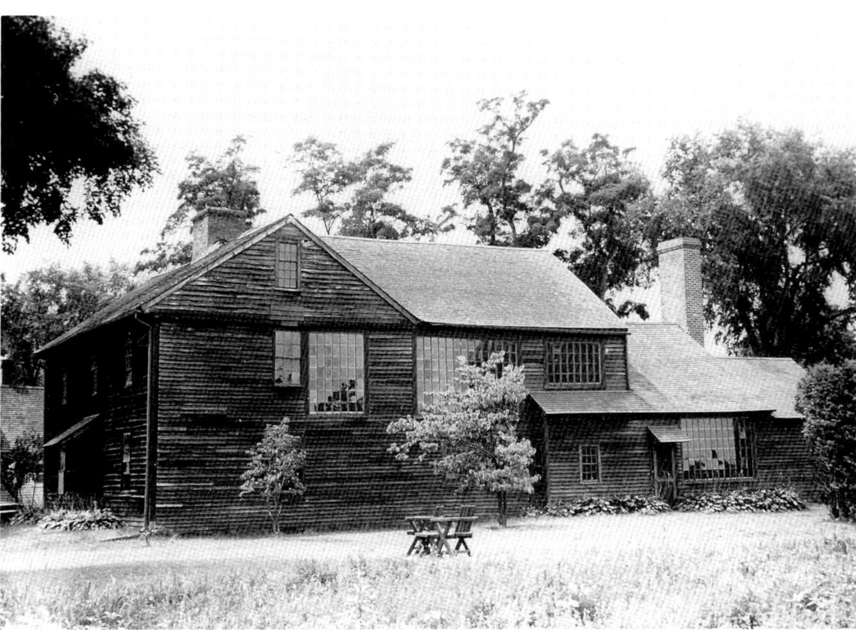

The Deerfield studio of George Fuller and subsequently Augustus Vincent Tack, ca. 1950, showing the studio's northern exposure, private collection

1930

Tack's decorative work for Phillips extends to the collector's new home on Foxhall Road, where he selects rug and paint colors to harmonize with a work he plans to execute for one of the rooms.

January: With Phillips's encouragement, Tack writes an article, "A Note on Subjective Painting," for Phillips's short-lived periodical, *Art and Understanding.* In it he makes a case for the "absolute" art of painting pure design, as a means of awakening the emotions—for Tack, the ultimate aim of art.

February: A religious panel, *Entombment,* is exhibited at the Nemzeti Salon in Budapest and, in the summer, at the Venice Biennale.

March: The Phillips Memorial Gallery exhibits Tack's panels. Phillips publishes a flyer in which he outlines the themes of the mural program and structure of the planned room where they will hang.

April: Phillips proclaims the exhibition a great success, noting John Marin's praise of Tack's color and originality.

May: Tack and fellow artist Thornton Oakley lecture at a dinner of the American Federation of Arts on "Two Definitions of Art." Their talk would be published in the *American Magazine of Art* in October. In his defense of subjective painting, Tack quotes the philosopher Jacques Maritain, artist Maurice Denis, poet and critic Roger Fry, and Leonardo da Vinci.

November: Phillips negotiates to have Tack's latest works included in the Museum of Modern Art's ninth loan exhibition of American painters, touting him as "one of the few Americans making original contributions."

1931

January: Tack has his first one-person show at the Century Association. During this month he travels to California and to Havana, Cuba.

June: Winthrop acquires nine of Tack's drawings through the Leonard Clayton Gallery. This New York gallery exhibits and purchases Tack's works throughout the thirties. The Indianapolis Art Association offers Tack a one-person exhibition of his new panels, including works from the library, in the autumn.

1932

Tack paints Winthrop's portrait, which the collector purchases the same year (*Grenville Winthrop,* Fogg Art Museum, Bequest of Grenville Winthrop).

January: Tack travels to England, where he views a French exhibition at Burlington House.

February: Phillips reissues his pamphlet on Tack's decorative panels, reflecting the addition of the monumental *Aspiration* to the lower gallery's cycle.

April: The Charles Johnson Dunlap Memorial at the First Presbyterian Church in New Rochelle, New York, for which Tack executed a mural of the Sermon on the Mount, is dedicated.

November: Tack's daughter, Agnes Gordon Tack, marries the businessman Elstner Hilton.

1933

June: Robert F. Tack marries Jean Proctor, daughter of sculptor Alexander Phimister Proctor (1862–1950), in his father's Grand Central Station studio.

August: Tack secures a commission from Ralph Adams Cram, architect of the Cathedral of St. John the Divine, to compose a study for a painting that will hang in the cathedral's All Souls Chapel. But no sponsor offers to pay for the painting itself. Instead, Winthrop buys it for his private collection (Fogg Art Museum).

1934

Tack continues to develop his life's work, the abstractions, experimenting with color and scale, between now and 1936.

March: In his efforts to procure Tack more portrait commissions, Phillips advises him in a March 24 letter to "volunteer to paint a panel for some Washington building . . . . It would give . . . conclusive proof of your capacity to get one of the big commissions and help your friends here in their efforts to overcome ultra-conservative timidity and political wire-pulling. Your Decorations in our Music Room are so abstract that it would be well to show what you can do with a figure painting on some American theme, preferably with landscape background."

April–May: In New York Tack has a major one-person exhibition of forty drawings at the Leonard Clayton Gallery as well as a large exhibition of over thirty paintings at Wildenstein's. Both receive favorable mention in the press.

1935

Tack devotes himself almost entirely to portrait painting, probably because of financial necessity. Yet he does not abandon his abstract style completely, as the expressive *Night, Amargosa Desert* demonstrates. Phillips purchases this panel shortly after it is painted.

September: Augustus and Violet Tack purchase Braeside, a large country house in Conway, Massachusetts, west of Deerfield, with 300 acres of farmland.

December: James W. Lane summarizes Tack's achievements in various genres and styles in an article for the *American Magazine of Art.*

1936

January: An exhibition of French paintings, organized by Tack, opens at the Century Association.

1937

February: On February 5, Tack writes to Phillips: "I have become more of a hermit than ever."

May–June: Phillips's experiments with various installations in the museum prompt him to propose further trades and exchanges with Tack, and he notes: "My experiment this month in combining your *Amergossa* and *Aspiration* with Van Gogh, Cezanne and Bonnard has been a huge success."

June: The final blow to the permanent installation of murals for "the Tack Room" is dealt in this year, when Phillips writes "our plans . . . have had to be indefinitely postponed since we lack both the funds . . . and the space. . . . [T]he whole plan was a beautiful dream."

July–August: An important retrospective of Tack's work is held at the Berkshire Museum, Pittsfield, Massachusetts, with a second showing held the following summer.

1938

Tack is appointed an honorary trustee of the Washington County Museum of Fine Arts.

October: Tack writes Phillips, "I have been making some experiments in painting I am most anxious to have you see," perhaps referring to his small abstract paintings, which Phillips may not yet have viewed in New York.

November–December: A retrospective exhibition of Tack's work is held in Hagerstown at the Washington County Museum of Fine Arts. Among his recent works are several small abstract paintings. A review in *Art News* states, "Despite this bewildering diversity of technical styles, there is a readily seen unity. . . . This comes from persistence of method—the artist's refusal to be limited to the representational and objective—and of subject. . . . Profound faith and a religious sense of beauty motivate much of Tack's work which ranges from . . . technique of modified pointillism, to the most recent, delicate designs . . . Chinese in character, which call to mind the quality of an antique rug."

1939

Sheldon Cheney includes Tack in a list of American abstract painters in his book, *A Primer of Modern Art,* along with Georgia O'Keeffe, Helen Torr, Raymond Jonson, and Andrew Dasburg.[22]

September: Richard Pleasant, director of the American Ballet Theater, invites Tack to create a backdrop for the choreographer Mikhail Fokine's debut ballet with the company, a production of *Les Sylphides.* Tack carries out the commission, despite Fokine's lack of enthusiasm.

1940

January 11: The American Ballet Theater opens with Tack's decor at the Center Theatre in New York; the design is based on the patterns of *Liberation.*

November 12: A dinner in honor of Tack's seventieth birthday is held at the Century Association. Phillips, Albert Gallatin, and Charles Downing Lay attend.[23]

1941

Homer Saint-Gaudens, director of the Carnegie Institute's Department of Fine Arts, publishes *The American Artist and His Times,* in which he devotes several paragraphs to Tack, describing his approach to painting taught at Yale: "Yale students have furnished a large complement of budding mural decorators to the American Academy in Rome . . . . Another onetime mentor in the Yale School and a man frequently in sympathy with and frequently opposed to the outlook of the Roman Academy is Augustus Vincent Tack. Possessed of rare culture this kindly dreamer has moved back and forth between religious designs . . . and abstract squares of vibrating pigment which have appealed greatly to the understanding of such forward-looking art patrons as Duncan Phillips in Washington. Tack has a sympathy with other years, but he is just not going to be hidebound."[24]

Tack completes a manuscript, "Reflections on Pictures. Some Painted and Some Unpainted." He dedicates the piece to the attorney Charles Stewart Davison, a fellow member of the Century Association.

January–February: A number of works are shown at the Macbeth Galleries in "Paintings and Drawings by Augustus Vincent Tack."

Spring: Tack takes a studio at the La Salle Building in Washington, D.C., across from the Mayflower Hotel, to produce wartime portraits. In the 1940s, he paints many prominent government officials, including Dwight Eisenhower, Harry Truman, Admiral William Leahy, and General George Marshall.

June: Phillips urges David Finley, director of the National Gallery of Art, to recommend Tack for a portrait commission of Chief Justice Charles Evans Hughes. Tack begins work on the painting a few months later.

July: Tack completes a portrait of Helen Keller.

November: Agnes Tack Hilton, Tack's daughter, dies in a car accident.

1942

March: Tack continues to paint numerous portraits of prominent government figures until his death. His last project, a portrait of Truman and his cabinet known as *The High Command,* was still in progress when he died.

1943

November: Grenville Winthrop bequeaths his collection, including Tack's paintings and drawings, to the Fogg Art Museum.

February: New York dealer Karl Nierendorf, one of Kandinsky's champions in America, deals briefly in Tack's work. He sells *The Crowd* to Phillips for the artist and hosts an important one-person show of recent work.

Spring: Phillips's exchanges, trades, and purchases of Tack's works continue, as he reconsiders his collection and even re-purchases works previously given up.

1944

Tack begins his final large-scale mural commission, another abstract entitled *Spirit of Creation,* for George Washington University's new auditorium.

Phillips donates Tack's recently executed portrait of Chief Justice Harlan F. Stone to the National Portrait Gallery.

March: Tack paints *The Spirit of the Hills* for Cloyd Marvin in gratitude for his backing on the George Washington University commission. Marvin later remembers: "[Tack] had asked me for my ideas [regarding the fire curtain] . . . . I told him I wanted the picture to represent 'Creation.' We then read together Genesis and ended our several meetings with [the French philosopher Henri] Bergson's *Creative Evolution.* Tack . . . took the idea from there. . . . In itself it [the mural] typifies the creative mind as Bergson portrayed it."

April 12: Tack suffers a heart attack.

1945

Tack donates a Chinese painting from his collection to the Washington County Museum of Fine Arts.

May: George Washington University honors Tack with the degree of doctor of fine arts.

1946

Spring–Summer: Tack paints several portraits for Williams College.

November: A mural for the Church of St. James in South Deerfield is in progress.

1947

January: Tack, who has been recuperating in western Maryland, grows well enough to return to Washington to paint portraits.

1948

Stephen Maniatty of Deerfield is hired as an assistant to Tack for his last commission, the triptych *The High Command.*

December: Tack enters George Washington University Hospital, and Phillips pays his expenses.

1949

February: Tack visits his exhibition, "Color Abstractions by Augustus Vincent Tack," at the Phillips Memorial Gallery. He is moved and writes to Phillips, "One is again reminded of [the composer] César Franck . . . . I would be happy if anything in the message of these paintings could be compared with the spiritual quality of his inventions . . . . You were the first to recognize me and it is to your lasting credit."

April: Tack's son, Robert, dies of complications of ulcers.

May: Tack's will reflects his great debt to Duncan Phillips: "All paintings and other objects of art owned by me at the time of my death, I give and bequeath to such museums, educational institutions or other charitable corporations . . . as my friend Duncan Phillips may appoint."

June: Tack suffers a second heart attack. His vision grows weak, which he claims is an advantage because "he was no longer bothered by non-essential details."

July 21: Tack dies in his Deerfield studio of coronary heart disease. According to Violet Tack, he was working on "the little Nativity . . . up to the morning of his death. His brushes were laid out and his paint ready to start in the morning. He simply did not wake up."

July 23: After a small funeral ceremony at St. James Church, Deerfield, attended by Phillips and family members, Tack is buried at Laurel Hill Cemetery, overlooking Deerfield.

1950

February: The depth of Tack's debt to Phillips is revealed after Augustus's death; left in great financial difficulty, his wife turns to the Phillipses, who sustain her until the end of her life. Phillips continues his lifelong campaign to enhance Tack's standing in America. "I shall continue," he wrote Violet, "as I have always done, to work for the realization of Augustus' aims and for the growth of his fame. He was very dear to me, and the paintings which I bought, 45 to be exact . . . were acquired because I loved him and wished to spread his reputation and to make his name in history and also his life secure." To this end, Phillips purchases numerous paintings from Mrs. Tack, many that are already his by deed of gift or earlier sale, and gives or sells them to other collections and museums.

1958

November: Violet Tack sends Phillips "the talking machine and the films Augustus made describing his latest pictures," vital documents on Tack's painting, which have since been lost.

1959

Upon Violet's death on September 2, the contents of the artist's studio that are not sold at auction as part of the estate come into the possession of The Phillips Collection, bringing the number of works by Tack in the museum's collection to some 260.

The remainder of the studio contents are auctioned off or destroyed, though some items, including Tack's 1941 manuscript and numerous drawings by both Tack and Fuller, are fortuitously saved by Deerfield historians.[25]

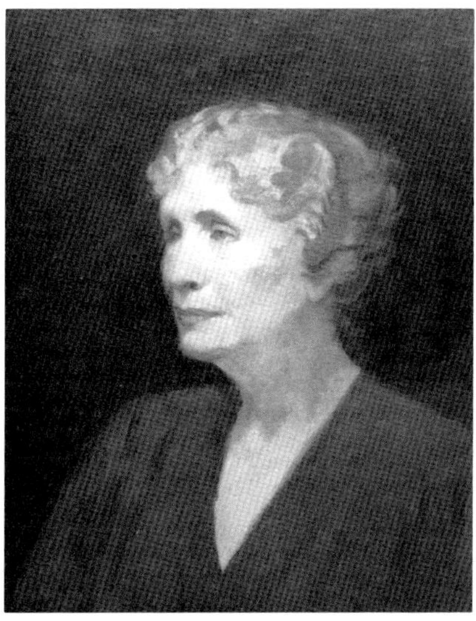

Augustus Vincent Tack, *Portrait of Helen Keller*, ca. 1944–45, Washington County Museum of Fine Arts, Hagerstown, Maryland

1968

The American Studies Group of Deerfield Academy students publishes a catalogue containing the most thorough biography, exhibition history, and list of paintings to date on Augustus Vincent Tack.

NOTES

1. Tack's name appears on the Art Students League registers for 1890–95 (Art Students League Records, reel NY 59–20, frames 371, 430, 491, 504, 576, Art Students League Papers, Archives of American Art, Smithsonian Institution, Washington, D.C. [hereafter ASL Papers]). He is elected to the Board of Control in 1892–93 (Minutes of Board of Control Meetings, reel NY 59–24A, frame 665). Tack competes for the Paris prize in 1890 (ASL Papers, reel NY 59–27, frame 635 forward). Typed petition for Chase's continued classes at ASL (ASL Papers, NY 59–29, frame 232). Tack became a member of the League in 1892, earning life membership in 1902 (ASL archivist Lawrence Campbell to Leslie Furth, January 8, 1986).

2. Emergency Passport Applications Issued Abroad, Miscellaneous Countries (France), 1894–98, nos. 337 and 338, National Archives, Washington, D.C. Tack was seeking a passport to travel in Europe and was intending to return to the U.S. within two years. Tack's arrival was remarked in the English-language paper, *American Register and The Morning News*, 7, published in Paris, as having been on April 27, 1895, with the rue Cassette address.

3. According to "Persons of Note," in *A New History of Old Windsor* (1935), Tuttle opened a studio in Greenfield, his hometown, in 1897.

4. Per Tack's own dating, the portrait's dates are 1897–98 (Archives, Metropolitan Museum of Art, courtesy of Jeanie James).

5. For further discussion of La Farge and Tack's association, see "Augustus Vincent Tack: A Mystic's Journey to Abstraction," in this catalogue. John La Farge was vice-president of the Society of American Artists beginning in 1892 and president from 1897 until 1906.

6. Tack probably submitted work to a preliminary jury for the Annual Exhibition at the United States Commission of the Paris Exposition of 1900. The decorations were for his sister and brother-in-law, Joseph and Mary Farley, for two New York houses (not located).

7. Augustus Vincent Tack to Violet Fuller, January 20, 1900: "It has a place of honor in the Philadelphia exhibition" (Fuller-Higginson Family Papers, Pocumtuck Vallery Memorial Association Library, Deerfield, Massachusetts).

8. His nomination and election are recorded in the Minutes of the Executive Meetings, April 19, 1900, Box 5, Archives of American Art, Smithsonian Institution, Washington, D.C.

9. The letters from Tack to Macbeth are preserved in reel NMc 11, frames 747–763; reel Z644, no frame numbers, Macbeth Gallery Papers, Archives of American Art, Smithsonian Institution, Washington, D.C. The scrapbooks also contain exhibition catalogues and reviews including Tack.

10. ASL Papers, Ledgers of Instructor Expenses, reel NY 59–28, frames 219; 239; 274; 299; 315; and 322. Tack also judged a scholarship competition along with Kenyon Cox, F. Luis Mora, and William M. Chase, among others, in 1908–09 (ASL Papers, NY 59–28, frame 621).

11. Tack's signature appears on the back of the menu for the dinner. Beckwith scrapbooks, New-York Historical Society, New York.

12. Courtesy of Nancy M. Cricco, archivist, University Archives, Elmer Holmes Bobst Library, New York University, correspondence with Leslie Furth, summer 1992.

13. Minutes, Nominating Committee, Century Association, New York, courtesy of W. Gregory Gallagher, librarian, Century Association. According to Margaret Stocker, National Academy of Design, Beckwith was taking a fatherly approach to many younger artists in this period. His diary notes Tack's election on December 3 (Stocker, conversation with Leslie Furth, January 1993)

14. Journal L, The Phillips Collection Archives.

15. Fourteen Tack paintings are listed in the June 1, 1921, published inventory. Paintings by Arthur B. Davies and Ernest Lawson almost rivaled this group, numbering thirteen each in 1921.

16. Metropolitan Museum of Art, "Centennial Exhibition of the Works of George Fuller," New York, Apr. 9-May 20, 1923, catalogue introduction by Augustus Vincent Tack.

17. Passport Application no. 331745, National Archives.

18. "Special Exhibition of Paintings by a Group of American Artists," April 26–May 18, 1924, included *Entombment* (cat. 26, lent by Phillips Memorial Gallery), and *Near Laggan, Mountain Landscape* (cat. 27), which was for sale for $1,500.

19. AVT to R. L. Cochran, secretary, Capitol Commission, State of Nebraska, December 5, 1924; courtesy of William Hansen, Capitol archivist, State of Nebraska.

20. Grenville Winthrop diaries, Fogg Archives, Fogg Art Museum, Cambridge, Massachusetts, courtesy of Abigail Smith. I am indebted to Marjorie B. Cohn, Carl A. Weyerhaeuser Curator of Prints, for pointing me to these diaries.

21. Mather, *The American Spirit in Art* (New Haven: Yale University Press, 1927), 160.

22. Cheney, *A Primer of Modern Art* (New York: Tudor Publishing, 1939), 171.

23. Courtesy W. Gregory Gallagher, Century Association Archives.

24. Saint-Gaudens, *The American Artist and His Times* (New York: Dodd, Mead & Co., 1941), 247–48.

25. Joseph Peter Spang III, interview with Leslie Furth, November, 24, 1992.

Leslie Furth with Vivien Greene

Selected Exhibition History

This selected exhibition record lists titles of only those paintings represented in the current exhibition.

1893

New York, Society of American Artists, "Fifteenth Annual Exhibition," Galleries of the American Fine Arts Society, April 17–May 13, 1893 (the first of nine exhibitions of SAA including Tack).

1895

Philadelphia, Pennsylvania Academy of the Fine Arts, "Sixty-Fifth Annual Exhibition," December 23, 1895–February 22, 1896, one painting (the first of eleven exhibitions to which Tack contributed between 1895 and 1934).

New York, National Academy of Design, "Seventieth Annual Exhibition," April 1–May 11, 1895.

1896

New York, Kraushaar Galleries, [Exhibition of twenty-five paintings by Augustus Vincent Tack], by March 13, 1896.[1]

1898

Boston, Boston Arts Club, "Fifty-Seventh Exhibition of Oil Paintings and Sculpture," January 22–February 19, 1898 (first of six exhibitions in which Tack was included between 1898 and 1906).

Pittsburgh, Carnegie Institute, "Third Annual Exhibition," November 3, 1898 –January 1, 1899.

1899

Philadelphia, Pennsylvania Academy of the Fine Arts, "Sixty-Eighth Annual Exhibition," January 16–February 25, 1899 (represented with four portraits).

New York, Society of American Artists, "Twenty-First Annual Exhibition," March 25–April 29, 1899

Illinois, Art Institute of Chicago, "Twelfth Annual Exhibition of Oil Paintings and Sculpture by American Artists," November 6–December 17, 1899 (the first of eight showings in which Tack was included, exhibiting there for the last time in 1934).

New York, Art Students League, "Twenty-fifth Anniversary of the Art Students League," May 10–May 19, 1900.

Worcester, Massachusetts, Worcester Art Museum, "Oil Paintings: Prize Exhibition," Summer, 1900 (first of seven submissions there between 1900 and 1920).

1901

New York, Architectural League of New York, Galleries of the American Fine Arts Society, "Sixteenth Annual Exhibition," February 17–March 9, 1901 (the first of five league exhibitions to which Tack contributed through 1930).

1902

Boston, Messrs. Doll and Richards, "Exhibition of Portraits and Landscapes by Augustus Vincent Tack," November 7–19, 1902. *New England Winter (Winter Landscape?), Twilight, Windswept, Dusk (Twilight?), The Coming Storm (Cloud Wrack?)*

1903

Worcester, Massachusetts, Worcester Art Museum [Loan Exhibition of Fifty Paintings], Winter 1903–04 (eleven portraits by Tack were included).

1904

Pittsburgh, Carnegie Institute, "Ninth Annual Exhibition," November 3, 1904–January 1, 1905. *Midwinter, Storm* (one of these works was *Winter*)

1905

Deerfield, Massachusetts, Arts and Crafts, Academy Hall, [Tack Portraits], July 1905

Boston, Copley Society of Boston, Copley Hall, "Loan Collection of Paintings by American Artists," June [possibly extended through September] 1905.

1906

Deerfield, Massachusetts, "Exhibition of Pictures and Textiles," Summer 1906.[2]

1907

New York, Macbeth Galleries, "Exhibition of Paintings by Augustus Vincent Tack," November 11–November 23, 1907 (Tack was included in seven group exhibitions at Macbeth's between 1908 and 1914). *Windswept, Cloud Wrack*

1908

Washington, D.C., Corcoran Gallery of Art, Second Annual Exhibition, December 8, 1908–January 17, 1909 (first of eleven contributions Tack made to group exhibitions there throughout his life). *Cloud Wrack*

1909

New York, Art Students League, National Arts Club, "Exhibition of Former Students of the Art Students League of New York," May 12–July 1, 1909.

1911

Hartford, Connecticut, Art Society of Hartford, "Exhibition of Paintings by Mr. Hermann Dudley Murphy, Mr. Augustus Vincent Tack, Mr. William Baxter Closson," sponsored by Connecticut Academy of Fine Arts, opening reception January 7; traveled to Michigan, Detroit Institute of Arts, February 23–March 10, and St. Louis, Missouri, City Art Museum, opening March 19, 1911.[3] *Cloud Wrack, City in Snow (Winter), The Dance (Deerfield in Twilight)*

1912

New Haven, Connecticut, New Haven Paint and Clay Club (held at Trowbridge House), "Eleventh Exhibition," April 8–20, 1912 (Tack served on the jury for this exhibition; he exhibited with the club on three subsequent occasions in the teens, serving on the jury once more).

1914

New York, Century Association, "Artist Members' Annual Exhibition," opening January 10, 1914. (Tack was a frequent exhibitor in the members' exhibitions, showing almost monthly throughout the teens).

New York, Century Association, "Artist Members Exhibition," February 8–19, 1914. *Mountain Slopes, Garden of Romance (Court of Romance), Across The Valley (The Valley)*

1915

New York, Worch of Paris, "A Special Exhibition of Paintings by Augustus Vincent Tack," February 15–28, 1915; (extended to March 15).[4] *Madonna of the Everlasting Hills*

1916

New York, Kraushaar Galleries, [An Exhibition of Paintings by Augustus Vincent Tack], by March 13–March 27, 1916 (the first of some eight one-person exhibitions Tack had at Kraushaar through 1929; he also participated in at least nine group exhibitions by 1926).[5]
The Valley

1918

New York, Kraushaar Galleries, "Exhibition of War Paintings by George Luks, John Sloan, Guy Pène du Bois, Augustus Vincent Tack, J. Mortimer Block, Charles S. Chapman, H. B. Fuller and W. Ritschel," June 2–29, 1918.
New York, American Art Galleries, Allied War Salon, December 8–24, 1918 (Tack exhibited a Landscape Target for use in the artillery schools).

1919

New York, Century Association, [Exhibition of Works Owned by Duncan Phillips], May 18–June 5, 1919. *Court of Romance*

Buffalo, New York, Albright Art Gallery, "Thirteenth Annual Exhibition of Selected Paintings," May 24–September 8, 1919 *Mother and Child (Allegory—Love and Life?)*

1920

Washington, D.C., Corcoran Gallery of Art, "Exhibition of Selected Paintings From the Collections of Mrs. D.C. Phillips and Mr. Duncan Phillips of Washington," March 3–31, 1920.

New York, Kraushaar Galleries, "Exhibition of Paintings by Le Sidaner and Tack," opening by March 22, 1920 until at least April 4, 1920.[6] *Madonna of the Everlasting Hills*

Cincinnati, Ohio, Cincinnati Art Museum, "Twenty-Seventh Annual Exhibition of American Art," May 29–July 31, 1920. *Madonna of the Everlasting Hills*

1922

New York, Kraushaar Galleries, "Paintings by August Vincent Tack," February 7–28, 1922 (first exhibition of *The Crowd*). *Barabbas! Barabbas! (The Crowd), Gethsemane, Many Hopes (As the Ships Go Sailing By)*

Washington, D.C., Phillips Memorial Gallery, [Second Exhibition of the Phillips Memorial Art Gallery], opening by November 22, 1922, checklist only, no catalogue (first showing of Tack's painting at the gallery).

1923

Canada, Art Gallery of Toronto, "Exhibition of Paintings by Contemporary American Artists," January 27–March 4, 1923. *New England, 1850 (Ox Cart)*

New York, Kraushaar Galleries, "Paintings and Decorative Panels by Augustus Vincent Tack," February 8–28, 1923 (first showing of the 1922–24 decorative panels). *Entombment, Magi's Journey (overmantel), Passacaglia (overmantel), Storm*

Cleveland, Ohio, Cleveland Museum of Art, "Third Exhibition of Contemporary American Painting," June 7–July 8, 1923.

1924

Venice, Italy, "XIV Biennale," Spring–Summer 1924.
Washington, D.C., Phillips Memorial Gallery, "Exhibition of Recent Decorative Paintings by Augustus Vincent Tack," March 26–April 26, 1924 (Tack's first solo exhibition at the gallery). *The Crowd, Canyon, Passacaglia, The Voice of Many Waters, Magi's Journey, Entombment, Storm, Madonna of the Everlasting Hills*

1925

New York, Art Students League of New York, "Golden Jubilee Exhibition," January 22–February 1, 1925.

New York, Durand-Ruel Galleries, "Altar Painting for the Church of St. James, South Deerfield, Mass.," April 6–15, 1925.

1926

Washington, D.C., Phillips Memorial Gallery, "Exhibition of Paintings by Eleven

Americans and an Important Work by Odilon Redon," February 1–28, 1926. *Storm*

1927

Louisville, Kentucky, J.B. Speed Art Museum, Louisville Art Association, "First Exhibition of Invited Paintings," January 15–29, 1927.

Baltimore, Baltimore Museum of Art, "An Exhibition of Expressionist Painters From the Experiment Station of the Phillips Memorial Gallery," April 8–May 1, 1927. *Passacaglia*

1928

Washington, D.C., Phillips Memorial Gallery, "Art is Symbolic," part of the Tri-Unit Exhibition, October 1928–January 1929. *Madonna of the Everlasting Hills, Storm*

1929

New York, Kraushaar Galleries, "An Exhibition of Decorative Inventions for the Phillips Memorial Gallery painted by Augustus Vincent Tack," November 19–December 3, 1929. *Liberation, Balance, Largo (others of the series for the Music Room)*

1930

Budapest, Nemzeti Salon, "Amerikai Muveszeti Kiallitas; Paintings and Sculpture by Contemporary American Artists," February 1930. *Entombment*

Washington, D.C., Phillips Memorial Gallery, Lower Gallery, "Decorations by Augustus Vincent Tack," March 9–June 1930. *Gethsemane, Crowd, Passacaglia, Storm, Voice of Many Waters, Decorative Panels (this group probably included Rhythm, Balance, Order, Allegro, Andante, Largo, Outposts of Time I and Outposts of Time II), Exaltation (Ecstasy), Liberation*

Venice, Italy, "XVII Esposizione Biennale Internazionale d'Arte," Summer 1930. *Entombment*

Washington, D.C., Phillips Memorial Gallery, [Works by Augustus Vincent Tack and Charles and Maurice Prendergast], Dining Room, PMG, October 5, 1930-January 25, 1931. *Storm*

New York, Museum of Modern Art, "Paintings and Sculpture by Living Americans: Ninth Loan Exhibition," December 2, 1930–January 20, 1931. *Largo (1928), Flight, Far Reaches*

1931

Indianapolis, Indiana, John Herron Art Institute, "Forty-sixth Annual Exhibition of Contemporary American Paintings," January 1–26, 1931. *Golden Morning (Untitled Oval?), Nocturne*

Indianapolis, Indiana, Art Association of Indianapolis, John Herron Art Institute, "Decorative Panels by Augustus Vincent Tack," [opening after September 30, 1931] *Passacaglia, Voice of Many Waters, Order , Balance, Flight, Far Reaches, Nocturne, Spring Night, Christmas Night, Magi's Journey, Aspiration*

New York, Leonard Clayton Gallery, "Drawings in Several Mediums by Augustus Vincent Tack," December 1–15, 1931.

1932

Washington, D.C., Phillips Memorial Gallery, "Decorations by Augustus Vincent Tack," Lower Gallery, February–June 1932. *Flight, Far Reaches, Christmas Night, Voice of Many Waters, Passacaglia, Aspiration, Gethsemane, Outposts of Time I, Rhythm, Order, Balance, Outposts of Time II, Liberation, Ecstasy, Largo, Blue Violet and Red Violet (Andante), Orange and Yellow (Allegro), Canyon (Mountains and Waterways)*

1934

New York, Leonard Clayton Gallery, "A Series of Recent Drawings by Augustus Vincent Tack," April 16–May 14, 1934.

New York, Wildenstein, "Exhibition of Paintings by Augustus Vincent Tack," April 28–May 11, 1934. *Ad Astra, Magi's Journey, Entombment, Canyon, Aspiration, Voice of Many Waters, Flight, Largo, Liberation, Ecstasy, Nocturne, Crowd, Dawn, Christmas Night, Andante, Winter, Far Reaches*

1935

New York, Arthur U. Newton Galleries, "Portrait of President Woodrow Wilson," October 29–November 9, 1935.

Deerfield, Massachusetts, Deerfield Valley Arts Association, [Exhibition of Paintings by Augustus Vincent Tack], October 25–October 31, 1936. *Daybreak, After Rain—Evening (Evening), Dawn, Cloud's Edge, Magi's Journey, The Crowd, Winter, Hilltop (Hill and Sky ?), Ad Astra*

1937

New York, Walker Galleries, [Paintings by Augustus Vincent Tack], March 22–April 3, 1937. *Abstractions*

Pittsfield, Massachusetts, Berkshire Museum, "Exhibition of Paintings by Augustus Vincent Tack," July 20–August 20, 1937, *Madonna of the Everlasting Hills, Entombment, Gethsemane, Court of Romance*

"New Decorations by Augustus Vincent Tack and European and American Colorists," Main Gallery, opening October 1 and continuing until at least November 6, 1937. *Aspiration, Night, Amargosa Desert*

1938

Pittsfield, Massachusetts, Berkshire Museum, "Paintings and Decorative Panels by Augustus Vincent Tack," August 2–September 17, 1938. *Winter, Dawn, Magi's Journey, Ad Astra, Amargosa, Far Reaches, Epiphany, Largo, Liberation, Rhythm, Nocturne, Symmetry (Balance), Ecstasy, Order, Spring Night, Voice of Many Waters, Christmas Night, Passacaglia, Evening After Rain (Evening), Daybreak*

Hagerstown, Maryland, Washington County Museum of Fine Arts, "Augustus Vincent Tack; Exhibition of Paintings and Drawings," November 17–December 19, 1938. *The Canyon, After Rain (Evening after Rain; Evening), Entombment , Gethsemane, Magi's Journey, Passacaglia, Storm, Madonna of the Everlasting Hills, The Crowd, The Valley (Canyon)*

1939

New York, Leonard Clayton Galleries, "Paintings and Drawings by Augustus Vincent Tack," January 8–February 4, 1939. *Gethsemane, Entombment, Love and Life (Allegory—Love and Life), Madonna of the Everlasting Hills*

1940

Washington, D.C., Howard Gallery of Art, "Exhibition of Christian Art," November 12–December 3, 1940. *Entombment, Madonna of the Everlasting Hills*

1941

New York, Macbeth Galleries, "Paintings and Drawings by Augustus Vincent Tack," January 14–February 13, 1941. *Gethsemane, Barabbas! Barabbas! (The Crowd), Entombment*

New York, James St. L. O'Toole Gallery, [Five Decorative Panels by Augustus Vincent Tack], by January 17, 1941, until at least February 27, 1941.

Washington, D.C., Phillips Memorial Gallery, "The Functions of Color in Painting: An Educational Loan Exhibition," February 16–March 23, 1941. *Storm, Amargosa*

Andover, Massachusetts, Abbott Academy, John-Esther Gallery, "Exhibition of Paintings by Augustus Vincent Tack," by November 3, 1941–January 16, 1942. *Madonna of the Everlasting Hills, Entombment, Christmas Night, Storm, Passacaglia, Spring Night, The Crowd (not on checklist; possible addition)*

1942

New York, MacDowell Club of New York City, "Exhibition of Paintings by Augustus Vincent Tack," March 22–April 12, 1942. *Madonna of the Everlasting Hills, Storm, Love and Life (Allegory—Love and Life), Christmas Night, Spring Night, Barabbas! Barabbas! (The Crowd), Entombment, Passacaglia*

1943

New York, Nierendorf Gallery, "Paintings by Augustus Vincent Tack," January 18–February 12, 1943. *Turmoil (The Crowd), Daybreak, Evening, Winter, Ecstasy, Liberation, Amargosa, Small Oval (Blue Oval?), Rhythm, Symmetry (Balance), Order, Andante, Spring Night, Storm*

Washington, D.C., Phillips Memorial Gallery "The Abstract Decorations of Augustus Vincent Tack," February 21–March 21, 1943. *Turmoil (The Crowd), Andante, Blue Oval, Voice of Many Waters, Liberation, Storm, Ecstasy , Amargosa Desert, Allegro, Spring Night, Christmas Night*

1944

Boston, Institute of Contemporary Art, "An Exhibition of Religious Art of Today," January 3–February 12, 1944. *Entombment* (dated erroneously to 1924)

New York, Century Association, "Exhibition of Work by Augustus Vincent Tack," December 7, 1944–January 8, 1945. *Night, Amargosa Desert, Blue Oval, Entombment, Gethsemane, Liberation, Passacaglia, Time and Timelessness*

1946

London, Tate Gallery, "Exhibition of American Painting," June–July 1946. *The Spirit of Creation (Time and Timelessness)*

1947

Washington, D.C., Phillips Memorial Gallery, "Early Paintings by Augustus Vincent Tack," Gallery A, December 7, 1947–January 5, 1948. *Passacaglia, Gethsemane, The Voice of Many Waters*

1948

Washington, D.C., Barnett Aden Gallery, "Contemporary Religious Paintings," October 17–November 1948, sponsored by Catholic Interracial Council of D.C., Fifth Anniversary Exhibition. *Gethsemane* (ca. 1920)

1949

Washington, D.C., The Phillips Gallery, "Color Abstractions by Augustus Vincent Tack," February 1–March 3, 1949. *Aspiration, Liberation, Spring Night, Ecstasy, Christmas Night, Amargosa Desert, Time and Timelessness, The Voice of Many Waters*

1950

Washington, D.C., The Phillips Gallery, "Memorial Exhibition: Abstractions by Augustus Vincent Tack," Main Gallery, June 25–September 16, 1950. *Aspiration, Liberation, Spring Night, Ecstasy, Christmas Night, Amargosa Desert, Time and Timelessness, The Voice of Many Waters*

Washington, D.C., National Gallery of Art, "Makers of History in Washington, 1800–1950," June 29–November 19, 1950.

1951

New York, Metropolitan Museum of Art, "75th Anniversary Exhibition, Painting and Sculpture by 75 Artists Associated with the Art Students League," March–April 1951. *Storm*

1952

Washington, D.C., George Washington University, Library, "Paintings by Augustus Vincent Tack from The Phillips Gallery," December 1952. *Christmas Night, Spring Night, Largo, Outposts of Time No.1, Allegro, Outposts of Time No.2, The Voice of Many Waters, Andante, Flight, Balance , Order, The Spirit of Creation (Time and Timelessness), Far Reaches, Ecstasy, Canyon, Liberation, Blue Oval, Passacaglia, Rhythm, Storm, Night, Amargosa Desert*

1953

Washington, D.C., The Phillips Gallery, "A Small Exhibition of Abstractions from the Studio of the Late Augustus Vincent Tack," March 3–May 2, 1953. *Canyon, Dawn, Nocturne*

1958

Washington, D.C., The Phillips Gallery, "Paintings by Augustus Vincent Tack," The Print Rooms, opening June and closing by October 1, 1958. *Outposts of Time II, Andante, Daybreak, Storm, Largo, Passacaglia, Ecstasy, Christmas Night, Liberation, Entombment, Outposts of Time I, The Crowd, Blue Oval, Spring Night, Mountains and Waterways (Canyon)*

1968

Deerfield, Massachusetts, Deerfield Academy, American Studies Group, Hilson Gallery, "Augustus Vincent Tack 1870-1949," April 1–June 6, 1968. *Gethsemane (1918), Entombment (c. 1923), Balance (c. 1930), Storm (1920–25), Time and Timelessness (c. 1944)*

New York, Whitney Museum of American Art, "The 1930s: Painting & Sculpture in America," October 15–December 1, 1968.

1970

Dayton, Ohio, Dayton Art Institute, "Color and Field: Abstract Painting in the Sixties and Its Backgrounds," traveled to Cleveland and Buffalo. *Time and Timelessness*

1972

Austin, Texas, University Art Museum, University of Texas at Austin, "Augustus Vincent Tack, 1870-1949: Twenty-Six Paintings from the Phillips Collection," August 27–October 3, 1972; traveled to College Park, Maryland, University of Maryland Art Gallery, October 19–November 19, 1972. *Court of Romance, Gethsemane, Voice of Many Waters, Storm, Largo, Rhythm, Allegro, Ecstasy, Daybreak, Canyon, Dawn, Time and Timelessness, Christmas Night, Spring Night, Blue Oval, Flight, Far Reaches, Balance, Outposts of Time I, Outposts of Time II, Andante, Order, Winter, Cloud's Edge*

1973

Kingston, Rhode, Island, University of Rhode Island Fine Arts Center, "Augustus Vincent Tack, 1870-1949: Loan Exhibition of Seventeen Abstract Paintings From the Phillips Collection, Washington, D.C.," October 9–28, 1973. *Gethsemane (c. 1918), Storm (c. 1920–25), Passacaglia (c. 1924), Crowd (Turmoil) (c. 1924), Liberation (c. 1929), Allegro (c. 1930), Flight (c. 1930), Canyon (c. 1931), Outposts of Time, No. 2 (c. 1931), Order (c. 1931), Rhythm (c. 1931), Dawn (c. 1934), Spring Night (c. 1934), Night, Amargosa Desert (c. 1937), Daybreak (c. 1938), Cloud's Edge (n.d.)*

1976

Washington, D.C., The Phillips Collection, "American Art From the Phillips Collection, Part 1," , May 29–August 21, 1976. *Storm, Largo, Canyon, Outposts of Time I*

Washington, D.C., The Phillips Collection, "American Art From The Phillips Collection, Part 2," September 4–October 24, 1976. *Storm, Passacaglia, Largo, Andante, Ecstasy, Outposts of Time II, Flight, Dawn, Daybreak, Winter, Hill and Sky, Voice of Many Waters, Christmas Night, Spring Night, Cloud's Edge, Gethsemane*

New York, Museum of Modern Art, "The Natural Paradise: Painting in America 1800–1950," October 1–November 30, 1976. *Canyon, Aspiration, Night, Amargosa Desert*

1977

Indianapolis, Indiana, Indianapolis Museum of Art, "Perceptions of the Spirit," September 20–November 27, 1977; traveled to Berkeley, California, University Art Museum, December 20, 1977–February 12, 1978; San Antonio, Texas, Marion Koogler McNay Art Institute, March 5-April 16, 1978; Columbus, Ohio, Columbus Gallery of Fine Arts, May 10–June 19, 1978. *Voice of Many Waters, Spirit of Creation (Time and Timelessness)*

1979

New York, New York University, Grey Art Gallery, "American Imagination and Symbolist Painting," October 24–December 8, 1979; traveled to Lawrence, Kansas, Helen Foresman Spencer Museum of Art, University of Kansas, January 20–March 2, 1980. *Madonna of the Everlasting Hills*

1984

Toronto, Canada, Art Gallery of Ontario, "The Mystic North: Symbolist Painting in Northern Europe and America, 1890–1940," January 13–March 11, 1984; traveled to Cincinnati Art Museum, Cincinnati, Ohio, March 31–May 13, 1984. *Storm (1920–23), Voice of Many Waters (1924), Flight (c. 1930)*

1986

Washington, D.C., The Phillips Collection, "Duncan Phillips: Centennial Exhibition," June 14–August 31, 1986. *Allegro, Andante, Aspiration, Ecstasy, Far Reaches, Flight, Largo, Liberation, Outposts of Time I, Outposts of Time II, Storm, The Voice of Many Waters*

New York, M. Knoedler & Co., Inc., "The Abstractions of Augustus Vincent Tack," November 5–December 4, 1986. *Aspiration, Balance, Blue Oval, Ecstasy, Far Reaches, Flight, Largo, Night, Amargosa Desert, Nocturne, Outposts of Time I, Outposts of Time II*

Los Angeles, "The Spiritual in Art: Abstract Painting 1890-1985," November 23, 1986–March 8, 1987; traveled to Museum of Contemporary Art, Chicago; Haags Gemeentemuseum, The Hague. *Storm*

1988

Southampton, New York, Parrish Art Museum, "American Modernism", July 16-September 11, 1988; traveled to Alexandria, Louisiana, Alexandria Museum, October 8–November 26, 1988. *Canyon*

Nashville, Tennessee, Cheekwood Fine Arts Center, "Augustus Vincent Tack: Eighteen Abstractions," December 3, 1988–January 22, 1989. *Blue Oval, Aspiration, Christmas Night, Ecstasy, Far Reaches, Flight, Liberation, Night, Amargosa Desert, Magi's Journey, Passacaglia, Self-Portrait, Spring Night, Storm, Time and Timelessness, Balance, Rhythm, Order, Allegro, Andante*

1989

Corpus Christi, Texas, Art Museum of South Texas, "American Modernism," January 12–February 12, 1989; traveled to Greenville, South Carolina, Greenville County Museum of Art, September 12–October 29, 1989; Memphis, Tennessee, Memphis Brooks Museum of Art, November 19, 1989–January 28, 1990; Palm Beach, Florida, Society of the Four Arts, March 16–April 15, 1990; Norfolk, Virginia, Chrysler Museum, May 11–July 8, 1990; Fort Wayne, Indiana, Fort Wayne Museum of Art, September 8–November 4, 1990. *Canyon*

1991

Atlanta, Georgia, Emory University, Michael C. Carlos Museum, "The Aftermath of Impressionism: Selected Works from The Phillips Collection," November 13, 1991–February 9, 1992.
The Crowd, Winter (New York in Snow)

NOTES

1. From exhibition review, *New York Times*, March 13, 1896, 4.
2. From exhibition review, *Greenfield Gazette and Courier* (Mass.), July 14, 1906.
3. Separate catalogues were published by Detroit and St. Louis; the numbers reflect those of the St. Louis catalogue.
4. From announcement card and reviews only; no gallery records or catalogue have been located.
5. From Duncan Phillips, "The Romance of a Painter's Mind, *International Studio* 58 (March 1916): 19–24.
6. Henry McBride, "Recent paintings by Vincent Tack now on view," *New York Sun*, April 4, 1920, sec. 4, 6; exhibition title from advertisement, same page.

Leslie Furth with Vivien Greene

Selected Bibliography

American Studies Group. Augustus Vincent Tack, 1870-1949. Deerfield, Mass.: Hilson Gallery, Deerfield Academy, 1968.

Baker, Marilyn. Manitoba's Third Legislative Building, Symbol in Stone: The Art and Politics of a Public Building. Winnipeg: Hyperion Press, 1986.

Dillenberger, Jane and John. Perceptions of the Spirit in Twentieth-Century American Art. Indianapolis: Indianapolis Museum of Art, 1977.

Eldredge, Charles C. American Imagination and Symbolist Painting. New York: Grey Art Gallery and Study Center, New York University, 1979.

Ferguson, John C. "The Influence of Chinese Painting on the West." The New Mandarin (1926): 4–5 (pamphlet).

Green, Eleanor. Augustus Vincent Tack, 1870-1949: Twenty-Six Paintings from The Phillips Collection. Austin: University of Texas, 1972.
—. Museums Discovered. New York: Shorewood Fine Art Books, 1981.

Haley, Carmel O'Neill. "Augustus Vincent Tack, A Knight in Quest of Beauty." International Federation of Catholic Alumni Quarterly Bulletin (December 1914): 14–15.

Lane, James W. "Augustus Vincent Tack." American Magazine of Art 28 (December 1935): 726–33.

Lemont, Jessie. "Old Subjects in New Vestments." International Studio 54 (November 1914): 3–10.

Luebke, Frederick C., ed. The Nebraska State Capitol. Lincoln: University of Nebraska Press, 1990.

McShine, Kynaston, ed. Natural Paradise: Painting in America, 1800–1950. New York: Museum of Modern Art, 1976.

Mechlin, Leila. "Notes of Art and Artists." Sunday Star (Washington, D.C.), November 16, 1930, 19.

Nasgaard, Roald. The Mystic North: Symbolist Landscape Painting in Northern Europe and North America, 1890-1940. Toronto: University of Toronto Press, 1984.

The Phillips Collection: A Summary Catalogue. Washington, D.C.: The Phillips Collection, 1985.

Phillips, Duncan. "The Romance of a Painter's Mind." International Studio 58 (March 1916): 19–24.
—. *A Collection in the Making.* New York: E. Weyhe and Phillips Memorial Gallery, 1926.
—. "Art is Symbolic." Introduction to *Tri-Unit Exhibition of Paintings & Sculpture.* Washington, D.C.: The Phillips Collection, 1928.
—. "Mystical Crucifixion." Pamphlet, 1928.
—. "Decorative Panels by Augustus Vincent Tack." Pamphlet, 1930.
—. *The Artist Sees Differently.* Washington, D.C.: The Phillips Collection, 1931.
—. *The Abstract Decorations of Augustus Vincent Tack.* Washington, D.C.: The Phillips Collection, 1943.

Rathbone, Eliza. Duncan Phillips: A Centennial Exhibition. Washington, D.C.: The Phillips Collection, 1986.

Rosenblum, Robert. "Resurrecting Augustus Vincent Tack." In The Abstractions of Augustus Vincent Tack. New York: M. Knoedler & Co., 1986.

Steele, John. "The Protean Talent of Augustus Vincent Tack." International Studio 89 (April 1928): 66.

Tack, Augustus Vincent. "George Fuller." In Centennial Exhibition of the Works of George Fuller. New York: Metropolitan Museum of Art, 1923.
—. "A Note on Subjective Painting." *Art and Understanding* 1 (March 1930): 240–43.
—. Foreword to *Exhibition of French Masterpieces of the 19th Century.* New York: Century Association, 1936.

Tack, Augustus Vincent, and Thornton Oakley. "Two Definitions of Art."American Magazine of Art 21 (October 1930): 576–78.

Tuchman, Maurice, and Judi Freeman; Carel Blotkamp; Flip Bool; John E. Bowlt; Charlotte Douglas; Charles C. Eldredge; Robert Galbreath; Linda Dalrymple Henderson; Rose-Carol Washton Long; Sixten Ringbom; W. Jackson Rushing; Harriett Watts; Robert P. Welsh. The Spiritual in Art: Abstract Painting 1890–1985. Los Angeles: Los Angeles County Museum of Art, 1986.

Unpublished Sources

Isaacs, Susan. "Augustus Vincent Tack." Ph.D. diss., University of Delaware, 1992.

McCready, Eric Scott. "The Nebraska State Capitol: Its Design, Background, and Influence." Master's thesis, University of Delaware, 1973.

Dehaney, Carolyn W. *Puvis de Chavannes and American Mural Painters.* Master's thesis, New York University, 1939.

Archives

Fuller-Higginson Family Papers, Pocumtuck Valley Memorial Association, Deerfield, Massachusetts.

Correspondence between Augustus Vincent Tack and Duncan Phillips. Archives of American Art, Smithsonian Institution, The Phillips Collection Archives.

Macbeth Gallery Papers, Archives of American Art.

Augustus Vincent Tack, "Some General Remarks About Paintings Called Abstractions," ca. 1942, typescript, Phillips Academy Archives, Andover, Massachusetts.

Collection of correspondence, interviews, notes, photographs and other memorabilia compiled by the American Studies Group in 1968, Deerfield Academy Archives, Deerfield, Massachusetts.

Art and memorabilia, including the 1941 manuscript by Augustus Vincent Tack, "Reflections on Pictures. Some Painted and Some Unpainted," from the artist's studio, collection of Joseph Peter Spang III, Deerfield, Massachusetts.

The Phillips Collection Archives

Foxhall Correspondence, The Phillips Collection, Washington, D.C.

Duncan Phillips, Journal L, 1914.

Duncan Phillips, Journal B, ca. 1923–24.

Duncan Phillips, Journal GG, 1924.

Exhibition Checklist

Where possible, the artist's titles are used. Dates are determined on the basis of the exhibition history and Tack's stylistic development. Measurements are given in inches with height preceding width. Inscriptions and signatures on the front of the images are provided. All works are in The Phillips Collection. The acquisition dates are determined from the museum's early records. Works given to the museum in 1959, on the death of Violet (Agnes Gordon) Tack, had been in Tack's studio on his death in 1949.

1. *Self-Portrait*
1897
oil on canvas
24 x 20
signed and inscribed lower left: To My Father and Mother/Christmas 1897
Acquired from the estate of Agnes Gordon Tack by 1959
Illustrated on page 102

2. *Winter Landscape*
ca. 1898–ca. 1902
oil on canvas
24 x 28
signed lower right: *TACK*
Acquired from the estate of Agnes Gordon Tack by 1959
Illustrated on page 23

3. *Deerfield, Spring Landscape*
ca. 1898–ca. 1902
oil on canvas
25 x 28
signed lower right: Tack
Acquired from the estate of Agnes Gordon Tack by 1959
Illustrated on page 24

4. *Twilight*
ca. 1898–ca. 1902
oil on canvas
24 ¾ x 27 ¾
unsigned
Acquired from the estate of Agnes Gordon Tack by 1959
Illustrated on page 25

5. *Cloud Wrack*
ca. 1900
oil on canvas
29 ⅜ x 36 ⅛
signed lower left: *AVGVSTVS VINCENT TACK**
Acquired from the estate of Agnes Gordon Tack by 1959
Illustrated on page 20

6. *Figure in Red with Beads*
ca. 1900
oil on canvas
29 ⅛ x 36
signed lower left: Augustus Tack
Acquired from the estate of Agnes Gordon /Tack by 1959
Illustrated on page 26

7. *Winter (New York in Snow)*
ca. 1900
oil on canvas
24 ⅞ x 27 ⅞
signed lower right:
AVGVSTVS. VINCENT. TACK
Acquired from the estate of Agnes Gordon Tack by 1959
Illustrated on page 30

8. *Windswept (Snow Picture, Leyden)*
ca. 1900–1902
oil on canvas
31 x 36 3/16
signed lower right: *AVGVSTVS VINCENT TACK*
Acquired from the estate of Agnes Gordon Tack by 1959
Illustrated on page 21

9. *Allegory—Love and Life (Mother and Child)*
ca. 1900–ca. 1907
oil on canvas mounted on hardboard
25 x 24
signed lower right: Tack**
Acquired 1919; traded 1924; reacquired from the estate of Agnes Gordon Tack by 1959
Illustrated on page 26

10. *Sea of Hills*
ca. 1905–ca. 1910
oil on canvas mounted on panel
15 x 30 ⅜
signed lower right: *AVGVSTVS VINCENT TACK*
Acquired ca. 1914 (?); first purchase of a Tack painting by Phillips
Illustrated on page 104

*The canvas was restretched by the artist; an earlier signature lies below the frame.

**The signature, added much later, lies on top of a layer of varnish.*

11. *Deerfield in Twilight (The Dance)*
ca. 1908; retouched after 1911
oil on canvas
14 7/8 x 30 1/8
signed lower right: *TACK*
Acquired from the estate of Agnes Gordon Tack by 1959
Illustrated on page 33

12. *New England, 1850 (Ox Cart)*
early teens
oil on canvas
15 x 30
signed lower right: *TACK*
Acquired ca. 1956
Illustrated on page 28

13. *Madonna of the Everlasting Hills*
1913–14
oil on canvas
55 3/4 x 46 1/8
signed lower left: *TACK*
Acquired 1920
Illustrated on page 34

14. *Court of Romance (Garden of Romance)*
ca. 1914
oil on canvas
15 x 30 1/4
signed lower right: *AVGVSTVS TACK*
Acquired 1919; traded 1924; reacquired 1933
Illustrated on page 27

15. *Canyon (The Valley)*
1914
oil on canvas
25 1/8 x 41 1/8
signed lower left: *TACK*
Acquired from the estate of Agnes Gordon Tack by 1959
Illustrated on page 36

16. *Mountain Slopes*
1914
oil on canvas
18 x 24
signed lower right: *TACK*
Acquired from the estate of Agnes Gordon Tack by 1959
Illustrated on page 104

17. *Elizabeth Hudson*
by 1914
oil on canvas
36 x 29 1/8
signed lower left: *TACK*
Acquired from the estate of Elizabeth Hudson, 1974
Illustrated on page 31

18. *Allegro Giocoso*
by 1917
oil on cardboard mounted on plywood panel
15 x 30
signed lower left: *TACK*
Acquired 1917
Illustrated on page 32

19. *As the Ships Go Sailing By (Many Hopes)*
ca. 1917
oil on canvas mounted on plywood panel
31 1/2 x 24
signed lower right: Tack
Acquired from the estate of Agnes Gordon Tack by 1959
Illustrated on page 37

20. *Gethsemane*
1921–22
oil on canvas mounted on plywood panel
16 x 37 1/16
signed lower right: *TACK*
Acquired 1922; traded 1933; reacquired 1941
Illustrated on page 46

21. *The Crowd*
1921–22
oil on canvas mounted on wallboard
25 x 45 3/4
signed lower right: *TACK*
Acquired 1943
Illustrated on page 40

22. *Entombment*
1922
oil on canvas mounted on plywood panel
29 x 40
signed lower left: *TACK*
Acquired 1924
Illustrated on page 41

23. *Passacaglia*
1922–23
oil on canvas mounted on plywood panel
43 7/8 x 49 3/4
signed lower right: *TACK*
Acquired 1924
Illustrated on page 45

24. *Magi's Journey*
1922–23
oil on canvas mounted on wallboard
48 x 47 3/4
signed lower right: *TACK*
Acquired 1924; traded 1930; reacquired from the estate of Agnes Gordon Tack by 1959
Illustrated on page 41

25. *Storm*
ca. 1922–23
oil on canvas mounted on wallboard
36 7/8 x 48 1/16
signed lower right: Tack
Acquired 1923
Illustrated on page 17

26. *Canyon*
ca. 1923–24
oil on canvas mounted on plywood panel
29 x 40
signed lower right: *TACK*
Acquired 1924
Illustrated on page 44

27. *The Voice of Many Waters*
ca. 1923–24
oil on canvas mounted on wallboard
77 3/4 x 47 7/8
signed lower left: *TACK*
Acquired 1924
Illustrated on page 18

28. *Portrait of Duncan Phillips*
commissioned 1921 or 1922; completed 1926
oil on canvas mounted on plywood panel
36 x 28
signed lower right: Tack
Collection of Mr. and Mrs. Laughlin Phillips
Illustrated on page 74

29. *Largo*
commissioned 1928; 1928–29
oil on canvas mounted on wallboard
43 7/8 x 35 9/16
signed lower right: *TACK*
Acquired 1930
Illustrated on page 85

30. *Balance*
commissioned 1928; 1929
oil on canvas mounted on wallboard
43 5/8 x 35 9/16
signed lower right: *TACK*
Acquired 1930
Illustrated on page 88

31. *Order*
commissioned 1928; 1929
oil on canvas mounted on wallboard
43 7/8 x 35 1/2
signed lower right: *TACK*
Acquired 1930
Illustrated on page 89

32. *Rhythm*
commissioned 1928; 1929
oil on canvas mounted on wallboard
43 5/8 x 35 1/2
signed lower right: *TACK*
Acquired 1930
Illustrated on page 83

33. *Liberation*
commissioned 1928; 1929
oil on canvas mounted on wallboard
47 7/8 x 64 1/4
signed lower right: *TACK*
Acquired 1930
Illustrated on page 90

34. *Ecstasy*
commissioned 1928; 1929
oil on canvas mounted on wallboard
47 ¾ x 64
signed lower right: TACK
Acquired 1930
Illustrated on page 53

35. *Allegro*
commissioned 1928; 1929
oil on canvas mounted on wallboard
43 ¾ x 35 7/16
signed lower right: TACK
Acquired 1930
Illustrated on page 86

36. *Andante*
commissioned 1928; 1929
oil on canvas mounted on wallboard
43 ⅞ x 35 13/16
signed lower right: TACK
Acquired 1930
Illustrated on page 87

37. *Outposts of Time I*
commissioned 1928; 1929
oil on canvas mounted on wallboard
43 ⅝ x 35 9/16
signed lower right: TACK
Acquired 1930
Illustrated on page 82

38. *Outposts of Time II*
commissioned 1928; 1929
oil on canvas mounted on wallboard
43 9/16 x 35 ½
signed lower right: TACK
Acquired 1930
Illustrated on page 92

39. *Flight (Fugue)*
commissioned 1928; 1930
oil on canvas mounted on wallboard
43 ⅞ x 35 ¾
signed lower right: TACK
Acquired 1930
Illustrated on page 93

40. *Far Reaches*
commissioned 1928; 1930
oil on canvas mounted on wallboard
44 x 35 ¾
signed lower right: TACK
Acquired 1930
Illustrated on page 91

41. *Nocturne*
1930
oil on canvas mounted on wallboard
43 ½ x 66 ⅝
signed lower right in oval: AVGVSTVS VINCENT TACK
Acquired from the estate of Agnes Gordon Tack by 1959
Illustrated on page 56

42. *Untitled Oval (Golden Morning?)*
1930
oil on canvas mounted on wallboard
68 ⅞ x 43 ⅛
signed lower right in oval: TACK
Acquired from the estate of Agnes Gordon Tack by 1959
Illustrated on page 57

43. *Aspiration*
1931
oil on canvas
76 ½ x 135 ½
unsigned
Acquired 1932
Illustrated on page 94

44. *Spring Night*
1931
oil on canvas mounted on wallboard
68 ⅞ x 43 ½
signed lower right in oval: TACK
Acquired 1934
Illustrated on page 60

45. *Christmas Night*
1931
oil on canvas mounted on wallboard
69 x 43
signed lower right in oval: *Tack*
Acquired 1932
Illustrated on page 55

46. *Blue Oval*
by 1933
oil on canvas mounted on wallboard
42 ½ x 34
signed lower right in oval: TACK
Acquired by 1938
Illustrated on page 54

47. *Winter*
1934
oil on canvas mounted on hardboard
23 ⅜ x 23 9/16
signed lower left: TACK
Acquired from the estate of Agnes Gordon Tack by 1959
Illustrated on page 61

48. *Dawn*
between 1934 and 1936
oil on canvas mounted on hardboard
23 ¾ x 24 ¾
signed lower left: TACK
Acquired 1953
Illustrated on page 8

49. *Hill and Sky (Hilltop?)*
between 1934 and 1936
oil on canvas mounted on hardboard
15 x 20 ⅛
signed lower right: TACK
Acquired from the estate of Agnes Gordon Tack by 1959
Illustrated on page 63

50. *Daybreak*
between 1934 and 1936
oil on canvas mounted on hardboard
26 x 33 ⅛
signed lower right: TACK
Acquired from the estate of Agnes Gordon Tack by 1959
Illustrated on page 105

51. *Above the Treetops*
between 1934 and 1936
oil on canvas mounted on hardboard
20 ⅛ x 30 11/16
signed lower right: TACK
Acquired from the estate of Agnes Gordon Tack by 1959
Illustrated on page 106

52. *Evening*
between 1934 and 1936
oil on canvas mounted on hardboard
23 ¾ x 23 ⅜
signed lower right: TACK
Acquired from the estate of Agnes Gordon Tack by 1959
Illustrated on page 59

53. *Night, Amargosa Desert*
1935
oil on canvas mounted on plywood panel
84 x 48
signed lower right: *Augustus Vincent Tack*
Acquired 1937
Illustrated on page 52

54. *Cloud's Edge*
between 1935 and 1936
oil on canvas mounted on hardboard
24 ¼ x 30 ⅛
signed lower right: TACK
Acquired ca. 1949–50
Illustrated on page 58

55. *Time and Timelessness (The Spirit of Creation)*
1943–44
oil on canvas
39 3/16 x 85 ¼
signed lower left vertically: AVGVSTVS VINCENT TACK
Acquired 1948
Illustrated on page 64

56. *Self-Portrait*
1940s
oil on hardboard
39 ¾ x 32 ¼
signed lower left: AVGVSTVS VINCENT TACK
Acquired from the estate of Agnes Gordon Tack by 1959
Illustrated on page 103

Elizabeth Steele

Technical Notes

FOR AUGUSTUS VINCENT TACK, painting was an evolutionary process. Almost all the pictures in this exhibition reveal the editing methods that he employed throughout his career: reworking of the surface, painting over certain elements, scraping others out, toning back bright passages. These additive and reductive techniques, which echo each other in appearance, signal the constant reevaluation of his process. Often the scraping back of paint occurred early in the development of a composition, so that the fabric weave is emphasized and the multiple layers of paint used to build up the surface are visible. Then, through additive methods—using rollers, cloths, and sponges—Tack sparingly applied paint that would only adhere to the tops of the canvas threads, visually breaking up the surface.

Tack's tools and methods probably related to his training as a mural painter. He appears to have followed H. Siddons Mowbray's "Suggestions for a beginner undertaking a decorative ensemble involving paintings, ornament and gold work": "Reduce the effect of an over-strong detail" and "modify the effect of gilt surfaces by lowering its key and curbing its brilliancy without hurting its relative value as gold."[1] The considerable attention Tack devoted to the borders and frames of his paintings is analogous to a mural painter's attention to architectural elements of an interior.[2] The use of stencils, cartoons, and projection methods to transfer imagery is a more obvious carry-over from mural painting.[3]

Tack's pragmatism is evident in his frequent reuse of canvases (nearly all the early paintings show signs of abandoned or unfinished compositions lying beneath the upper paint layers) and in his adoption of building materials. He used several types of wallboard, plywood, and hardboard as supports and auxiliary supports. Tack was oblivious to small nicks, tears, cuts, and losses in the surfaces of his pictures. He made little attempt to try to hide these scars, choosing instead to simply paint over them. Perhaps he even appreciated these accidents, feeling that they added to the textural and surface qualities with which he was so concerned elsewhere. Therefore, the conservation of these paintings involved preserving these anomalous marks as idiosyncratic signs of the artist's hand.

Self-Portrait (cat. 1)
Paint on all four tacking margins indicates that the portrait was painted on an unstretched canvas or stretched onto a larger auxiliary support before being attached to its present stretcher. Unrelated brush strokes beneath the upper paint layers indicate that this painting may be painted on an unfinished composition.

Winter Landscape (cat. 2)
This composition appears to have evolved through several states. Green paint on the left, right, and bottom tacking margins indicates a different color scheme from an earlier state. At some point, the upper tacking margin was folded out, the canvas was restretched onto a larger stretcher and the composition was extended; tack holes from the earlier stretching are visible in the paint along the top edge. There are strong pentimenti in the lower left and texture in the paint film unrelated to the composition, all evidence of changes. An artist's card bearing the name of one of Tack's colleagues was found affixed to the inner side of the bottom stretcher bar. One side is engraved with his name, Edward McDowell; on the other, presumably in his hand, is written: Title: The close of day/Artist: Edward McDowell/126 E. 28th Street/N. Y. Stretcher plier marks on both sides of the auxiliary support attest to Tack reusing his friend's stretcher.

Deerfield, Spring Landscape (cat. 3)
Brush strokes in the paint film that are unrelated to the composition indicate that the landscape evolved in imagery or that it was painted on an unfinished or abandoned composition, particularly visible in the lower left quadrant.

Twilight (cat. 4)
The landscape passages have been blocked in using a warm, orange-pink hue, which shows through thinly painted areas and gives a sense of depth to the composition. Textured brush strokes in the foreground that do not relate to the upper paint layers indicate that the composition underwent changes before reaching its final state.

Cloud Wrack (cat. 5)
Two sets of tack holes on the margins indicate that the canvas was stretched twice. The dimensions were reduced along the lower edge in the second stretching, evident on the bottom margin where the larger composition was wrapped around the stretcher bar. A signature can also be found wrapped around the bottom member. *Cloud Wrack* seems to have been painted on top of another abandoned composition. An infrared photograph reveals large shapes and brush strokes that are unrelated to the landscape; the image revealed is unclear but may be a figure or another, very different, landscape. This earlier composition can also be detected by the textured brush strokes that lie beneath the upper layers of paint and are unrelated to this landscape. Small damages to the canvas appear to have been retouched by the artist without regard to ameliorating their distracting physical appearance.

Figure in Red with Beads (cat. 6)
Tack scraped back the paint around the figure's hair to soften the transition between it and the face. An infrared photograph (fig. 33) reveals shifts and changes in the composition as it evolved (see Leslie Furth's essay, "Augustus Vincent Tack: A Mystic's Journey to Abstraction," in this catalogue).

Winter (New York in Snow) (cat. 7)
An infrared photograph reveals an unfinished portrait beneath the city scene (fig. 34). On the canvas reverse is an inscription in black paint: "Winter"/ A.V. Tack/ 939 8th Avenue (Tack's studio address from 1894–1901).

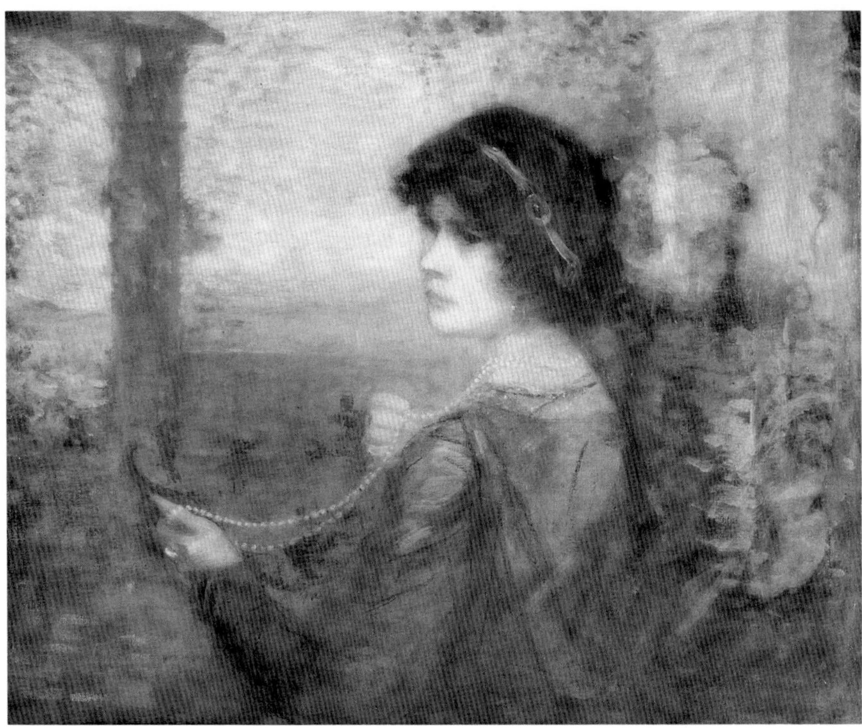

Fig. 33. An infrared photograph of *Figure in Red with Beads* (cat. 6) reveals an evolution of form in and around the sitter's left hand and large changes in the composition to the right of the figure. Charcoal underdrawing is visible in the dress.

Windswept (Snow Picture, Leyden) (cat. 8)
The irregularly shaped rocks were developed in the early stages of the composition, evident in the negative spaces surrounding these idiosyncratic forms and the white brush strokes that overlap their edges.

Allegory—Love and Life (Mother and Child) (cat. 9)
The image was cut down from a larger canvas and attached to the hardboard. The type of cracks present in the paint film would only develop on a stretched canvas. An early photo from the Art Students League Archives shows this painting as a slightly larger format and presumably on a stretcher. Age cracks take a number of years to develop, so considerable time must have elapsed between Tack's completion of the painting and his cutting it down and attaching it to the hardboard. The hardboard mat is an integral part of the work. It was painted using a white, oil-resin–type paint and textured brush strokes; the mat was toned back after the picture was framed, using a brown wash, evident in the unaltered white edge that was covered by the rebate of the frame.

Sea of Hills (cat. 10)
The horizon line was raised at some point during the development of the composition. Examination under ultraviolet light shows a build-up of form from an earlier state. The trees in the foreground and isolated white brush strokes lie on top of a varnish layer, applied by the artist between states. Use of a cloth to apply the paint is visible in the white clouds.

Deerfield in Twilight (The Dance) (cat. 11)
A thinly painted, dark underpainting delineates the trees, on which heavy impastoed brush strokes were daubed to build up the branches. Examination under the microscope reveals instances in which these impastoed marks in the upper layers lie over cracks that developed in the lower, more thinly painted layers. The marks and the cracks indicate two different states of execution and a space of time between execution dates.

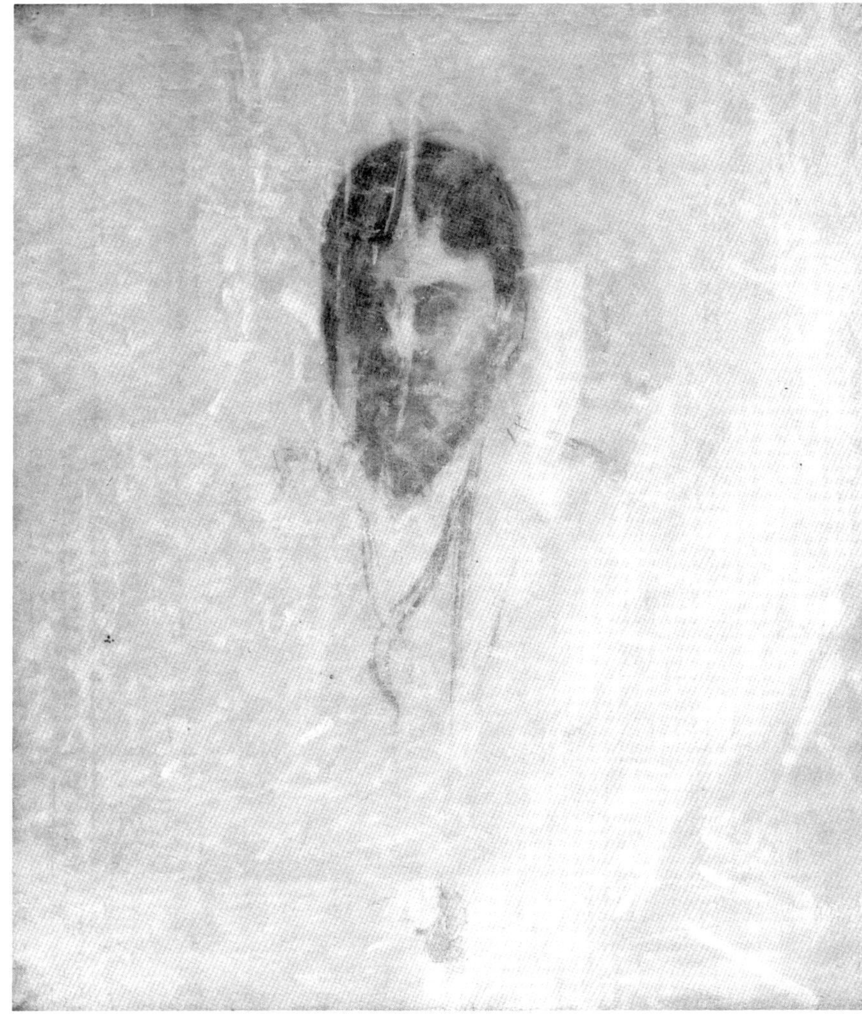

Fig. 34. An infrared photograph of *Winter* (*New York in Snow*) (cat. 7) shows the abandoned portrait of a man beneath the landscape.

New England, 1850 (Ox Cart) (cat. 12)
Tack's editing process is quite obvious in this painting. Sky was painted over tree branches, the central tree trunk was slimmed down, and pictorial elements were removed in the middle ground (left of center). Examination under ultraviolet light reveals the sky to have changed dramatically: it was originally composed of multicolored, wet-into-wet daubs of paint, similar to the sky in *Canyon (The Valley)* (cat. 15).

Madonna of the Everlasting Hills (cat. 13)
The vertical dimensions of the picture were increased about four and one-half inches by adding a strip of preprimed canvas to the bottom edge. Pinholes are visible on either side of the seam, probably a consequence of attaching the two fabrics together. A piece of wood was affixed to the bottom stretcher bar to accommodate the enlarged canvas size. Green and blue paint is found on the right tacking margin, which appears to lie beneath the impastoed, upper layers of paint. Remnants of gold paint in the lower layers are found in both upper corners of the composition. All of these signs of change point to an earlier state or another painting beneath.

Court of Romance (Garden of Romance) (cat. 14)
Sensitivity of the paint to both aqueous and solvent-based cleaning solutions points to the medium being one that Tack used in mural painting.[4]

Canyon (The Valley) (cat. 15)
Brown paint on two of the four tacking margins indicates that this picture was painted on top of an abandoned or unfinished composition, which was then cut down to fit the present stretcher. A commercially prepared ground is visible on the other two margins. Two small tears in the center right hill and in the lower left hill have been repaired, presumably by the artist based on the characteristics of the brush strokes, which strongly resemble his own.

Mountain Slopes (cat. 16)
Dark paint around the edges of the painting indicate that the picture was painted over an abandoned composition. In the upper right quadrant, some of the dark color shows through the thinly painted white layer that Tack used to cover the earlier picture. Under ultraviolet light the composition is revealed to have gone through two different states. First, the general landscape forms were developed, and a varnish was applied. Then, the bold, impastoed brush strokes in the sky and hillside were added.

Elizabeth Hudson (cat. 17)
Distinctive drying cracks developed in the coat and fur collar as a result of a fast-drying glaze being applied over slower-drying underpaint. The artist's changes in the positions of the feather, hat, and chair are visible as pentimenti. He incised the paint to indicate the stem of the feather. The hat, fur collar, and red areas of the coat were selectively varnished using a water-soluble coating that has the physical characteristics of a gum.

Allegro Giocoso (cat. 18)
The medium is an extremely matte oil type.[5] The support is a cardboard that the artist adhered to a plywood panel, presumably to make it more substantial. He then painted white around the edges of both the cardboard and the panel, probably to make them appear as a single unit.

As the Ships Go Sailing By (Many Hopes) (cat. 19)
The composition was begun on an unstretched fabric or stretched onto a larger auxiliary support before being cut

to its present dimensions and affixed to the plywood panel. The panel and frame were gilded with a metal leaf and then painted over with a white paint. Curiously, little of the gold color remains visible on the panel, most likely because Tack's intention changed. He distressed the frame surface, revealing gold beneath the white paint. He varnished both frame and panel at the same time.

Many changes were made in the evolution of the picture. A tree was painted out (right) but is still visible as impastoed texture beneath the upper paint layers. The positions of the figure's feet have been altered, as have the locations and sizes of several sails. In the center foreground, broad strokes of green paint cover what was initially an area with swirling brushwork. The dresses of the first and third figures from the right appear to have undergone large transformations.

Gethsemane (cat. 20)
The composition was built up from forms blocked in in washes of red and purple. This underpainting is visible in negative spaces. An early photograph from the Kraushaar Galleries archives indicates that the painting was later altered by the artist. The sky, originally a light color, has been repainted a dark blue. This alteration necessitated changes to the spears, which now slant to the left rather than to the right, and both the figures and bushes have been reworked in places. Use of a sponge or cloth to apply the paint in the final stages of working is apparent as gray and yellow daubs that break up the surface.

The Crowd (cat. 21)
The irregularly cut edges reveal that Tack was either working on a scrap of prepared canvas or that the painting was haphazardly cut down from a larger size. It was then adhered to a wallboard, and a tricolored border of gray, metal leaf, and green was painted around the canvas. Along the top edge, the green border is painted over cloud shapes and a blue sky, indicating a reduction in the vertical dimension of the composition. Random pinholes painted over by the artist can be found throughout the canvas and wallboard. They are likely to be the result of a preparatory study being attached to the surface.

An abstract underpainting, confirmed by an infrared photograph, appears to be the structural guide for *The Crowd* (fig. 35). It is composed of fragmented shapes painted in several shades of red, blue, and off-white and is most clearly visible in the lower right corner and in negative spaces. Viewed under high magnification, the shapes appear devoid of underdrawing and bear sharp edges that may result from the use of a stencil. Freely painted red lines seem to be the next step in the underpainting; Tack did not paint over some of them, and they can be seen in the figural shapes to the right.

Examination under ultraviolet light shows that the sky was painted at least twice. The cerulean blue passage was apparently added later; in the infrared photograph the reworking of the sky is visible as dark paint (fig. 35). The second layer lies over a more thinly painted blue sky, separated by a varnish layer. There were large flake losses early in the evolution of the work, especially along the top edge. These losses may have occurred when the painting was cut down from a larger size and attached to the panel. The lacunae do not seem to have disturbed Tack, as he liberally painted over them without concern for hiding the voids created in the paint film. The texture of the moderately coarse-weave fabric is emphasized by the use of rollers, cloths, or sponges to apply the paint. Texture is also created by scraping back paint and letting the underlayers show through. The acutely straight edges of several striated red passages appear to have been made using a stencil. One such area with horizontal red lines is located left of center.

The frame and hardboard mat that surround the painting are an integral part of the work. The wallboard to which the canvas is affixed is in turn attached to the reverse of the hardboard mat. The frame and mat were gilded and painted together, but at some point they were separated, hence the broken painted edge between the two. The first layer was a red size, on which was laid an aluminum leaf. In places, the leaf appears to have wrinkled when it was laid down, creating weblike lines on the mat. The surface of the mat and frame were then distressed. Next, Tack covered the surface with a translucent off-white followed by treatment with rollers and cloths using a gray paint to further break up the surface visually. The mat and frame were then varnished simultaneously.

Entombment (cat. 22)
This painting was begun on an unstretched canvas or stretched onto a larger auxiliary support before being adhered to a plywood panel. The bottom edge of the painting was extended with a strip of canvas, cut to fit its irregular edge. No attempt to disguise the seam was made. In fact, a blue border along the bottom was painted over when the strip was added, and the blue line was then reinstated at the bottom.

The forms were initially laid in using red painted lines with no visible graphite underdrawing. Some of these lines are allowed to show through in the final composition. An early photograph from the Kraushaar Galleries archives reveals additions of paint to the pillow, face, and neckline, presumably to add a sense of depth to these areas. Vertical, overlapping lines are visible evidence of the use of a roller in the final stages of painting.

Passacaglia (cat. 23)
Charcoal pounce marks exist beneath the red lines that serve as the underpainting for this composition. A red wash was used to block in many of the forms prior to painting. The technique involves scraping back and the use of sponges to apply the paint.

Magi's Journey (cat. 24)
Pinholes can be seen to follow the contours of the various shapes. Viewed under high magnification, they are dark pinpoints on top of the red underpainted lines. They appear to be the result of laying a tracing paper over the painting and making a cartoon from the composition by perforating the paper and paint film with the point of a graphite pencil. The cartoon would then be used to pounce imagery onto another canvas. However, Tack continued painting the lower half of the work after the cartoon was made; his procedure is evident in the graphite pinpoints that have been painted over

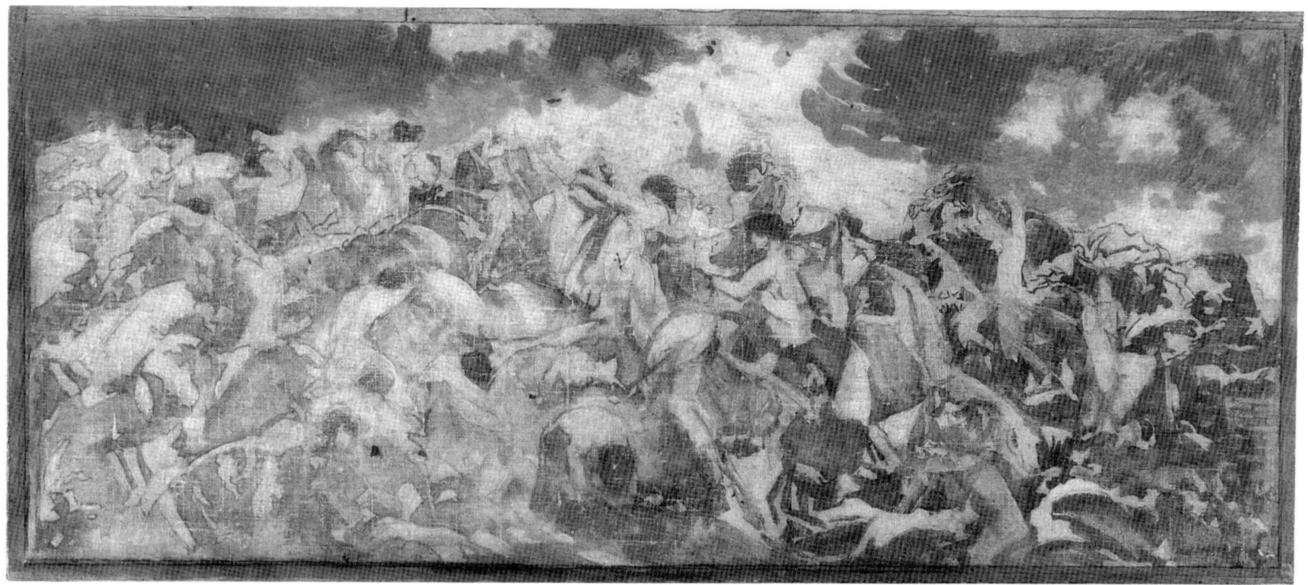

Fig. 35. An infrared photograph of *The Crowd* (cat. 21) reveals the abstract underpainting composed of fragmented shapes. The artist's repainting of the sky is visible as the darker brush marks.

and are only partially visible as small indentations. Under ultraviolet light, a varnish layer can be seen to lie between the upper and lower sections of the painting, further attesting to two states. The diagonal orientation of the canvas weave as placed on the panel is emphasized by Tack's use of a roller to apply the final paint layers.

Storm (cat. 25)
As with *Magi's Journey*, Tack made a cartoon from the imagery and then seems to have continued painting, attesting to two states of the work. The red lines that establish the forms are visible throughout, as is a red wash underpainting used to block in shapes. The paint surface is scraped and distressed, emphasizing the coarse weave of the canvas and revealing the consecutive layers of paint. A roller was used to apply paint to the tops of the threads. Using daubs of blue paint, Tack broke up the strong vertical lines created by the roller in the lower center of the composition.

Canyon (cat. 26)
An infrared photograph shows that some small abstract shapes were painted over in the sky. Dark pinpoints following the red contour lines of some of the imagery indicate that forms in this composition were used to make a cartoon.

The Voice of Many Waters (cat. 27)
The painting was begun on an unstretched canvas or stretched onto a larger auxiliary support before being attached to the wallboard. The support was made from two pieces of canvas. Initially, the composition was only the size of the lower section, as evidenced by the yellow border visible as pentimenti along the top edge of the larger canvas. A second piece was added at the top that has the same weave as the canvas on the bottom. The handling of the paint is uniform from top to bottom, so that the enlargement must have been made early in the painting's evolution. Three random cuts along the top edge occurred before the canvas was adhered to the auxiliary support; Tack painted over them with no attempt to conceal them. In the same fashion, he painted over irregularly placed pinholes, presumably the result of cartoons being attached to the surface. Charcoal pounce marks lie beneath the red painted lines used to establish the composition. Light red washes are then used to block in the forms. Both reductive and additive techniques of applying the paint are visible in this picture.

Music Room Series

Largo, Balance, Order, Rhythm, Liberation, Ecstasy, Allegro, Andante, Outposts of Time I, Outposts of Time II, Flight (Fugue), Far Reaches (cats. 29–40)
Tack adopted similar techniques for the paintings in this series. With the exception of *Aspiration* (cat. 43, discussed separately), they are all painted on a fine-weave canvas mounted to wallboard. (The trade name of the building supplier, UPSON, is found on the reverse of several of these boards along with step-by-step instructions for attaching them to a wall.) A fine particulate matter has been added to the preparation layer to lend surface texture. All the pictures bear some pounce marks, which guided the establishment of the composition. On some of the paintings dark pinpoint pounce marks are strongly evident, while on others they are barely visible as faint brown spots. *On Far Reaches, Flight (Fugue), Ecstasy,* and *Liberation,* the pouncing has a mechanical appearance, resulting from the use of a perforated wheel (fig. 36). The imagery in *Far Reaches* and *Flight* is small in scale compared to the other lunettes and most likely reflects a one-to-one transfer from the primary source. The imagery on the other eight lunettes has been enlarged from the primary source. On these

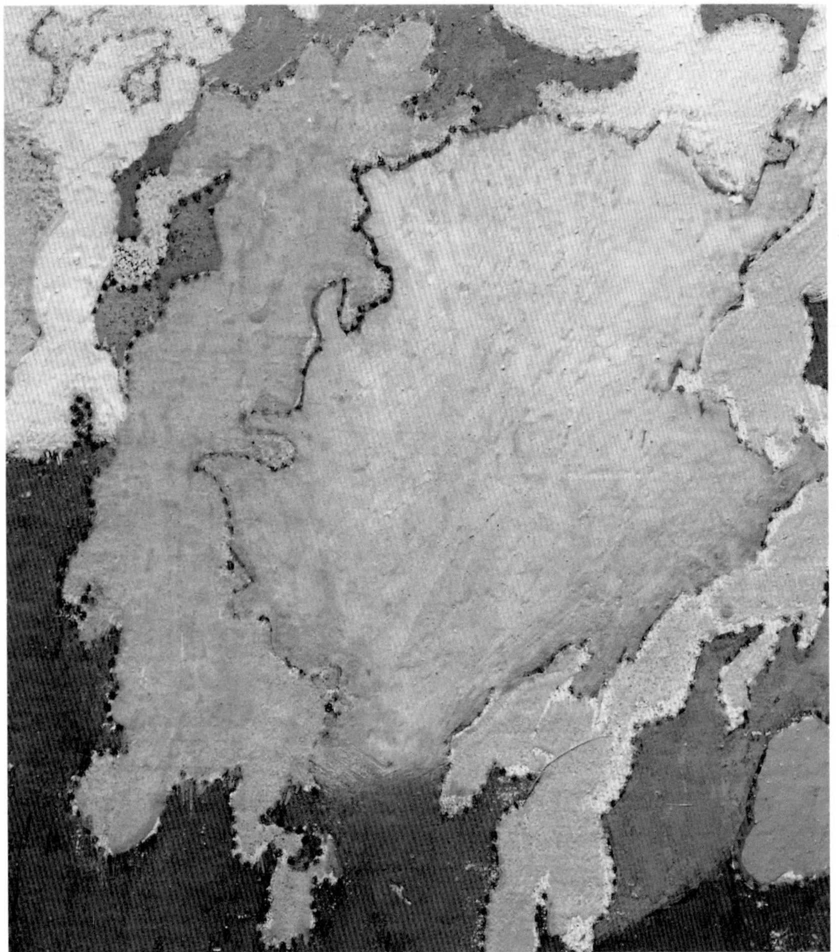

Fig. 36. A close-up photograph of *Flight (Fugue)* shows the pounce marks made using a perforated wheel to prick the cartoon.

paintings the pounce marks exist only sporadically beneath the contour lines, suggesting that Tack abandoned the cartoon and used a combination of transfer and scaling up techniques. The lines that follow the pounce marks appear much more freely and loosely painted than in Tack's previous abstractions. Overall, the paint is less built up on the Music Room paintings than on some of the earlier abstractions, with only two to three layers of paint. Reductive technique is generally abandoned in favor of additive methods to break up the flat surfaces.

The spandrels and the frames are treated similarly. The spandrels are gilded using two or more types of gold-colored metal, apparent in the different toned and sized leaves. The architectural shapes are delineated by painted gray lines over the gilded area. The same frame profile is found on all the paintings; it has been gilded in a gold metal leaf and toned back with dark glazes.

Nocturne (cat. 41)
The preparation of the canvas and the establishment of the composition are the same as on *Spring Night.* Application of the paint is relatively thin and uniform overall with a heavy dependence on rollers and cloths to apply the final layers. At the lower right, however, Tack used opaque, wet-into-wet brushwork, perhaps to put a sense of distance into the composition. The silver-colored metal leaf on the border is probably aluminum. The straight edges of the individual sheets of leaf are clearly visible. It was laid on a slow-drying red size layer, which created the round-edged, drying cracks. Tack apparently did not like the red underlayer showing through the cracks, so he daubed gray paint over them; perhaps he was also trying to imitate the tarnish that would develop on silver leaf. The entire gilded area was toned back with a gray wash. The frame is aluminum-gilded and toned back with gray and yellow glazes.

Untitled Oval (Golden Morning?) (cat. 42)
The preparation of the canvas, establishment of the composition, and application of the paint are the same as for *Spring Night.* The border is gilded similarly to the Music Room paintings.

Aspiration (cat. 43)
The canvas was prepared with a pink imprimatura. There are no pounce marks beneath the red contour lines. The painting has an orange border that is no longer visible, as it has been stretched around the stretcher bars. Many of the shapes have been edited out in the sky area but are visible as pentimenti.

Spring Night (cat. 44)
A pink imprimatura lies beneath the entire oval shape. There are no marks to indicate the transference of shapes, so it may be presumed that the red painted lines are the result of a projected image. Although there is some scraping back of the paint, the surface effects are mainly additive rather than reductive. Use of the roller in the final applications extends over the flatly painted border. Its orientation is both vertical and horizontal and crooked in certain places. There is a red and green painted border around the canvas and a brown border around the edges of the panel with a cartouche element on the bottom edge.

Christmas Night (cat. 45)
The entire canvas has been covered with a gold metal leaf. The absence of any marks to transfer the shapes, outlined in red, points to the use of projection for establishing the composition. Drying cracks, which would have been apparent in the paint surface early in the work's history, are presumably caused by the

metal leaf substrate; they function to break up the surface as the additive paint technique does in other paintings. The gold color is allowed to show through in many places, covered by only a thin wash. The borders are similar to those found on *Spring Night.*

Blue Oval (cat. 46)
The preparation of the canvas and the establishment of the composition are the same as on *Spring Night.* A gold metal leaf used on the border is painted over in a blue-green color and shows through only as a warm tone. The frame is gilded with aluminum leaf and has been toned back with a tinted yellow glaze.

Night, Amargosa Desert (cat. 53)
Texture is derived from the coarse weave of the fabric and particulate matter in the ground layer. Broad, sweeping, circular strokes arising from the preparation layer can be seen in the paint film. Red lines establish the composition, with no transfer marks visible. Modulation of form is carried out using the brush rather than additive or reductive techniques. The larger shapes are formed by uniting smaller ones. The border is embellished with textured, swirling brush strokes.

Small, Late Abstractions

Winter, Dawn, Hill and Sky (Hilltop?), Daybreak, Above the Treetops, Evening (cats. 47–52)
The small, late abstractions are all similar in their construction and technique. The compositions are begun on an unstretched canvas or stretched onto a larger auxiliary support. They are then cut down and affixed to a hardboard with a gessoed border.[6] The canvases are trimmed through a painted surface, evidenced by small losses on the edges that were retouched by the artist after he affixed them to the hardboard. As on *Night, Amargosa Desert,* the preparation is characterized by the inclusion of particulate matter and by broad, sweeping strokes in the ground layer. The same ground layer on all the canvases points to the use of a single commercially prepared fabric or to the replication of method in preparing the fabrics. A warm pink imprimatura lies beneath all the compositions and can be seen at the edges of many of the shapes. There are no visible transfer marks from a preparatory study. Painted red lines, freely executed, establish the composition. Generally, the paint is built up in one to three layers with only isolated instances of additive or reductive technique. Pentimenti of shapes that were reduced or edited are visible on several of these pictures. Painted borders of two lines surround the canvases. On *Winter* and *Evening,* the gessoed borders are distressed intentionally. After being placed in their frames, they were toned back with gray washes. *Dawn, Daybreak, Hill and Sky (Hilltop?),* and *Cloud's Edge* appear to have had gessoed borders similar to *Winter* and *Evening,* but these borders were erroneously overpainted at some point in their history. The present mats and frames were made to approximate the originals.

Cloud's Edge (cat. 54)
The preparation of the canvas and the establishment of the composition are the same as in the other late abstractions. This work is also mounted on hardboard, but the border is painted with an oil paint and not gessoed. The border was painted after the picture was placed in its frame, which was also painted by the artist.

Time and Timelessness (The Spirit of Creation) (cat. 55)
Pounce marks made with a perforated wheel are visible beneath the red painted contour lines. There are numerous layers of blues, greens, and purples, applied by both a brush and a cloth, to render a modulated surface.

Self-Portrait (cat. 56)
Highly textured brush marks in the surface appear to correspond to a loose blocking in of the figure. The abstracted shapes were painted after the yellow background, as evidenced in both the paint texture and an infrared photograph.

NOTES

The technical observations reported in this essay were formulated during the fall of 1992 while examining the paintings with Leslie Furth.

1. H. Siddons Mowbray, "Suggestions for a beginner undertaking a decorative ensemble involving paintings, ornament and gold work" (Rome: printed for the American Academy in Rome, 1916), 8, 13.
   Augustus Vincent Tack, 1870–1949 (Deerfield, Mass.: Hilson Gallery, Deerfield Academy, 1968), 14–17. A studio assistant, the Reverend William Wilfrid Bayne, recalls preparing canvases for mural paintings and relates the use of tools and techniques, evidence of which can be found in Tack's easel paintings.

2. Mowbray, "Suggestions for a beginner," 5, 9.

3. Stephanie Wiles, "The American Muralist H. Siddons Mowbray and His Drawings for the Larz Anderson House," *Master Drawings Quarterly* 31, no. 1 (Spring 1993): 29–31. "Enlarging Mural Decorations," *Harper's Weekly* 41 (November 13, 1897): 1122.

4. See note 5.

5. Drying oil was confirmed to be the medium in analysis of the paint by E. René de la Rie and Susana Halpine, Scientific Research Department, National Gallery of Art, Washington, D.C. During the conservation of the picture, the paint film was found to be unusually sensitive to both solvent and aqueous cleaning solutions for oil. One possible explanation is that Tack was using a medium developed specifically to produce a matte finish as desired in mural paintings, made of equal parts linseed oil, turpentine, and water, as described by Bayne (see n. 1). This mixture would result in a very under-bound medium, which would make the paint vulnerable to any type of surface action. This paint is also found on *New England, 1850* (*Ox Cart*), *Deerfield in Twilight* (*The Dance*), *Court of Romance* (*Garden of Romance*), *Madonna of the Everlasting Hills,* and *Canyon* (*The Valley*), although its matte appearance has been altered by the application of a varnish, presumably by the artist.

6. Medium analysis of the borders by Susana Halpine confirmed the presence of an animal glue as the binder, as would be found in traditional gesso grounds.